The Highlands
and Islands of Scotland

A New History

Also by Alistair Moffat

The Borders: A History from Earliest Times

The Great Tapestry of Scotland

The Hidden Ways: Scotland's Forgotten Roads

Islands of the Evening: Journeys to the Edge of the World

The Reivers: The Sory of the Border Reivers

*Scotland's Forgotten Past: A History of the Mislaid,
Misplaced and Misunderstood*

Scotland: A History from Earliest Times

The Secret History of Here: A Year in the Valley

To the Island of Tides: A Journey to Lindisfarne

The Wall: Rome's Greatest Frontier

War Paths: Walking in the Shadows of the Clans

The Highlands
and Islands of Scotland

A New History

ALISTAIR MOFFAT

BIRLINN

For Jan Rutherford and Andrew Simmons,
the best of friends and the best of professionals

First published in 2024 by
Birlinn Limited
West Newington House
10 Newington Road
Edinburgh
EH9 1QS

www.birlinn.co.uk

Copyright © Alistair Moffat 2024

The right of Alistair Moffat to be identified as Author of this work has been asserted
by him in accordance with the Copyright, Designs and Patents Act 1988.

ISBN: 978 1 78027 857 5

British Library Cataloguing-in-Publication Data

A catalogue record for this book is available from the British Library

Typeset by Initial Typesetting Services, Edinburgh

Papers used by Birlinn Ltd are from well-managed forests and other responsible sources

Printed and bound by Clays Ltd, Elcograf S.p.A.

Contents

Acknowledgements

Over many years now, I have published books with Birlinn, and one of the major reasons that has been so enjoyable has been the pleasure of working with Jan Rutherford and Andrew Simmons. We have become good friends and happy collaborators.

I started writing after a twenty-year career in television because I wanted to work on my own, to be responsible directly for all I did instead of managing hundreds of people, and while I was putting words on a page, that was how it was. But I very quickly realised that publishing, if not writing, is highly collaborative, and I could not have had better, more sympathetic, more creative collaborators than Jan and Andrew.

When I submitted the manuscript for this book, it was even longer than the doorstop you now hold in your hands and it needed the excellent comments it had from Andrew. From others, I should be ashamed to say (but I'm not), I rarely accept suggestions, but I trust Andrew's judgement and this book is very much the better for his quiet insistence. Also, James Rose did an excellent job with the copy edit, and I'm very grateful for his hard work.

But you might not have the book in your hands were it not for the skills of Jan Rutherford in marketing, publicising and guiding authors on how best to present their work to the public. I am grateful to her for her tact, kindness and acute observation.

Finally, I'm very grateful to Carcanet Press for permission to quote from the poetry of Sorley MacLean and Iain Crichton Smith; to Calum Macdonald for permission to reproduce lyrics from various Runrig songs (copyright © C&R Macdonald and published by

Chrysalis/BMG); to Polygon for permission to reproduce extracts from the poems of Norman MacCaig.

Alistair Moffat
Selkirk
March 2024

Introduction

Introductions are sometimes best written last. Like maps of recently discovered lands rather than manifestos of intent, they can guide readers better as they embark on long exploratory journeys. What you have in your hands is not only a new history of the Highlands and Islands of Scotland, but a long story of much that is unlikely and unexpected. Events and processes follow a broadly chronological sequence, one thing after another, but the narrative occasionally takes surprising turns.

History can be like memory. What stays in our collection of recollections is often made vivid by colour, atmosphere or the unexpected, and just as splashes of sunshine on a grey mountainside make the whole landscape seem to come alive, memory can illuminate the past powerfully. Often, we have to work out when whatever we remembered took place after we have remembered it. Was it before or after important turning points in our lives?

Consequently, this substantial book is arranged much like a mosaic, a long frieze illustrating a journey from the primeval and the prehistoric to the present day. What links it all is of course people, from the pioneers who came north after the retreat of the ice, the first Highlanders and Islanders, to those who now live in the same beautiful places. The bright, red, wind-burned faces of the fishermen who fire the engines of their boats and sail out of Hebridean harbours in search of lobster, crayfish and crab are the heirs of the oarsmen of the birlinns of the Lords of the Isles, the Shetland fishermen out on the haaf and the monks who rowed their curraghs along the ragged Atlantic shore. *Linn gu linn, bho ainm gu ainm,* 'from one generation to the next, from one name to another', people make this story what it is.

In the Highlands and Islands, geography made history. The mountains, glens, straths, lochs, the islands and the seas that linked them all are unique and the nature of the land and sea, *muir is tir*, made the people utterly distinctive. And the people named the land and sea. Beinn Nibheis and Loch Laomainn are not part of a wide scatter of wild and rainswept words few people now understand or can pronounce. The names of Ben Nevis and Loch Lomond not only tell us what Gaelic speakers called them, they mean something, names that placed people in the landscape. Maps are the language of the earth and place names are the litany of history, and the great scholars who made and catalogued them in the Highlands and Islands – William Roy, Edward Dwelly and W. J. Watson – are all deservedly venerated in this history. Their work helped greatly in its telling.

From the middle of the nineteenth century onwards, there was much more history, more material, more information about ordinary people for the first time. In 1841, the modern census began, a thorough and generally accurate account of the population of Britain. More than arithmetic, it not only located people, but it also offered a much more concrete sense of the nature of their lives. Successive censuses listed marital status, family relationships, occupations and whether or not children attended school. They also supplied addresses and showed how dense occupation could be as large families crammed into farm cottages and croft houses. It was possible for the first time to do more than imagine what living conditions were. Newspapers began to proliferate and include much of the detail of what changed in the north, and what stayed the same. And many more written records of all sorts survived.

This welter of data, a cornucopia compared to the long silences of the past, forces choices and a more selective, more kaleidoscopic approach to the story of the Highlands and Islands. So, whilst it still follows the broad chronological sweep, the later chapters of the book focus more on social, political and cultural fundamentals: how and why life changed for Highlanders and Islanders, what affected the day-in, day-out rhythm of work, belief, and also what made people smile and what roused them to action.

Histories of the Highlands and Islands have often, and with very good reason, seemed to be elegiac, a mourning for loss and departure, and the passing of a distinctive set of cultures. And there is no denying that the recent past in particular saw terrible wrongs done. But in what follows, you will read of much that is to be celebrated. The glories of the north are to be found here, the warmth and humour of Highlanders and Islanders, stories of their resourcefulness, their dignity and their ancestral courage. These qualities remain undimmed, and the story of these remarkable communities burns brightly.

I

The Weather Man

At 4.40 a.m. precisely, on the morning of 1 June 1881, a tall, red-haired man closed the front door of his lodgings at Banavie, a hamlet between Corpach and Fort William. Carrying a pack containing instruments, notebooks, some food and waterproofs, he crossed the Caledonian Canal near the series of locks known as Neptune's Staircase. Once across the bridge over the River Lochy, he found a path on the south bank of a fast-flowing stream, the Allt a' Mhuilinn, and began to climb Ben Nevis. It was the first of 153 consecutive ascents of Britain's highest mountain. Every day between 1 June and 31 October, whatever the conditions, Clement Wragge climbed 4,411 feet from sea level to the top of the great mountain.

The variable weather conditions were the point. Clement Wragge was a meteorologist, uncharitably known to some of his associates as 'Inclement Rag', who was absolutely dedicated to the gathering of accurate, sequential data that would inform the developing science of weather forecasting. It was the invention of the telegraph in 1835 that made forecasting viable and the safety of British shipping that made it highly desirable. The volume and value of sea traffic around the Empire was vast and if meteorologists could warn mariners about impending storms, then fewer lives and fewer cargoes would be lost. A network of weather stations was set up by the coastguard service and coordinated by the Board of Trade. When the Scottish Meteorological Society mooted the idea of an observatory on the summit of Ben Nevis, there was great enthusiasm for the project. The mountain stood directly in the path of storms blowing in off the Atlantic and consistent readings of air pressure, temperature, rainfall, cloud and fog cover, and much else, would create an unrivalled bank of data that would allow meteorologists to discern patterns and issue good forecasts that could immediately be telegraphed great distances to shipping and elsewhere.

When Clement Wragge heard of the Scottish Meteorological Society's proposal, he immediately volunteered to climb Ben Nevis every day for five months. The readings he took would prove the value of a permanent observatory and also help raise the funding needed to build it. Independently wealthy, Clement did not seek payment for this remarkable, punishing and sometimes dangerous programme of work, and nor did his wife, Leonora. While Wragge climbed the mountain, she took hourly readings, despite having two children to look after, at what they called their sea-level station at Banavie. These allowed simultaneous comparisons of data gathered on the same day. It could be sunny and calm at sea-level and windy and raining on the summit of Ben Nevis at the same time.

As he climbed the mountain, Clement stopped at regular intervals to take readings. At Lochan Meall an t-Suidhe, what he called the Halfway Lake, he would later set up a Stevenson Screen. Designed by Thomas Stevenson, the father of the great novelist, Robert Louis Stevenson, and the builder of spectacular lighthouses around Scotland's coast, these were essentially instrument shelters. Square boxes with double-louvred sides, they were always painted white in order to reflect sunlight and set up on supports that stood between four and six feet off the ground. The screens sheltered thermometers, barometers and other instruments.

In good weather, Clement could reach the summit in less than four hours, not counting his stops at six points on the way up to take readings. But conditions could change quickly and suddenly become very dangerous, especially in thick fog. The summit is a stone- and boulder-strewn plateau with sheer cliffs on three sides and in his diary Clement recorded that he sometimes took a guide, a local man called Colin Cameron. Here is part of an account of the end of the first season of ascents (Wragge wrote reports of his work for the scientific periodical, *Nature*):

The conditions of weather on Ben Nevis are now such as to render it impracticable and hazardous to continue the daily observations satisfactorily. I have therefore judged it best to discontinue them, after a very successful season, under the auspices of the Scottish Meteorological Society, of five months from June 1, without the break of a single day. The work at the six intermediate fixed stations has, I am very pleased to say, been well and generally punctually kept up throughout, and I trust that much goodwill will result. Simultaneous observations were of course made at the observatory at Achintore [near Banavie], Fort William. The Stevenson's screens at these stations have now been made firm by wire stays to withstand the storms of winter. Yesterday Colin Cameron, the guide, accompanied me. The track was snowed up, and it was necessary to force a way through great banks and drifts of snow. The average depth was two feet; once we got off our course in the blankness of thick cloud-fog and trackless snow. To-day the weather was very bad on the summit, the hut was partly filled by drift, and the south-east gale was so violent at times that I could hardly make way. Possibly I shall attempt weekly or periodical ascents during the winter to keep up the registrations of the rain-gauges and self-recording thermometers.

In the course of the first summer, gangs of workers had climbed Ben Nevis to install instruments in a shelter built from sturdy angle-iron and covered it with a tarpaulin. Its skeleton can still be seen, stayed and securely anchored, having survived the gales of more than 140 winters. The hut mentioned by Clement was a rudimentary shelter built as a last, safe resort in bad weather and a place to shelter from the icy winds and make notes. There exists a photograph of him coming out of the door, preceded by his dog, a Border collie. He wears a double-breasted jacket, a cloth cap, what might be jodhpurs and knee-length leather boots. Clamped in the corner of his mouth may be a pipe. The slightly blurry photograph looks as though it was not posed and Clement seems a wiry, leathery, thin, even cadaverous man; the physique of a marathon runner, perfect for an amazingly arduous programme of work.

The sun shines in the shot, but the design of the shelter speaks of extreme weather. Built with massive boulders and stones picked up on the summit plateau, it is little more than six feet high, with no windows and not much bigger than a garden shed. The roof is a tightly tethered tarpaulin. It has been roped to what might be wooden beams wedged about halfway down the walls and kept securely in place by the weight of five or six courses of the large stones laid over them.

Nature published details of the beginning of the second summer of data gathering in 1882:

> . . . the heavy work of reopening chiefly consisted in digging out from the vast accumulations of snow the barometer cairn, hut, and thermometer cage which here, as a safeguard, incloses Stevenson's screen. The snow, in fact, was nearly four feet deep, and it was necessary to cut out wide areas around the instruments . . . I had also to fix a new roof of ship's canvas to the rude shanty that affords some little shelter from the piercing cold and storms.

Through articles like these and other reports, Clement Wragge's work caught the public imagination and funds were quickly raised for the building of the observatory. Both Queen Victoria and the Prince of Wales contributed. The job of superintendent was advertised but despite his pioneering and voluntary efforts, Clement was not appointed. It seems that he was an eccentric, irascible man who perhaps spoke his mind too readily. Nevertheless, the data he so doggedly gathered and was carried on for thirty years by the observatory was a unique model, still the most complete record of high-altitude mountain weather that exists in Britain. No doubt stung by such a blatant rejection, Clement and Leonora sailed with their children to live in Australia. He continued his work in meteorology and we have him to thank for the irritating habit of giving people's names to hurricanes.

What Wragge saw from the summit of Ben Nevis on clear, graphic, sunlit summer days must often have been spectacular. He saw the Highlands. In every direction, he looked out over spectacular and unique geography. And in the Highlands and Islands geography made history. To the north the Torridon mountains of Beinn Eighe and Liathach are visible, to the north-east the peak of Morvern in Sutherland, to the south Ben Lomond can be clearly made out and beyond it, the Irish coast. Over to the west, Clement saw Loch Eil snake into the Moidart mountains and Loch Linnhe lead the eye south-west to the ocean and the Hebrides. But perhaps most important to an understanding of Highland geography was what lay immediately at the foot of the great mountain, what Clement crossed every morning to climb it.

The Great Glen, An Gleann Mòr, the fault-line that runs north-east from Fort William to Inverness is a memory of an immense, slow-motion collision that took place hundreds of millions of years ago, one of three that formed the geology, the geography and the history of the Highlands.

Hugh Miller was fascinated by the age of the earth. Born in 1802, a Cromarty stonemason to trade, he was a geologist by vocation. His work in the quarries and his walks along the rocky shorelines on the Moray and Cromarty Firths had long stirred his curiosity. The strata he saw, making 'a right use of his eyes', and the fossils he picked up convinced him that the earth was very old, despite his deeply held religious beliefs. Miller's famous book, *The Old Red Sandstone*, described sedimentary rocks laid down hundreds of millions of years ago when the crust of the planet was forming. Vast palaeocontinents with names that might have been invented by science-fiction authors were moving very slowly across the face of the earth. Avalonia, Baltica and Laurentia were once part of a giant land mass called Gondwana. When it broke apart, as volcanoes roared, the earth quaked and convulsed and oceans opened up, these vast pieces of the craton, the earth's mantle and crust, shifted and started to collide. Bits sometimes broke off and three of these shards of ancient rock, known as terranes, came together very slowly, grinding and pushing against each other, to create the mountains, lochs and glens, to make the singular geography of the Highlands and Islands.

The Great Glen shows the angle at which two of these terranes collided. It was north-east to south-west, a virtually straight line now mostly filled with a string of lochs; Ness, Oich, Lochy and Linnhe. On the eastern side of the glen is the Grampian terrane and to the west is the North Highland terrane. Beyond it is a third terrane. It is based on a very hard and very old rock called Lewissian gneiss and it includes the Western Isles, much of Skye, Coll, Tiree and most of the north-west Atlantic coastline. To the south-east of all of these lies the geological definition of the Highlands and Islands. What is known as the Highland Boundary Fault runs north-east from the island of Arran at the same diagonal angle as the Great Glen until it reaches Stonehaven on the North Sea coast. South of the Boundary Fault is the Lowlands and another Scotland.

The weather patterns so painstakingly recorded by Clement Wragge had been changing for millennia, sometimes dramatically. Recorded history offers many examples. In 1303 and again in the winter of 1306/07 the Baltic Sea froze over and almost ten years later the very bad spring weather of 1315 caused widespread crop failure and Northern Europe found itself in the grip of a devastating famine. It was the beginning of a very long series of periods of cooling across the North Atlantic. Temperatures dropped sharply, winters were more severe and lasted longer until the middle of the nineteenth century. Sir Henry Raeburn's famous painting of the Reverend Robert Walker Skating on Duddingston Loch near Edinburgh is emblematic. That winter of 1795/96 saw episodes of very cold weather but the minister and his friends made the best of it, setting up the Edinburgh Skating Club, the first to be formed anywhere in the world.

Others were not so fortunate. Famine stalked the Highlands frequently and the 'Ill Years' of the last decade of the seventeenth century persuaded many that political union with England was desirable. The Scottish economy was badly in need of revival as farming contracted, land became unmanageable as growing seasons shrank and the rain seemed incessant. Clement Wragge will have been aware of these patterns. The winter of 1849–50 was very severe with heavy snow across the Highlands piling up drifts as high as fifteen feet, and tremendous storms raced in off the Atlantic, smashing into coastlines. High winds and tides blew away large sand dunes on the coast of Orkney Mainland to reveal the prehistoric settlement at Skara Brae. In August of 1850, the Cairngorm Plateau was still covered in deep snow that reached down to lower altitudes in the glens and as far as Braemar. The following two winters saw more dreadful and damaging weather as well as widespread disruption. But by the end of the decade, the cycle appeared to have shifted and it may have seemed to meteorologists that what became known as the Little Ice Age was at last ending.

As predominantly rural communities concerned with food production, Highlanders and Islanders have long been at the mercy of the weather and, like geography, it has shaped their history, where they lived and how they lived their lives.

In 1159 BC the Icelandic volcano known as Hekla suddenly blew itself apart. A huge tonnage of ejecta, of debris, rocketed into the atmosphere. Much of this was dust and it immediately screened the sun. The tremendous force of the eruption sent the ejecta so high that it became trapped in the stratosphere, too high for rain to wash it out but so dense that the sun could not fully penetrate. The immediate impact of the eruption of Hekla was almost certainly a tsunami that crashed onto the shores of the Hebrides and the north-west Highlands. When prehistoric communities looked up and heard the roar of the great wave before they saw it hurtling towards them, they could not have known what had caused it. The eruption of the Icelandic volcano though would have much longer lasting and even more devastating effects.

A deadly darkness descended over the mountains, glens and islands, a perpetual twilight that must have seemed to many like the evening of the world, as though it was ending. Tree ring analysis of ancient Irish oaks confirm that the volcanic dust screened the sun for several summers. In those years, the rings were very, very narrow, showing little or no growth. Temperatures dropped and the cultivation of crops, especially at higher altitudes, became impossible. Before this catastrophe, archaeology suggests that the north-west and especially the islands were relatively heavily populated, were good places to live. Fish and game were abundant and prehistoric farmers grew enough corn to feed themselves and the cattle, sheep and goats they had domesticated. But after Hekla exploded, it is likely that a series of great migrations began, the first in a recurring pattern of departure. In the dim, half-dark of the sunless summers, families and communities trekked over the mountains to settle in eastern Scotland where the effects of the eruption were much less severe. The cold and the rain accelerated the formation of peat as good grazing and crop-raising land became bleak, damp and soggy moors. At the magnificent Calanais Stones on the Atlantic coast of Lewis, archaeologists removed a four-foot layer of peat in 1857 that had formed around the megaliths in the centuries since Hekla, restoring the monument to its former splendour.

Profound changes in the weather shaped the Highlands and Islands even more dramatically in the deeper past. About 26,000 years before Clement Wragge climbed Ben Nevis and gazed out over the mountains of the north, they were buried under a thick sheet of ice. Sometime around 24,000 BC, the climate began to grow colder. Mean annual temperatures plummeted, winter snow lay on higher ground all year round and the growth of vegetation shrank. The animals who browsed the grasslands and the woodlands of the north began to retreat southwards and they were followed by the first Highlanders and Islanders, hunter-gatherers who depended for their food, clothing and much else on the herds of wild horses and deer. The last ice age was beginning.

Huge ice-domes formed. Hemispherical and symmetrical and often accumulating around land mountains like Ben Nevis, they could be several miles thick. Hurricanes howled around the smooth slopes of these vast ice-mountains as their great weight pressed down hard on the land, crushing the crust of the earth. When the skies darkened over a dazzling, white landscape, these high points attracted precipitation. Ice formed on the summits and as it began to solidify, gravity pulled it radially downwards to become the slow-moving frozen rivers known as glaciers. Over millennia they gradually began to shape the Highland and Island landscape we see now.

Invisible under the frozen rivers was a slick of meltwater, and as the mass of ice moved, it acted as a lubricant. Locked inside the glaciers was all sorts of debris: boulders, silt, gravel and even plant matter. This geological rubbish acted like primeval sandpaper. As the glaciers inched forward, they scarted and planed the land underneath them, gouging out the glens, and the lochs and shaping the mountains and their ridges. On the islands of Lewis, Harris and the Uists, there are wide inland areas known as *cnocan agus lochain* – hillocks and small lochs. Thousands of large rock pools filled with brown, peaty water pattern the landscape and they are mirrored by small hills that look as though they have been scooped out of the lochans. These were formed by relatively fast-moving glaciers towards the end of the last ice age. Sometimes, these changes were much more immediate as the ice domes began to melt about 11,000 years ago.

*

In the summer of 2022, I went to the scene of one of the most dramatic events in the making of the Highland landscape. I'd driven often on the A86, along the banks of Loch Laggan and below the glories of Creag Meagaidh to the Braes of Lochaber and through the dappled shade of its beautiful woodland. It was a good, alternative route to the west, to Fort William and the Atlantic shore beyond. I'd seen signs for Glen Roy and knew something of the history that had made its way down by the River Roy to Keppoch and the foot of Glen Spean, but I'd never been up the glen. Events of great moment in much more recent history had taken place there. In January 1645, James Graham, Marquis of Montrose, and the MacDonald general, Alasdair mac Colla, had led their clan army through the deep snows of the winter mountains and down Glen Roy on a flanking march to surprise the Campbells and their allies at Inverlochy Castle. On a bright summer morning, I turned off the A86 and drove up the glen in search of a different, much more ancient kind of drama.

After a few difficult miles on a winding, fraying single-track road, I found where the map had plotted a car park and a viewpoint. It was stunning, an epic landscape, a direct and clearly visible legacy of the last ice age.

Running along the steep flanks of Glen Roy are what are known as the Parallel Roads. For centuries their origins were held to be mysterious, even mystical. Three ribbons of precisely parallel tracks run at different altitudes from the head of the glen to its mouth, a distance of about eight miles. Each is about thirty-five feet wide and so consistent in width that it was believed that they were made by hands of giants or ancient heroes, like the fearsome Finn McCuil. Or perhaps they were the work of gods. Highland geography was sometimes thought to be made by the divine, wrought by the Queen of Winter, the Storm Hag, An Cailleach nan Cruachan, as she flew through the night air. Having inadvertently created Loch Awe (by forgetting to cap a spring on the summit of Ben Cruachan), she might also have been the magical builder of these remarkable roads. More down-to-earth assessments insisted they were man-made, one for walkers, a second for carts and a third for livestock. But that made no sense to me either. Why not build one track that all could use, and in any case, wouldn't it have been much easier to set that on the floor of the glen and not on its steep sides? In 1838 Charles Darwin was so fascinated by the Parallel Roads that he made the long and arduous journey by coach from London to examine them. But even a scientist with his gifts and insight could not unravel the web of mystery around these extraordinary features.

As I looked up Glen Roy, I understood why drawings and engravings had lured Darwin into the heart of the Highlands. The roads did look like divine decoration, as though a deity had leaned down from the clouds with a stylus and drawn these marks on the steep hillsides, following their folds and curves in perfectly parallel lines. Two years after Darwin's bemusement, the Swiss-American geologist, Louis Agassiz, was driven up the winding road in a pony and trap. Perhaps from the viewpoint where I stood, he made, in Hugh Miller's apt phrase, 'a right use of his eyes'. Almost immediately, the geologist understood exactly what he was looking at.

In 1837 Agassiz postulated a new theory: that the earth had endured a relatively recent ice age that covered much of the Northern Hemisphere. His particular interest was the behaviour of glaciers, how they had shaped the land and carried rocks and gravel far from their places of origin. With the English geologist William Buckland he toured the Highlands and recorded clear evidence of glacial action and its effects. In Glen Roy he saw how the ice had done something different, and spectacular. When Agassiz looked at the Parallel Roads, he realised immediately that these were not tracks at all but a series of three prehistoric shorelines. Steep-sided Glen Roy had once been a vast and very deep loch.

Near the end of the last ice age, as the domes groaned and cracked, the ice began to melt and move more quickly. A glacier known as the Lochaber Ice Lobe had shifted and dammed the mouth of Glen Roy. The very cold and fast-flowing waters of the River Roy slowly built up to form the loch up to the level of the lowest of the three Parallel Roads. Almost certainly by a combination of wind-driven wave action in the summer and intense frost in winter, the thirty-five-foot wide, flattish beaches were created on the flanks of the ridges on either side of the glen.

As the ice age ended there were fluctuations when the intense cold advanced and then retreated. When a cold period began, the Lochaber Ice Lobe grew larger and pushed the waters of the loch further up the glen. And its level rose to form the second or middle of the three Parallel Roads. When temperatures dropped even lower, the level of the ice-cold loch rose once more and created the highest of the roads.

From the viewpoint car park, I could see that the lowest of these ancient shorelines was perhaps only two or three hundred feet above me. As a string of well-washed ewes lifted their heads from the lush summer grass, they watched me puff and struggle up the steep incline. The lowest road was, I discovered, not absolutely flat but in fact a very shallow slope, like most sandy, seaside beaches. Below me the ground fell away sharply to the bottom of the glen and I realised that Loch Roy must have been very deep at its fullest.

When the temperature fluctuations ceased to be so extreme and the earth began to warm at the close of the last ice age, the slow-moving changes that took centuries, even millennia, suddenly accelerated. In only a few catastrophic hours the great ice-dam at the mouth of Glen Roy broke down, and with a mighty roar, a huge volume, a tsunami, of extremely cold water burst out and raced towards the frozen wastes of the Great Glen. Carrying everything in its path, the raging torrent probably first drained to the northeast towards what became Loch Ness and into the Moray Firth. The Parallel Roads are the relic of a cataclysm, but also the moment when the last ice age ended and life in the Highlands and Islands began.

In the late summer of 1993, a group of archaeology students were fieldwalking near the village of Bridgend on Islay. It lies at the head of Loch Indaal, and the students were looking to see if recent ploughing had turned up anything of interest. A sharp-eyed individual spotted something glinting on the top of a furrow. It was a flint arrowhead, and most significantly, it could be dated to around 10,800 BC, at least a thousand years before the ice age finally ended.

The prehistoric archer who loosed an arrow near Bridgend almost thirteen millennia ago may have been one of the first pioneers to set eyes on the Highlands and Islands. It seems that as temperatures fluctuated, some of the mountain peaks poked through the ice. Known as nunataks, similar peaks can be seen standing out clearly from the frozen, white landscape of Antarctica. It may be that Islay was easier to find because the mountains of Beinn Bhàn, Beinn Bheigeir and Beinn Sholum could be seen easily from the sea. The flint found at Bridgend may have belonged to one of a summer hunting party who sailed from the south in search of seasonal game, or perhaps seals. There is evidence to suggest that the western part of Islay, the Rinns, may have escaped glaciation entirely and the party that made their way north, almost certainly in early versions of the skin boats known as curraghs, probably came back each summer. Another flint, dating to 10,000 BC, was picked up near Port Askaig after it had been unearthed by rootling pigs. When these hunters looked to the east, all they will have seen was ice and snow as the Highlands and Islands lay buried, waiting for their people, waiting for the bands of pioneers to come and to stay.

*

The deposit of all this geological drama, what was left after the ice melted, was the soil of the Highlands and Islands. A clear understanding of its nature and the distribution of different types was much advanced by sentiment and a generous donation.

In 1930, Thomas Bassett Macaulay remembered his heritage. Descended from the Macaulays of Uig, a crofting township on the Atlantic coast of Lewis, he was born in Hamilton, Ontario, the son of an emigrant. Thomas worked his way up to become the chairman of Sun Life Financial Inc., making a great deal of money in the process. He gave £10,000 to found the Macaulay Institute for Soil Research, mercifully known as the Macaulay, and it was based in Aberdeen.

The land, its quality and what it can produce is clearly central to understanding farming and food production in Scotland. In the mid 1960s the Institute developed a Land Use Capability System that divided the country into four main classifications: land capable of supporting arable farming, mixed arable, improved grassland and rough grazing. This in turn allowed a fascinating and revealing map of Scotland to be drawn, as much a historical document as something created by geology and geography. Different colours indicated degrees of fertility. Russet denoted the best land and areas of arable farming were heavily concentrated in the Borders, the Lothians, Fife, lowland Perthshire, Angus and the Mearns, Aberdeenshire and a small group of patches around the Beauly Firth and the Black Isle. Mixed arable was shown in green and included Ayrshire, Dumfries and Galloway, Lanarkshire, Orkney, parts of Caithness and around the fringes of the best land. There are no areas of russet or green anywhere in the Hebrides, the Atlantic coastlands or the Western and Central Highlands, not a spot. Improved grassland, a shade of red, was concentrated in the Southern Uplands, Easter Ross and the eastern glens of the Grampians. On the Macaulay map, purple identifies areas of rough grazing, and apart from significant swathes of the Galloway Hills, almost all of it is plotted in the Hebrides, the Highlands and Shetland.

This immensely detailed and thoroughly researched map is an important snapshot. It offers an underlying and undeniable fact of life. When the ice finally melted in the Highlands and Islands, it revealed poor and difficult land, as well as the drama and great beauty of the mountains, sea lochs, glens and islands. The Macaulay reveals this in its definition of rough grazing:

> This land has very severe limitations in that it prevents sward [short grass] improvement by mechanical means. This land is either steep, very poorly drained, has very acid or shallow soils and occurs in wet, cool or cold climate zones. In many circumstances, these limitations operate together. The existing vegetation is assessed for its grazing quality . . . and is of very limited agricultural value. Nonetheless, this ground often has a high value, for example in terms of storing carbon in its organic soils and supporting rare species and habitats.

There is also 'Rocky and boulder strewn ground of very limited agricultural value . . . [and] it covers 4,035,800 hectares [almost 10 million acres] or 51 per cent of Scotland's land area.'

Even allowing for the amount of rough grazing in Galloway, these statistics are stark, and absolutely determinant. In the Highlands and Islands, geology made geography and geography would make history.

2

The Forest

Just to the north of Oban, below the ruined ramparts and the massive keep of Dunollie Castle, there is a sea-stack. A tall, massive finger of rock with an unlikely tree growing out of its top, it sits not in the waters of the bay but on a green, grassy ridge above it, on what is known as a raised beach. The sea-stack is a relic of a geological phenomenon known as isostatic rebound. When the ice domes at last cracked and disintegrated and the glaciers melted, a massive weight was lifted off the land and it began to rebound, to rise up, outstripping the level of the oceans as they filled with melt-water. Scotland is still rising, 11,000 years after the ice. Slight isostatic rebound can still be measured in East Lothian and elsewhere in the Central Belt.

In the centuries following the ice, the rebound was much more dramatic. A huge area of what is now the North Sea was dry land, a subcontinent known as Doggerland, named after the Dogger Bank, once a range of hills. It lay between what are now the coasts of Denmark and Germany and much of the eastern shoreline of Britain. The coastline was ragged, breached by wide estuaries and fringed with large areas of wetland, a rich habitat for the people who lived to the south of the Dogger Hills. Undersea maps plotted by the North Sea oil and gas companies and wind farm builders have discovered a varied landscape, one ribboned with rivers and ranges of hills, and with a large lake near the centre called the Silver Pit. It was one of the richest hunting grounds in prehistoric Europe and probably relatively heavily populated. Similarly, a land bridge linked Caithness with Orkney, plains extended for a hundred miles to the east of the

Highland massif, and the Rivers Ness and Conon were once much longer. With its disappearance, the influence of Doggerland on early Highland and Island history can be easily underestimated, even ignored. And the effects of the ice and its legacy have sometimes been forgotten.

North of Ullapool, just off the A837, now part of the famous and notorious North 500 tourist route, polar bears once hunted on the ice sheets. Near the hamlet of Inchnadamph on the shores of Loch Assynt, a grassy glen leads into the mountains, and down it rushes the foaming white water of the Allt nan Uamh. The Gaelic place name means 'the Mountain Stream of the Caves'. At the base of a 200-foot limestone cliff there are four dark, shaded entrances, each of them accessible by tracks up a gentle slope. Behind these openings, one of them very wide, is the longest cave in Scotland. Uamh na Claonaite stretches back into the mountainside for almost two dark, damp and dangerous miles and the Gaelic description makes clear that it is steeply sloping, and probably very slippery.

In 1889, Dr John Horne and Dr Ben Peach walked up the slope with spades and picks and undertook a careful, methodical exploration and excavation of the great caves and discovered remarkable survivals from a lost history. On the floor of the caves, they came across the remains of the fauna of the ice age and its last centuries. They were able to identify the bones of Arctic fox, brown bear, reindeer, a lynx – and a polar bear. In the late nineteenth century there was no way of dating the bones accurately, but it was clear to Horne and Peach that their finds remembered a landscape emerging from the ice, and indeed before then. All of these species had been long extinct in Scotland.

In 2009 the techniques of carbon dating revealed fascinating results. The polar bear had padded over the ice sheets and survived the extreme cold of the height of the ice age as it hunted for seals sometime around 16,000 BC. One of the brown bears had prowled in a Scotland that has disappeared. It lived in the centuries around 45,000 BC, long before the coming of the ice, before the ice domes and the glaciers that scoured, sheared and planed the landscape we see now. The bear hunted and scavenged in a lost world. The remains of another bear were 35,000 years younger. It lived at the end of the last ice age and may have died when it was hibernating in one of the caves. Its bones were found some distance from the entrances and its body may have been washed by meltwater down into the deep interior of the cave system where its skeleton was preserved.

Human remains were also found and dated and it is possible that Uamh na Claonaite was an ice-age refuge, a place where early settlers or seasonal hunters could shelter when blizzards whistled down the glen and temperatures plummeted. In the famous ice-age refuges of the Pyrenees, our ancestors painted on the walls the animals they hunted and stalked beyond the caves. When the thaw came at last, about 10,000 or 11,000 years ago, those cold-adapted animals, like reindeer, could not evolve quickly enough to cope with higher temperatures and so they were forced to chase the retreating ice northwards. And the hunters from the southern refuges who depended on the herds followed them.

When the reindeer bones found at Uamh na Claonaite were carbon dated, they turned out to be about 12,000 years old, the last phase of the ice age in Scotland. There were also the remains of wild horses from about the same era. Both of these herd animals could easily outrun human predators and they could only be brought down at vulnerable moments in narrow or difficult places. These came when the herds moved to begin the annual journeys of transhumance, making their way upcountry from winter pasture to fresh summer grazing in the hills and on the mountainsides. Each year, they followed the same routes and in defiles or crossing places over rivers, or where there was cover, the hunters would be waiting. Old reindeer or horses might sometimes straggle, unable to keep up with the herd and be attacked by spearmen or bowmen. Flint arrowheads or sharpened wooden spears charred hard in the embers of a fire would not kill an animal but might wound it. There then followed a blood pursuit as the pumping heart of an injured and slowing horse or reindeer might make it bleed out and finally collapse. Archaeologists have speculated that the high country at the head of the glen of Uamh na Claonaite might have been a calving ground for reindeer and when the herds came down off the summer pasture in the late autumn, hunters will have tried to pick off young animals.

The finds in the caves beg an obvious question. These dates for human activity in prehistoric Scotland are very early. Was Assynt at least partly ice-free before the thaw began over the rest of the Highlands and Islands, like the Rinns of Islay? Or were the hunters who butchered their kills in the caves seasonal visitors from the south? Whatever the unknowable answer, these people were amongst the first, the earliest to see the Highlands and Islands after the ice.

*

A sense of what the prehistoric landscape looked like had to wait thousands of years until the Roman Empire crossed the English Channel and the legions marched north to the ends of the earth, to the land they called Caledonia.

Pliny the Elder was interested in everything, and in AD 79 his curiosity killed him. He was an extraordinary individual; not only a naval and cavalry commander, and a friend and advisor to the Roman Emperor Vespasian, he also compiled the first encyclopaedia. *Natural History*, as it is now known, was an attempt to gather together all knowledge in one place, in a single volume. A large Roman fleet was based at Misenum on the Bay of Naples, and as Praefectus Classis, its commander, Pliny lived in a grand villa near the shore with a vast library of scrolls. It was there that he wrote much of his great work. When Vesuvius erupted and engulfed Pompeii on 24 August 79, the great scholar had a grandstand view, watching from the safety of his terrace at Misenum as the mountain exploded, raining down ash and pumice, sending clouds of toxic gases rocketing into the atmosphere. Having received a desperate plea for help from a friend, and also wanting to get close to the volcano to observe the course of the eruption, Pliny ordered a ship to put to sea and sail as close to the harbour at Herculaneum as possible. But the crew and the Prefect were themselves overwhelmed as a fiery emission of poisonous gas enveloped them. It appears that Pliny was asphyxiated rather than burned, for when his body was recovered the following morning, it was unmarked.

Many posthumous copies of Pliny's *Natural History* were made and survived the collapse of the Western Roman Empire, sometimes preserved in monastic libraries. The great encyclopaedia turns out to be important in the history of the Highlands and Islands because it contains the earliest documentary mention of the north of Britannia, and gives it a name that has endured.

Pliny's friend, Vespasian, had campaigned as a legionary commander during the Claudian invasion of Britannia in AD 43, and when he became emperor he ordered 'the whole island' to be conquered and brought into the Roman Empire as a new province – all incoming emperors needed the glow and prestige of military success to help consolidate their authority. It was sometime after AD 75 that Pliny wrote of the advance of imperial armies in Britannia, noting that 'as yet they have not penetrated beyond the vicinity of the Caledonian Forest'.

This is a fascinating footnote. Clearly the Silva Caledonia was a place so well known in the Roman world as not to require any further explanation. And in the *Natural History*, Pliny does a lot of explaining. What was the Caledonian Forest, and why did its existence appear to denote a limit, a boundary, even a problem?

Roman generals were very wary of forests. Terrible things had happened to Roman legions in the dark, dangerous depths of impenetrable woods. In 391 BC, Celtic warbands had cut a Roman army to pieces in the Ciminian Forest in what is now southern Tuscany. After that disaster, the Senate was so spooked that it passed a law forbidding commanders from leading their men into the woods. In AD 9, another great slaughter took place. A huge army, whose core comprised the XVII, the XVIII and the XIX Legions, commanded by Gaius Varus, was ambushed in the Teutoburg Forest by hordes of barbarians led by the German tribal leader Arminius. On hearing the news, Emperor Augustus was appalled, humiliated. He tore his clothes and went about unshaven and in rags for months. The three lost legions were never reformed. And the Romans never lost their fear of forests.

That is why they did not make the mistake of marching into the Caledonian Forest. The army that invaded the north of Britannia in AD 79 appears to have very deliberately gone around it. Pliny says nothing more about the great wood, but someone who knew him and was friendly with his son, Pliny the Younger, adds more than a little to the story.

Publius Cornelius Tacitus did not live up to his name, or rather, his cognomen. Tacitus means 'Quiet Man', and mercifully for the first glimmers of the documentary history of the Highlands, he was no such thing. Writing concise prose full of well-turned, memorable phrases, certainly as talented a stylist as Cicero, if not even better, he published a great deal towards the end of the first century AD. Perhaps Tacitus' most famous work is the *Agricola*, a brief biography of his father-in-law, Gnaeus Julius Agricola, the governor of the province of Britannia between AD 77 and AD 84 and the man who led an army into Caledonia. It reads fluently, the narrative fresh, exciting, clear and succinct, and many scholars believe that much of it is eyewitness reportage. Provincial governors often appointed family members, men who could be trusted, to their staff, and it is likely that his son-in-law accompanied Agricola on his campaigns in Britannia as a military tribune.

By AD 80 Roman legions had marched north of the Cheviots and were building forts and roads to consolidate their conquests and strengthen their alliances with Lowland native kindreds and their kings. A Roman fleet shadowed the advances north and kept the army supplied by sea. In AD 82 Agricola led his troops further north, 'beyond *Bodotria*', the Latin name for the Firth of Forth. It was not terra incognita. Two thousand years ago military intelligence was just as vital as it is now, and Tacitus wrote that Roman ships had made voyages and reconnoitred the northern coasts and potential harbours. The report in the *Agricola* of what their sailors and captains saw was one of the earliest recorded and earliest surviving eyewitness accounts of the Northern Isles and of the western sea lochs of the

Atlantic shore – it is a brief snapshot of the Highlands and Islands seen from the sea:

> It was then that a Roman fleet for the first time circumnavigated this coast of the remotest sea and established that Britain is in fact an island. Then it too discovered the islands, hitherto unknown, which are called the Orcades [Orkney], and subjugated them. Thule [Shetland] was thoroughly viewed, as well, but no more, for the fleet's orders were to go no further, and winter was approaching. It is reported, however, that the sea there is sluggish and difficult for the rowers, and is not even stirred up by the winds as happens elsewhere. The reason is, I believe, that land and mountains, which create and feed storms, are further apart there, and the deep mass of broken seawater is set in motion more slowly. It is not the purpose of the present work to investigate the physical properties of the Ocean and tides, which have in any case been dealt with by many writers. I would add only one point. Nowhere is the dominance of the sea more extensive. There are many tidal currents, flowing in different directions. They do not merely rise as far as the shoreline and recede again. They flow far inland, wind around, and push themselves among the highlands and the mountains, as if in their own realm.

When Agricola led his army beyond the Tay, Tacitus noted that in the previous summer's campaigning season, the governor had prudently consolidated his gains south of the firths of Clyde and Forth. These were separated from Caledonia 'by a narrow neck of land' around what is now Stirling, and 'the enemy had been pushed back, as if into a different island'. Although not explicitly stated, it seems that Caledonia was then the name for only the north of Scotland, the lands beyond the Forth and Clyde.

The route to the north taken by the legions can be securely traced by a string of defensive camps they dug at the end of each day's march. From their frontier posts on the Gask Ridge, not far from Bertha (Perth), the Romans skirted the great forest and its mountains and glens, more or less following the line of the Highland Boundary Fault, establishing a fort at Raedykes, close to Stonehaven. They then turned north to Kintore and then north-west through the Moray coastlands as far as Bellie, near Fochabers. The marching camp there may have been substantial (a great deal of archaeology was destroyed by the building of a much later army camp during the Second World War) at thirty acres and it lay close to the River Spey and could have been easily supplied by ships anchored in Spey Bay. The only native kindred noted by Tacitus in the *Agricola* is the Boresti, and the name may be cognate to Forres, a town not far from the camp.

In AD 83 the governor of Britannia launched his seventh and final campaign. The enemy was the Caledonian kindreds, what may have been a confederacy of Highland warbands (Tacitus called them 'states'), and once more the advance of the Roman army skirted the fringes of the great forest. Somewhere in the Angus glens, Agricola appears to have made a near-fatal tactical blunder – although Tacitus does not call it that (he is always supportive of his father-in-law's reputation). Agricola divided his forces 'into three divisions and advanced'. In one of his most brilliantly written, most authentic passages, Tacitus recounts what happened next:

> When the enemy discovered this [that Agricola had divided his forces], with a rapid change of plan they massed for a night attack on the Ninth Legion, as being by far the weakest in numbers. They cut down the sentries and burst into the sleeping camp, creating panic. Fighting was already going on inside the camp itself when Agricola, who had learned of the enemy's route from his scouts and was following close on their tracks, ordered the most mobile of his cavalry and infantry to charge the combatants from the rear and then the whole army was to raise the battle-cry. At first light the standards gleamed. The Britons were terrified at being caught between two fires, while the men of the Ninth regained their spirits and now that their lives were safe began to fight for glory. They even ventured on a break out and a fierce battle followed in the

narrow passage of the gates. Finally the enemy were driven back before the rival efforts of two armies. The one wanted to show that it had come to the rescue, the other that it had not needed help. Had not marshes or forests covered the retreating enemy, that victory would have ended the war.

Agricola might have ended the war, and not with Rome as the victor, if he had not remembered the fate of Gaius Varus and had instead allowed his army to pursue the Caledonians into their deep, dark forest. As it was, he regrouped and marched further north. Probably at the foot of the singular hill of Bennachie, not far from Inverurie, the Caledonians made their own, fatal, tactical blunder. Instead of retreating to the sanctuary of the great forest and conducting a guerrilla campaign of attrition, they gave Agricola what he wanted, a battle in open field. Below what Tacitus called the 'Graupian Mountain', the disciplined, tight formations of Roman auxiliaries and legionaries slaughtered the charging warriors of the Caledonian Confederacy. They were led by Calgacos, perhaps the first Highlander to be named in the historical record. His name means 'the Swordsman', and he was the earliest in a long line of famous swordsmen from the north, the last of them being defeated at Culloden in 1746.

There was one other arrival from the Mediterranean who cast a long, ancient and very intriguing shadow over the history of the Highlands and Islands. Pytheas of Massalia (Marseilles, then a Greek colony) wrote a *periplus*, a route guide for traders, known as *On the Ocean*, meaning the Atlantic and the North Sea. Compiled sometime after 320 BC, it has very sadly not survived but was much quoted and even plagiarised by later writers. Pliny had read it and included information from the intrepid author in the *Natural History*, and he informs us that in Britain, 'the tide rises 80 cubits [about 120 feet]'. It may be that Tacitus' reference to other writings about the ocean and its tides is an oblique reference to the Greek adventurer's work. Copies of *On the Ocean* were still circulating in the first century AD.

It was the tin trade that brought Pytheas to Britain. It is a rare metal in Europe and was necessary to make the very valuable alloy known as bronze. The traveller was also the first to call Britain 'Britain'. When he reached the Channel coast of what is now France, he probably asked the natives what the peoples across the sea called themselves. *Pretannikai* was how he rendered the answer. It means the 'People of the Tattoos', and though body decoration was clearly still widespread amongst the ancient British, it had probably died out in what became Gaul. Pytheas wrote down the name of the island as *Pretannike* and the Romans changed it only a little to Britannia, before it finally settled and became Britain.

The Greek was making notes for a guide for merchants and was an explorer who took accurate measurements as he circumnavigated Britain. He wanted others to follow him. Reckoning in *stades*, about 200 yards, Pytheas believed that the circumference of Britain was about 40,000 stades. That works out at about 4,830 miles and shows that he was taking very accurate measurements. The actual circumference of the British coastline is 4,710 miles.

Just as Agricola's naval captains were to do almost 400 years later, Pytheas saw the Highlands and the Islands from the sea. Using a measuring stick called a *gnomon*, he took readings of latitude as he travelled further and further north. Given his accuracy, it is almost certain that he landed on the Atlantic shore of the island of Lewis, very close to where the standing stones of Calanais were set up almost 2,000 years before. Even though they had long been abandoned, they must still have impressed this remarkable, brave and endlessly curious Greek traveller. He was also the first to note the name Orkas, his version of Orkney. It almost certainly means something like the 'Boar Islands'.

From Pliny's *Natural History*, Tacitus' crisp prose and other noted Roman historians (some of whom, like Diodorus Siculus, lifted whole passages from *On the Ocean*), the Caledonian Forest passed from documentary history into the half-light of Celtic myths and unreliable narratives. The *Historia Brittonum*, the History of the Britons, was compiled by Nennius, an Old Welsh-speaking monk probably working in the eighth century. His name looks like a Latin version of Ninian. In the preface to his history, he cheerfully admits that 'I have made a heap of all that I have found' and includes tales of dragons and other fables. But there is also material in the book that deserves to be taken more seriously. In particular, Nennius wrote of the wars between the native British and the Anglo-Saxon immigrants of the late fifth and sixth centuries. 'Then Arthur fought against them in those days, with the Kings of the Britons, but he himself was the Leader of Battles.'

Not a king, as in popular legend, but a general, a *dux bellorum*, a war leader, Arthur fought a campaign of twelve victorious battles which other sources suggest may have checked the advance of Anglo-Saxon power across what is now England. The seventh battle appears to have been fought in the north, perhaps against Anglian warriors, more likely against Highlanders, the peoples who became known to history as the Picts. Nennius wrote: 'The seventh battle was in the wood of Celidon, that is, Cat Coit Celidon.' The last three words are a version in Old Welsh of the 'Battle of the Wood of Caledonia'.

Forever associated in the popular imagination with King Arthur is Merlin, both as a wizard and as an advisor. He too is not an invention, but he could never have met Arthur since the wisps of such records as exist have him living seventy years after the great general died. There exists an early cycle of Welsh language poetry known as *The Prophecies of Myrddin*, the name an early version of Merlin. Much that was passed on in an oral tradition and then written down can be fanciful, but there are nuggets of history in these ancient poems, events that are noted by other sources. In 573 a bloody battle was fought at Arthuret, between Carlisle and Longtown. The defeated King Gwenddolau was killed and his bard, Myrddin, was said to have been driven insane by the slaughter and he fled to the north, to the safety and cover of the great forest.

I slept alone in the Woods of Celyddon,
Shield on shoulder, sword on thigh.

From this moment, in the late sixth century, the story needs to rewind back to the end of the last ice age and to rely not only on Old Welsh poetry or Roman and Greek prose but on the painstaking work of palaeoclimatologists. They help us understand what the Caledonian Forest looked like and the landscape of the Highlands and Islands around its fringes. The trees began to grow about 10,000 years ago, following the melting of the ice and the warming of the climate. The forest was once vast and dense, reaching high up the mountainsides and it covered a staggering 3.7 million acres, a primeval wildwood. Stretching from the Highland Boundary Fault, its green horizons extended as far north as a line drawn from the Dornoch Firth to Ullapool but did not cover the Moray coastlands or the straths of Aberdeenshire or Angus, the relatively open country through which Agricola's legions marched. The forest also did not spread south to Cowal or Kintyre, and trees were not abundant on any of the islands of the Hebrides or the Northern Isles. It was most dense amongst the mountains and glens of the mainland, and the green corridor of the Great Glen dividing the two ancient terranes was also covered by the great wood.

Now, only a little more than 1 per cent of the Caledonian Forest has survived. Remnant woodlands can be seen in Strathspey and Glen Affric, and in small areas scattered across the Highlands, but the lonely stands of trees can offer no real sense of scale. Ten thousand years ago, when the forest was at its greatest extent, the north looked very different.

The remnant trees form a tiny part of the taiga biome, the snow forest. It covers a huge area, 11.5 per cent of the earth's land surface, stretching across Siberia, Scandinavia, North America and Alaska. The first seeds of the Caledonian Forest were carried on the winds that blew across the now-drowned subcontinent of Doggerland or were dropped by the birds and animals who ate them. And the green tide also came from the south because the English Channel was dry land for at least three millennia after the ice.

Scots Pine was the staple of the Caledonian Forest and many of its seeds travelled east from Scandinavia in the centuries around

7,000 BC to grow amongst the glens and the mountains. When the North Sea reclaimed Doggerland and forced its way through the English Channel, the pines became genetically isolated. The remnant trees are therefore the direct descendants of the original arrivals. Scots pines can be monumental, often growing as high as 100 to 120 feet even in the poorest soils on the Macaulay scale. And they are beautiful, magnificent. As the trees grow, they tend to shed lower limbs as the canopy spreads, and this allows the development of underbrush, bushes of berries and sometimes a lush, green and mossy carpet. The bark of mature pines is heavily ridged, rough and gnarled, almost layered, the heartwood is a glorious russet-orange and the scent of Scots pines is unmistakable. Some live long, up to 700 years. These are sometimes known as granny trees and many of the remnant woods have several still surviving.

Once the taiga, the snow forest, was established in the Highlands, the weather changed once more. Warmed by the waters of the Gulf Stream, the western coasts in particular saw temperatures rise even higher between 6500 BC and 6000 BC in what is known as the Atlantic Warm Period. This marked change brought deciduous trees north, such as birch, aspen, willow, rowan and oak. The famed oak forests of Lochaber were seeded at that time. Beyond the fringes of the Caledonian Forest, the Hebrides, the far north-west, the Northern Isles and in the south Cowal and Kintyre, became green landscapes as growing seasons lengthened and average temperatures climbed.

The bounty of the great forest and the woodland around it attracted all manner of animals. Most spectacular was the aurochs, huge wild cattle with seven-foot horn-spreads who thrashed their way through the undergrowth in search of succulence. There were elk, almost as large, and wild boar snuffling after acorns and beech-mast. On the seashore and in the rivers there were otters, and beavers felling trees to make dams, build their lodges and make good places to fish. Up in the canopy, squirrels skittered along the branches with pine martins, wildcats and polecats. Predators lurked in the shadows of the trees, waiting and watching. There were lynx, brown bears and packs of wolves. Above the wildwood's green horizons, raptors such as golden eagles and buzzards quartered the silent Highland skies, soaring in the updraughts, searching the ground for movement. It was a time of abundance, almost Edenic, the millennia after the ice, and as predators quietly patrolled the woods and in the great forest in the mountains, they were followed by the most dangerous and deadly predator of all, by human beings, our ancestors.

3

The Gates of Eden

8000 BC–3700 BC

It was an evening of high summer, windless and a westering sun lighting the tree-lined single-track road along the north shore of Loch Carron. I was looking for a cottage at Ardaneaskan. The Ordnance Survey map showed it at the end of the road, a fraying, unclassified little road that swung abruptly around rocky outcrops and dived down and then up out of steep declivities. But the little cottage turned out to be at the beginning of another road, a sea road, and it looked out over a wide and watery intersection. Once I'd worked out how to extract a key from the combination safe by the front door, dumped my bag, taken a bottle of Glenlivet from it and furnished myself with a reward for a long drive from the Borders via Inverness, I sat down on a bench and gazed at magnificence.

Ardaneaskan lies at the end of a peninsula that forms part of the southern shore of the Inner Sound, a wide stretch of sheltered water between the long islands of Raasay and Skye in the west and the mainland coastline of Applecross in the east. Speckled with a scatter of smaller islands, Scalpay, Pabay, Longay and the Crowlins, the sea, the mighty Atlantic, glimmered in a flat calm, the sun slowly sinking behind the mountains of Wester Ross. I was surrounded with a silence broken only by the lapping of the waves on a stony beach below the cottage. Across Loch Carron were the only signs of other people, the distant string of twinkling lights that picked out the little village of Plockton in the gathering gloaming. The huge and darkling sky was becoming a starry canopy, and I thought of the phrase 'the vaults of

Heaven'. Out to the west, the hills of Raasay and the jagged ridge of the Cuillin behind them were becoming shadowy silhouettes.

In the woodland behind the cottage, owls began answering each other, their hooting seeming to echo on the water as territory was marked out. After a day's drive on difficult or busy roads, I needed just to sit, clear my head and think about nothing. All the questions and any answers could wait for the morning. I knew that after I'd gone indoors, eaten what I could be bothered to cook and then climbed into a welcome bed, I'd be asleep in moments.

The sign at the bottom of the pass was eye-catching, even arresting: ROAD NORMALLY IMPASSABLE IN WINTRY CONDITIONS. I'd driven from Ardaneaskan on a still, crystal blue morning, one of many in the dry summer of 2022 when no rain fell for weeks on end. With the sun at my back and the colours of Highland Scotland rich and subtle on the mountain and lochsides, I was on my way to Applecross. Not for the last time on the Atlantic shore, where 'the tides flow far inland . . . as if in their own realm', according to Tacitus, I thought my journey would have been faster and safer by boat as I wound my way along and around sea lochs. From a rotting old jetty close to the cottage I'd rented, I reckoned I could have sailed between the Crowlin Islands and the southern tip of the Applecross peninsula and tied up at Camusteel in less than an hour. And I wouldn't have had to drive over a mountain.

I had stopped the car at the foot of Bealach na Bà, 'the Cattle Trail', to take some photographs. It is Britain's steepest ascent over the shortest distance, rising 2,000 feet from sea level at Loch Kishorn to the summit in less than two miles. And the cattle would have made the climb more quickly, and more safely. Even though the road is said to be two-way, it is not only very narrow in places, places where there is often a forty-five degree drop on one side, it is also extremely busy. As a mobile home, far too wide, came barrelling round a blind corner, far too fast, I was forced to stop right on the fraying edge of the tarmac. And as it whooshed past, its wing mirror cracked into mine, knocking it flush with the driver door. If the idiot driving this bus had been inches closer, I'd have been pushed over the edge and the somersaulting descent would only have stopped at the loch shore a thousand feet below me – if the car hadn't blown up before then. The Bealach na Bà is part of the North 500, and it should not be. Hairpin bends and extravagant, looping, zigzagging roads, especially where there are no safety barriers, need careful driving and not people gazing at the spectacular views, forgetting to steer or brake, thinking only of themselves.

But when I reached the summit almost all was forgiven.

In a welcome car park, I climbed out of my car and looked southwest to Raasay, the Cuillin and the Red Hills below them. To see mountains across the brilliant blue sea from the top of other mountains is for some reason breathtaking, as though we are standing closer to the gods with the earth below us, the clear, clean air filling our lungs, the vistas graphic and long, and perhaps I could see the curve of the far horizon. In places like the summit of the Bealach, there can be a sense of purity and of peace.

Where the road swings around a bend beyond the car park, it seemed to me that I had passed into another world. Far below me was the wide sweep of Applecross Bay. Beyond woodlands and green fields was a white church and what might have been its manse beside it. And beyond all of that distant splendour lay the eternities of the ocean. After a hellish ascent, I felt as though I was passing down through the gates of Eden.

When I reached the foot of the road that wound gently down from the summit, I saw that Applecross village was strung out to my left along the shoreline. But I turned in the opposite direction to drive around the wide bay, cross the river, pass the church and its manse and make my way to a small inlet with an immense story to tell.

Sand Bay is a prosaic name for an idyllic place. In a small indent that looks on the map as though it was bitten out of the Applecross shore, there is a beautiful, broad beach and dunes behind it. What interested me was neither. I walked across the grass to a large humpbacked rock half engulfed by bracken. On one side of it there is a shelter, not a cave like those at Allt nan Uamh, but an overhang that would have kept out the worst of the wind and bad weather that blew in off the Inner Sound. Recent archaeology has discovered that more than 8,000 years ago a hunter-gatherer band lived here, some of the very earliest people to settle in the Highlands and Islands after the ice.

A rubbish heap turned out to be eloquent. In the summer of 2000, on the grassy slope below the rock shelter, archaeologists began to excavate what they call a shell midden. About thirteen feet wide and sixteen feet long, it was the residue of a menu, what the band of hunter-gatherers caught, cooked and ate. Most of the shells were limpets prized from the rocks around the bay, a job that could have been done by children while adults fished offshore or in the nearby river. Sand was a good place to overwinter and limpets and other shellfish were a staple in the cold months when days were short and game not plentiful. But eaten raw, they are chewy and the excavators found fragments of stone boilers amongst the debris outside the rock shelter. Limpets can also be roasted in the embers of a fire. When the shells are gathered and while the limpet is still alive, it can be set on a wet and flat stone where it will re-attach itself. When a dozen or so are securely on the stone, it is then placed in the centre of a dying fire and hot ash and embers are heaped over it. Twenty-first-century limpet roasters are always careful to remove the bitter-tasting gut sack before eating what they have cooked.

A steady and convenient supply of firewood was vital to a family of hunter-gatherers and in the lee of the humpbacked stone, there will always have been a blaze burning under the overhang. Not only was the heat needed for cooking, but it was important to keep the winter's chill at bay. Modern human beings complain bitterly if they are cold and do all they can to wrap up and keep warm. But for our ancestors, who had yet to perfect the skills of spinning and weaving, animal skins and fleeces were all they had to wear and being cold in winter will have been normal, something to be tolerated. Analyses of later prehistoric skeletons have shown that many people, even in their twenties and thirties, suffered from arthritis probably brought on by being persistently cold and damp. But there were ways of warding off the night chill. Just as in unheated tenements in cities and farm cottages in the recent past, people slept as close together as possible to warm each other – the single bed is a modern invention. In the circle of firelight, on a winter night when the seawind howled down the Inner Sound, mothers and fathers will have held their little ones close, covering them with fleeces and pelts, cuddling them if they shivered.

Firewood and food gathering was a daily business and the shell midden at Sand was found to contain debris from other crustaceans. Crabs can be very simply cooked by placing them in the centre of a flaming fire. Once the shell is blackened, and it has cooked in its own juices, parents will have been careful not to spill these as they opened it. Bird bones were also found, yet more evidence that Sand was a good place to overwinter. There are low cliffs nearby and with care and some stealth, nesting sites can be approached in the spring for eggs and later for young and flightless chicks. In addition to a few other animal bones such as deer, tools also turned up in what is called a lithic scatter, a place where flints were knapped to make arrowheads and sharp edges for cutting and skinning.

Some of the stone that the people at Sand worked and used came from the island of Rum, almost twenty miles to the south. At Kinloch, at the head of Loch Scresort, sheltered and east-facing, archaeologists have found the marks made by bender tents or tipis. Dating to around 7000 BC, these shelters were made by pushing rods of whippy green wood into the ground, bending them to form a curved roof framework, lashing them together and then covering them with large animal pelts like deerskins. The people who built the tipis may have been engaged in prehistoric industry. Scotland has few deposits of flint but igneous rocks like bloodstone are workable substitutes. Around the tipis at Kinloch on Rum, archaeologists found many thousands of microliths, the waste produced by knapping the stone to make blades.

It may be that the people of Sand sailed, in better weather, to the island to acquire the bloodstone they needed for hunting and preparing meat. Perhaps they bartered for it. But how did they make the forty-mile return voyage?

In 2003 I saw how they did it. On the bank of the River Lee, opposite the Beamish Brewery in the city of Cork, is the Michel Mara boatyard. Amongst the clutter of stacks of seasoned planking and offcuts of wood, amidst the thud of hammering and the buzzing whine of electric saws, Pádraig Ó Duinnín was making a boat designed 10,000 years ago. Under the corrugated iron roof of a lean-to, he was bending thick, green hazel rods into the oval shape of the gunwales of a small boat. With twine he lashed the rods together, putting some tension on each to widen the oval. Then he bored a series of small holes into each rod, being careful not to pierce them. In a flurry of activity, Pádraig then pushed a series of thinner hazel rods into the holes, lashed them tightly together and trimmed them into what was beginning to look like the skeleton of the hull of a boat. With the help of Michael, a young enthusiast who worked part-time in the boatyard, Pádraig then stretched black, toughened canvas over the frame and lashed it as tightly as possible to the gunwales. Both men then picked up the little boat, flipped it over and forced two benches between the gunwales to act as thwarts and to keep the frame rigid and the canvas taut.

It had taken Pádraig and Michael little more than a morning to make a seagoing curragh, a boat that has sailed the coastal waters of the Atlantic for millennia. The only major difference between the curragh made in Cork and those that were rowed across the Inner Sound was the fabric. The hunter-gatherers at Sand would have used deerskins, the pelts of wild horses or the hide of an auroch if one could have been brought down with arrows and spears. For caulking, they may have used warmed resin or animal fat.

Most of the voyage south to Rum and its bloodstone was between the mainland and Raasay and Skye. Tides at the narrows of Kyle of Lochalsh and at Kylerhea might have been tricky to navigate, but if the wind ran behind them, the oarsmen in a curragh might have made good time. The only stretch of relatively open water was the five or six miles from the Aird of Sleat to the sanctuary of Loch Scresort on Rum. If at any stage on the voyage the weather had become difficult, the oarsmen could have quickly rowed to the shorelines of Skye or the mainland and picked up their curragh to turn it over to make a shelter from the squalls.

The team of archaeologists who excavated the shell midden at Sand also conducted a survey of potential hunter-gatherer sites around the Inner Sound. Four had already been identified at Redpoint, south of Loch Gairloch, at Staffin on Skye, at Shieldaig at the head of Loch Torridon and at Loch a' Sguirr on Raasay. But meticulous new research revealed a staggering 104 new sites around the sound. Of these, seventy-four were rock shelters or caves, twenty-one were lithic scatters and there were nine more shell middens. Even though these places were occupied by different people over a long span of time, it is difficult to escape the conclusion that there was a prehistoric community around the shores of the Inner Sound.

On still days the people of Sand will have seen the smoke of the fires of their neighbours on Raasay to the west and elsewhere around the coast. And they must have communicated and met. Curraghs rowed expertly can skim across the top of the waves because they are so light and have a shallow draught, and exchanges of all sorts will have been made; food and materials bartered, information given and taken, and perhaps marriage partners sought for growing children. The hunter-gatherer population of the Highlands and Islands was likely very small and most bands seemed to live on the coast, with occasional summer hunting parties venturing inland after deer and other large mammals. The sea and its shorelines were bountiful. There were nesting birds on the cliffs, fish traps could be set at the mouth of rivers to catch migrating salmon, brown trout could be pulled out of lochs and in some places particular wild harvests could be gathered. On the island of Colonsay, south of Mull and a long voyage from Sand, hazel trees grew in abundance. On the old, raised beach at Staosnaig a pit was found filled with hundreds of thousands of charred hazelnut shells, too many to be accurately counted. They were carbon dated to *c.*6,700 BC. When the harvesters had picked all the hazelnuts, they roasted them to improve the flavour and also to allow them to be mashed into a paste, like a prehistoric version of Nutella. This nourishing paste kept well and could be eaten through the winter.

But then something surprising, inexplicable, came to light. It seems that after ingathering their rich harvest, the pickers destroyed the trees on Colonsay, not pruning them or cutting them back, but cutting them down. Why the harvesters would do that is hard to fathom, but there is a whisper of ritual, of some sort of religious rite. Was the bounty of the gods being somehow acknowledged, or denied? It is impossible to tell.

More mystery was uncovered very close at hand. Oronsay is a small island linked at low tide with Colonsay. It is a curious, wind-swept, atmospheric place and when I walked across to the island at low tide, I found I was the only person there. Sheep were contentedly grazing and had cropped the lush grass right down to the shoreline. There were low ruins here and there, an old cottage and perhaps a barn. I walked inland a little way to find what I'd come to look at, a series of large and grassy mounds. They looked as though they might have been found on a landscaped golf course, but in fact they are what remains of huge shell middens. There are five on Oronsay and one on Colonsay. Far larger than the middens at Sand, they are also later, dating to around 5300 BC and used for a thousand years after then. As well as hundreds of thousands of mussel, clam, oyster, limpet, razor and scallop shells, archaeologists found fish bones, bits of antler – and human remains.

When human fingers were discovered deliberately laid on seal flippers, the image resonated with me. I had read of and seen photographs of a remarkable burial near Vedbæk in Denmark, linked at that time by the subcontinent of Doggerland with Britain. Near an encampment of bender tents, a grave had been dug for a woman whose corpse had been decorated in all her finery, including a necklace made from the teeth of forty-three different stags. Beside her lay the body of her baby, nestled in a white swan's wing. It is an image of great power and tenderness that speaks of a sense of an afterlife, perhaps even of the migration of souls. Was it thought by the people of Vedbæk that the spirit of the baby might fly with the great birds in the huge skies above the encampment? And did the hunter-gatherers of Oronsay believe that their dead would swim with the seals in the deeps of the world?

At Sand the archaeologists found that life was not solely concerned with survival, with the quotidian routines of firewood and food gathering. The hunter-gatherers made jewellery. Two pierced and decorated cowrie shells were found in the midden. They might have formed part of a necklace. There were also shell beads and a square plaque had been cut from a large scallop shell.

Life around the shores of the Inner Sound was not Edenic, perhaps, but it could be good. In summers of plenty, when wild harvests of roots, fruits and berries had been gathered and stored, when game had been caught and smoked, when salmon and trout had been brought ashore and a crab roasted on a fire, there was time not only to make jewellery but also to talk, tell stories, gossip, laugh, play pranks and sit on the humpbacked rock in the warmth of a summer evening and look out over the glories of the Highlands and Islands, the place these people called home. We can never know what our ancestors said or believed 8,000 or 9,000 years ago, but we can be sure that life could be rich and joyful and that they were not always shivering around the flicker of a winter fire. Nevertheless, it was a world that could be shattered by the deadly drama of natural disaster.

*

In the autumn of 2020, I was walking up Castle Street in Inverness to see how building work was proceeding. Transformed from a courthouse and a prison, always a dour, dismal set of buildings to find in the middle of a vibrant and growing city, Inverness Castle was to become a visitor centre for those who wanted to find out about the history and the culture of the Highlands and Islands. I remembered reading about other, earlier building work when numbers 13 to 24 Castle Street were demolished in the 1980s to make way for more modern architecture. As often in the centre of historic cities, and especially on a site so close to the castle, archaeologists undertook a rapid dig to see what might be discovered. And they found something unexpected. Under the remains of what they reckoned were early medieval houses, they found a lithic scatter and other tell-tale signs of a hunter-gatherer encampment from the sixth millennium

BC. But mixed with those there was a layer of sand, but not just any sort of sand. It was white, pelagic sand, the sort found on the seabed and not on the beach. And in it there was a great deal of debris, many stones and pebbles. It turned out to be the residue of a cataclysm.

Sometime around 5840 BC there was a huge undersea earthquake. Off the western coast of Norway, along the edge of the continental shelf, the seabed suddenly shuddered with a massive landslip when many millions of cubic yards of rock slipped into a gap that opened up in the earth's crust. The effect was unimaginably dramatic, belly-hollowing, terrifying. An enormous volume of water surged into the gap in moments and the sea receded very fast from coastlines, sounding like a monstrous vacuum-cleaner, revealing great expanses of the seabed, leaving fish flapping, seals, whales and other mammals stranded. That band of hunter-gatherers at the mouth of the River Ness will have watched this elemental drama open-mouthed, wondering if the world was about to end. But it was nothing compared to what happened next. Far in the distance, beyond the eastern horizon, a faint rumble rapidly grew into a mighty roar as a tsunami raced towards the shore. It travelled at an extraordinary speed, perhaps 300 miles an hour. And when the giant wave crashed down on the coast, smashing all in its path, raining down boulders, snapping trees like matchsticks and sweeping all before it, many died. Any who had somehow survived may then have been pulled out to sea by the ferocious undertow that followed. The white sand, the stones and the pebbles found at 13 to 24 Castle Street in Inverness remember that prehistoric catastrophe.

Traces of what became known as the Storegga Slide (the name of a deep-sea trench that curves around the Norwegian coast) were found on the western shores of Continental Europe and as far south as Amsterdam. But the consequences of the massive landslip for another community were probably more than catastrophic. They were terminal.

Doggerland had been shrinking slowly for some time as sea levels rose faster than isostatic rebound, and the area around the Dogger Hills may have become a large island by 5840 BC. But it is very likely

that the tsunami, and others that came behind it, inundated the dry
land and what remained of the subcontinent to the south in a matter
of hours. Many will have been drowned, much lost and it could
be that at this time Britain did become the British Isles as the sea
roared into the valleys between the cliffs of England and France,
broke through to the Atlantic and made the English Channel.

Geographical isolation was not followed by a break in contact. In
the centuries after the Storegga Slide and its devastating tsunamis,
people sailed between Europe and Britain, most making way across
the Channel where they could stay within sight of land.

In the summer of 2003, the National Trust for Scotland decided
that the footpaths on its Mar Lodge estate in Highland Aberdeenshire
were in need of repair. The River Dee rises in the shadow of Ben
Macdui, Scotland's second-highest mountain, and where it is joined
by the Geldie Burn, the glaciers and their meltwater shaped a raised,
triangular terrace known as the Chest of Dee. The footpath there was
fraying and when workers set about restoring it, they noticed – and
recognised – something unusual. It was a lithic scatter, mostly debris
and a few flints that had clearly been knapped. When archaeologists
arrived to assess and then excavate the site, they discovered something very surprising. Carbon dating of pieces of charcoal from a
firepit told them that a band of hunter-gatherers had made camp on
the river terrace around 8000 BC, not only an astonishingly early date
but also clear evidence of pioneers penetrating the interior, travelling
far from the abundance of the sea-coast, and entering the shadows of
the Caledonian Forest.

Ten thousand years ago, Chest of Dee looked very different.
Instead of open, wind-scoured moorland, much of it peaty and
heather-covered, the terrace lay well below the tree line. It was likely
open woodland with dense stands of Scots Pine mixed with copses
of birch, good cover for animals, and for those who hunted them.
Even the higher altitudes and places with snowfields that lasted for
most of the year were a sanctuary of sorts for the cold adapted animals who had followed the melting ice northwards, such as reindeer,
who suffered in the summer heat. Bitten by insects and attacked by

parasites, they fled to the high places on the Cairngorm plateau. And the hunters followed them.

These were family bands who probably left their overwinter refuges on the sea-coast or perhaps even in Doggerland to make their way up the River Dee in skin boats. They could be used as water and windbreak shelters on the journey and were perhaps dismantled when the family reached the river terrace. The hide hulls of curraghs or coracles can easily be adapted to make bender tents. At Chest of Dee the archaeologists found a small hearth that may have burned in the centre of a tent or a tipi. Whole families, not just parties of men, travelled along what prehistorians call 'lifeways', annual or frequent journeys in search of life's essentials: food, flints, hides, pelts and firewood. There is strong evidence that people came to Chest of Dee for 5,000 years, 250 generations of families or more. Because of their diet of roots, fruits, berries and meat, babies and toddlers whose teeth developed only slowly depended on their mother's milk as a source of essential protein. Women can be infertile while nursing and some children will have had breast milk as a dependable staple for three to five years. That had the effect of making the birth interval long and hunter-gatherer families small. Assuming a short life span, twenty-six to thirty years at most, women were fertile for perhaps only fourteen to sixteen years, perhaps enough time to have four children. And by no means all would have survived. It is also likely that complications in giving birth, such as breech, resulted in early deaths for both mothers and babies.

Evolution was at work here. The long birth interval allowed the families to travel the lifeways. With a baby and one or two toddlers, these journeys would have been impossible. With either a baby carried in a papoose, or a toddler walking and being carried when tired, a small family could travel. And if there was an older child of four or five, he or she could gather berries, fungi, dig up roots, search for eggs or knock limpets off the rocks on the seashore.

For millennia, flint brought families to Chest of Dee. It is rare in Britain, but deposits of rhyolite, a very hard, silica-rich volcanic rock could be found nearby. It often occurs at or near the points of collision of terranes or tectonic plates. With meticulous excavation, sifting through the peaty soil for tiny artefacts, the archaeologists found some skilfully knapped blades and points of rhyolite. Acidic soil dissolves a great deal of organic material, and these slivers and chips of igneous rock can be eloquent. Other lithic scatters have been found nearby at Caochanan Ruadha and Sgor an Eoin, 'the Red Streams' and 'the Rock of the Wildfowl'. Excavators are convinced that there are many more sites waiting to be discovered and they have appealed to hill walkers to keep an eye open for more signs of lithic scatters. The finds at Mar Lodge and elsewhere are redrawing the geography and rewriting the prehistory of the Highlands and Islands. It used to be thought that hunter-gatherers settled on the coasts, around shores such as those of the Inner Sound where food could be found all year round. It now seems that bands ventured into the Caledonian Forest and the high country above it on more than summer expeditions. At Chest of Dee they made a base and each spring, for thousands of years, bands kept coming back to exactly the same place.

The climate was still fluctuating and there was a particularly cold period in the centuries around 6200 BC, but the forest is likely to have been home to many species of fauna and flora that flourished there. Populations of animals far outnumbered human beings and paths through the woods will have been made by animals and not by men or women. Since deer, wild horses, wild boar and most other four-legged creatures would always outrun human pursuers, it is highly likely that trapping was the prime means of predation. Along the paths followed by animals, pits will have been dug and sharp stakes placed in them before they were covered over. Nets and snares will have been used, and occasionally there might have been opportunistic kills. Few animals ever saw human beings in the Caledonian Forest and might have been fatally hesitant before they recognised a predator. But there was danger too. Bears and wild boars are not to be trifled with and no doubt some hunters became the hunted.

*

Archaeology can be eloquent about the lives of early peoples, but so can language when it is seen as a deposit of history, as can a study of place names because they speak of long experience in one place.

Two figures tower over any serious attempt to understand of the story of the Highlands and Islands, and neither of them were historians. Edward Dwelly was an unlikely lexicographer who compiled a vast, sprawling, idiosyncratic and immensely valuable dictionary of the Gaelic language. Born in 1864 in Twickenham, now a suburb of London, Dwelly was an Englishman who did not speak the language. But after being stationed in Scotland as a soldier and working on surveying for Ordnance Survey maps, he fell in love with the Highlands, learned to play the bagpipes and learned the language. In 1896 he married Mary McDougal, a native Gaelic speaker from Kilmadock near Stirling, and she helped him become fluent.

Dwelly began work on his dictionary in 1901. It was a pioneering enterprise, there being no definitive lexicon. A great difficulty was that Gaelic speakers often could neither write nor read their language as a result of generations of suppression. Into the yawning cultural void Dwelly poured immense labour and love. His dictionary is much more than an alphabetical wordlist with meanings attached. It is also a narrative, a history of understanding and describing a way of life. He included drawings and wrote snippets of description. For example, Dwelly's magisterial analysis of the Gaelic colour spectrum – very different from and much wider than English – includes notes on different pigments and how they were extracted from plants, roots, shellfish and lichen, and then goes on to describe how yarns were dyed before weaving. The dictionary is a treasure-trove, a thesaurus in all senses, but its compiler was neither liked nor lauded by the native Gaelic speech community. Edward Dwelly died in obscurity in 1939 at Fleet in Hampshire, about as far away from the Gàidhealtachd as it is possible to be.

Gaelic has described the Highlands and the Hebrides for at least 1,500 years and is eloquent on the precise nature of geography and how people used it. From my research and writing about the Scottish Borders I knew that the place names of Eildrig, Elrick and

even Ellig remembered an ancient method of hunting. Very different
from the popular image of riding around the countryside behind
a pack of hounds, it became known as the drive and sett. Much
more efficient than the chase, this method involved driving prey
animals towards a confined narrow place where hunters waited to
kill them. The Borders place names sounded Gaelic-derived to my
ear and Dwelly confirmed that instinct. *Eileag* means 'a v-shaped
structure wide at one end and narrow at the other into which
deer were driven and shot with arrows as they came out'. I wasn't
convinced by 'structure'. Perhaps Dwelly was referring to fencing
or hurdles of some kind, but badly frightened deer can clear even
very high fences. Suitably confining geography sounded much more
likely although the point made in the dictionary about the narrow
end of the v-shape being open must be right. To keep on coming
towards the hunters, no doubt concealing themselves as best they
could, the fleeing deer had to believe there was a means of escape. A
closed end would have had them wheel and even turn back on those
driving them.

Wondering about how the names of places can tell stories, especially about prehistory, a time long before written record, I turned
with great pleasure to the second towering figure in the historiog-
raphy of the Highlands and Islands. Published in 1926, *The Celtic
Place-names of Scotland* is a canonical work. Unlike Edward Dwelly,
its author, William J. Watson, was a native Gaelic speaker and came
from Milton in Easter Ross. The son of a blacksmith, Watson became
Rector of the Royal High School in Edinburgh and later, Professor
of Celtic at Edinburgh University. His prodigious intelligence and
great gifts of insight propelled him up the academic ladder even
though his origins were humble. The great toponymic survey is the
product of thirty years of research, much of it derived from oral traditions, correspondence and fieldwork. Watson's ear for connections
between different and sometimes widely dispersed place names is
pitch-perfect.

When I looked for references to *eileagan*, his work and the
deep research behind it offered a rich response. Writing in 1795,

the minister at Assynt mentioned a place in his huge parish called 'Fe-na-hard-elig'. This is a characteristic example of transliteration by someone who understood Gaelic but was unable to write it, a difficulty that dogged Edward Dwelly's work. Watson supplied the correct spelling as Féith na h-Airdeileig and it means 'the Bog of the High Eileag'. The minister went on to explain that it was 'a track of soft boggy moor in which, in times of old, the natives gathered deer, and when entangled, they killed them'. He added that there were other deer traps in Assynt: at Allt Eileag, 'the Trap by the Stream', at Loch Eileag and Mointeach Eileag, another boggy place. On his own account. W. J. Watson supplied even more *eileag* names from all over the Highlands, from Gairloch to southern Banffshire.

What all of these place names have in common is the use of appropriate geographical features to entrap the deer and indeed other large mammals. Dwelly's 'structure' must be a reference to more modern practices. And even though these Gaelic names were not attached until the fifth and sixth centuries AD at the earliest, that does not mean the narrow places and bogs were not used by hunter-gatherers thousands of years before then. The geography did not change very much.

In 1949 the great French historian Fernand Braudel published *The Mediterranean and the Mediterranean World in the Age of Philip II*. Although it was ostensibly concerned with the King of Spain, Portugal, Naples and Sicily between 1544 and 1598, the book and the thinking behind it reached much further back in time. Braudel created the concept of the *longue durée*. In similar geographical, social and economic circumstances, he argued, groups of people maintain habits of life and mind over immense periods. When deer traps were renamed as such in Gaelic, many had probably been deer traps for much, much longer, perhaps five or six millennia. Edward Dwelly described the drive and sett method of hunting as *timchioll na sealg*. It was still being used in the Highlands into the early modern period. In 1618 an English poet, John Taylor, travelled to Scotland and published in his *Pennyles Pilgrimage*, an account of a deer hunt he saw in the mountains:

The manner of the hunting is this: five or six hundred men do rise early in the morning, and they do disperse themselves divers ways, and seven, eight, or ten miles compass, they do bring or chase in the deer in many herds (two, three, or four hundred in a herd) to such or such a place, as the Nobleman shall appoint them; then when day is come, the Lords and gentlemen of their companies do ride or go to the said places, sometimes wading up to their middles through bournes and rivers: and then: they being come to the place, do lie down on the ground, till those foresaid scouts, which are called the Tinchel, do bring down the deer: but as the proverb says of a bad cook, so these Tinchel men do lick their own fingers; for besides their bows and arrows, which they carry with them, we can hear now and then a harquebuss or a musket go off, which they do seldom discharge in vain. Then after we had stayed there three hours or thereabouts, we might perceive the deer appear on the hills round about us, (their heads making a show like a wood) which being followed close by the Tinchel are chased down into the valley where we lay; then all the valley on each side being waylaid with a hundred couple of strong Irish grey-hounds, they are let loose as the occasion serves upon the herd of deer, so that with dogs, guns, arrows, dirks, and staggers, in the space of two hours, fourscore fat steer were slain, which after are disposed of some one way, and some another, twenty and thirty miles, and more than enough left for us to make merry withal at our rendesvous.

Clearly, what became known as tinchel hunting on this scale was impossible for tiny bands of hunter-gatherers, even if several came together to cooperate. The population of the Highlands and Islands in prehistoric times is a matter of pure guesswork, and my own instinct is that, given the long birth interval, it grew very slowly from small numbers of pioneer settlers. There may have been fewer than 3,000 people over a vast area, certainly too few to mount a huge deer hunt. But it may be that groups of twenty or thirty could achieve a high kill rate in the right *eileag*, if they had help in the *timchioll na sealg*.

*

Far to the south of the Highlands, a chance discovery shone a bright light on the lives of the hunter-gatherers who chased the deer into the *eileag*. It seems that they might have had help.

In the afternoon of Sunday 18 December 1994, three friends were walking in the Ardèche Gorge in southern France. Christian Hillaire, Eliette Brunel Deschamps and Jean-Marie Chauvet were amateur cavers and they were looking for ice-age refuges, places where our ancestors had survived the millennia of cold and frost. The walls of some of them had been painted with wonderful images of lions, mammoths, wild horses and other ancient fauna. On that winter afternoon, the three friends found a spectacular, undiscovered cave, perhaps the most beautiful of all. Named Chauvet Cave, it had paintings of rhinoceros, bison and hyenas, but perhaps their most remarkable discovery was not the friezes of beautiful art and all its still vibrant colours, but a set of footprints, and pawprints.

In a remote chamber of the large cave, lit by their head torches, the friends came across something remarkable, haunting and moving. Walking into the darkness across the damp clay floor were the footprints of a little boy, probably one of the last to see the paintings before a rock fall sealed the cave sometime around 24,000 BC. He was not alone. Walking beside the little boy was his dog. The pawprints convinced scientists that this was not a tame wolf cub but a canid, a very early domesticated dog.

Many of us in Scotland are descended from the people of the ice-age refuges and as they came north, following the herds who chased the cold, they must have brought their dogs with them. They were not pets (although his companion in the cave might have kept the little boy warm on a very cold night – amongst the Australian Aborigines that is what is known as 'a three-dog night') but probably hunting dogs. With half a dozen well-trained deerhounds to help with the *timchioll na sealg*, the circle could have been wider and more animals would have been driven into a bog or a narrow defile where hunters were waiting with arrows, spears or nets. John Taylor's account mentions deerhounds at the end of the drive attacking the herds but with a small group, it would make more sense for them to snap at the heels of the fleeing animals.

In the ancient world, British hunting dogs were much prized. Writing in the first century BC, the Greek geographer Strabo thought them the best he knew of and when Tacitus listed the exports from Britannia, he added 'clever hunting dogs'. The third-century AD writer, Oppian, had something to say about their origins of what sounds like a different breed and a different method of hunting:

There is a strong breed of hunting dog, small in size but no less worthy of great praise. These the wild tribes of Britons with their tattooed backs rear and call by the name of Agassian. Their size is like that of worthless and greedy domestic table dogs; squat, emaciated, shaggy, dull of eye, but endowed with feet armed with powerful claws and a mouth sharp with close-set venomous tearing teeth. It is by virtue of its nose, however, that the Agassian is most exalted, and for tracking it is the best there is; for it is very adept at discovering the tracks of things that walk upon the ground, and skilled too at marking the airborne scent.

The reference to wild tribes wearing tattoos almost certainly places these dogs in the Highlands, and their skills make them sound like woodland hunters, perhaps mastiff or bulldog-style animals used on a wild-boar hunt rather than chasing the deer in the open. It also draws an important distinction between sight and scent hounds. The former were used in hunts such as John Taylor described and the latter in tracking prey, and perhaps attacking it. It is significant to note that Oppian mentions a breeding programme, more evidence of the great value of hunting dogs in chasing or tracking prey.

Sometimes prey did not move, but instead was difficult and dangerous to reach. Each September, a trawler casts off from the Port of Ness at the Butt of Lewis, the most northerly point of the Hebrides. It is a voyage back in time, back to the prehistoric past. The skipper sets a course for Sulasgeir, an uninhabited rock lashed by the waves of the Atlantic that lies thirty miles to the north. The hunters' prey are the guga, the young and, as yet, flightless chicks from a large colony of gannets that nest on the island's cliffs. There is no quay or convenient landing-place at Sulasgeir and so the hunters must climb the sea-washed, windy and slippery cliffs.

With long poles that have a loop of rope at one end, the men lift the young birds out of their nest by their necks and quickly kill them. Once the annual quota has been reached, the hunters pluck the birds, their feathers flying away on the seawinds. Then they burn off the down, holding the guga by their wings over roaring blazes. With an axe, the wings are chopped off and the rib cage is pulled out so that the young birds look like spatchcocked chickens. At that point, in what resembles an assembly line, the guga are salted and then stacked like peat on the flat ground at the top of the island cliffs to make sure they are completely dry.

The oily flesh of the young gannets is considered a great delicacy, and not only on the Isle of Lewis. In the past, the hunt was more than a proud tradition, it was an essential source of protein and a welcome supplement to a diet dominated by oatmeal, potatoes and fish. It is also a rare surviving example, at the farthest edge of north-west Europe, of Braudel's *longue durée*, and the journey to Sulasgeir may be thought of as a hunter-gatherer lifeway.

Two hundred years ago, the MacKenzie Lairds of Lewis demanded that the men of Ness pay a tithe of the guga or a cash equivalent. They refused, saying that they needed no one's permission to hunt the young birds. It was an ancient right and they would not desist from its exercise.

4

The Temple

3700 BC–AD 43

Early on a crisp spring morning I walked between grandeur and mystery, and began a journey into the darkness of the long past. On the evening before I'd caught the car ferry from Scrabster to Stromness and landed in Orkney after my first voyage across the Pentland Firth. Having stayed overnight in a comfortable guesthouse in the little port, I was up early to drive north to the twin lochs that lie close to the heart of Mainland. On their banks stand the magnificent Stones of Stenness and the astonishing and spectacular Ring of Brodgar. I wanted to be there at first light and by the pale blue on the eastern horizon I could see that I would be blessed with the good fortune of a clear day's dawn. As the sun crept over the low hills, it cast long shadows when it reached the Stones of Stenness.

They are tremendously impressive. Three of the stones stand sixteen feet high, nearly three times the height of a man, and they formed part of the earliest henge monument in Britain. It was raised many centuries before Stonehenge. There were originally twelve tall, wafer-like stones arranged in an ellipse and surrounded by a rock-cut ditch which long ago filled up. There are other, smaller stones around them and in the centre of the elliptical circle is what archaeologists believe was a large hearth. Beyond the survivors is the tallest of all. The Watch Stone is eighteen feet high and was raised to the north-west. It seems to stand guard over the approach to the henge.

Like a blank prehistoric signpost, it is close to the road that crosses a stretch of water linking the two lochs. After the bridge, it begins to snake along the isthmus between them. The road leads to more prehistoric grandeur. The Ring of Brodgar is unique, the only large henge in Britain to have been laid out in a perfect circle. There were once sixty stones set up around it sometime between 2500 BC and 2000 BC, at least half a millennium after Stenness and at about the same time as Stonehenge was begun. Twenty-seven stones still stand and around them the clear remnants of the encircling ditch can be seen. It must once have been massive. There exists a photograph taken in 1941 of the army committing sacrilege as bren gun carriers drive through the circle, into the ditch and up out of it, and the extreme angle of the vehicles showing how deep and steep-sided it is.

Having parked in the half-dark, I'd been alone at Stenness and also on my own as I walked up the road to the Ring of Brodgar. On that still, crystal morning as the low sun glinted off the lochs, I was able to make my way slowly around the perfect circuit of the stones and touch them without anyone wondering what on earth I was doing. I laid the palm of my hand flat on their surfaces. Why that seemed important, I'm not sure. Something pretentious occurred to me, like reaching back across millennia to join hands with the people whose immense effort and completely mysterious beliefs raised the stones and hacked the rock out of the surrounding ditch with antler picks. But perhaps it was something much simpler, and something I wanted to do by myself, before the tour buses arrived. I had an urge to touch history, touch the stones so many of my ancestors had laboured over, the stones that carried deep and almost certainly powerful symbolic meaning for them. It wasn't like hugging a tree – although I have – it was a way to make a connection.

History is not only something I read about or watch and listen to in television documentaries, it's a very personal matter, something I can sometimes feel and intuit. And more than that I believe strongly that we are all part of it, every one of us. What's attractive about prehistory is that it is anonymous. Of course, there must have been elites, leaders, warriors, kings, perhaps queens, but their names are all lost and none of their actions, no battles, no laws, no great deeds, no important days or dates have come down to us in the historical record. All we can see are consequences, like these extraordinary stone circles in the Northern Isles, lying on the edges of Britain, made by the hard labour of many thousands and millions of man-hours. They are a common monument and probably not something raised to celebrate the glory of a single individual. And I think that's very attractive.

What the purpose of the henges was is difficult to work out beyond a few generalisations. Stenness and Brodgar were clearly prehistoric cathedrals, places of worship designed to impress, although who or what was worshipped is impossible to know. It's like trying to piece together the medieval Catholic Mass by looking at the empty ruins of Kelso Abbey. But rituals did take place inside the stone circles and these may have been connected to death, and like the burials at Oronsay and Vedbæk, there are echoes of a belief in an afterlife. Aubrey Burl devoted his working life to a study of what were labelled as megalithic monuments, and below is an interesting quote that I think is far from fanciful:

> Let us imagine, then, families approaching Stenness at the appointed time of year, men, women and children, carrying bundles of bones collected together from the skeletons of disinterred corpses – skulls, mandibles, long bones – carrying also the skulls of totem animals, herding a beast that was one of several to be slaughtered for the feasting that would accompany the ceremonies.

When I visualise these eloquent images, my sole hesitation revolves around the notion of exclusivity. The area enclosed not only by the circles of tall stones but also protected by the ditches so laboriously cut out of rock, and perhaps with a bank of upcast beyond them, as was the case with other henges, was without doubt sacred ground. It was different, not part of the everyday world. Instead, this was the sanctum sanctorum, the holy of holies of the sort understood by Christians, the place from where songs, prayers, incantations or chants, and sacrifices were offered up to the gods or god or ancestor-gods, perhaps with faces tilted skywards and arms raised. But it was not a place for everyone. Otherwise why circle and screen it? I think that only those whose role or magic or status allowed them to commune with the divine entered the holy of holies. It is easily forgotten in an age of relative openness and inclusivity that until recently the mysteries of the Catholic Mass were conducted behind a rood screen, out of sight, an essential mystery the faithful could hear but not see, and the rituals were performed in a language few understood. I think something of the kind went on at Stenness and at Brodgar as well as in the many later henges in the south of England.

After the principals, priests or a ruling priestly elite, processed into the circle, ceremonies began, possibly with music, drums, chanting and perhaps fire, something that might have been especially dramatic in the evening or at night. Ordinary people remained outside the sacred precinct and listened to what went on, or perhaps watched it at a distance at the Stones of Stenness. Even though archaeologists have found no trace of a bank of upcast, this elliptical circle may have had screens built up between the great stones to help deepen the mystery of the unseen rituals. And Burl was right. There is evidence of animal sacrifice and feasting around these and other monuments.

In 1999 the Ring of Brodgar, the Stones of Stenness, the chambered cairn at Maes Howe and the houses uncovered by the storm of 1850 at Skara Brae were designated as parts of a UNESCO World Heritage Site. That change in status prompted a survey of the whole area, much of it done by non-ground-penetrating radar. When I visited Brodgar and Stenness I remember walking back to my car on the far side of the bridge as the tour buses passed me going the other way. I noticed a small farm with a modern bungalow by the side of the road, next to the narrow stretch of land lying between the Ring of Brodgar and Stenness, what's known as the Ness of Brodgar. The ground seemed slightly mounded, a hummock rather than a hillock. That was where the surveyors identified features below the topsoil that were not natural, and a test dig was undertaken. It was the beginning of an extraordinary story.

In 2003 the fields around the little farm at the Ness of Brodgar were ploughed and a large rectangular stone was turned up. Along one edge there was a series of notches and it was first thought that the farmer had skinned the lid off a kist, a stone-lined prehistoric burial. But when excavators arrived from Glasgow University, they uncovered something quite different, something completely unexpected. What they found looked more like the foundations of a building. Its rectilinear zigzag resembled the remains of a prehistoric settlement found at Barnhouse, less than a mile away, beyond the Stones of Stenness. Between 2004 and 2007 a series of test trenches came across the archaeology of structures built from Orkney flagstone well worked and dressed by masons who were clearly very skilled. By 2012 a much larger area was opened up and something remarkable came to light – part of a unique and sophisticated complex of large buildings was revealed.

These discoveries are unparalleled in northern Europe. The Ness of Brodgar has upended the story of prehistoric Britain. Because Stonehenge is the most famous, most monumental stone circle, its construction was assumed not only to have been the zenith of megalithic culture but also its origin, its centre. But the finds at Ness of Brodgar have shown conclusively that Orkney was where the building of stone circles began and where the cult that created them and the context of artefacts around them were also first made. The Ness was the focus of new and vibrant world-changing ideas that swirled around the archipelago and these moved southwards down the length of Britain to create the first unified culture in these islands, a different way of understanding the world. And Stonehenge and the ritual landscape around it was the ultimate, the grandest expression of these new beliefs and ideas that originated 500 miles to the north. Far from being peripheral, Orkney was the centre of Stone Age Britain, the beating heart of the culture that ultimately supplanted the old life of hunting and gathering.

The large area opened up on the Ness in 2012 is perhaps only 10 per cent of what lies beneath the soil. It is thought that fourteen substantial structures were contained inside a massive wall, perhaps sixteen to eighteen feet thick and at least six feet high. The buildings are rectilinear with rounded corners and their walls are supported by a series of interior buttresses that may also have created enclave spaces. They were roofed with stone slates, something completely new and unique to Orkney. All of the masonry techniques are drystone (the invention of mortar lay a long way in the future). But construction was made much easier by the nature of Orkney flagstone. A series of sedimentary strata that can be easily and evenly split with wedges, it is naturally straight and soft enough to be dressed with stone tools. Often, recently excavated walls look fresh, tidy and as though they were built much more recently. The flagstone also splits into thinner sheets that are light enough to be used as slates.

What is striking about the complex is that the buildings are not funerary, not tombs. They appear to have been lived in, except perhaps one of them. In the south-west corner of the main trench is Structure Ten. At more than eighty feet in length and sixty-five feet wide, it is the largest prehistoric building yet found in Britain. There is a central hearth, a series of four dresser-like installations similar to those in the houses at Skara Brae, and it contained art. The excavators have called it the Temple and, in reconstructions, it looks magnificent, with a high, ridged roof and it seems that there were standing stones incorporated into its walls. Outside the entrance there may have been more standing stones and there was a paved walkway around the perimeter of the building. If the Ness of Brodgar was where a new way of seeing the world was invented, that cult's focus was Structure Ten, the Temple.

One of the most striking discoveries at the Ness was colour. In the Temple there appears to have been a paint shop, a place where pigment was made from minerals and possibly ochre. When mixed with egg-white or other fixatives, it became paint and was used to decorate the stonework. Faded yellows, reds and oranges have been traced on the flagstone and it may be that colour was widely used on the exterior of buildings. What we now think of as grey stonework has been stripped of decoration by time, by thousands of winters, but in its pomp, much of it was probably brightly painted. It may be that the standing stones at Stenness and Brodgar were also painted on important occasions. Greek and Roman classical sculpture was not thought complete until colour had been added and what we think of as the monochrome dignity of the likes of the Parthenon frieze looked very different when the Athenian temples were in use. Free-standing Celtic crosses such as those on Iona were also vividly coloured, the paint probably renewed after every winter. In a landscape of natural, muted greens, greys and blues, buildings and objects devoted in some way to the divine, or at least the unearthly, gained power and significance with bright reds, yellows and oranges. They were designed to look different, be literally outstanding.

A distinctive pottery was also made at Ness of Brodgar. Grooved ware was so called because of its incised decoration and it became associated with the spread of megalithic culture down the length of Britain. It too was coloured, and shards with beautiful shades of red have been uncovered. On several buildings, both inside and outside, patterns were cut into stone faces and along edges. These were always geometric, abstract and never figurative. Beautifully made objects have also been found, such as a carved stone ball and highly polished stone axeheads. Whatever the specific purpose of the Temple and the other buildings in the complex, it appears to have been a busy, productive place where time was found to make beautiful things and enhance and enliven the world with colour.

Despite the diligence and care of ten years of digging at the Ness of Brodgar, albeit over short, two-month annual seasons, the archaeologists are no nearer understanding the purpose of the site. As with stone circles only generalisations are possible. The Ness was clearly central. Recent work on the first, the earliest layer of building has pushed back the date of its inception to *c*.3500 BC, well before the raising of the Stones of Stenness and the laying out of the Ring of Brodgar. Was it a meeting place for the people of the whole archipelago? Stones for the Ring of Brodgar came from different places on Orkney and there is a faint sense of representation. Was the Ness a focus for pilgrimage? If the Temple was indeed a temple, and nothing on its scale had ever been built before, then that sort of reverence is likely. Was it a tribal meeting place? That is more difficult to imagine, but it may be that some of the larger islands off Mainland such as

Hoy, Rousay, Westray and South Ronaldsay were seen as distinct communities, the home places of different kindreds.

My own view is that the Ness of Brodgar was a royal palace. The King of Orkney held court in the Temple and his role was not only secular but also priestly. In the other thirteen structures in the compound behind its high and wide wall lived his courtiers and his band of warriors. Those who gathered at the Ness, or more likely at the Ring of Brodgar and the Stones of Stenness, may have taken part in seasonal rituals, perhaps at the equinoxes, and brought tribute and affirmed loyalties.

This, I readily concede, is almost pure conjecture but it is not completely without foundation. The huge communal projects undertaken at and around the Ness required, in my view, a controlling mind or minds. There needed to be organisation and coordination of a detailed kind and an ability to compel reluctant prehistoric Orcadians to do work for what was seen as a common purpose, and one that was not related to the essential business of food production.

In 1958, Ronald Simison, a farmer on the island of South Ronaldsay, found a large, chambered tomb on his land. In it were the disarticulated remains of 324 individuals, the earliest dating from the third millennium BC. Alongside the human bones and skulls were the talons and bones of between eight and twenty sea eagles – lending the burial site the nickname Tomb of the Eagles. A recent analysis of the skulls produced a surprising result. Almost half showed clear evidence of serious physical violence, having been hit so hard on the head with stone maces or other weapons as to leave traces of depressed fractures that were severe but did not kill them. There are other examples of these sorts of injury that have been found elsewhere on the archipelago. Interpersonal violence on a considerable scale appears to have been a fact of Orcadian life when the Ness of Brodgar and the monuments around them were being built and used. This very high percentage more than implies coercion, and takes no account of the victims of violence who did not survive, and therefore can be seen as clear evidence of a ruthless social hierarchy. I believe that those in power were compelling many people who were weaker to do as they were told.

The presence of the bones and talons of the sea eagles in the tomb also supports the notion of the Ness of Brodgar as a tribal meeting place. If the great birds were, as seems likely, the totem animals of the people who lived on South Ronaldsay, then that suggests other places with different totems. There are large, chambered tombs on Mainland, Stronsay, Eday, Sanday and Papa Westray that hint at the territories of tribal kindreds across the archipelago. There is a sense of these prehistoric mausolea as a physical, hereditary claim of owner-ship, a belief that where the ancestors are planted was the kindred ground of their descendants. There are seventy-six chambered tombs across Orkney and all are located near pockets of good farmland. Echoes of these notions of ownership can still be heard on the windy island of Rousay, north of Mainland. Archaeologists found that the number of chambered tombs matched exactly the number of mod-ern farms. Based on this settlement pattern, estimates of that island's population at the end of the fourth millennium BC vary between 300 and 650.

Even though this historical notice lies three and a half millennia in the future, there was indeed a king of Orkney. When the Roman Emperor Claudius came to Colchester in AD 43 after his legions had conquered the south-east of what is now England, a king sailed from Orkney to offer his allegiance. This was recorded because it was important. To bolster Claudius' shaky hold on power and create some badly needed military prestige, the arrival of this man was said to demonstrate a new and unparalleled reach of imperial power. It could stretch as far to the north as it was possible to be, to the very ends of the earth, the edge of the ocean.

Perhaps the most compelling evidence for the Ness of Brodgar as a royal palace was the manner of its destruction. Sometime around 2200 BC, the Temple was closed and the complex around it aban-doned. The reasons for this are long lost but there is evidence of what happened at that important moment. Archaeologists have discovered a mass of cattle bones, particularly on the paved walkway around the Temple. It appears that an enormous feast that may have fed thousands was mounted as the life of the Ness came to an end. Four hundred head of cattle were slaughtered, cooked and eaten; their bones split so that the succulent marrow could also be consumed. And this huge number of cows, in an act of conspicuous consumption, all came from one herd, the herd of the most powerful and wealthy individual on Orkney, surely from the royal herd.

How many people could feast on 400 cows? Perhaps five or six thousand? Some of the excavated bones were very large and may be a genetic inheritance from the aurochs, the huge wild cattle who were their ancestors. If the numbers are even remotely accurate, then they must represent the whole population of the archipelago and perhaps also people from beyond its shores. Or, alternatively, the feast may have gone on for several days and fed fewer. Whatever the historical reality, this was an enormous event and an example of massive consumption, a statement of power on the part of leaders, and a practice that has not died out entirely.

Potlatches are feasts organised by the chiefs of the native kindreds of British Columbia. They were vast and could last for days, involving the consumption of so much food, much of it salmon, that guests vomited frequently. Rich clothing was worn and occasionally host chiefs would cut their robes to pieces and give them to guests. During these bouts of gluttony, important announcements were made: dynastic marriages, the affirmation of heirs or the marking of an important death. Perhaps something of this kind went on at the Ness of Brodgar when the royal complex was abandoned *c.*2200 BC.

The King of Orkney ruled over communities of cattle farmers. They were the descendants of recent immigrants, new people with new ideas and new skills who had sailed from Europe to the islands of Britain. Their arrival in the Northern Isles was the last ripple in a revolution that radiated from the east. Sometime after 9000 BC, the most profound transition in the world's history began to happen. In Mesopotamia, the lands between the Rivers Tigris and Euphrates, and the uplands extending towards the Mediterranean coast, the

place once known as the Fertile Crescent and perhaps the inspiration
for the myth of the Garden of Eden, men and women began to do
more than hunt and gather in the wild landscape. They began to
farm it.

The lands between the two rivers turned out to be ideal for the
raising of crops, the primitive strains of wheat known as einkorn and
emmer. They also learned to grow barley. On the banks of the Tigris
and Euphrates a short rainy season with some helpful flooding was
followed by a long, hot and reliable summer. The seeds planted by
the first farmers began life as wild grasses and through a process of
selection the most calorific became the early cereal crops.

At the same time animals were domesticated. Species that were
sociable, docile and meaty were chosen. Cattle, sheep, goats, pigs
and chickens were all reared and selectively bred. Apart from pigs,
kept solely for their meat, all of the others had secondary uses, con-
tributing milk, wool and eggs. Hunting and gathering did not cease
as farming developed, but it became less important – a secondary,
seasonal source of food.

The production of cereals in particular had a profound effect, as
the invention of porridge changed the world. When mothers began
to make a pappy, porridge-like food from grain that was high in
protein as well as calories, and that their babies and toddlers could
digest without chewing, it meant they could be weaned much earlier
than the children of hunter-gatherer bands. This in turn reduced the
length of the birth interval and the populations of farming communities expanded quickly. The effect was dynamic. Land has a defined
carrying capacity, an ability to feed only so many mouths. People were
forced to move out of the Fertile Crescent, bringing new ideas and
new skills with them. Many walked westwards. By 5500 BC farming
had advanced up the Danube valley, reaching the Hungarian plains
where it acquired an archaeological profile. Soon afterwards, groups
of these early farmers reached the edge of the land, the western coasts
of the continent, what is now the Low Countries and France. And
then they crossed the sea. And in the centuries around 4000 BC, they
reached Orkney. As did other, much smaller creatures.

Voles have a story to tell about the origins of these immigrants. The Orkney vole is genetically different from the British vole, or the Irish vole. They did not somehow swim across the swirling, racing currents of the Pentland Firth and colonise the archipelago – the Orkney voles came from somewhere else. They came from what is now Belgium in the boats of the first farmers who made landfall on the islands. There is a close DNA match between Orcadian voles and their cousins, the Belgian voles.

As the skills and knowledge needed to establish a farming economy spread west over Europe, the migrants followed the coastline of the Mediterranean or the great river valleys of the interior. Sometime in the fifth millennium BC, they reached the mouth of the Rhine. Doggerland had been swept away by the Storegga Slide but there was still sea traffic between the British Isles and the Continent. Neither was terra incognita. When families took the decision to emigrate, to cross the sea, they will have taken advice and hugged the coast and sailed in good, safe weather. Only when they saw the cliffs of what is now the English coast will they have struck out into open water and crossed the Channel. In each boat, probably hide boats like curraghs, they carried the seeds of a new life and a new way of life, pots of emmer and einkorn, and barley seeds. They must also have brought domesticated animals in these small and fragile craft. Only the pig was native to Britain, the descendant of the wild boar. Domesticated cattle, sheep and goats will probably have been hobbled to make them as immobile as possible when the oarsmen pulled out into the open sea. It was a time of great danger, but enough of these voyages must have succeeded.

The ancestors of the Orkney vole either arrived as accidental tourists, hidden in animal fodder or amongst pelts and hides. Or perhaps they were brought along as meat. The Romans enjoyed specially fattened dormice as a delicacy. Whatever their status, Orkney voles did not make landfall in Britain on their journey from Belgium. What must have happened is a voyage up the eastern coasts, a series of short hops, putting in at safe places for fresh water and to set up cooking fires on the shore before quickly moving on and making landfall on the archipelago, where the voles disembarked, escaped and began to breed in wild and glorious isolation.

The oldest surviving house in Northern Europe was built by these early farmers at Knap of Howar in Orkney. In the 1920s, erosion on the eastern coast of Papa Westray nibbled at the edges of what turned out to be a farmstead. There were two well-preserved, flagstone-built houses and radiocarbon analyses dated them to *c.*3700 BC, close to the time when work began at the Ness of Brodgar. Evidence from the middens at Knap of Howar showed that they reared cattle, sheep and pigs (these were large and close in ancestry to the wild boar and may be why Orkas or Orkney got its name) and they grew wheat and barley as well as harvesting shellfish from the seashore. It seems that the immigrant farmers established themselves quickly and studies of ancestral DNA show the population expanding, driving the indigenous hunter-gatherers to the margins or absorbing them through intermarriage into the creation of a new society, one that was in the process of inventing a new cosmology, the megalithic culture that would sweep down Britain to create Stonehenge, Avebury, Silbury Hill and the ritual landscape around them. It lasted 1,500 years, until the great cattle feast at the Ness of Brodgar signalled change.

*

Just off the A9 in Caithness, not far south of its terminus at Thurso, is Achavanich – the Gaelic place name means the Field of Stones. Thirty-six standing stones, survivors from an original total of sixty, they are not set in a circle like Brodgar or an ellipse like Stenness. Instead, Achavanich is a horseshoe shape with one end left open. The stones themselves are unusual in another way. Unlike most others they were not erected with the broadest side facing inwards but side-on and they resemble a set of dominoes arranged so that one can topple them all. Archaeologists have dated Achavanich late in the period for such monuments, created about 2000 BC. It is not clear how long it was in use and its layout hints at a search for different meaning, a new interpretation of the function of such places. In any case, a cultural sea change was waiting to wash over the henge builders and their chambered tombs. A fascinating harbinger of a different society was accidentally discovered just across the road from the horseshoe stones.

Towards the end of the third millennium BC there is a sense of recession and abandonment. Not only stone circles and chambered tombs went out of use, it seems that cultivation retreated in the north as the skies darkened and the weather grew wetter. Cleared areas that show the criss-cross marks of the ard, the early wooden plough, were reverting to woodland. The trees of the Caledonian Forest were reclaiming the land.

Burial practice was also changing. Instead of the large communal tombs like the Tomb of the Eagles, there was a new emphasis on individual interments, what are called kist burials. One of these was accidentally broken into during quarrying operations at Achavanich. Sometime around 2250 BC, a woman had died and been laid to rest in a kist with some ceremony and honour. She must have been a person of status. Near her head a pot had been placed. Almost intact, it was quickly identified as a beaker, or a bell-beaker. These pots are signifiers of an important cultural shift across Western Europe. Decorated by twisted cords pressed into the clay and shaped like an upturned bell, they are closely associated with a new group of immigrants. Quickly dubbed 'Ava', the woman's DNA was very informative about her origins. It turned out that she had dark hair, brown eyes and a sallow complexion. Ava was a recent immigrant from Europe, perhaps somewhere in the south. Her grave had been strewn with flowers and the pollen residue of meadowsweet was recognised. It is an early example of the long tradition linking flowers with funerals.

Another beaker kist was found at Culduthel in Inverness, and it contained eight tanged and barbed flint arrowheads and an archer's wristguard made from bone and studded with gold rivets. The richest beaker burial ever found in Britain was excavated near Stonehenge, in Wiltshire. Dating to about the same time at Achavanich, it contained the body of a man who became known as the Amesbury Archer, or, by the more excitable, as the King of Stonehenge. Before this discovery in 2002, the maximum number of beakers ever found in a kist was two. Arranged around his crouched body, the Archer had five pots and a great deal more. There were three copper knives, two full sets of archery kit, fifteen flint arrowheads and two gold hair clasps. The association with archery at Amesbury and Inverness is interesting. Was it a memory of the millennia of hunting, or was it a military association? It certainly was a mark of status. In all there were a hundred artefacts, and no beaker burial to that date had more than ten. The most intriguing find was, however, not made from copper or gold, but was a square piece of greenish stone. It was recognised by the archaeologists as a cushion-stone, a last used by metalworkers when working gold, copper or bronze objects. DNA analysis showed that the Archer was another immigrant from Europe.

The Beaker people had come to Britain with a new technology. They could work metal with fire and magically make lustrous and beautiful objects out of dull ore. Ava was laid in her kist in Caithness at the beginning of what became known as the Bronze Age.

Gold may have been the first metal to have been worked. It was almost certainly the first to be noticed. In the Highlands and at the foot of the mountains, gold can sometimes be found in the form of relatively pure nuggets often picked up from the gravel of a stream or a river. Bright and eye-catching amongst the grey stones, small pieces of gold, known as placer deposits, were probably first prized as decorations, perhaps as part of a necklace or a bracelet. Gold is also soft and when heated only a little, it can be worked easily.

Our ancestors also saw small grains or flecks in streams and they worked out a means of extracting that form of gold that gave rise to a glittering legend. Experiments with a wicker frame and a sheepskin in Ireland have suggested how prehistoric prospectors went about their business. Held fast by the frame, the sheepskin is inserted into the gold-bearing stream at a point where the current flows fast. Gravel is then shovelled on to it, the current pushes it through the sheepskin sieve, and, in theory, the heavier nuggets or grains of gold are trapped. In Greek mythology, attractive echoes of this method of prospecting are preserved in the tale of Jason and the intrepid

Argonauts who sailed to the Black Sea city of Colchis to find a golden fleece hanging from a tree.

In Scotland, gold was just as enduring a magnet as it was for Jason and his sailors. More sophisticated, if less romantic, methods of extraction were used in Scotland's only known gold rush. In 1868 Robert Gilchrist came home to the Strath of Kildonan in Sutherland. He had spent seventeen years prospecting in the goldfields of Australia, and he was struck by the similarities between the configuration of the creeks around Ballarat, Bendigo and Forest Creek in Victoria and those of the Strath of Kildonan. Finds in those and other areas had produced two tonnes of gold a week at their peak and the city of Melbourne had grown prosperous on the work of the prospectors.

With the Duke of Sutherland's permission, Gilchrist methodically surveyed these Highland burns. And on the very first day, he found gold. Not nuggets, but in the gravels of the Kildonan Burn, he panned out tiny granular flecks of gold in what was called 'a paying quantity'.

The secret soon got out, and a Wick newspaper, the *Northern Ensign*, ran a story on 17 December 1868, saying that 'the presence of gold is indisputably proved'. It was followed by stories in the *Inverness Courier* and *The Scotsman*. The gold rush began almost immediately. More than 600 men raced up to Helmsdale, including a few who had prospected in California and Victoria. Local people joined in. Two shanty townships sprang up in the strath, Baile an Or ('the Town of Gold') and Carn na Buth ('the Hill of the Huts'). The Duke of Sutherland's factor was quickly in on the act too and Joseph Peacock began to issue monthly licences for prospectors at £1 apiece. They were eagerly taken up.

Gold was found in the gravel of the burns, but not as much as was hoped and nothing like the yield in Australia. As winter approached in late 1869, miners drifted away and it seems that Robert Gilchrist returned to Victoria. By the end of the year the duke had decided that gold mining on his estates would cease, deer-stalking was much more important. Like a fever, the gold rush had seen frenetic activity and then a rapid collapse of interest.

Elsewhere on the edges of the mountains gold is being sought once more and Australian expertise is once again involved. At Cononish, near Tyndrum, a commercial gold and silver mine has opened and 'a paying quantity' is being extracted. Run by Scotgold Resources Ltd (headquartered in Australia), its larger purpose is to use the proceeds to fund more exploration of the Grampian terrane. It seems that the make-up of the rock formations that collided hundreds of millions of years ago contain treasure. In 2023, Scotgold announced that several new seams of gold had been discovered and that the pace of extraction would accelerate.

More humble prospects exist in Glen Orchy, also not far from Tyndrum. The restrictions and lockdowns of the Covid pandemic saw a revival in the solitary activity of amateur gold panning and flecks of gold have been found in the River Orchy. Scotgold Resources believe that there is even more to be found.

*

In time, other metals came to have value as techniques for extracting them from ore and working them developed. Bronze is an alloy of tin and copper, relatively rare metals in Britain. Cornish and Devonian miners produced by far the bulk of the prehistoric output of tin. It was what brought Pytheas north from Massalia. Copper was mined on the north coast of Wales and a few other places, but it was not plentiful. It appears that the techniques of smelting and making the alloy crossed the Channel with the Beaker people. Bronze could be highly polished to a rich, gold-like lustre and also sharpened into fearsome edges. But at first metal working affected only elites, and working farmers went on using flint for some time.

Scotland's most impressive and mysterious Bronze Age site is Kilmartin Glen in Argyll. It lies on an approximate north–south axis between the sea at Loch Crinan and the southern tip of Loch Awe. Around 3000 BC, a chambered cairn was built at Nether Largie, the ditch of a henge was dug and laid out at Ballymeanoch and a stone circle at Temple Wood was in use. But it was not until the end of the third millennium BC that the development of the whole glen began to gather pace. There were beaker burials, a huge cursus monument (a series of long parallel ditches whose function remains stubbornly obscure) and many burial cairns were piled up, some to sixteen to eighteen feet high. By 1500 BC what archaeologists call the 'linear cemetery' had been laid out.

Perhaps three miles long when complete, running the whole length of Kilmartin Glen, it was created on an epic, theatrical scale. Many older monuments were reused and reshaped and an original alignment of seven cairns (only five survive) was strung out in a line down the glen. Its landscape had probably been completely cleared of woodland to reveal the relationship between the entire series of monuments, and their great scale could easily be seen. On either side of the glen are hillsides and those who gathered there on important occasions in the year could see the ceremonies play out below them. It was a traverse theatre of ritual and sanctity.

There is also a sense of a sacred precinct on a vast scale. It may be that avenues were cut through the trees on the hillsides to allow processions to descend and join those on the valley floor, nearer the monuments. If Kilmartin drew its congregation from a wide area, much like Ness of Brodgar did on Orkney, perhaps different communities will have gathered in particular places before going down to the glen and its cairns and stones.

The boundaries of the precinct may have been delineated by cup and ring marks on rocks and outcrops. Within six miles of the glen there are more than a hundred groups of these, many of them much closer to the monuments. Pecked into the rock are round, sometimes teacup-sized holes and these are often surrounded by rings, perhaps as a way of identifying them as man-made. Some of the cups near and in the linear cemetery are deep, and it may be that on special occasions they were filled with libations or perhaps flowers and the rings coloured with ochre. This was done in Ireland as late as the tenth century AD when cups were filled with libations of milk. If this hypothesis is correct then it further feeds the notion of different but parallel worlds, a boundary between the everyday and the sacred.

The extraordinary scale of what went on in this valley of death is worth a moment's consideration. In contrast to the Orkney monuments, Kilmartin was not built for an elite, although only important people were buried in its kists and under its cairns or officiated at its ceremonies. It is far too large. Small and exclusive groups would have been lost in this vast ritual landscape. Having climbed the low ridges immediately to the west and looked down through the winter trees, I could see many of the funerary monuments or their sites – and all the cairns will have been much larger 3,500 years ago. That was the point. Many hundreds, perhaps thousands passed from the temporal world into the great linear cemetery, and not necessarily solemnly. Perhaps processions sang, played drums and flutes, prayed or chanted, or danced on the days and nights when the priest-kings summoned them to the ceremonies. Perhaps great fires blazed by each of the string of cairns, their sparks spiralling into the night sky. Perhaps the ancient drama of full moonlight darkness enhanced the rituals as the spirits swirled in the night air as torchlit processions moved along ancient pathways between the seven cairns.

Dunchraigaig Cairn is not considered to have been a major part of the cemetery, but in 2021 it turned out to have a unique significance. Hamish Fenton, a keen photographer and an archaeology graduate, visited Kilmartin and noticed something that had been hidden for millennia. When he looked inside the kist that had once been covered by the cairn, he shone his torch on the underside of the capstone. At first he thought he was looking at a pattern, something like a laurel wreath, the sort of thing worn by Julius Caesar. But as he looked more closely, Hamish realised he was looking at antlers. He had accidentally discovered the earliest figurative art ever made in Scotland. Carved on the capstone, which had probably been a small reused standing stone, were two stags complete with antlers and three other deer that looked smaller and younger and might have been hinds. The sculptor created these remarkable images between 4,000 and 5,000 years ago. And what could be more appropriate or enduring? One of the most readily recognisable images of the Highlands of Scotland was painted by Sir Edwin Landseer in

1851: though *The Monarch of the Glen* is rather easier to see than the monarchs of Kilmartin Glen since it hangs in the Scottish National Gallery in Edinburgh, on a wall, the right way up.

The prehistoric peoples of the Highlands and Islands clearly revered their dead and great monuments were raised to their ancestors. But few people lived with their corpses. On South Uist there is a beautiful and spectacular cemetery at Cladh Hallan. It lies on the machair, a meadow that blooms each spring with a multitude of wildflowers, and it looks west over the eternities of the Atlantic. My old friend, Peter MacLellan, a native Gaelic speaker from the Islands is buried there. I had the honour of saying something at his funeral mass and I chose to recite the first verse of Donald MacIver's great lyric 'An Ataireachd Ard'. Its rhythms echo the shushing of the waves, pitiless and unceasing. Peter's wife, Mairi, wanted the language of his ancestors to be heard at the service and I was glad to do that before my friend found his last resting place beside the endless horizons of the ocean.

The first element of Cladh Hallan means what it is – a burying place – but it refers to more than the cemetery. Between 1998 and 2002 archaeologists began to dig on a site very close by. They came across a much more ancient cemetery as they excavated a seaside settlement of seven conical-roofed roundhouses that were occupied around 1100 BC. The village had been built directly on top of the cemetery and those who constructed the houses knew that. The hearth of one had been carefully placed over a cremation burial. But even more striking, and unique, was the discovery of several corpses that had been buried inside the houses, while they were being constructed.

In a small pit under the floor of one, the skeleton of a man had been placed with his knees tucked up under his chin and his arms folded over. In another part of the house a woman had been buried, and under a post near the entrance was the corpse of a baby. These seemed to be part of some sort of foundation ritual, perhaps a posthumous blessing on the new house from the ancestors. But once the bodies were removed for more detailed examination in a laboratory, the mystery of these silent witnesses only deepened.

The skeleton of the man turned out to be a composite: the torso and the limbs came from one individual, the skull and the neck from another and the lower jaw from a third. Even more extraordinary, these three men had all died at least 400 years before the house at Cladh Hallan was built. The woman and the baby had been dead for 200 years before they were buried under the floor. What explained how this was possible, and what also amazed the archaeologists was that the bodies were not true skeletons. Each had enough soft tissue and sinew left to show that something remarkable had happened. They had all been mummified.

These finds were unique, the earliest example of deliberate body preservation in Europe, and they were older than the early mummies of the Egyptian pharaohs, Seti I and Ramses II. Soon after the man, or men, the woman and the baby had died, their bodies were buried in peat bogs. The cold, anaerobic conditions prevented bacteria from degrading the flesh and it preserved them. When the bodies were retrieved, probably some months later, their skin will have become brown and leathery, but their faces would still have been recognisable. The archaeological team believes that at Cladh Hallan there may have been at first a house of the dead where mummies were placed and perhaps worshipped. Then something changed. Perhaps after the immense destruction caused by the eruption of Hekla, the Icelandic volcano that blew itself apart in 1159 BC, the mummies were buried under the floors of the houses in this village of the dead.

*

Almost forty-four feet high, perched on a low promontory on the rocky shore of the Shetland island of Mousa, a long way to the north-east of Uist, is what might be called a statement in the landscape. The broch is magnificent. Like a stone version of a cooling tower, it tapers from fifty feet in diameter at the base to forty feet at the parapet at the top. Mousa was built sometime around 300 BC by an extremely skilful gang of masons. It is an entirely drystone structure, using weight and the size and shape of stones to build an exterior wall that is pinned to an interior wall for support, and to carry a staircase that winds to the top. The broch has no windows and a single, low entrance that leads along a sixteen-foot passageway to the living areas. What probably preserved Mousa was the immense thickness of the walls as well as a relatively remote location. In the *Orkneyinga Saga*, there is a tale of a failed siege. A man called Erlend runs off with Margaret, the mother of Earl Harald Maddadsson, in 1153, and holes up with her in the broch. When the pursuing earl arrives, he finds Mousa 'an unhandy place to get at' and agrees that Erlend could marry his mother. 'Broch' sounds like a Gaelic word, but in fact it derives from Old Norse for a castle, a *borg*.

In the last few centuries BC more than 500 brochs were built, almost all of them in the Highlands and Islands. The uniformity of design and the comparatively brief period in which they were raised implies specialism. There may well have been gangs of itinerant masons who could offer to run up a broch for local grandees. On Shetland, it may have been a neighbour who inspired whoever commissioned Mousa to keep up with the Joneses. There are 120 brochs on the archipelago, almost a quarter of the total in Scotland. Who were these masons and how were they rewarded? Whatever they received, it had to be portable and exchangeable but that is about as far as speculation about the economics of the late first millennium BC building trade can take us.

The itinerant masons certainly knew their business. Like Mousa, many brochs were built at exposed locations on or near the shore. The inner and outer walls also acted as necessary insulation, helping to create a barrier of warm air generated by the fire burning in the central hearth. As the wind howled in off the North Sea, brochs may have been snug enough. Despite their commanding locations, the derivation of their name, and their massive construction, they were unlikely to have been used or been seen as fortresses. They could withstand a foray like Earl Harald's in 1153, but not a siege. Brochs were probably built to impress and act as a focus for local leadership. Society was changing, becoming more polarised, because new technologies had developed.

At the beginning of the first millennium BC knowledge of iron working came to the Highlands and Islands. Much more readily available than copper or tin, iron was also more difficult to extract from the ore. The very high temperatures needed to smelt and smith the metal meant that charcoal had to be used in forges. By the seventh century BC, the process known as 'blooming' was becoming widespread. Smiths extracted a bloom of iron from the lumps of ore by smelting and continually discarding the slag until they achieved an acceptable level of purity. Then they melted the iron before pouring it into clay moulds for swords, daggers or axeheads. Once these had cooled and been turned out of the moulds, smiths quickly began to hammer them into shape, occasionally reheating whatever they were making before it was plunged into water.

Because of the wider availability of iron, useful tools, especially axes, became much more accessible to many more people. Timber could be felled more quickly than with sharp but brittle flint axes and that contributed to what might be seen as a prehistoric housing boom in the Highlands and Islands. At Kilphedir, near the east coast north of Brora, the footprints of very large roundhouses have been found, some of them thirty-three to thirty-six feet in diameter. They were excellent examples of the characteristic domestic architecture of the Iron Age.

The roundhouses at Kilphedir had an internal circle of posts, often substantial, trimmed tree trunks that supported a thatched roof and were surrounded by a low outer wall of stone. Some very large houses had a first floor reached by a ladder. Like brochs there were no windows, only an entrance, and they were lit and warmed by a central hearth. Roundhouses would have been smoky, but the design of the conical roof prevented sparks from rising up to set light to the thatch. The cone encouraged a layer of carbon dioxide to form and it extinguished anything that spiralled up on the warm air from the hearth that might have been dangerous. People only stood up in a small roundhouse for short periods. I once cooked my lunch (sausages that spat fat at me) in a faithful replica of one of these Iron Age houses and wondered why the benches around the fire were so low, until cramp forced me to stand, and I immediately began to cough and my eyes watered with smoke. But like brochs, roundhouses could be warm, spacious, even comfortable.

Some brochs became villages. On the north coast of Orkney Mainland work began at Gurness between 500 BC and 200 BC. Around a central tower that rose to an impressive thirty-three feet, there were numerous smaller stone houses with yards. A 'main street' led from a gate and bridge over an encircling ditch to the entrance to the broch. Like Ness of Brodgar, Gurness was almost certainly a royal palace and also where a king received emissaries from an emperor.

Pieces of Roman amphorae were discovered in the ruins, and they were not just any old amphorae but a type that had become obsolete by AD 60. These were used as containers for a fancy sweet liqueur enjoyed by elites, and the nearest similar example was discovered 600 miles to the south, at Colchester, where Emperor Claudius waited to receive the submission of the King of Orkney.

In AD 43, after the successful invasion of the south-east, the Roman emperor was in Britain for only sixteen days and so prior diplomacy had to have taken place. Well in advance of the arrival of the imperial court, diplomats who came north to Orkney brought a sweetener in their ship. And also a return voyage had to be planned and undertaken from Gurness to Colchester in plenty of time for the king to join the other ten British kings in swearing their allegiance to Claudius. It was important that this was all choreographed properly. The submission of the kings was inscribed on a triumphal arch set up in Rome in AD 51, and the achievement endured. In the fourth century, the historian Eutropius compiled a list of Roman emperors and he took care to note Claudius' greatest, most spectacular achievement: 'He added to the Empire some islands lying in the Ocean beyond Britain, which are called the Orkneys.'

Historians long believed that the appearance of the King of Orkney in Colchester to be so unlikely as to be impossible, and in any case the source must have been a scribal error. But it is absolutely clear that the archipelago's elite were in contact with rulers in the south, and the scholars' hesitation says much about their own assumptions, and frankly, prejudices. The Northern Isles were emphatically not peripheral, as they may seem now to some. It is clear that the Orcadians invented a megalithic culture and transmitted its ideas southwards not through some mysterious process of osmosis but through direct contact. I believe that people came to Orkney to witness the ceremonies and see the great monuments – and were impressed and converted. All that happened in AD 43 was that the Romans arrived, wrote down what occurred and it survived. As will become clear in the pages that follow, the Highlands and Islands were never marginal, always central to the story of the British Isles, and sometimes to the story of Europe.

5

The Kindred Ground

AD 43–793

No one had ever visited the Isles of the Blessed but one man knew where they should be. They were said to be a winterless earthly paradise that Pliny the Elder believed to 'abound in fruit and birds of every kind', but more importantly they were the place where an accurate understanding of the world's geography began. Marinus of Tyre needed to find the right place for the prime meridian, zero longitude, and in his *Geography*, published in AD 114, he set it on the Isles of the Blessed even though he had never been there or indeed spoken to anyone who had. But that didn't matter. Marinus realised that the location of zero longitude could be arbitrary because he knew exactly where he would place zero latitude. The island of Rhodes was his choice, somewhere familiar and close to his home at Tyre on the Syrian coast.

Once the prime meridians were fixed, on the widely held assumption that the Isles of the Blessed lay out in the Atlantic Ocean, off the coast of Africa, Marinus came up with the notion of equirectangular projection. This simple system set lines of longitude and latitude in constant spacing, which in turn allowed a flat map to represent the globe without too much distortion. This meant that the locations of places could be plotted, and found by travellers, using a straightforward series of coordinates of degrees of latitude and longitude.

Like Pytheas' *On the Ocean*, where only latitude was measured with a gnomon, Marinus' great work was lost, but it did influence the man who produced the coordinates that led to the first detailed map of the Highlands and Islands to be drawn. Working in Alexandria around AD 150, Claudius Ptolemy revised and added greatly to Marinus' *Geography* with many names of places, peoples and geographical features, all with coordinates attached. He also listened to the testimony of sailors who had visited far-flung coasts and scholars attribute his accurate mapping of the Bay of Bengal to interviews of this sort. A Greek sailor known as Alexandros gave an account of a voyage to a place he called Cattigara, now identified as Oc Eo in the Mekong Delta in Vietnam. Remarkably, remains of Roman trade goods from the middle of the second century AD were recently unearthed nearby.

Ptolemy's own maps were lost, but his list of names and coordinates survived and monks working in the scriptoria of Constantinople in 1295 recreated them. After the fall of the Eastern Roman Empire and the migration of surviving scholarship to the West, a detailed map of Europe that included Ireland and the British Isles was made by Francesco di Antonio del Chierco in Florence sometime between 1450 and 1475. He worked as an illustrator of manuscripts, including a beautifully made copy of Pliny the Elder's *Natural History*, for wealthy patrons such as the de' Medici. Francesco's map was widely copied and it is very revealing, the first glimpse of the Highlands and Islands, its peoples and places, a snapshot that is almost 2,000 years old. Marinus and Ptolemy almost certainly relied heavily on data collected by Agricola's sailors, scouts and military intelligence officers between AD 80 and 84. These soldiers may indeed have made rough charts of their own as they circumnavigated the northern coasts.

Ptolemy's map looks very odd, as though a fundamental miscalculation of the coordinates had been made. At approximately where the Cheviot Hills might have been plotted, what is now Scotland abruptly lurches to the right and is drawn not on a north to south axis but west to east. It looks as though the long island of Britain is bowing from the waist to Europe, not an attitude, in all senses of the word, some contemporary politicians might be happy to see. This bizarre piece of cartography was probably not a mistake but a misconception. Living in the warmth of the Mediterranean, Greek geographers believed that human life was impossible in latitudes north of 63 degrees. It was simply far too cold. And so to explain the inconvenient fact that people could in fact survive in what is now Scotland, they bent it through 90 degrees.

The map is very much Scotland seen from the sea, just as the sailors on Agricola's reconnaissance ships had plotted the bays, the promontories, islands and estuaries. There were coordinates for seventeen rivers, ten islands, seven capes, three bays, sixteen towns (or more likely, substantial settlements), four other places and finally, and perhaps most interesting, the names of seventeen kindreds and their territories.

Only one major feature did not lie on or near the coast. Planted in the middle of the Highlands, often illustrated in versions of the map by a dense stand of woodland, is Caledonia Saltus, the Caledonian Forest. The use of *saltus* is odd. Pliny called it the Silva Caledonia. *Saltus* carries the more precise meaning of 'an upland, wooded pasture', perhaps a more accurate description of a depleted forest cleared for grazing and populated by herdsmen rather than the dense, deep, dark woods so feared by Roman generals. The word can also mean a pass or a passage through mountains or forests. Entertainingly, my small Chambers Latin–English Dictionary also notes that 'coarsely' it can also mean 'the female pudenda'.

Following Agricola's sailors around the coasts of the Highlands and Islands, Ptolemy plots the 'Venicones' people in Fife and north of the Tay. But before we embark on this philological and toponymic voyage back in time, steered and guided through the fogs of half-forgotten history by the peerless work of W. J. Watson, it is worth pausing for a moment. How did the Roman scouts get their information about the likes of the Venicones? Clearly, on the journey of Claudius' diplomats to Orkney in AD 43, there would have been interpreters and probably pilots who knew the offshore waters, their tides, reefs and shallows. The questions asked by Pytheas on the southern shore of the Channel around 320 BC must often have been repeated. Who are these people, and by what name are they called?

How far does their territory and the power of their kings or lords extend? How many of them are there?

All sorts of qualifications need to be entered at the moment of these exchanges. Watson opens his analysis with the observation that the name of the Venicones and all of the kindreds on the Ptolemy map are similar to the tribal names the Romans encountered in Gaul, modern France. That strongly suggests that the languages were cognate. Elements of ancient Gaulish may survive in Breton, now spoken by only 210,000 in Brittany. Because of the migrations across the Channel in the fifth and sixth centuries (people probably fleeing from the Saxon invasions, and also supplying the origin of the place name: Brittany means 'Little Britain') the language is much more closely related to Cornish and, more distantly, to Welsh. At this point, it is important to draw attention to a crucial distinction: Welsh, Breton and Cornish, the last all but extinct, are known as P-Celtic languages, related to, but very different from, Q-Celtic, that is Irish and Scots Gaelic and Manx, the last also almost extinct. The difference is usually encapsulated in the words for 'head'. In P-Celtic it is something like *pen* and in Q-Celtic it is *ceann*, there being no letter *q* in Gaelic, the sound is rendered as a combination of a *c* and an *e*. The distinction is not, sadly, the origins of the phrase, mind your *p*s and *q*s. That comes from teaching children the alphabet, although it could equally have applied to *b* and *d*.

Which, eventually, brings us back to the Venicones. It is a P-Celtic name and it means the Kindred Hounds. They may have been related to the Votadini of the Lothians and the Borders. Both names make it clear that the language spoken in the north of Britannia was a version of Old Welsh. Venicones is also the first of many animal names listed by Ptolemy. It's also important to bear in mind that the plotting and scale of a kindred's territory by a naval expedition must have relied on the accounts of natives and some of these may have been vague, unreliable and outdated by the shifts of local politics.

Beyond the Venicones and the Tava Aestuarium, the Firth of Tay, lay the lands of the Vacomagi. It is not an animal name, or very informative either. Watson reckoned it might mean something like 'the people of the great prince or king', or possibly 'the people of the plains'. However unlikely philologically, the latter does fit with the nature of their territory. The Vacomagi appear to have occupied lowland Perthshire, the valley of the Spey and the Moray coastlands as far west as Varar Aestuarium, the Beauly Firth.

West of them and into the mountains of the Grampian massif lay the 'Caledones'. Some versions of Ptolemy's map draw their name across the eastern fringe of the trees, implying that they lived in the great forest. It is always named after them. To the west their territory extended to the Lemmanonian Bay. An exotic-sounding name more redolent of the eastern Mediterranean than the West Highlands, it is linked by Watson to the Lennox, the area of the Vale of Leven and the great loch of Lomond. In Gaelic it is Leamhnachd, clearly a cognate name but in Q-Celtic and not P-Celtic. It probably represented the area around the River Leven, or Leamhn, with the *mh* sounding like a *v*. And if the toponymic coordinates are correct, it looks as though the Caledonians controlled the largest territory in the north, most of the central Highlands, the lands of either side of the Great Glen. Their south-eastern boundary is marked by a string of surviving place names. Dunkeld means the Fort of the Caledonians, Schiehallion is the Magic, Shape-Shifting Mountain of the Caledonians, and Rohallion is another Fort of the Caledonians. The use of the kindred name in such a tight cluster seems to Watson to imply a boundary. The people south of Dunkeld were not Caledonians.

The name of the Caledones appears to have a simple root. *Caled* means 'hard'. Whether this refers to the nature of the people, or the mountainous territory they occupied is unclear. How one should interpret that is largely a matter of taste.

I could, and have, spent many happy days staring at maps with Watson and Dwelly (at the back of his great lexicon is a very handy gazetteer of place names and a glossary of proper names) at my elbow and many more detailed pages on ancient toponymy could follow the above. But there is an immense story still to tell, time is pressing in all senses and so the tour around Marinus' and Ptolemy's map will need to become whistle-stop.

East of the Vacomagi were the Taexeli, a name nothing can be made of, and their territory was Aberdeenshire and the Garioch. Beyond the Beauly Firth lay the Decantae, and their name means something like 'the Noble People'. North of them, in Sutherland and Caithness, were the Lugi, 'the Raven People', another animal name that might have been a totem. Inland from this kindred was one that sounded decidedly sinister. The Smertae means 'the Smeared People', smeared with blood, that is, perhaps a description rather than what they called themselves, a reference to warriors who shed a great deal of the stuff. The Cornavii occupied the north-west and their name may be a reference to Cape Wrath because it means 'the People of the Promontory'. It is cognate to the root of the first element of Cornwall and may have been conferred in passing rather than reported by native guides. On the Atlantic coast were the Caereni, 'the Sheep Folk', and again this is likely not a native name, but one that was conferred, an exonym. South of them were the Carnonacae, 'the People of the Cairns', and below them lay the land of the Creones, which may mean the Borderers. South of this kindred is a final name that suggests a series of remarkable and very ancient continuities. In Kintyre were the Epidii, 'the Horsemen'. For much of the historic period these were the clan lands of the MacEacherns. The name means 'the Son of the Horse Lords' in Gaelic.

The islands to the north and west are often erratically plotted on versions of the Ptolemy map, but some of the names also show 2,000-year-old links with the past. Sketis is the earliest record of the name for Skye, Malaios was shortened to Mull and the Aebudae acquired an r, probably through a scribal error, to become the Hebrides. The same sort of thing happened to Mons Graupius. When Tacitus' *Agricola* was first printed between 1475 and 1480 in Florence, Francesco dal Pozzo mistook a 'u' for an 'm' and the enduring typographical blunder of Grampian was born.

Perhaps the longest continuity was marked on the map as 'Orcades'. Pytheas called the islands Orkas and Watson believes that it came from a kindred name, the Orcoi, the Boar People. Like the Venicones and the Lugi, and arguably the Caereni, it derived from a totem animal whose spirit and characteristics were felt to embody a communal identity. During his fascinating discussion of the origins of these and many other names, and their lineage, W. J. Watson made another connection that can be brought forward to the recent past.

In 1890, Scotland's greatest artist was decorating his bedroom at 2 Firpark Terrace, Dennistoun, a suburb of Glasgow. Around the walls he painted a frieze of cats; long-backed and slightly stylised, they looked less like domestic moggies and more like cheetahs or lynxes. Whether he knew it or not, Charles Rennie Mackintosh was remembering an immense past, a thread of identity that ran through Highland history for at least 2,000 years and reached him. The Mackintoshes were part of the ancient Clan Chattan federation, the Clan of the Cats. At Culloden in April 1746, one of their officers, Major Gillies MacBean, showed an extraordinary, feral courage. Despite having his leg broken by grapeshot, he cut his way out of the ruck of the fighting, knowing the battle was lost, to retreat with his clansmen. But, unable to keep up, he was surrounded by government dragoons. With his back against a dyke, MacBean fought like a fury until the dragoons finally rode him down, trampling this courageous warrior under the hooves of their horses.

According to Watson, Clan Chattan originally derived from the ancient name for Shetland. On the Ptolemy map it is marked as 'Thule' and was similarly identified by Pytheas, but from very early Irish sources it was Innse Catt, 'the Islands of the Cats', 'of the Cat People'. They also appeared to control territory on the mainland and this name was applied to Dunnet Head. It was Cat Cape and then Katanes, the ultimate source of Caithness. Sutherland is known as Cataibh in Scots Gaelic, 'the Land of the Cat People'. Machair Cat was the eastern coastal land down to Dunrobin and until modern times the occupant of Dunrobin Castle, the Duke of Sutherland, was Diùc Chat, and a man from Sutherland was known as a Catach, a 'Cat man'.

Perhaps Rennie Mackintosh knew exactly what he was painting in his bedroom. The Cat People's totem was almost certainly the now-extinct Scottish lynx.

*

Marching under the eagle, the imperial totem animal, the Romans were ruthless, and they did not hesitate to slaughter enemies, men, women and children, or burn and destroy farms and houses in pursuit of conquest. The leaders of the Caledonian Confederacy in AD 83 may have made a fatal error when they offered battle in open field at Mons Graupius, but perhaps they believed they had no option. Gnaeus Julius Agricola's legions and auxiliaries will have devastated the countryside as they marched north, and starvation must have stared native communities in the face. But the battle was a disaster, and as always more died in the flight than in the fight. Agricola remembered how the ancient tinchel method worked and 'he ordered strong, light-armed cohorts to form a kind of huntsman's cordon, part of the cavalry to dismount and scout the forest where the trees were dense, the remainder to range through the clearings ... when the enemy saw their pursuers coming forward again in good order with closed ranks, they turned to flight'.

In the next paragraph Tacitus reports that 10,000 Caledonians were killed, a suspiciously round number but probably not much of an exaggeration: 'At dawn the next day the scale of the victory was more apparent: the silence of desolation on all sides, the hills lonely, home-steads smouldering in the distance, not a man to encounter the scouts.'

Agricola marched in into the territory of the Boresti, possibly around Forres, and it seems that part of the army overwintered in the north, no doubt consuming enormous amounts of food. Terrible suffering must have followed for the people of the north. And yet they were not daunted.

In common with other Roman commentators and historians, Tacitus is not always precise about the identity of the enemies of the empire. He occasionally wrote of Caledonians and Caledonia, but most of the time he used the generic terms of Britons and Britain, and sometimes barbarians. But it is very likely that when it came to conflict, he and those who followed him were referring mainly to Caledonians, to Highlanders.

If a longer view is taken, it becomes absolutely clear that Caledonia and its peoples were a continuing problem for the Roman Empire. At its zenith in the second century, when its borders ran from the banks of the Euphrates in the east to the Atlantic shore of the Iberian Peninsula in the west, then to the coast of the Solway Firth in the north and eastwards on to the southern banks of the Rhine and the Danube, there were thirty-four provinces in all. And yet 12 per cent of the entire Roman army was based in a single, peripheral province, in Britannia. Two walls, both huge building projects, were raised in the north at the instigation of Hadrian and Antoninus Pius, and six emperors, or generals who would become emperors, came to Britain. One of them, Septimius Severus, established the imperial court at York between AD 208 and AD 211. There he massed a vast force to invade Caledonia, between 40,000 and 45,000 soldiers, the largest army ever seen in Britain until the twentieth century. And of course, following all that expense and commitment, there is an obvious question. Why?

Capable Roman emperors were decisive and unhesitating. After Agricola was recalled to Rome in AD 84, a huge legionary fortress began construction at Inchtuthil. It lay close to the Tay in lowland Perthshire, in the shadow of the Caledonian mountains. Its role was to house a garrison large enough to consolidate the conquest of the north, but it was never completed. In AD 87, Emperor Domitian decided that he needed reinforcements on the Danube frontier, the legion at Inchtuthil was immediately withdrawn, the buildings of the fort destroyed, the ditches filled in and the walls cast down, and, in an amazing archaeological find, a million nails were unearthed from a deep pit that had been sealed with clay. Iron in that quantity could not be allowed to fall into the hands of the Caledonians.

The Romans not only behaved savagely in battle and in its aftermath, they were also ruthless decision makers, not hesitating to protect the integrity of the empire, and were prepared to throw military resources quickly at places where they were needed.

In one simple sense, the reason why 12 per cent of the entire Roman army was stationed in Britain was not because what is now England

and Wales were likely to see insurrection or trouble of some kind. The province was settled and becoming increasingly Romanised as towns were built and villas set up. The north was the problem. All of these soldiers and all of the building work associated with the two walls and their forts were thought to be absolutely necessary to keep the Caledonians and the other northern kindreds in check. There can be no other credible reason.

But that begs another question. Caledonia was not like the rich eastern provinces of Egypt or Syria. It was a relatively poor part of north-western Europe, much of it mountainous and cold. Tacitus complained that 'the climate is miserable, with frequent rain and mist'. Why then were such expensive efforts made to conquer or subdue such a worthless place? Or was this enormous and sustained military commitment made to protect southern Britain from the savages from the mountains and the forests? Perhaps. Or was it a matter of imperial prestige, like the submission of the Orkney king and his people from the ends of the earth? Possibly.

Whatever their motivation and despite the commitment of arms and men, it didn't work. The Roman historian Cassius Dio wrote about the events of 197: 'The Caledonians, instead of honouring their promises, had prepared to defend the Maeatae, and Severus at that time was concentrating on the Parthian War; so Lupus [governor of Britannia] had no choice but to buy peace from the Maeatae for a considerable sum of money, recovering a few captives.'

The Maeatae do not appear on the Ptolemy map, but place names in the Ochil Hills help to locate them. One of these is the glowering hill of Dumyat, which means 'the Fort of the Maeatae'. From the passage above it looks as though there was a confederacy of northern kindreds and that the Caledonians were probably the major players, coming to the aid of their southern allies, the Maeatae. Clearly there had been hostilities of some sort, and the Romans had been defeated and captives taken, but whatever silver or gold Lupus handed over, it was not enough. By 207, his successor as governor, Lucius Alfenus Senecio, was in despair, as can be seen in part of his dispatch to Rome: 'There was a rebellion amongst the barbarians and they were laying waste the country, plundering and causing widespread destruction.' The governor went on to say that he did not have the resources in the province to deal with this problem and either more troops had to be sent, or the emperor himself should mount an expedition. Septimius Severus decided to act. He moved the entire imperial court to York and mustered his huge army. But when the juggernaut lumbered north, the Maeatae and their Caledonian allies realised that giving battle or even fighting a guerrilla campaign would be futile. They sent emissaries to sue for peace, but Severus would have none of it. His army harried and devastated the countryside in the north before returning to its base at York. Cassius Dio reported the extraordinary sequence of events that followed. In 210, the northern kindreds were defiant and war flared once more: 'The Britons having broken their agreements and taken up arms, Severus ordered his soldiers to invade their territory and put to the sword all that they met, adding the Homeric quotation that "they should let nobody escape, not even the children hidden in their mothers' wombs".'

It was genocide. The orders were absolutely clear. But still it did not succeed. Perhaps the Caledonian kindreds took more than a generation to recover from the slaughter and destruction visited on them by Rome, but recover they did. By the end of the third century, there was war again in the north and a new name was coined.

In order to make the government of the Roman Empire more manageable and more stable, Diocletian decided to divide it. In 286 he designated Maximian as co-emperor to rule over the western provinces while Diocletian retained the east. Each man appointed a junior Caesar as a deputy and a potential successor in an attempt to avoid the usual conflict when a reign ended. Emperor Maximian's Caesar was Constantius Chlorus and his earliest priority was to bring Britannia back into the empire. Under a general known as Carausius, the province had broken away and then had passed to another usurper, Allectus. Constantius defeated the rebels, massacring their Frankish mercenaries somewhere near London, then restored and reinforced Hadrian's Wall and brought Britannia back under imperial control. A praise-poem, *The Panegyric of Constantius Caesar*, was declaimed in his honour in 297, comparing him to Julius Caesar. It made references to the vanquished enemies of the empire, to *Picti et Hiberni* and said they often fought against the Britons, even during Caesar's time.

Picti – the Painted or Tattooed People – was almost certainly a soldiers' nickname, an exonym that had probably been coined by a new garrison on Hadrian's Wall installed by Constantius Chlorus at the end of the third century, men who had never seen warriors who wore tattoos that must have been clearly visible. The name stuck, and was in frequent use because in the fourth century wars burst over Britannia from the north again and again. The Picts raided and invaded between 305–6, in 312, 342, 367, 382 and 400. It was a century of intense pressure and the empire often struggled to deal with it.

Roman commentators described in more detail what these warriors looked like, even before the nickname itself came into common use. Here is Herodian, writing around 237: 'They are ignorant of the use of clothes ... they tattoo their bodies not only with the likenesses of animals of all kinds, but with all sorts of drawings. And this is the reason why they do not wear clothes, to avoid hiding the drawings on their bodies.'

Tertullian wrote of the 'stigmata Brittonum', and at the end of the fourth century the poet Claudian personified Britannia as a woman with her cheeks tattooed. When he praised the resilience of the Roman army, he called them 'this legion which curbs the savage Scot [meaning Irish or perhaps Gaelic speakers] and studies the iron-wrought designs on the face of the dying Pict'.

Much later, at the end of the sixth century, Bishop Isidore of Seville, often regarded as the last genuine classical scholar in the west, set down what he believed the tattoos signified: 'The race of Picts have a name derived from their bodies. These are played upon by a needle working with small pricks and with the squeezed-out sap of a native plant, so that they bear the resultant marks according to the personal rank of the individual, their painted limbs being marked to show their high birth.'

All of these observations are more than interesting, they say something about Pictish society. The totem animals hinted at on the Ptolemy map may have been tattooed on the bodies of a kindred's warband. Other cultures did this and like most men of my age, I well remember James Fenimore Cooper's wonderful *The Last of the Mohicans* and the shock when Uncas's tattoo of a turtle on his chest, a signifier of his fading tribe, was revealed. It may well be that warriors believed their totem animals might simultaneously protect them and give courage. Chingachgook and Hawkeye certainly thought so.

What Isidore of Seville wrote in his *Etymologiae*, a kind of encyclopaedia, about tattoos as a means of showing rank, like a sergeant's stripes, suggests that this cultural habit changed over time and became embedded in all senses, the Picts continuing with body decoration long after most others had ceased to do it. There were also perceived overtones of paganism and as late as the eighth century, at a Church synod held in Northumbria, a bishop railed against the peoples of the north with their 'hideous scars' on their bodies, which had suffered 'the injury of staining'.

There are no written or inscribed records in the Pictish language to agree or disagree with these interpretations, or indeed supply any more information. It has been almost entirely lost, a remarkable disappearance. No one can now utter a sentence in Pictish. Virtually all memory of the language has vanished. Scholars have tried to piece together scraps from place and personal names. For example, the prefix 'pit' in the likes of Pittodrie, Pitreavie or Pitlessie might mean 'a portion of land', but that is hardly much of an advance. It had been concluded that Pictish was a P-Celtic language, but little more can be said.

Nevertheless, the silence can be broken in other ways. Much more information is to be found by the sides of the roads in the north, in churchyards, on the edges of woodland, in the grounds of grand houses, on a suburban street or in museums. Two hundred Pictish standing stones have survived in the north. No doubt many more were raised in the centuries between 400 and 900. Striking, beautifully carved, they show battles, hunting scenes, seated and standing figures, riders and a menagerie of what must surely be totem animals: there are eagles, salmon, bears, deer, wild boar, snakes, hawks, wolves, horses, geese, bulls and what is known as the Pictish Beast. To my eye, it looks very much like a stylised representation of a dolphin.

Some historians believe that the stones were raised on boundaries, especially where arable land meets hill country, and that must reinforce the notion of totems. Like the body tattoos, they needed to be seen. Clearly there are also links with the kindreds on the Ptolemy map, the boar with Orkney is only the most obvious, and it is not beyond the bounds of possibility that these animals were commonly tattooed on human beings in much the same style as they were carved in stone.

The most common carvings on the stones are also the most mysterious. Some appear to be high status objects like a mirror and a comb, others may be associated with work, like a blacksmith's hammer and tongs, or a pair of shears that might have been used to clip sheep. But most are abstract, and most common are rods, but they are never straight. Some are shaped like a V or like a Z. There are many crescents, often decorated, double discs, what looks like a tuning fork, and a scatter of random rectangles and squares. Often the V and Z rods seem superimposed on these other designs and perhaps relate to them in a lost language of symbolism.

What do they mean and why were they carved on standing stones designed and placed where they could be seen? The apparently abstract symbols seem to hark back to a pagan past. All over Scotland and elsewhere in Britain, Iron Age peoples made ritual deposits of valuable metalwork, often weapons and often in considerable volume. In some kind of ceremony these were usually thrown into watery places with no intention to retrieve them. At Duddingston Loch in Edinburgh, where Henry Raeburn's minister skated so elegantly, there appears to have been a jetty, a place from where a priest or an important leader of some kind could throw these objects into the water. They were almost certainly sacrifices to the gods and before swords, daggers, shields, spears could be deposited, they had to be broken, bent, slighted, and in a sense, killed.

I think that what we see on the Pictish stones are stylised representations of damaged weapons: spears or swords bent or broken at 90 degrees, or bent twice to make the Z-rod, shields slighted and so on. By the time the symbols began to be carved on the stones, Pictish society was beginning to change, moving from paganism to Christianity. The symbols seem to me to be an inheritance of pagan ritual deposit, which, increasingly, could not actually be practiced. But instead, it could be carved where it could be seen as a representation of pagan piety. Carvings of the Christian cross rather than an actual cross work in the same way. Many of the stones that have symbols also carry Christian iconography and references. The 200 surviving stones have been classified in three groups and they show this transition from paganism clearly. The earliest have only the symbols, the second group has both symbols and Christian iconography, and the third group has no symbols, only Christian iconography.

As W. J. Watson has so brilliantly shown, place names are another way of reading history and detecting cultural change, but the attachment of names is very difficult to date and may have been more of a gradual process as older examples faded and new ones gained currency. Argyll used to compass a much larger area than the boundaries of the modern local authority or the old county, reaching from the tip of Kintyre as far north as Loch Broom. But borders in the early medieval period were much more porous than they are now. There were no frontier posts and guards, no checks on movement, little uniformity and some fluidity. Three Pictish symbol stones have been found in Skye and they are clear cultural markers, but all they indicate is ebb and flow, not an emphatic permanence. In modern Gaelic, Argyll is rendered as Earra-Ghàidheal, 'the Coast of the Gaels'. An older name was Oirer Ghàidheal, with the first element have the sense of being on the edge of the land, the coast. In medieval sources the lands north of Ardnamurchan were known as Oirer a Tuath, 'the Coasts of the North', and those to the south were Oirer a Deas, 'the Southern Coasts'.

Traditions hold that Fergus Mor mac Eirc led a migration from Ireland to found what became the kingdom of Dál Riata sometime around the beginning of the sixth century. 'Dál' is like 'pit' and means a portion of land. 'Riata' seems to have been a personal name whose identity is now long lost. More likely than some sort of invasion is that Gaelic had probably been spoken on both shores of the North Channel for a long time, the sea being much more of a highway than a barrier.

Sometimes Dál Riata was known as Alba, the modern Gaelic name for Scotland, and indeed in the recent past for the whole of Britain. Napoleon Bonaparte complained about 'perfidious Albion' and an unlikely memory of the name is preserved in English football clubs like West Bromwich Albion, and Brighton and Hove Albion. Alba means something like White Land, and perhaps an image of the snow-capped Highlands seen from Ireland, or the white cliffs of England seen from the Channel, were prompts. It is impossible to do more than speculate.

What is accepted is a remarkable document known as the *Senchus fer n-Alban*, 'The History of the Men of Alba'. Compiled in the middle of the seventh century, it is a long genealogy of Dál Riatan kings, and also a muster roll for a navy and a census of sorts. More than 400 years before the Domesday Book, it lists property and also the obligations attached to it. The kingdom of Dál Riata was made up of four kindreds who held different territories along the Atlantic coast. Only three are listed in the *Senchus*, the fourth, the Cenel Comgaill, based in Cowal, a cognate name, and perhaps Bute, is missing. It had probably been absorbed into the Cenel nGabrain. Here is a summary of the census:

Cenel nOengusa [the Kindred of Angus on Islay]	430 houses
Cenel Loairn [the Kindred of Lorne in Lorne and Appin]	420 houses
Cenel nGabrain [the Kindred of Gabran in Kintyre]	560 houses

Houses almost certainly denoted farmsteads. These could be of varying size and the compiler of the *Senchus* noted that 'small are the lands of the houses of the Cenel nOengusa'. The main motive behind the survey was to make an informed assessment of military obligations and strengths – even though the numbers are suspiciously round. Each group of twenty houses was bound to supply twenty-eight oarsmen, sufficient to row two seven-bench seagoing curraghs and the *Senchus* showed that Dál Riatan kings could command a navy of seventy vessels carrying a force of almost a thousand marines. The first recorded naval battle in British history was fought in 719 in the Hebrides when the Cenel nGabrain and the Cenel nOengusa attacked each other in some forgotten dispute.

These records, unique in north-western Europe at the time, give a sense of an established state, well-organised and relatively settled. There is no mention in the *Senchus* of territory held in Ulster, even though there were strong dynastic, linguistic and historical connections. What also emerges is a developing sense of political geography. From the writings of Adomnán, Abbot of Iona from 679 to 704 and the biographer of St Columba, it is clear that there were frontiers, if not frontier lines, and contact between two different cultures in the Highlands and Islands. He noted 'the Mountains of the Spine of Britain', what Gaels call Druim Alban or Drumalban. The high ranges from Arrochar north to Ben Nevis and beyond were seen as a formidable barrier breached only by the Great Glen and a few passes. Drumalban seems to me to have been a clearly understood border. Broadly speaking, to the west lay the lands of the kingdom of Dál Riata and to the east was Pictland. And they were different.

No symbol stones have ever been found in Argyll and their greatest concentration is in the east, from the clusters around the head of the Moray Firth to Aberdeenshire and south to Angus and around the shores of the Tay. According to Adomnán, St Columba travelled up the Great Glen in 565 to visit the court of Bridei, King of the Picts. His mission was one of conversion, and, significantly, the saint had to bring an interpreter with him. He had passed from one country into another. And there is, incidentally, no record that Columba succeeded in converting Bridei to Christianity, and some that he failed to get his message across.

Between the sixth and eighth centuries, the high kingship of Dál Riata passed between the three major kindreds, with Cenel nGabrain usually dominating. On the other side of Drumalban, Pictland appeared to be divided into provinces or subkingdoms, all of which were intermittently ruled by a high king. Bridei was almost certainly one such. A list of these provinces survived in Irish sources. Here is W. J. Watson's translation:

Seven of Cruithne's children divided Alba into seven divisions,
the portion of Cat, of Ce, of Cirech, children with hundreds of
    possessions,
the portion of Fib, of Fidaid, of Fotla, and of Fortriu.
And it is the name of each man of them that is on his land.

The matching of seven divisions with the seven children of Cruithne, a legendary first king of the Picts, sounds equally mythic in its symmetry, and the alliteration is deeply suspect. But despite these hesitations, there is a link with later geography. In the twelfth century a recension of this list appeared, known as *De Situe Albania*. Here is how Watson combined the two sources:

Cirech [also written as Circenn]	Angus and the Mearns
Fotla	Atholl and Gowrie
Fortriu	Strathearn and Menteith
Fib	Fife with Fothreue
Ce	Mar and Buchan
Fidaid	Moray and Easter Ross
Cat	Caithness and South East Sutherland.

The author of *De Situe Albania* noted that each of these seven provinces was held by a king and that under him there was a petty king, a *subregulus*, perhaps a deputy of some kind. The twinning of a larger region with a smaller seems to reinforce that arrangement and in Ireland this sort of hierarchy was common, and over all of these regional kings, there was often a high king, the office Bridei may have held.

The old Scottish counties were swept away in 1974 in a spasm of local government reform, and a great deal was lost, not least some echoes of the old Pictish provinces. In several parts of the country, a large county lay next to a small one. There was Angus and Kincardineshire, known as the Mearns, Perthshire and Kinross, and Morayshire and Nairn. They may be the shadows of parts of the list in the *De Situe Albania*.

*

A century before the *Senchus fer n-Alban* was compiled, Pictland had begun to change as men who brought the word of God walked eastwards through the mountain passes of Drumalban. In the summer of 2019, I sailed in search of sanctity. From the harbour at Easdale, on the island of Seil, off the Atlantic coast to the south of Oban, I boarded a RIB, a bright orange rigid inflatable boat. The skipper had agreed, for an eyewatering fee, to take me across the Firth of Lorne to Eileach an Naoimh. It is an uninhabited, jagged rock, an *eileach*, at the mouth of the great firth, that was once close to paradise, a portal found and founded by a saint, *an naoimh*. He was St Brendan the Navigator, more famous for his voyage of exploration in the Atlantic, in a seagoing curragh, looking for Marinus of Tyre's Isles of the Blessed.

He found Eileach an Naoimh sometime around 542, twenty years before Columba landed on Iona. History has seen both holy men as missionaries bringing the word of God to pagan Scotland, but in truth their voyages were more than that. The early Church was much influenced by the teachings of the Desert Fathers, groups of Christian ascetics who fled from the cities, and the persecution, of the Roman provinces of Egypt and Judaea to seek refuge and solitude. In caves, and even in an abandoned Roman fort, they sought peace and silence in the desert. There, through prayer, fasting and privations of all kinds, they hoped to achieve a transcendental state so they might draw closer to God, know the mind of God. It was essential to withdraw from the distractions and temptations of the temporal world to a place of solitude. The Latin *monachus*, from the original

Greek, *monakhos*, meant not a community of monks but instead a person who chooses to be alone, and the earliest monasteries in the desert were groups of solitaries who only occasionally came together and who lived lives of brutal privation.

So influential were the Desert Fathers in Western Europe that the Gaelic word for a monastery is *diseart*, from 'desert'. It survives in Scottish place names, notably Dysart in Fife, and there is another near Forfar, and, according to W. J. Watson, there are older, now unused *diseart* names near Pitlochry and in Argyll. When Brendan crossed the North Channel in his great curragh and made his way up the Atlantic shores of southern Dál Riata, that was what he was searching for. In place of deserts, the early Irish saints thought of the wastes of the sea as a barrier against the temporal world. Rocky, remote islands amongst the Hebrides became *diseartan* and all I'd read told me that Eileach an Naoimh would take me back fourteen centuries because there on this uninhabited, wind-battered place, I'd see what Brendan saw.

When the skipper of the RIB cut the engine below a low cliff of wave-washed black stone, he pointed out two iron rings attached to it. 'That's it', he said, smiling at me. 'That's how we'll get you ashore'.

The other crew member turned out to be as agile as a mountain goat. Having nudged the RIB closer to the cliff, the skipper shouted, 'OK', and the young man leapt onto a ledge no more than a foot deep. He caught the line the skipper threw, threaded it through the iron ring and pulled the RIB close enough so that the stern could be attached with another line to the second ring, before jumping back on board. The skipper turned and looked at me. 'OK?'

Right, I thought, OK. I've driven a long way and spent more than the cost of a return plane ticket to New York on this short, thirty-minute voyage. OK. So I waited until the RIB bobbed upwards on the swell and jumped. I made the ledge and grabbed one of the lines. After steadying myself, untying both and throwing them back, I crawled, scrambling rather than climbing, and clambered up the cliff face. Sometimes on all fours, I probably looked like a much less agile lower primate, one that knew a lot of swearwords.

'See you about five o'clock,' shouted the skipper as he wheeled the RIB around and skimmed over the waves back to Easdale, fast disappearing into the distance.

A jagged, angry deposit of geology thrust up through the waters of the firth by an ancient convulsion, Eileach an Naoimh looked forbidding. When I reached the top of the low cliff and was able to stand up straight on sure footing, I looked along the shore of this little island. Instead of coves or inlets, or even small beaches, shingle or sand, it looked like a rampart. Strung out in a line was what resembled a row of huge standing stones that had been scattered by the careless hands of giants. Some stood at drunken angles, others looked as though their tops had been snapped off, while more lay on their sides having apparently collapsed. As I looked along the coastline cliffs and stones, it occurred to me that St Brendan might have liked that, a rampart made by God to keep not only the sea but the temporal world at bay.

And yet amidst all this seismic drama, there was detail and beauty. Growing in fissures between the black rocks were little flowers. Blue, pink, white and star-shaped, I guessed, unhampered by any horticultural knowledge, that these might be alpine plants, certainly ones that could withstand salt spray, of which there is not a lot in the Alps. Maybe they could be found only here, in the middle of the Firth of Lorne. The only name for an alpine flower I could remember came swimming up from the depths of juvenile memory. 'Edelweiss' was a song I'd heard in the early 1960s. Was it from *The Sound of Music*? It was hard to picture Julie Andrews in her pinafore skipping over the rocks of Eileach an Naoimh.

There was no path I could find and so I made my way into the interior of the little island very carefully, for the ground was obscured by tall and dense stands of ferns. They may have hidden ankle-breaking holes or declivities. I rounded a strange rock formation where a much larger stone perched on a smaller, as though placed there and then forgotten by one of the giants while he scattered the crooked standing stones on the shore ramparts. And suddenly, there, right in front of me, was what I'd come to see.

In the lee of a low hill were two beehive cells, one much larger than the other. Surrounded by a rickety fence to keep out the sheep that grazed the island's summer grass was a magnificent, and unique, example of drystone building, more impressive even than Mousa Broch. Shaped like old-fashioned straw skeps, the ancestors of modern, wooden beehives, the cells were like a large, upturned pudding bowl attached to a smaller one. It was as though one was an extension of the other, an afterthought.

Like the brochs, there was a low entrance under a massive lintel. Even lower than I thought as I scraped my scalp on it. But I managed to suppress any more expletives. I knew I was entering a holy place, Britain's oldest surviving chapel, oldest surviving ecclesiastical building of any kind. When I stood up inside the beehive cell, I could see that it was a surprisingly large space. Perhaps eight to ten monks will have been able to kneel in prayer and sing psalms. For inside, out of the sea wind, there was peace and a stillness in the half darkness, an ancient air, the unmistakable atmosphere of an austere sanctity.

It was what I had come to the island to understand, to stand in a place where Brendan had stood, where he led worship, where he and his monks recited the Jesus Prayer, counting the number of repetitions on their prayer ropes, early versions of a rosary. I had come to the place where the word of God was first heard in the Highlands and Islands of Scotland. When I looked up at the wide hole the centuries had made in the roof, I saw the grey clouds scud across the sky but could not hear the sigh or saugh of the wind. The cell seemed otherworldly to me, a place apart and somewhere I felt the turning world unwind and slow down.

When at last I sat down on the beaten earth of the floor, my back to the drystone corbelling as it curved upwards and inwards to make the miracle of the roof, I listened for what Gaelic speakers call 'the music of the thing as it happened'. There is no feeling, nothing like being alone in the turn of history, in the hypnotic silence as fourteen centuries fall away. Instead of the skill and industry of Brendan and his hardy monks building this ancient chapel, I heard faint echoes of their solitary lives. I was alone where they had been alone, searching the huge Highland skies for glimpses of Heaven, listening to the eternal music of the wind and the waves for the voice of their God, whispering to them and them alone. With every prayer, every day of fasting, every mortification of the flesh, they moved closer to salvation, to the glories of eternal life, to being gathered up in the arms of angels.

Remembering to crawl low enough, I made my way out of the chapel and walked up the hill behind it. In the middle of the little island was what made life possible: perhaps three or four acres of flattish ground where animals might graze and oats might be grown. There was the upstanding, rectilinear ruin of a medieval chapel, a strange underground chamber known in Gaelic as *am prìosan*, 'the prison', and beyond it a low mound that would take the story of early Christianity in the West forward by a generation. At the side of the path was a well-weathered Historic Scotland sign:

Eithne's Grave

Traditionally identified as the grave of St Columba's mother. This round enclosure seems to have been intended for burials, as the early Christian cross-marked stone indicates. Who was buried here remains unknown.

*

St Columba has come to dominate the early history of Dál Riata, and before Andrew supplanted him in the later Middle Ages, he was seen as Scotland's patron saint. To some he still is. In 563, with twelve companions (probably a common trope, certainly in imitation of Christ's twelve disciples), Columba sailed from Ireland in search of another *diseart*.

Iona is much larger, greener and more welcoming than Eileach an Naoimh, but has become a magnetic tourist attraction. Only when the crowds have left on the last ferry to Fionnphort is it possible to catch a fleeting impression of the island's *genius loci*, what I think of as a place of spirits. George MacLeod, who re-established the Iona Community in the 1930s and 1940s, called it 'a thin place', where the veil between worlds can sometimes be like gossamer. And he was right. Away from the crowds around the rebuilt abbey and the cafés and shops of the little village, across the spine of the island to the machair on the west coast, spirits sometimes swirl in the evening air. Once, I slept the night on the sandy shore of the meadow, listening to the shushing of the waves, drifting in and out of formless, shifting reveries about the long past before I closed my eyes.

Several significant and substantial holy men sailed from Ireland in the sixth and seventh centuries to found communities of solitaries in the Hebrides or the Atlantic shore: Moluag on Lismore, Donan on Eigg, Maelrubha at Applecross and others. But Columba overshadows them all, and not necessarily because of his achievements but because he had a gifted and influential biographer. Adomnán was the ninth Abbot of Iona and it was his *Vita Columbae*, probably written between 697 and 700, that established the saint's powerful cult. But in some ways, he was a more substantial figure in his own right; a politician and lawyer, as well as a writer.

The Life of St Columba was not a biography in a modern sense, although it did contain precious biographical details. Adomnán's purpose was to establish sanctity and the main method of achieving that status was the recounting of miracles wrought by 'the praiseworthy man'. Those demonstrated Columba's closeness to God, his innate sanctity. On his visit to Bridei's court, probably at Craig Phadraig, on the fringes of the city of Inverness, the saint was said to have rebuked the Loch Ness Monster, no less. When one of the Iona monks swam across the River Ness to retrieve a boat moored on the opposite bank, the fell creature reared up from the deeps, its jaws agape. But when Columba made the sign of the cross, it turned and fled and was not seen again until 1933. The saint could change the direction of the wind to bring curraghs safely back to Iona, heal disease and even bring the dead back to life.

In 697 Adomnán was sufficiently powerful and influential to convene a conference of churchmen and kings. With the help of the

High King of Ireland, Loingsech mac Oengusso, he persuaded all sorts of notables to come to a meeting at Birr in what is now County Offaly. There, Adomnán produced his *Cáin Adomnáin*, better known as the *Law of the Innocents*. It is a remarkable document that demonstrates the growing power of the Church. Irish, Dál Riatan (or Scottish Gaelic speakers) and Pictish bishops all agreed that in addition to monks, women, children and non-combatants should also not be at risk during times of warfare. The sanctions were strict, even savage: 'whoever slays a woman . . . his right hand and his left foot shall be cut off before death, and then he shall die'. Order and the rule of law were slowly being introduced to what might be seen as a society where only military might mattered. It may be no coincidence that the *Law of the Innocents* came into force on the centenary of Columba's death in 597.

As a politician as well as a churchman, Adomnán attempted to heal an important rift in the early British Church. In 664, at a synod convened by King Oswiu of Northumbria at Whitby in Yorkshire, it had been agreed that the monasteries of the Hebrides and their foundations at Lindisfarne, Melrose and elsewhere, needed to come into conformity with Roman religious practices. The date of Easter, the most important festival in the Christian calendar, and one from which all others were dated, was reckoned differently in the north and Oswiu ruled that this should cease. The underlying argument was almost militaristic. What mattered was not only the power of prayer but also its volume. To defeat and keep at bay the hellish hosts of Satan, all Christians needed to pray at the same time. When Celtic Easter and Roman Easter were celebrated on different dates, the forces of Heaven were divided. The primacy of the Bishop of Rome, where St Peter and St Paul had 'lived, taught, suffered and are buried' was also insisted upon. And finally, the Roman tonsure, where the top of a monk's head was shaved to leave a fringe of hair at the temples and at the back so that it resembled Christ's crown of thorns, was to be made universal. Columba and all of the northern monks had what has been suggested was the ancient druidic tonsure: the hair shaved across the crown of the head to the forehead and worn long at the back. The decisions of the synod took a long time to be enforced, but Adomnán appears to have succeeded at Iona.

Conflicts of a more deadly kind flared between Northumbria and Pictland in the later seventh century. A unique record of one of these has come down to us on a symbol stone. In the graveyard at Aberlemno Church, near Forfar, scenes from a pivotal battle are depicted on a massive stone.

In the afternoon of Saturday 20 May 685, a Northumbrian cavalry force was drawn into a trap in a landscape that has largely disappeared. Near the town of Forfar, the ruins of Restenneth Priory overlie an earlier monastery founded by Pictish kings. It was probably seen as a *diseart*, a place apart from the world because it was surrounded on three sides by a lake that was drained in the late eighteenth century. Loch Restenneth lay to the east and south of the old *diseart*, and in the Pictish language it was probably known as something like Linn Garan, the Crane Lake. To the west was a narrow piece of land and beyond it another loch, Loch Forfar, which has also been drained. Between the two bodies of water and the boggy ground at their edges, a troop of Pictish cavalry pretended to retreat, and, spurring on their horses, scenting a quick victory, a force of about 500 warriors led by King Ecgfrith of Northumbria gave chase – and rode into a trap, into a place where they were confronted by ranks of infantry commanded by the High King of Pictland, Bridei mapBili.

These two men, adversaries from what were apparently two distinctive cultures, were in fact cousins. Bridei was the son of Bili, King of Alt Clut, what became the Old-Welsh-speaking kingdom of Strathclyde. His mother was a daughter of Edwin, who had succeeded to the throne of Northumbria half a century before the battle at the Crane Lake. It appears that the kings of Pictland paid tribute to the Angles, and what almost certainly brought Ecgfrith and his cavalry north was default, the refusal of Bridei to continue to send valuables to Bamburgh. The Venerable Bede, a famous and often reliable historian based at Jarrow and Monkwearmouth, related what happened next: 'For in the following year King Ecgfrith, ignoring the advice of his friends and in particular of [St] Cuthbert, rashly led an army to ravage the province of the Picts. The enemy pretended to retreat, and lured the king into narrow mountain passes, where he was killed with the greater part of his forces.'

The stone in Aberlemno churchyard adds welcome detail to that brief account. It shows three ranks of Pictish infantry, probably drawn up on the slopes of Dunnichen Hill, as they wait for the charge of the Northumbrian cavalry. Holding up his spiked shield high and carrying a sword, the warrior in the front rank is supported by his comrade behind him who pushes out his spear beyond the first rank so that he can stab at the enemy. Behind both of these men stands a third warrior, apparently in reserve. Horses will wheel away from a solid phalanx of infantry who stand fast and close up quickly if men fall and gaps appear. Bridei lured the Anglian cavalry to fight on ground of his choosing, a narrow place where he could not be easily outflanked and surrounded. The Aberlemno Stone shows that the Pictish infantry did indeed stand fast, for in another scene their own cavalry chase a fleeing Northumbrian, his shield thrown away. And in the bottom left-hand corner a figure, who may be Ecgfrith, is shown lying dead, pecked at by the symbol of battlefield carnage, a raven.

The victory at Dunnichen, or in early English, Nechtansmere, or in Old Welsh/Pictish, Linn Garan, was a pivotal moment, famous in two languages perhaps because it influenced their spread. The juggernaut of the Anglian advance was halted and rolled back south of the Forth, and Pictish kings continued to act independently.

*

In the early decades of the eighth century, the mountain spine of Drumalban became less of a barrier, certainly to dynastic ambition. Pictish and Dál Riatan kings were often related to each other and there is a sense of the Gaelic language drifting eastwards. The Cenel Loairn, based in Appin, Lorne, Morvern, Mull and the south-western end of the Great Glen, began to fade from history. In the past they had contended for the high kingship of Dál Riata with Cenel nGabrain but, after the 730s, their ambitions appear to have been thwarted, permanently. But in fact the Cenel Loairn did not disappear, they moved. Migrating up the Great Glen, their warbands and their leaders began to assert themselves in northern Pictland, along the fertile littoral of the Moray Firth. Eventually a powerful kingdom of Moray emerged. Much larger than the old county, it compassed all of the coastlands, east to Aberdeenshire and north up to Wick and perhaps beyond, as well as stretching west to Skye and the north-west.

Kings of Moray emerged in the tenth century and their power centre seems to have been at Forres. It is the location of the grandest and most monumental of all the symbol stones. Known as Sueno's Stone, it stands more than twenty feet high, and four panels seem to show several stages of a battle. Squadrons of cavalry trot in single file, ranks of soldiers and archers surround what might be a broch. Decapitated, defeated soldiers are depicted and on the bottom panel, it looks as though a victory parade departs the battlefield. Whatever the historical detail, Sueno's Stone is a display of military power.

Royal genealogies show a coherent series of chronologically correct links between the powerful kings of Moray and the Cenel Loairn. This was important because it allowed the Moray kings to challenge credibly the kings of Alba, the descendants of the rival Cenel nGabrain. In 1040, one of them famously succeeded. Far from the blood-spattered usurper portrayed by William Shakespeare, Macbeth was a legitimate and successful king who ruled in the north for fourteen years.

But that is to anticipate events, and by some distance.

On 8 June 793, the Vikings sailed out of nowhere and attacked the much-loved monastery on Lindisfarne, as recorded in the *Anglo-Saxon Chronicle*: '793. Here terrible portents came about over the land of Northumbria, and miserably frightened the people: there were immense flashes of lightning, and fiery dragons were seen flying in the air. A great famine immediately followed these signs; and a little after that . . . the raiding of heathen men miserably devastated God's church in Lindisfarne by looting and slaughter.'

When sea lords roared for their oarsmen to row hard for the shore and rasp up the keels of their dragon ships on the shingle beach below the monastery, the monks will have fled for the safety and sanctuary of God's holy church. There the shrine of Cuthbert, the great saint of the north, would surely protect them. But as Viking warriors hacked with their axes and smashed down the doors, the defenceless, terrified monks will have been appalled at the impiety. These raiders were pagans, defilers of the sacred ground where Cuthbert walked and the place where he knelt to pray. The Anglo-Saxon chronicler wrote of slaughter and the looting of the church's treasures, the ransacking of places so revered that they had needed no protection except God's. The shock of this first contact reverberated around the shores of Britain and Ireland. Monastic annalists came to call the Northmen the Sons of Death.

After the raid on Lindisfarne, Viking dragon ships rounded Cape Wrath and left a trail of destruction in their wake all down the Atlantic shore. Iona was attacked repeatedly, in 795 and 802, and in 806 sixty-eight monks were slaughtered at what became known as Martyr's Bay. St Donan's and St Maelrubha's communities on Eigg, Skye and at Applecross suffered, all of them defended only by prayer and sanctity, no barrier to the pagan Northmen. Iona was eventually abandoned, the monks seeking refuge inland at Kells in Ireland and Columba's precious relics taken over the Drumalban mountains for safekeeping at Dunkeld.

In 839 there was a bloody and defining battle in northern Pictland. Here is the entry from the Annals of Ulster: 'The heathens won a battle over the men of Fortriu [a Pictish province in the north, usually held by the high king] and Eoganan, son of Oengus, and Bran, son of Oengus, and Aed, son of Boanta, and others almost innumerable fell there.'

Although the exact location is uncertain, the outcome of the battle was not. It seems that the Viking army decapitated Pictish leadership as many of the royalty and nobility fell in the face of a furious onslaught. After 839, Gaelic appears to move further eastwards as Dál Riatan kings establish themselves over the whole of the north, and Pictish and Pictland begin to fade from the map.

6

Thralls

793–1058

In the Temple Bar district of central Dublin, archaeologists came across what at first they thought was a small stock pen, a wattle-and-post outhouse that measured about ten feet by eight. Analysis of the remains of animal droppings dated the little structure to the eleventh or twelfth centuries and the beginnings of the medieval city. But something unexpected came up in lower layers. The diggers found a small hearth and evidence of human fleas that suggested the stock pen was considerably older, perhaps early ninth century. What they had found were faint traces of a story of unimaginable misery, of centuries of horror and humiliation. More than a thousand years ago, Dublin was one of Western Europe's busiest slave markets. At the Temple Bar was not a stock pen, but a cramped hovel where captives shivered around a hearth, waiting to be sold or transported.

In the spring of 870, lookouts on Dumbarton Rock searched the northern horizon, scanning the mouth of the Firth of Clyde for movement. And they saw something that hollowed their bellies with fear. The sails of a huge fleet, 200 ships, were rounding the headland at Gourock and making way quickly towards the royal citadel of the kingdom of Strathclyde. When the lookouts roared down to the garrison below, the gates were clanged shut and barred, and King Artgal no doubt joined his soldiers on the ramparts.

Standing in the prows of their ships were two Viking sea lords, Amlaib and Imar, the sons of the King of Dublin. They anchored their fleet and set about laying siege to Alt Clut, 'the Great Rock of the Clyde', and after four months of attrition, they took it when the garrison's well ran dry. But there was no great slaughter. Instead the Strathclyde nobility and their retinues were taken captive, their king, Artgal, having managed to escape. They were dragged out of the citadel, probably beaten into submission and bundled into the ships of the Viking fleet either to be ransomed or sold at the Dublin slave market. Many would become 'thralls', the Norse word for a slave that survives in the English phrase, 'to be in thrall', or the verb 'to enthral'. The latter now carries a quite different meaning.

In the first shocking and blood-spattered raids around the coasts of Scotland, Ireland and the rest of the British Isles in the early ninth century, the Viking warbands stole whatever portable valuables they could find, sweeping aside those who tried to protect them. Churches and their treasures were easy, defenceless and lucrative targets. The pagan sea lords may have learned something about the Christian calendar and attacked at Easter, when valuable cups, plate and bejewelled bibles would be on the high altar, having been taken out of their hiding places. But as time passed, the raiders found that slaughter was a wasteful last resort – much better to take captives and sell them on for silver or bartered goods. Vikings often counted their wealth in arm silver, usually coins melted down to make armlets worn around the biceps. Dublin was central, easily accessible by sea from the south and in the first half of the ninth century was a focus for the trade in human beings. Like the much later slave castles on the west coast of Africa, Dublin's stock pens were where buyers and sellers gathered to do business.

Slavery is often invisible to archaeologists, but other finds and records in Dublin have added colour and context to this cruel picture. Iron slave collars and shackles have been found, and a rare entry on trafficking confirms an early date. For the year 821, the *Annals of Ulster* noted that 'Etar [the Howth peninsula in Dublin Bay] was plundered by the heathens and they carried off a great number of women into captivity.'

Because women often had saleable domestic skills, such as textile making, they were attractive to the Viking slavers, as well as more easily controlled and intimidated. And often groups of women were systematically raped before being put up for sale because those who were pregnant fetched higher prices. The *Life of S: Wulfstan*, from the end of the eleventh century, describes a long and sad history:

> There is a maritime town called Bristol, which is on the direct route to Ireland, and so suitable for trade with that barbarian land. The inhabitants of this place with other Englishmen often sail to Ireland for the sake of trade. Wulfstan banished from among them a very old custom which had so hardened their hearts that neither the love of God nor the love of King William could efface it. For men whom they had purchased from all over England they carried off to Ireland; but first they got the women with child and sent them pregnant to market. You would have seen queues of the wretches of both sexes shackled together and you would have pitied them: those who were beautiful and those who were in the flower of youth were daily prostituted and sold amidst much wailing to the barbarians.

Some product descriptions used at the Dublin market survive: 'a foreigner who does not know Irish' may have been a Pictish or English captive, or 'a woman from across the great sea' might have been abducted from further afield, perhaps from across the North Sea or up from the Bay of Biscay. Slaves from the Iberian Peninsula and North Africa were sold in Dublin, and there is powerful ancestral DNA evidence that a huge proportion, perhaps two-thirds, of the foundation female population of the Scandinavian colony of Iceland were women with Highland and Islands and Irish genes. In 875, the largest slave rebellion since the fall of the Western Roman Empire erupted in Iceland. The captives killed their masters and fled to the peninsula of Vestmannaeyjar where they were all caught and slaughtered. Slaves were also taken back to Norway and other Viking homelands. Ancestral DNA supplies strong evidence of this direction of trafficking. A characteristic early British Y-chromosome marker, carried only by men, is found at a significant frequency of 5 per cent in all Norwegian men, and it is specifically concentrated along the western coasts, those closest to the Northern Isles. In Hordaland, the district around Bergen, the frequency rises to an average of 15 per cent of the modern population.

On the southern fringes of the Highlands and Islands, a unique image of the Viking slave trade has recently come to light. Sometime in the seventh century, a holy man not from Ireland but perhaps a native Scot, St Ernan, founded a *diseart* on the little island named after him. Inchmarnock lies north of Bute, just off the coast of the Cowal Peninsula and it became an early medieval school, a scriptorium. Just as they were used in my lifetime when children were taught to write, slates have survived with the efforts of novice monks scratched on them. But one of them carries something much more sinister. Above an inscribed illustration of what is clearly a dragon ship, there are three men wearing mail armour. The largest figure has a captive trailing behind him, a monk taken in a Viking raid. His hands are held out in front of his body and his wrists appear to be handcuffed or manacled as he is taken off to the ship to be sold into slavery.

Literate slaves like this poor man were valuable, especially in the east, both in the Byzantine Empire and in the courts of the Arab caliphates (probably 'the barbarians' in the extract from the *Life of St Wulfstan*). Fair-haired and fair-skinned Christian slaves attracted even more of a premium. As did another grisly, unspeakably cruel practice. Slaves bought in the market at Dublin sometimes travelled long distances as they passed through the hands of several merchants, but for some, horror waited en route. Venice was an entrepôt where Irish and Scottish slaves were sold on to eastern buyers. For their courts and especially their harems, caliphs and other Muslim potentates preferred to buy eunuchs, but castration was forbidden by Islamic law. And so, when likely young men arrived in Venice on the slave ships, they were taken to castration houses, where they screamed as the gelding knife sliced off their genitals. After the blood had been staunched, a tube was inserted into the urethra so that they could urinate, but only by squatting, like a woman. Slavery is utterly dehumanising, converting people into objects, but castration must be one of the most profound humiliations, to say nothing of the agony. And the Vikings ruthlessly fed the demand for eunuchs as they raided monasteries and carried off young monks to meet a horrific fate.

Slaves were also used as human sacrifices by the pagan Vikings and there are appalling accounts of women being raped and killed before joining their masters as they were buried. Atrocities spatter the early accounts of these raiders and what magnified the horror and the fear was their paganism. It meant that they were capable of anything. A society that had adopted Adomnán's *Law of the Innocents* only a century before was at first stunned by what early medieval chroniclers called 'a shower of Hell'.

*

From Muckle Flugga, off the tip of Unst, the most northerly of the Shetland Islands, to the North Foreland Point on the coast of Kent, Britain presents a long target. At almost 900 miles, it was hard to miss. In the ninth century, navigation was not precise but most Viking sea lords were very competent sailors and when they went 'westoversea', their dragon ship usually made safe landfall somewhere along the eastern coast of Britain, even they were not sure exactly where. Shetland is closest, and Unst much closer to Norway than it is to the mainland of Scotland. In good weather and with a fair wind, a dragon ship could sail the 190 miles from Hordaland to Shetland in less than twenty-four hours. Orkney is only fifty miles further.

The Vikings seem to have been the first to use a large sail, and when a dragon ship ran before the wind it will have made tremendous headway, the spray flying over the bows. Long before these ships were seen off British coasts, their construction had become very sophisticated. Made from overlapping strakes of wood that had been shaped to form a hull, these *dreki* could be very large, much larger than the curraghs of the *Senchus fer n-Alban*, at eighty feet in length and seventeen feet wide. The keel was usually made from the trunk of a single oak and that helped to make the structure so elastic that in heavy seas, the gunwales could twist six inches out of true and still remain watertight. Like the curraghs, the *dreki* had a shallow draught, and that, and their speed over the water, was what made the Vikings dangerous. Their ships gave them the crucial element of surprise. They could row up rivers, and even after lookouts had made out their sails on the horizon, the dragon ships could be rasped up onto a beach before defences were organised or valuables hidden.

For navigation out of sight of land, the sea lords relied on observation, sea lore and common sense. In the absence of charts, distance was measured by the number of days under sail or in becalmed weather, shifts at the oars. A floating log was attached to a line with knots tied in it at regular intervals and put over the side to estimate the dragon ship's speed. Widely adopted in the Middle Ages, this practice supplied the names of two characteristic items of seafaring technology: a ship's log and its speed measured in knots. The open-decked ships offered little shelter, and in bad weather another enduring maritime item was invented. To keep rain, wind and cold at bay, the Vikings slathered the skin side of fleeces with fat or fish oil, and invented oilskins. No one will have cared about the stink if they were kept dry.

At Rubha an Dùnain, an uninhabited peninsula in southern Skye that reaches into the Hebridean sea roads, an extraordinary discovery has recently been made. Between the Atlantic seacoast of the Sound of Soay, a stone-lined canal was dug so that ships could be rowed into the freshwater Loch na h-Airde for repair and shelter, and also to overwinter in dry docks known as 'noosts'. From the evidence of chance finds, it seems likely that boats were not only serviced at the quays around the loch but also built there, and the foundations of several buildings have been found along the sides of the canal and on the shore of the loch. There seems also to have been a means of regulating the levels of the loch. Landing places and noosts have been recorded elsewhere in the Hebrides, but what had been found at Rubha an Dùnain is unique: it was a Viking shipyard.

After the ferocity and raiding of first contact, Vikings began to settle. Closest to Norway, Orkney and Shetland became their earliest colonies, but after the abandonment of Iona and the attacks on other communities down the Atlantic shore, written records dry up and it is very difficult to chart the process of Viking settlement. The very word makes it sound like a peaceful process, but recent research into ancestral DNA suggests the opposite. The Pictish population of Orkney appears to have disappeared, geneticists being unable to detect any significant signal from a male Pictish population after the ninth century. It looks very much as though a great deal of blood was spilled and the slave ships were filled with native Orcadian farmers in the decades after the raids on Lindisfarne and Iona. It seems also that there was genocide, something perhaps more easily achieved on an archipelago where there was nowhere to run. The M17 Y-chromosome marker of the Vikings persists very powerfully in the modern male population of Orkney and especially amongst old surnames such as Isbister, Clouston, Flett, Rendall, Linklater and Foubister. Men who have these names are the direct descendants of the Vikings who brought fire and sword to the islands in the early ninth century and changed their culture utterly.

The process of colonisation gathered momentum, and after subduing the Northern Isles (the Nordreyjar), Vikings took over what they called Katanes, 'the Cape of the Cats', Caithness and Sutherland. The latter seems northern rather than southern to most Scots, but not to Viking Orcadians. All of the Hebrides, even the islands in the Firth of Clyde and as far south as the Isle of Man, were eventually settled, and Norse place names completely obliterated the original Pictish and Gaelic. Stornoway is only the best known example of this – it was Stjornavgr, 'the Steering Bay', now Steòrnabhagh in modern Gaelic. A dialect of Norse known as Norn was spoken in Orkney and Shetland until the nineteenth century, persistent probably because there was no competing indigenous language. But down the Atlantic shore, where the genocide seen in the Northern Isles seems not to have occurred – and DNA evidence supports this supposition – it may be that Gaelic and perhaps fading communities of Pictish speakers coexisted with the Norse of the conquerors. Shreds of data suggest this. The same individuals in different sources are recorded with somewhat different names, some of them more Gaelic sounding depending on the context.

By the end of the eleventh century the Sudreyjar, the Norse name for the Hebrides, Kintyre, the Clyde islands and the Cowal Peninsula, were all in the hands of Viking sea lords and settlers. Strangely, the name of the Sudreyjar, the Southern Isles, survives in the see of the Bishop of Sodor and Man. The well-established earls of Orkney asserted a degree of control over the Southern Isles in the early Middle Ages and eventually these territories were welded into the kingdom of Man and the Isles – but that is to let the story run some way ahead of itself.

In the ninth century, the effect of the Viking invasion was to drive the power base of Dál Riata eastwards into the Highlands and the Lowlands beyond the mountains. After the defeat and the destruction of the Pictish nobility in 839, a famous name stepped into the vacuum. All Scottish kings are numbered from Kenneth macAlpin because he was widely considered the founder of Scotland, the first king of both Picts and Scots, the creator of Alba. The reality is, of course, much less emphatic and much more messy. Two years after he succeeded his father, Alpin mac Echdach, Kenneth seized the shaky throne of Pictland and held the combined realm until his death in 858. But Kenneth was not the first Gaelic speaker to rule over the Picts and Alba was not Scotland as it is understood now. In addition to the Viking incursions in the west and north, the territory to the south of the Forth–Clyde line was divided between Strathclyde in the west and Northumbrian kings ruled in the Lothians, the Borders and Galloway.

What macAlpin's reign does suggest is the increasingly successful takeover of Gaelic from Pictish in the eastern Highlands and the Lowlands beyond. Scone, near Perth, became the symbolic focus of the combined kingdom, and on its Moot Hill, new reigns were acclaimed and inaugurated, but not according to primogeniture. Tanaiste is the Old Irish name used as a title for the deputy prime minister of Ireland, and it is a resonant echo of a different way of ensuring continuity. Edward Dwelly defined *tanaisteachd* as 'the regulative law of Celtic succession'. It embraced certain main features, one of which was that the succession was always continued in the family of the chief within three degrees of relationship to the main line. Brothers succeeded preferably to sons to provide the tribe with a leader in all enterprises.' And that is what happened on the death of Kenneth macAlpin. Instead of being succeeded by a relatively inexperienced young man, he was replaced by his brother, Donald I.

The destructive, piratical instincts of the early Vikings did not fade as they settled in the islands off the Scottish coasts. Svein Asleifsson was born in Caithness in the early twelfth century but spent much of his time on Orkney. But not all of his time.

> This is how Svein used to live. Winter he would spend at home on Gairsay [off the coast of Orkney Mainland] where he entertained some eighty men at his own expense. His drinking hall was so big, there was nothing in Orkney to compare with it. In the spring he had more than enough to occupy him, with a great deal of seed to sow, which he saw to carefully himself. Then when that job was done, he would go off plundering in the Hebrides and in Ireland on what he called his 'spring trip', then back home just after midsummer, where he stayed until the cornfields had been reaped and the grain was safely in. After that he would go off raiding again, and never came back until the first month of winter was ended. This he used to call his 'autumn trip'.

It all sounds so matter of fact, a routine, two annual 'trips'. But of course it meant nothing but pain and loss when Svein and his drinking friends rowed hard for a beach and tumbled out of their dragon ships, screaming war cries as people fled for their lives.

*

The greatest surviving work of art ever made in early medieval Scotland is to be found in the wrong place, in Ireland, in the library of Trinity College, Dublin. And it also has the wrong name.

The Book of Kells should be known as the Book of Iona, or better, *Leabhar Chaluim Chille*, the Book of Columba. Its 680 pages of staggering, stunning, vibrant beauty are made up from the four gospels of Mathew, Mark, Luke and John. Written and painted on calfskin, what became known as vellum, it is acknowledged as the greatest of all the illuminated manuscripts made in the eighth and ninth centuries in the monasteries of Britain and Ireland, the most glorious blossom in an extraordinary flowering of religious art. And it was made on Iona, not in Ireland. Just as the Viking raids and later settlement drove Dál Riatan kings eastwards, they also persuaded monks to take their great treasures to safety and the monastery at Kells, a daughter-house of Iona, became a sanctuary for the great book.

More than anything, Christianity is a religion of the word. The first lines of the Gospel according to St John are: 'In the beginning was the Word, and the Word was with God, and the Word was God.' And the Book of Iona, as we must learn to call it, was less a gospel to read, more one to be revered. Laid on the high altar, opened at one of the many gorgeously decorated pages, it was a sacred object, the word of God to be worshipped as well as read.

The making of the gospels was itself miraculous, a blaze of rich colour that came alive against the waves of the steel-grey ocean. It began with an enormous investment that must have brought involvement from many across the Hebrides and the mainland, especially for a society that counted its wealth in cattle. Three hundred and eighty calfskins were needed to make the pages, not counting those that were discarded as blemished in some way. The skins were stretched, scraped, cleaned and then trimmed into rectangles, double pages, incidentally establishing the shape of modern printed books, very different from the scrolls of ancient Greece, Rome and Egypt.

Once the calfskin was ready, it was pinned tightly onto a writing board or into a frame. The scribe then ruled the pages with a stylus that left an impression rather than a mark. In the later eighth century, when this gospel was made, the monks of Iona lived in cramped, dark cells and neither their scriptorium nor church would have been large or have large windows. And so, on bright, settled days, most of the work of writing and painting would have been done out of doors.

The text in the Book of Iona is itself very beautiful, so regular that it might have been printed. When the scribe sat down in a sheltered, sunny place with his board, before he began to write, he made his quill pens. With a penknife he cut his nibs from the long feathers of geese, swans and even crows, to a uniform width so that there would be no variation in the lettering when he discarded a spent quill and picked up a new one.

When the pages were ruled, the decorative scheme had already been worked out. The *incipit* letters (the Latin verb for 'it begins') of the gospels, could crowd out almost all of the lettering on that page, they were so elaborate. The scribe-painters on Iona then did something surprising. On the reverse of the calfskin *incipit* pages, and the many other pages that carry illustration, they did outline drawings with a stylus. They needed these to guide their work on the other side. These drawings must have therefore been done in mirror-image and to make out the lines through the calfskin, there needed to be a light behind it. In this very early version of a lightbox, a candle was probably used or perhaps the pages were set up so that the sun shone behind them.

Under the headword *dath*, meaning 'colour', the great Edward Dwelly listed not only the traditional native plant sources of natural dyes and the colours they gave up, but he also described the process of using them. Monks will have scoured the island of Iona and they must have crossed to the mainland, to the glens and shores, to look for what they needed. Purple could be got from blaeberries or sundew, claret red from crotal (the lichen that grows best on the rocks of the seashore) and green from the bark of whin bushes.

Once crotal had been scraped off the rocks, it was steeped in buckets of urine that was at least three months old. After it was taken out and patted into cakes, the lichen was hung up in bags to drip and dry. Before being used to paint, the dried cakes were crumbled into powder and mixed with a fixative such as egg white.

Acid or alkaline materials were combined with other plant and root extracts and still more colours could be extracted from mineral deposits. The deep black ink of the text came from oak galls, sometimes known as oak-apples, growths on older trees that held the larvae of a species of wasp. This was probably found locally, perhaps in the Lochaber forests. Whatever the source, the colours were well made and fast, and, over twelve centuries later, they have faded only a little.

Works of art gain a great deal from context, from being seen and understood in the place where they were made. Masaccio's great fresco *The Tribute Money* glows in the Brancacci Chapel in Santa Maria del Carmine in Florence partly because those who gaze at it are standing where the painter himself stood half a millennium before. The Book of Kells should once again become the Book of Iona. It should be returned to the island so that it too can glow even brighter in the place where all that love, skill and devotion was poured onto its gorgeous pages. It was inspired by the unique *genius loci* of that island of spirits where, as George MacLeod said, the veil between worlds is thin.

*

When Kenneth macAlpin shifted the axis of Alba eastwards, a hefty and much less colourful lump of cultural and political luggage was trundled across the mountains of Drumalban. The Lia Fáil, 'the Stone of Destiny', was said to have come to Dál Riata from Ireland, from the Hill of Tara, and, sometime in the middle of the ninth century, it was placed on another hill. Scone may have been the centre of a Scottish sect of severe ascetics known as the Culdees, the Companions of God, and their presence may have blessed the place, made it suitable for sacred and solemn ceremony. Near their church, an artificial mound was raised that became known as Moot Hill, meaning 'the place of assembly', and it was there that the Stone of Destiny became the Stone of Scone and a symbol of a new kingdom.

Gaelic remembered what happened on the hill, for bards sang of ancient rites at Scoine Sciath-Airde, 'Scone of the High Shields'. It spoke of the habit of warriors of raising up a new king on their shields. As this precarious ceremony was enacted, another bardic name told what happened next. These were the chants and shouts of acclamation that rang around the Moot Hill as lords and their warbands roared their support and approval.

The earliest written record of the ceremonies at Scone was made after 13 July 1249, when Alexander III, a direct descendant of the macAlpin kings, was crowned and anointed. The boy was only eight years old and may easily have been carried aloft by the warriors on their shields. When he sat on the Stone of Destiny, the royal bard, *an t'ollaimh righ*, stood forward and fell on his knees to call down God's blessing and then enact what may have been the most important part of the ceremony. He began the recital of a vital list, the *sloinneadh*, 'the naming of the names'.

Beginning as far back as the time when Fergus macErc sailed out of the sea mists of the North Channel to found the kingdom of Dál Riata in Argyll, the bard intoned the sonorous formulae as king followed king, beating out the ancient rhythm of the royal genealogy until he arrived at the boy who sat before him on the great stone. More than anything the *sloinneadh* laid down the king's right by blood to rule.

In 906, on the Moot Hill, there occurred a rare moment when history seemed to stand still. Constantine II was king and had come to Scone with Bishop Cellach of St Andrews, an event recorded in the *Annals of Ulster*: '[They] pledged themselves on the Hill of Faith near the royal city of Scone that the laws and disciplines of the Faith, and the rights in churches and gospels, should be kept in conformity with [the customs of] the Scots.'

It was the moment when the Gaelic-speaking Scots became the Scots (and not the Irish), the moment when the Picts at last faded from history and the moment when Alba became the focus for the emerging nation of Scotland.

Not that Scotland after 906 was inevitable. Events could have fallen out differently and we might all have been living at addresses in Norseland, New Ireland or Pictland, or indeed northern England. It is important to resist the temptation to read history backwards, but for all that, Scone in 906 was witness to change, and that change eventually led to a destiny we all recognise as Scotland.

*

In the Highlands and Islands, that destiny may not have seemed a likelihood. Political gravity tugged in at last three opposing directions at the outset of the tenth century. While Constantine II aspired to greatness, his regnal name a nod to the ancient glories of imperial Rome, and climbed the hill with Bishop Cellach, the Vikings were lengthening their reach down the Atlantic shore and the Cenel Loairn were laying down the foundations of the kingdom of Moray.

Moreb is one of the earliest versions of the region's name. W. J. Watson leads us through the stages of change to modern Gaelic, which expresses Moray as Moireabh, the 'bh' sounded like a 'v' and therefore directly derivative of the Latin, Moravia. In a language Watson calls 'early Celtic', he translates the first element of *mor* as 'the sea' and links it with modern Gaelic *muir*. Prefixed to the second element, Watson gives *moritreb*, meaning 'sea-settlement' or 'seaboard settlement'. If the definition is widened to the plural then that describes Moray as the settlements by the sea. Which seems reasonable enough. But modern scholars with no Gaelic have had the effrontery to disagree and they connect the name to the Middle Welsh, *moreb*, and the Cornish *morab* – both meaning 'low-lying land by the sea'. This can also be applied happily to the fertile Moray coastlands and perhaps, somewhere in the shadows, Watson might have nodded his agreement.

Compiled at the Priory of Lanercost, near Carlisle and not far from Hadrian's Wall, the chronicle of the same name was usually dispassionately well-informed about events in medieval Scotland. For the year 1230, the scribe recorded a brutal incident. Knights in the service of King Alexander II arrived in the marketplace of the town of Forfar: 'And after the enemy had been successfully overcome, a somewhat too cruel vengeance was taken for the blood of the slain: – the same [Gillespie] MacWilliam's daughter who had not long left her mother's womb, innocent as she was, was put to death in the burgh of Forfar, in view of the market place, after a proclamation by the public crier: her head was struck against the column of the [market] cross, and her brains dashed out.'

The killing of the baby girl was the last, shocking, act in the long and contentious history of the kingdom of Moray, the creation of Gaelic speakers from the Atlantic shore.

What appears to have sparked the migration of the Cenel Loairn up the Great Glen was the Pictish invasion of Dál Riata. Here is the entry for the year 736 in the *Annals of Ulster*: 'Oengus, son of Fergus, King of the Picts, devastated the territories of Dál Riata, and won Dunadd [a fortress immediately south of Kilmartin Glen] and burned Creic [perhaps the Craignish Peninsula]; and he bound with chains two sons of Selbach [High King of Dál Riata and of the Cenel Loairn], namely Dungal and Feradach.'

No doubt the movement of the kindred from its homelands around the Firth of Lorne, and on Colonsay, Mull, Morvern and Ardnamurchan was piecemeal, patchy and it almost certainly was not an event but a process. Aristocratic intermarriage may have taken place in Moray, and that will have strengthened a warband and its hold over territory. Also, it is important to note that the annalists left no record of a battle or war of any sort between incoming Dál Riatans and the Picts of the north. Except perhaps in one place.

Sueno's Stone may not only have been a display of military might. Like the Aberlemno Stone, it might also be a record of a battle. One eminent archaeologist has interpreted the carvings as those of 'a Pictish sculptor working for a Scottish [meaning Dál Riatan] patron'. And the location might also be telling. Set up near Forres, it stood at the heart of the Pictish kingdom in the north, exactly the place where a new, incoming ruling elite would want such a statement to be made.

Amidst all this talk of the doings of kings, of kingdoms and conflict, it is important to enter some definitions and qualifications. Dál Riata and Pictland were not unitary nation states in the sense that we understand the notion now. There were no frontier posts and border guards, nor any sense of separate sets of distinct institutions, or even completely separate identities or languages. Instead, kingdoms were shifting networks of relationships, webs of personal loyalties and obligations, almost certainly with oath-taking as their binding agent – and Highland and Island society may well have been multilingual as a matter of course. When Constantine II climbed the Hill of Faith at Scone, he trailed behind him a series of interlinked networks, and his power depended on the strength of those links. Like Svein Asleifsson's eighty drinking buddies who caroused, roared and then snored in the straw by the fires in his hall at Gairsay, each lord had his retinue. Most of them were fighting men whom he maintained with food and a place to sleep off all that ale and mead. And when Svein came back from his spring and autumn trips, he divided the proceeds of raiding, including slaves, between them, keeping the lion's share for himself as the general provider. Even though it was less well advertised, and perhaps less brutal, raiding and larger scale warfare was of course frequent in Pictish and Dál Riatan society as kings led their warbands beyond the territory they already controlled. Success in battle bred success, and failure in war saw authority disintegrate. Something of the kind appears to have been going on in Pictland – for the year 750, the *Annals of Ulster* reported the 'ebbing of the sovereignty of Oengus [King of the Picts]'.

Below the aristocracy and their warriors were the people who made it all possible. In return for protection, farmers, both free men and unfree, ploughed, sowed and reaped, herded, pastured, milked and slaughtered cows, goats, sheep and pigs so that they could pay the food renders demanded by their lords. And everybody both hunted (the Pictish nobility seems to have been addicted to the chase since symbol stones show several scenes of horsemen, and even a horsewoman riding side-saddle, in pursuit of game, mostly deer) and gathered a wild harvest.

The limits of the reach of the kings of Moray must have fluctuated, but its eastern bounds were approximately along the banks of the River Spey, running south-west from its mouth into the mountains. The first surviving mention of the name of Moray occurred in the *Chronicle of the Kings of Alba* and it noted that Malcolm I, King of

Alba from 943 to 964, 'crossed into Moray and slew Cellach'. There is a sense of crossing a river and a clear indication that Moray was not part of Alba. It did not end well. King Malcolm was 'killed by the Moravians by treachery' at Blervie, a fortress two miles south of Forres. The town probably became the inland centre of the kingdom of Moray, safer from the Vikings after the disastrous battle in 839, probably when the ancient sea-citadel at Burghead was destroyed by the fury of the northmen.

Not until the early fourteenth century do the bounds of Moray become clearer. Two years before Bannockburn made the grant less provisional, King Robert Bruce gave the earldom of Moray to Thomas Randolph. It probably mirrored the shape of much of the old kingdom. Randolph's territory included the lands of Fochabers on the Spey and a great deal of the low-lying territory to the west as far as the River Ness and on north to the shores of the Beauly Firth, where the mainland holdings of the earls of Orkney began. All of the upland lordships of Badenoch, Abernethy and Kincardine, Glencarnie and Lochaber belonged to the earldom, and further north on the Atlantic seaboard, the territory of Glenelg was included, what used to be northern Argyll. It was a vast area of the Highlands in the fourteenth century, and probably even larger in the tenth.

Moray was worth fighting for, and the kings of Alba made repeated attempts to bring the rich and fertile coastlands under their control. The alternating use of two titles may chart the ebb and flow of their power in the north. The Cenel Loairn lords who eclipsed the Pictish nobility in the ninth and tenth centuries were known to the annalists either as *mormaers* or as kings, and sometimes both. The former is a Gaelic and Latin hybrid. *Maer* derives from *maior* which means 'greater' or 'bigger' and became the modern English mayor. And it is that sense of an office or a role that is present in the term. The first element is Gaelic and also, confusingly, means 'big' or 'great'. And so, *Mormaer* probably deserves a capital M because it may be taken to mean Great Steward. But on whose behalf did the Steward act? The overlord must have been the King of Alba and it may be that when he successfully exerted his power over Moray, that role was appropriate. When he did not, Mormaers also called themselves kings.

In 1032 the most famous – and notorious – king there ever was in Scotland gained control of Moray, probably at first as Mormaer. When King Duncan came north in the summer of 1040, almost certainly to collect tribute, Macbeth challenged him. At Pitgavey, near Elgin, on 14 August, there was a battle. Duncan was killed and Macbeth immediately had himself proclaimed King of Alba. And his claim was not spurious or opportunistic, but legitimate since he could trace his royal ancestry through the Cenel Loairn back to Selbach, High King of Dál Riata in the eighth century.

At this point the story, and perceptions of the story, race ahead by six centuries. Macbeth is the most famous of Scottish kings because William Shakespeare defamed him, miscalled him a usurper (having no knowledge of the principles of *tanaisteachd* so eloquently explained by Edward Dwelly) and spattered his allegedly brief reign with blood and treachery born of vaulting ambition. He made a demon king out of a Highland king, a man who lived by savagery and a ruthless, reckless courage.

Timing was everything in the process of creating this monstrous fiction. The play is thought to have first been staged in 1606, three years after the accession of James I. As King of Scots, he had devoted much energy in curbing the power of the Highland clans in an effort to promote the creation of a modern state that left behind the barbarities of the north and blood-soaked usurper-kings like Macbeth. All of this was done for cosmetic reasons. To succeed to the Crown of England, his own vaulting ambition, James had to look as though he could control the Gaelic-speaking barbarians of the Highlands. Shakespeare wrote wonderful dialogue and created great drama, but he did not invent this version of the story. To find favour with the Stewart dynasty, medieval Scottish chroniclers such as Andrew de Wyntoun and John of Fordun called the Moray king a usurper and claimed he killed poor old Duncan in cold blood. Hector Boece transformed Queen Gruoch into the appalling Lady Macbeth. This pro-Stewart propaganda eventually found its way into

Ralph Holinshed's *Chronicles of England, Scotlande and Irelande*, and from there into William Shakespeare's luminous imagination.

The play also did not create the enduring antitype of the savage, unprincipled, wild Highlander, but it is the most famous example. Tacitus had written of barbarians in the north and medieval lowlanders had embellished the image, but Shakespeare's *Macbeth* cemented existing attitudes in the popular perception of Highlanders that carried on through to the Jacobite rebellions of the eighteenth century. It took genocide, clearance and the inventiveness of another great writer, Walter Scott, to finally shift the stereotype from threatening to romantic as the sad, wistful music began to play and mists began to float around the bens and the glens.

In fact, Macbeth reigned as King of Alba from 1040 to 1057 and was secure enough to go on pilgrimage to Rome in 1050, where it was said 'he scattered money like seed'. War came when Earl Siward of Northumbria, a character used by Shakespeare, moved to install Malcolm, the son of Duncan, as ruler over Lothian and Strathclyde. Macbeth retreated to his heartland in Moray and sometime in the summer of 1057 he was killed in battle with Malcolm's forces. His stepson, Lulach, succeeded and reigned for less than a year. The Irish *Annals of Tigernach* were in no doubt about his status, as it turned later perceptions upside down: 'Lulach, King of Scotland, was treacherously slain by Malcolm, son of Duncan.'

But so powerful was the impact of Shakespeare's fiction that Macbeth is seen as an aberration, and rarely accorded the title of king in old-fashioned royal genealogies. And King Lulach is ignored entirely.

Superstition still swirls around the play, perhaps as a faint echo of the lies and misrepresentation. No actor is allowed to mention it by name except in a rehearsal or a performance. Macbeth is routinely referred to as 'the Scottish Play', and if there is a slip of the tongue in a theatre, there are cleansing rituals to ward off bad luck.

The deaths of Macbeth and Lulach did little to diminish the independent spirit of the men of Moray. In 1058 Máel Snechtai succeeded his father, Lulach, not as King of Alba but as King of Moray, but he was pursued and apparently defeated by King Malcolm III 'Canmore'. The Moray king's name is more than intriguing. Máel Snechtai means the Follower of the Snows. Was it a reference to his retreat into the mountains? His successors continued to press their claims to what was beginning to look more and more like the kingdom of Scotland. In 1018, Malcolm II had defeated an army of Northumbrians at Carham on the River Tweed and pushed the bounds of his realm much further south, but in 1130 at Stracathro, near Brechin, Oengus, King of Moray and son of Máel Snechtai, was defeated by the army of David I of Scotland. It was the beginning of the end of the independent history of Moray.

The continuing pretensions of the Moray dynasts prompted radical action, a programme of colonisation, the introduction of another theme that would haunt Highland history as new people arrived and displaced indigenous communities. David I of Scotland's social engineering would leave a lasting legacy in Moray.

*

Between Strachan's the newsagent and Clark's home furniture shop in Nairn's High Street there is an invisible frontier. To the north, clustered around the bridge over the River Nairn, Scots was spoken, and to the south, the town's inhabitants lived their lives in Gaelic.

Only a little over a hundred years ago J. A. H. Murray, a Borderer who compiled and edited the first edition of the *Oxford English Dictionary*, wrote about the survival of Gaelic in northeastern Scotland: 'The town stands across the division between the highlands and the lowlands which intersects High Street at about Rose Street.' The precision is surprising, but the origins of this divided community are not. They lie in the dynastic politics of Scotland in the twelfth century.

After the battle at Stracathro, David I of Scotland decided on radical action. He brought a man called Freskin the Fleming to the north, gave him the lands of the Gaelic-speaking rebels and many Lowlanders followed in his wake. The ancestor of the earls of Moray, Freskin transformed the political and linguistic map.

The divide between the descendants of Freskin's Scots English speakers and Gaels ran through the middle of Nairn until the early twentieth century. The census of 1891 was the first to ask a question about language. At that time 25 per cent of the population of the old county of Nairn spoke Gaelic. Further west the numbers climbed dramatically and 83 per cent in Invernessshire had the language, although it should be borne in mind that the county used to include Skye, Harris, North and South Uist, Benbecula, Barra, Rum and Eigg.

As the twentieth century dawned, the picture began to change rapidly. The Act of 1880 had made education compulsory and the school leaving age was set at twelve in 1899, and of course children were taught only in the medium of English. The advent of mass communication through newspapers, radio and eventually television only encouraged the learning of English even more. But the frontier in Nairn High Street remained. Until recently it was between the dialect of Scots known as Doric and what was considered the pure, unaccented English of Invernessshire. In reality it was unaccented because it was being spoken by people who had recently learned the language, former Gaelic speakers.

Far to the south, Gaelic had a very visible frontier. At the head of Loch Lomond, on the watershed ridge of Glen Falloch, there stands a singular, massive boulder. It is called An Clach nam Breatann, the Stone of the Britons. They were the people of the Clyde whose capital place was the great Rock of Dumbarton that was attacked by the Dublin Vikings in 870. There is another huge stone at the head of Loch Goil with a similar name, An Clach a' Breatannach. Below this frontier, in the south-western pocket of the Highlands around Loch Lomond and Cowal, people spoke Old Welsh, a dialect that would have been understood in early medieval Wales.

The Gaels called the speakers of this language the Britons because it was spoken not only in Wales but all over England until the coming of the Anglo-Saxons. Old Welsh survived much longer on the fringes of the Highlands and in the valleys of the Clyde, Forth and Tweed, and it may have conferred a famous clan name. The

Campbells gradually took over the northern parts of the kingdom of the Britons and may have spoken their language. The name derives from *caimbeul* in Gaelic, and it means 'twisted mouth'.

Around 1000, six languages were spoken in the Highlands and Islands. In addition to Gaelic, Old Welsh and Scots English, Norn was spoken in the Northern Isles and Caithness. By about 1100 Pictish appears to have become extinct. French would come later to the north, spoken by the Anglo-Norman elite, men such as King David who was raised at the court of Henry I of England. And Latin was spoken to God.

At least on the fringes of each of these speech communities, multilingualism must have been the norm and centres such as Inverness are likely to have been places where traders and administrators spoke some Gaelic, Scots, Norn and perhaps even Pictish.

When the king's knights rode into the market square at Forfar in 1230 and committed the shocking, ruthless murder of the baby girl, it was the final act in the story of the kingdom of Moray. She was the last in a long line of descent from the kings of the Cenel Loairn and after her there would be no more claimants to the throne of Alba and Scotland. Instead of looking north, the Canmore kings and their successors would see threats to their throne in the west.

7

The Kings of the Islands of the Strangers

1058–1306

In February 1953, two excited young men rushed into the Eagle pub in Cambridge and announced to the lunchtime clientele that they had just discovered the secret of life. It was the sort of thing that young men sometimes say after many hours in the pub. But in the case of Francis Crick and James Watson, it was true. That morning they had completed a wholly convincing and coherent model of the molecular structure of DNA, deoxyribonucleic acid. It is indeed the secret of life, because DNA is the basis of heredity, a biochemical blueprint for reproduction. Everything that lives has DNA, from a daffodil to an aphid, from bacteria to a whale. Crick and Watson's discovery laid the basis for new scientific disciplines, radical new medical research and techniques, and much else. In very recent times, it enabled the rapid production for vaccines for the Covid 19 virus because the DNA of the disease could be sequenced and ways to suppress it quickly found. DNA can also help us to understand history.

Two small parts of the human genome have allowed geneticists and historians to collaborate in developing the field of ancestral DNA. Men pass on the Y chromosome to their sons, and so on down the fatherline, the male line of descent. Mothers pass on mitochondrial DNA, mtDNA, to both their sons and daughters, but it dies with men because only women can pass it on. In the 1980s, Professor Allan Wilson, a New Zealander of Scots descent, noticed that mtDNA mutated more readily and more regularly than the rest of our DNA. This made it easier to track changes over relatively short periods of time, rather than the millions of years of evolution. Wilson also discovered the molecular clock, the fact that mutations of mtDNA happen at regular intervals, and this created a new chronology, a new way of understanding history.

The seeds of these stories of the past lie in the DNA of modern human beings. By comparing the Y chromosomes of different men, geneticists can judge how closely or distantly they might be related, and can also move the story of their ancestry back in time, using the molecular clock. They can find a recent common ancestor, a man from whom modern men are certainly descended. This sort of research will become helpful in telling an important story when it is combined with other ways of understanding the past.

Place names are one of the few reliable methods of charting the process of culture and language shift. When Viking warbands began to settle in the Hebrides, it seems that they colonised the Isle of Lewis heavily. Out of 126 names of villages, 99 are Norse names. On the northern, Trotternish peninsula of Skye, 60 per cent of the place names are Norse, on Islay the proportion is 30 per cent. This clear pattern is also found in the origins of personal names. Northern Hebrideans called MacLeod, MacSween or MacAulay are the sons of Ljot, Sweyn and Olaf. Further south are clan names that owe their origins more to Ireland or are indigenous to the Atlantic seaboard. But after the ninth century, the Outer Hebrides, what is now known as the Western Isles, were renamed Na h'Innse Gall, 'the Islands of the Strangers', the Vikings.

After the flight of monasteries in the face of the early Viking raids, written sources from the ninth to the twelfth centuries are distant, patchy and often laconic. Norse poetry can sometimes paint vivid pictures. When Magnus Barelegs, King of Norway, took over Orkney from its earls and sailed his fleet down through the Hebrides to establish control over what became known as the kingdom of the Isles, the skald or bard, Björn Cripplehand, charted the swathe he cut:

In Lewis Isle with fearful blaze
The house-destroying fire plays;
To hills and rocks the people fly
Fearing all shelter but the sky.
In Uist the king deep crimson made
The lightning of his glancing blade;
The peasant lost his land and life
Who dared to bide the Norseman's strife.

The hungry battle-birds were filled
In Skye with blood of foemen killed,
And wolves on Tiree's lonely shore
Dyed red their hairy jaws in gore.
The men of Mull were tired of flight;
The Scottish foemen would not fight
And many an island girl's wail
Was heard as through the Isles we sail.

On Sanda's plains our shields they spy:
From Islay smoke rose heaven-high,
Whirling up from the flashing blaze
The king's men o'er the island raise.
South of Kintyre the people fled
Scared by our swords in blood dyed red,
And our brave champion onwards goes
To meet in Man the Norseman's foes.

Despite the destruction, Norwegian control appears to have been fleeting and in the early decades of the twelfth century, local sea lords seem once more to have asserted themselves. One name in particular emerged from the sea mists.

Somerled is a Norse name that means 'Summer Warrior', a Viking. And indeed, some recent historians have repeated the nickname, 'Somerled the Viking'. But his father had a Gaelic name, Gilla-Brigde, 'the Follower of St Bride', and his grandfather was Gilleadomnan, 'the Follower of Adomnán'. The *Chronicle of Melrose Abbey*, compiled on the banks of the Tweed, far from the Hebrides, noted that Somerled was *regulus* of Argyll, the King of Argyll, perhaps between 1120 and 1150. Sometime before 1150 the scribes wrote that he married Ragnhild, the daughter of Olaf, the King of Man, but it seems that he had a previous wife, and many children. In 1164 Somerled sailed with a huge fleet of 160 warships up the Firth of Clyde to contend for control of Scotland, or at least the west – Malcolm IV, David I's successor, was young and perhaps his authority was uncertain. Battle was joined at Renfrew and an eyewitness reported disaster. It seems that early in the fight, Somerled was 'wounded by a thrown spear and cut down by the sword'. With the loss of their general, the Islemen lost heart, retreated to their ships and sailed back north.

Very little else is known from written records about Somerled, but large claims for his significance are often made. He is said to have founded the Lordship of the Isles, the powerful maritime principality controlled by Clan Donald, and he was also the progenitor, the name-father of that dominant surname, as well as several others. It seems to many that Somerled was the father of the Highland and Island clans as famous names emerged from the darkness of the past.

In 2011 I joined Dr Jim Wilson of Edinburgh University (now Professor of Human Genetics) in a research project. We wanted to discover whether or not the notion of a common name-father for the clans was a reality or just traditional wishful thinking. We also wanted to look into the origins of the Y chromosomes of different clans and match results to what is essentially oral history. The geographical origin of a Y-chromosome marker (the mutation that makes it different from others) is relatively simple to work out. The place where the marker is most common and where it has seen the most mutations is where it first arose.

Added to this genetic and statistical mix is a cultural phenomenon known politely as 'social selection'. In essence this was the ability and, frankly, the habit of powerful men to have sex with many different women and thereby father many more children than someone who was monogamous. The most remarkable example was the great

Mongol warlord Genghis Khan. No fewer than 16 million men are directly descended from him, 0.5 per cent of all men on the planet. The number is so vast because Genghis's sons were also powerful and they too were in the habit of having sex with many women and so the pyramid grew exponentially.

When Jim Wilson and I concluded our research, we reckoned that more than 50,000 men now living are direct descendants of Somerled, a modest number by comparison with the great Khan, but nevertheless very significant. Most carry the surname of MacDonald or its variants, and most live in Britain. These numbers do not presume a Highlands and Islands version of *droit de seigneur* or *ius primae noctis*, the right of the lord or the right of the first night (meaning of married life for a bride), two unpalatable notions hiding behind French and Latin phrases. Instead, they probably reflect the fertility of a man who had many sons, certainly by modern standards, who were fathered on a relatively small number of women who were equally fertile. And it must also be remembered that in the twelfth century, many babies will not have survived birth or infancy, and nor will some women.

A more recent and better-documented example of social selection from Ireland gives a clear idea of how the arithmetic might have worked out. Lord Turlough O'Donnell died in 1423, presumably of exhaustion. He had fourteen surviving sons by ten different women (and probably many daughters) and fifty-nine male grandchildren. From this well-attested example, it is easy to see how a Y-chromosome marker could quickly multiply. Assuming similar and continuing levels of enthusiasm and fertility, Turlough might have had 1,040 great, great grandsons. In a very short time, by the end of the fifteenth century, the old man could have bred an army. And that was part of the point. Blood ties mattered in Irish and Highland society. Notions of legitimacy mattered less, despite the efforts of the Church. It seems, although attitudes are hard to chart, that it made little difference whether or not a son was born in wedlock. Sources talk of children 'begotten in brake or bush', but that is not always an indication of illegitimacy. Given the relative lack of privacy indoors in the small dwellings used by many people, most begetting, legitimate or otherwise, was done out of doors in a thicket or brake, or behind a bush.

From DNA tests on 164 men with the name of MacDonald or its variants and a securely traceable lineage that told us where their recent ancestors had been born, Jim Wilson discovered a fascinating twist to the story. A large number of the sample directly descended from Somerled, 23 per cent, carried a specific signature type within the Norse subgroup of M17, the marker so characteristic of a high percentage of the male population of Orkney who had old Orcadian surnames. That meant that Somerled's epithet was more than a tradition. Whatever the convolutions, repetitions and fantasies of the genealogies, this man was undoubtedly of Norse descent. Somerled the Viking was the epitome of the new Hebridean hybrid, the Gall-Gaidheil, 'the Stranger Gaels', men and women of mixed Scandinavian descent who would come to dominate the medieval history of the Western Highlands and Islands and beyond. And he made himself King of the Islands of the Strangers.

Furthermore, in a pleasing historical continuity, all five of the Clan Donald chiefs have the same Y-chromosome marker. Glengarry, Clanranald, Sleat, Keppoch and MacAlister of Antrim are all direct descendants of Somerled. Their particular hierarchy may be a faint echo of the ancient governance of the Lordship of the Isles. Lord Godfrey Macdonald of Sleat is the High Chief of Clan Donald, and the other four are independent but lesser. No other Highland clan thinks of itself in this way.

Our research produced a great deal of data that lit the shadowy process of cultural change. Two of the mainland chiefs with the Somerled marker of the Gall-Gaidheil, Glengarry and Clanranald, may well have been lords over a largely Pictish population. Of the whole Clan Donald sample, a large cluster, 12 per cent, carry the classic R1b-Pict marker and it may be that they are descended from a powerful Pictish lord whose identity is now lost or was subsumed, but who chose to join with Clan Donald and adopt the name. And that is unlikely to have been an isolated example.

To the south lies another surprising set of genetic discoveries.

Clan Gregor's lands lay to the east of the dorsal ridge of Drumalban, in Highland Perthshire, formerly part of Pictland. The clan motto is *'S rioghal mo dhream*, 'My race is royal', and MacGregors traditionally claim lineage from Alpin, the father of Kenneth macAlpin. At first, the testing looked promising. From a sample of 144 MacGregor Y chromosomes, a very large proportion, 53 per cent, clearly indicated descent from a single individual. But it turned out not to be Alpin. These men all carried the S145-Pict marker. Whoever Gregor, or more likely something like Griogar was, he is unlikely to have been a Gaelic-speaking Dál Riatan. Clan Gregor's origins are emphatically Pictish and indeed probably do descend from royalty – Pictish royalty.

To the north, another set of assumptions was put to a DNA test. Clan MacLeod claim descent from Ljot, a Norse aristocrat related to Olaf, King of Man and Somerled's father-in-law. Despite this, the sample we tested did not carry the classic M17 Viking marker. Instead, almost half, 47 per cent, turned out to be descended from a single individual and to carry a subgroup marker, S68. It is very specifically located in Lewis, Harris and Skye, the traditional lands of Clan MacLeod. Some S68 shows up in Orkney and Scandinavia, and it is almost invisible over the rest of Scotland and Britain. It looks as though Ljot did exist and was indeed the name-father of Clan MacLeod.

These genetic findings loosely reflect the general pattern of place name change with Viking or Scandinavian influence more pronounced in the north and more diluted further south. They also show a cultural mix: the rise of the Gall-Gaidheil and the clear absorption of Pictish communities into the Highland clans, especially in the east.

*

As Somerled forged a sea kingdom in the decades leading up to the disastrous battle at Renfrew, he created a network of stunning landmarks, perhaps better described as seamarks. On promontories, where there were safe anchorages and long views, he had castles built. At Duart on the eastern tip of Mull, a splendid fortification looks

down on a sheltered bay and across the Firth of Lorn to Dunstaffnage
Castle and its anchorage to the east. From the high battlements at
Duart, lookouts could signal to the garrison at Ardtornish on the
mainland shore of the Sound of Mull. To the north, guarding access
to long Loch Shiel as it snakes into the heart of the mountainous
interior, Castle Tioram stands on a rocky tidal island. There were
many more at the likes of Castle Sween, at Castle Stalker and elsewhere. Somerled cast a network of sea castles over his new realm
that were accessible not by roads or tracks but by ships. The inshore
waters were the Hebridean highways, how people travelled and how
the King of the Islands of the Strangers policed and defended his
maritime possessions. Movement on water was faster and safer. Just
as the Romans patterned much of Europe with roads, ships and sea
castles drew the new sea kingdom together.

Twenty years ago, I was researching a book I called *The Sea
Kingdoms*. It was an attempt to understand not only the Hebrides
but the whole of the west of Britain and Ireland as a series of Celtic-
language speaking regions who shared a different history from the
rest of Britain. In a collection of Scottish historical documents
I came across something surprising: the Treaty of Westminster–
Ardtornish, an unlikely coupling of the familiar with the forgotten. I
was intrigued, and more reading told me it was agreed in 1462 by two
powerful men, King Edward IV of England and John MacDonald of
Islay, Lord of the Isles and King of Man, the descendant of Somerled.
If the boy king of Scotland, James III, could be deposed, Edward and
John agreed to divide his kingdom between them.

No road leads to Ardtornish, or at least not one any sensible
driver who cared about their axles and tyres would follow. I remember parking at a net-drying station on the shore of Loch Aline and
beginning a long hike to the castle. The potholes on the track were
deep with jagged edges, and in any case, it seemed to stop well short
of Ardtornish. Walking was the only option. After passing some cottages, serviced by a jetty rather than the track, I turned uphill and
it was as though a curtain had been drawn. The sun appeared from
behind clouds, long vistas up and down the Sound of Mull opened

before me and on a low hump near the shore stood the ruins of the castle.

Its positioning was perfect. The promontory it sits on projects into the busy seaway and when I reached the castle, I immediately saw traffic, the ferry crossing from Lochaline to Fishnish on Mull. To the south I could see Duart Castle clearly and if I'd thought to bring binoculars, I am sure I could have made out Dunstaffnage across the wide Firth of Lorn and the town of Oban beyond it. Below lay a bay fringed by mixed forestry, a wide anchorage where many ships could have sheltered. It was said that on John of Islay's accession to the lordship at Ardtornish in 1449, 10,000 warriors mustered and 250 ships bobbed at anchor below the castle, and many pavilions were erected in the fields on the landward side. Power pulsed from this ruin 500 years ago. After the kings of England and Scotland, Lord John may have been the greatest landowner in the British Isles, his writ running for 300 miles, from the Calf of Man to the Butt of Lewis and in the islands and coastlands between. John was also the Earl of Ross, a vast area in the north that compassed much of the old kingdom of Moray. He could treat with kings, and attempt to take a motive hand in the fate of the Stewart dynasty.

And yet there was no plaque at the castle, no information board, nothing to tell of these ancient glories when mighty Clan Donald ruled in the west. Even the ruins themselves seemed to me anonymous; low, dumpy walls and the remains of a gable pierced by a window. Overgrown and tumbled down, Ardtornish felt almost abject, perhaps mirroring the hubris and the ultimate, ignominious fall of John of Islay. The terms of the Treaty of Westminster–Ardtornish were cynically leaked in 1475 after Edward IV had allied himself with the Scottish Crown. The revelations forced John to surrender the earldom of Ross, and when in 1491 his proxies failed in an attempt to retrieve it, James IV was powerful enough to force the abolition of the Lordship of the Isles. John never saw Ardtornish again and was compelled to spend what remained of his life as a royal pensioner in the Lowlands before he died in Dundee in 1503. No one is sure where his body was buried. It was an ignominious end to a majestic story.

Somerled's military reputation was based not on his prowess in land battles – despite having a large army at his back, Renfrew in 1164 was a disaster – but on his skill as an admiral. There is some evidence that he defeated his brother-in-law, Godred, King of Man, in a naval engagement off the coast of Islay in January 1156. The two fleets appear to have fought each other to a standstill, even though Somerled may have commanded fewer ships. After negotiation, Godred was forced to grant Somerled Mull, Jura and Islay to add to his holdings in Argyll. The kingdom of Man retained what they called the 'Out Isles', Lewis, Harris and the Uists down to Barra as well as Skye, but the fact that Somerled's new territories lay between Man and the northern Hebrides must have loosened Godred's hold on them.

It may well be that technology forced these concessions in 1156. The eighty ships in Somerled's navy were described as galleys, but in Gaelic, they were *birlinnean*. Although their basic design was based on the Viking dragon ships, they differed in two important ways. Instead of a steering oar at the stern, birlinns had hinged rudders. These made them much more manoeuvrable, something that was vital in the close-quarter melee of medieval sea battles.

Somerled's major naval base was at Dunyvaig on the southern shore of Islay, at Lagavulin Bay. On a small, rocky promontory, he had a fort built. It overlooks a series of small inlets strewn with rocky reefs, and a wider bay to the west. It was a difficult place to navigate, especially in bad weather and if your ship did not have a responsive rudder to avoid shattering the wooden hull on jagged rocks. But that is probably why Somerled chose Dunyvaig. The name means 'the Fort of the Little Ships'. Birlinns were not only easier to steer and quicker than dragon ships, they were also smaller and, having a shallow draught, faster, able to skim across the water under sail and pushed on by banks of oarsmen. In the shallow water below the fort and behind the ridges of reefs, they were safe from attack.

When we came to make a television series based on *The Sea Kingdoms*, history sailed back up the Sound of Mull to weigh anchor at Ardtornish. In 1991, a boatyard in Donegal had built a replica of a birlinn. No design or drawing survived to guide the draughtsmen's hands and so they turned to tombstones for information – because of its central role in maintaining the power of Hebridean lords, a birlinn was sometimes carved with their coats of arms on their gravestones. The best preserved and most detailed example was found at St Clement's Church at Rodel in Harris, where the MacLeod chiefs are buried.

Alasdair Crotach MacLeod's last resting place is magnificent. His byname means humpbacked, and the deformity was not genetic but inflicted, the result of terrible wounds in battle. On Skye, the MacLeods of Harris attacked the men of Clanranald in a late-fifteenth century skirmish in the chaos that followed the fall of the Lordship of the Isles. Ewan, the chief of Clanranald, set on Crotach with a Lochaber axe and as MacLeod fell to the ground, severely wounded, he dragged his assailant down with him and stabbed him to death with his dirk. In triumph, Crotach cut off Clanranald's head as a trophy.

In later life, it seems that the MacLeod chief repented – and he had a great deal to be repentant for. Before his death in 1547, the old warrior retired to the monastery at Rodel, endowing it with land and paying for the building of the beautiful church that now houses his tomb. He was no doubt seeking burial in holy ground, for it was widely believed that the soil upon which saints had walked and where they had prayed had been made sacred. As his corpse rotted, the holy ground would cleanse Crotach of his (many) mortal sins and reduce what would certainly be a long sentence in purgatory. He was said to be ninety-seven when he departed this life and no doubt many dutiful masses were said by the monks for MacLeod's immortal soul.

Said to be the finest medieval wall-tomb in Scotland, the old chief paid for sculptors to decorate the arch above the effigy of his body with biblical scenes. In the centre of the panels below, the Virgin Mary sits enthroned beside a strangely baby-faced bishop, perhaps the Pope Clement for whom the church was dedicated. But on either side of these figures, Alasdair could not resist references to his secular life. To the left there is a hunting expedition, probably a drive and sett, led by the chief in a full-length mail coat, wearing a conical steel helmet and holding a claymore. Behind him are three leashed dogs held by huntsmen and in the next panel three deer flee for their lives. To the right of the baby-faced bishop there is a beautiful carving of a birlinn, the vehicle of MacLeod's power. And it was this birlinn that supplied the blueprint for the replica built in Donegal.

With all the bag and baggage of a film crew trailing behind, and vehicles able to negotiate the terrible, potholed road sufficiently well to get us and all the kit as close to Ardtornish Castle as possible, we walked the last mile. And once again, it was as though the clouds were waiting to part. When we reached the promontory, the sun came out. Lying at anchor in the glinting bay below the castle was a birlinn. Named *The Aileach* after a mythic Dál Riatan princess who crossed to Ireland to marry a prince, the little ship had been sailed up the Sound of Mull the day before. I had agreed with the trust who owned and managed it that we would film the birlinn under sail and oars, and with its crew in twelfth-century costume. One man had splendid flowing fair hair, and he was encouraged to stand in the prow, as Somerled might once have done in the same stretch of water.

The Aileach looked beautiful. The rich, reddish brown of its larch strakes swept up to a high prow. At the straight stern-post was the hinged rudder with two curved tillers on either side and poking through the gunwales were two banks of oars. When its saffron sail was rigged, billowing in the breeze the following morning, and the birlinn glided out into the Sound of Mull, it was as though the words of the great Gaelic poet of the eighteenth century, Alasdair macMhaighstir Alasdair, came alive. As the crew pulled on the oars to move it out of the shelter of the bay, the verses of *The Birlinn of Clanranald* seemed to echo their steady beat:

The smooth-handled oars, well-fashioned,
    Light and easy,
That will do the rowing stout and sturdy,
    Quick-palmed, blazing,

That will send the surge in sparkles,
  Up to skyward,
All in flying spindrift flashing,
  Like a fire-shower!
With the fierce and pithy pelting
  Of the oar-bank,
That will wound the swelling billows,
  With their bending.
With the knife-blades of the white thin oars
  Smiting bodies,
On the crest of the blue hills and glens,
  Rough and heaving.

All that long day at Ardtornish we were blessed with sunshine, the water sparkling as the oars of the birlinn dipped in and splashed out, as they had for Alasdair macMhaighstir Alasdair.

For the title sequence of the television series, we needed to film a glorious Hebridean sunset, and despite the long day, the cameraman was willing to wait at the castle for the last glimmers in the west. It was the perfect vantage point. As the sun began to dip behind the mountains on Mull, I lay on a warm grassy bank by the ruined walls looking down at the birlinn in the bay, its mast casting a long shadow over the water towards the trees that fringed the shoreline. Not for the last time in the Highlands and Islands, it occurred to me that in history beauty mattered as much as anything, as much as John of Islay's great power or Alasdair Crotach's feral courage, as much as the saints who walked on Eileach an Naoimh or the warriors who roared their acclamation around the Moot Hill at Scone. The elemental, eternal beauty of *muir is tir*, 'the sea and the land', of the sweep and drama of the lochs and the high mountains, that is what stirred the hearts of men and women who walked their lives under these huge Highland skies, what made them act in heroic defence of their homeland, what moved Alasdair macMhaighstir Alasdair to do that and also to write what follows below. As the birlinn of Clanranald nosed its way out of Loch Eynort in South Uist and into the Minch at sunrise, the weather began to change:

> The sun bursting golden yellow
>   From his cloud-husk;
> Then the sky grew tawny, smoky,
>   Full of gloom;
> It waxed wave-blue, thick, buff-speckled,
>   Dun and troubled;
> Every colour of the tartan
>   Marked the heavens.
> A rainbow 'dog' is seen to westward –
>   Stormy presage;
> Flying clouds by strong winds riven,
>   Squally showers.

In the original Gaelic, this poetry of the sea and the sky is even more mouth-filling and rich, and it rises out of something not easily expressed in English. Many of Alasdair's images, and instincts, are bound up with the ideas inside the word *dùthchas*. It is difficult to translate. *Heimat* in German comes closer than any English equivalent. It means 'homeland' but also has notions specific to German culture and language attached, and not necessarily national German culture and language. *Heimat* can also include detail and regionalism. Like *dùthchas*, it does not easily translate.

A series of films written and directed by Edgar Reitz about life in a village in the Rhineland between the 1840s and 2000 attempts to capture the essence of *Heimat* as it views national and world events through a rural lens. The series takes *Heimat* as its title and its tone can be sentimental, even simplistic, but somehow that works. In 2022, Kirsty MacDonald and Andy MacKinnon made a film for BBC Alba called *Dùthchas*, which they translated as *Home*. It opens with shaky footage filmed from a departing boat. People walk along a concrete quay. They are waving goodbye, and that turns out to be a powerful theme in the film. It intercuts amateur colour film shot on the island of Berneray, off North Uist, in the 1960s and 1970s, with recent interviews, many of them in Gaelic. The film-makers wrote: 'This film is about the yearning for their birth home felt by those who have left Berneray . . . and the remembrance of the ever-living past for those who have stayed or returned when the home in their heart is also where they live.'

The film is quietly powerful, and it does more than show great beauty. It recreates a world of *dùthchas/Heimat* that needs few words. It can be read on faces, in body language. Shot in sunshine and silent, it describes an idyll, certainly, images of the rhythms of the past, of rural life on the little island. The present is far away across the sea. But there is drama of a sort. A set-piece is the wedding of Berneray's Australian district nurse to a local man, someone from the other side of the world entering a community that understands itself in a language she does not know. Those native to the island attempt a definition of *dùthchas*. 'It is the culture that is around you, but also everything in you.' The same interviewee introduces the world of *Cò às a tha thu?* It is the question that Gaelic speakers ask when they meet someone they don't know. It means not 'where do you come from?' but literally, 'who are the people you are from?'

Geography also matters, I think, in any wider definition of *dùthchas*. Edward Dwelly noted that it means 'native place', but it is much more than that. It is impossible to escape geography in the north and west of Scotland. The sea, the mountains, lochs, glens and straths are never out of sight, even in the streets of Inverness. This is a different experience of place from where most people live – in the sprawl of cities, conurbations and large towns where the view from a house or a flat is often of another house or flat, a street, a shopping centre, a bus or railway station. Hard concrete, stone and tarmac townscapes. Everything is man-made and often made in the recent past.

Dùthchas is softer and more pliable, and seems to be bound up with the landscape and how it works on the spirit of the people who live in the midst of all the glories of the land and seascapes of the north. It is the constant working of an elemental beauty on the senses even when the weather is bad (although Alasdair macMhaigh-stir Alasdair makes bad weather beautiful) and the winters harsh. Distances, low population density and the need to engage constantly with surroundings make time turn in a different way. Leaving to one side all the hoary prejudices, people in the Highlands and Islands seem to have time, take time to talk, to transact with each other. Geography and the weather persuade people not to rush. What would be the point? That slower, softer, more considered pace seems to me to be a living element of *dùthchas*.

The cycle of the seasons matters, the weather is much more important in the Highlands than it is in cities where it is usually possible to avoid it. These necessary sensitivities to the elements can induce a greater and more sympathetic understanding of the past, of the generations who have gone before. They travelled the same roads down the Great Glen, saw the same unchanging horizons of mountain and ocean. The continuity of history, from the stones at Calanais to the ceremonies at Scone, whether known or intuited, is part of *dùthchas*.

Tha mise a' dol dhachaigh means much more in Gaelic than simply 'I am going home'. Highlanders and Islanders instinctively know that.

After three days at Ardtornish, we completed our schedule, having captured, I believe, a real sense of what the Hebridean past looked like eight centuries ago. History as much as geography can be part of *dùthchas*, and Somerled's story as the name-father of Clan Donald and King of the Isles is a source of pride, a time when Gaelic culture was strong and vibrant. But there were reverses as well as advances.

After Somerled's death in 1164, three of his sons appear to have contended for all or part of his great sea kingdom. Angus took control of Garmoran, the territories of Knoydart, Morar, Moidart, Ardnamurchan, the Small Isles and the Uists and Barra. Dugald became Lord of Lorn and the name-father of Clan MacDougall, while Ranald ruled over Kintyre and the southern islands. Godred of Man seized the opportunity to recover Lewis and Skye. Despite this fragmentation, which cannot have been as tidy as sources suggest, the idea of the sea kingdom of Somerled did not fade and would flower once more.

By contrast there was unusual continuity in the kingdom of Scotland. Three kings reigned for 121 years, as long-lived sons succeeded long-lived fathers. William the Lion sat on the throne between 1165 and 1214. Alexander II reigned for almost thirty-five years and his son, Alexander III, for over thirty-six. Relations with England were settled. In 1237 the Treaty of York conceded substantial possessions in England, including the great Honour of Huntingdon, to the Scots kings in return for a formal renunciation of their claims to the earldom of Northumberland and Cumbria. Peace with England allowed the macMalcolm dynasty to turn its attention to the north and to the west.

Scottish kings had long insisted that their dominion extended over the whole of the mainland, and in 1197 William the Lion led an army up to Sutherland, the first king to venture so far north. His aim was to push the Earl of Orkney, Harald Maddadsson, out of territory that belonged to the Crown, and to limit his power in Caithness. Thurso was taken, and while allowed to retain a presence on the northern mainland, the Orkney earl was forced to do homage to William. But despite this apparent acquiescence, atrocities were subsequently committed in Maddadsson's name, and in his presence.

Scottish kings insisted on imposing their own bishops on the Church in the north and this was met by a savage response. In 1201, Bishop John of Caithness refused to collect Peter's Pence, a tax paid directly to the papacy, because he believed that many were too poor to afford it. Using this dispute as a pretext, Maddadsson's real objection was to King William using the bishop as an informant. The earl arrived at the bishop's castle at Scrabster with a group of armed men. When John went to greet Harald, he was seized and tied to a pillar. And then his mouth was forced open, his tongue clamped by tongs, pulled out and cut off. That rendered the bishop mute so that he could no longer inform the Scots king about Maddadsson's doings. Then the earl's men gouged out John's eyes so that he could no longer see anything that his scribes might record.

A year later, William the Lion marched north once more and forced Maddadsson to give up a quarter of all his revenues from Caithness to the Crown. His son, Thorfinn, was captured and probably in a grisly reprisal for Bishop John's hideous fate, the young man was also blinded and then castrated. He died soon afterwards in prison.

But the appalling acts of cruelty did not abate. In 1222, Bishop Adam was seized in his house at Halkirk by a band of Caithness farmers who 'stripped him of his proper vestments, stoned him, wounded him . . . with a double-sided axe and roasted him to death in his own kitchen'.

Alexander II acted swiftly and harshly against the Earl of Orkney, who was behind the attack. Jon Haraldsson, the son of Harald, died in 1231 and with him the line of Viking earls ended, cruel and ruthless to the last. Scottish lords thereafter succeeded to Orkney but it remained firmly part of the kingdom of Norway.

Haakon IV was determined to consolidate Norwegian control over all of Scotland's islands. He already held Shetland directly, and in 1263 he set sail with a huge fleet of 120 ships to seize the Hebrides. Having made landfall on Orkney, Haakon sailed his fleet around Cape Wrath and down through the Hebrides where he left a place name to mark his passage south. The Norwegians probably dropped anchor in the sheltered straits between Skye and the mainland, between Kyle of Lochalsh and Kyleakin; the latter means 'the Narrows of Haakon'. The sight of the fleet, with its sails billowing and colours flying must have been memorable for all who saw it from the shore, and the name endured.

When the Norwegians sailed south, many of their ships were badly damaged in a storm before an indecisive battle was fought at Largs. Much more decisive was the fact that two months later, having decided to overwinter on Orkney, King Haakon died. As the succession was decided and instability followed, the Scots took the opportunity to attack Caithness and Skye in 1264, forcing the Norwegians to negotiate. In the Treaty of Perth of 1266, they agreed to give up their claims to the Hebrides (but not the Northern Isles) and the Isle of Man in exchange for 4,000 merks.

*

As power politics played out in Perth, farmers and their families followed the ancient rhythms of the year: sowing, growing, pasturing, harvesting and laying in stores for the hungry months of the winter. All over Scotland, and particularly in the Highlands and Islands, there was one harvest that never failed, one that is still emblematic of life in the north.

The founder of the dynasty of Orkney earls that died out with Jon Haraldsson had a surprising nickname. Einarr Rognvaldson ruled the archipelago from about 895 to 910 and the Norse sagas remembered him as tall, ugly and blind in one eye, and of course utterly ruthless. When he captured his enemy, Hálfdan, on North Ronaldsay, he had him sacrificed to Odin in the obscene ritual of the blood eagle, as recorded in the *Orkneyinga Saga*: 'Einarr made them [his men] carve an eagle on his back with a sword, and cut the ribs all from the backbone, and draw the lungs there out, and gave him to Odin for the victory he had won.'

But it was not blood-spattered cruelty or his ugliness that gave Einarr his nickname. It was the cutting of peat, or turf, not ribs. The sagas claim that Torf or Turf Einarr was the first to dig peat and use it as fuel because wood on Orkney was so scarce. This cannot be true. Peat must have been harvested long before Einarr is said to have had the idea. What does sound authentic is an account of a trip to Tarbat Ness, a long spit of land at the mouth of the Dornoch Firth. Wilkhaven Muir was probably where the Orcadian earl set his men to cut peat because it was close enough to the sea for ships to be used to carry it off.

Since the ninth and tenth centuries and long, long before, peat digging has been a defining, characteristic element in Highlands and Islands culture; as is the warming glow of its red and gold embers and the sweet and musky smell of peat smoke, of peat reek. But recently it was a legacy that needed defending.

In the early twenty-first century, Anne Campbell, Finlay MacLeod, Catriona Campbell and Donald Morrison fought a war with words.

A multinational company proposed to erect a huge wind farm of 234 turbines on Barvas Moor, a wide area in the middle of the Isle of Lewis. They were to be 140 metres tall, the height of a thirty-storey building. The villages around the edge of the moor had cut their peats there for a time out of mind and had intimate knowledge of what most people would see as an empty and barren landscape. But the winds whipped straight off the Atlantic and in this bleak place would turn the sails of the turbines almost every day to generate a great deal of electricity and at last make the moor productive.

The four authors of 'Some Lewis Moorland Terms: A Peat Glossary' told a different story. They listed 120 terms and words used in only three villages that described richness, diversity, a moor that was far from empty, and one that had been productive for millennia. And their lexicon did more than that. If the bulldozers and cable layers had moved in, a unique and precious world would have been destroyed and its language would have become an epitaph, nothing more than a memory. Here are five words and phrases from the 'Peat Glossary':

> *Cuochan* – a slender moor-stream obscured by vegetation such that it is virtually hidden from sight.
> *Feith* – a fine, vein-like watercourse running through peat, often dry in the summer.
> *Eit* – the practice of placing quartz stones in streams so that they sparkle in moonlight and thereby attract salmon to them in the late summer and autumn.
> *Teine biorach* – the flame or will-o'-the-wisp that runs on top of heather when the moor burns during the summer.
> *Rionnach maoim* – the shadows cast on the moorland by clouds moving across the sky on a bright and windy day.

In the millennium and more between Torf Einarr and the successful rescue of Barvas Moor in 2008, a culture grew up around the annual harvest of peat in the Highlands and Islands. Crofters have parts of the moors allocated to their families, often passed down many generations, and with names particular to them. It is customary to cut new peat before the lambing and its long nights begin in later March. Whole families go out to begin the work, and it was a precise operation, not just a case of digging at random. Edward Dwelly lists dozens of words for the different parts of a peat bank, and also describes the process of cutting. First, the *barr fhada*, the top, tussocky, heathery layer, is removed and laid to one side. Crofters need to care for and preserve their banks and once a winter's supply is cut, they will re-cover the bank with the top turf to protect it.

Using a *toirsgian* – literally a peat-knife, a long-bladed spade – a cutter lifts out rectangular slices from the bank and they are tossed up onto the heather for the first part of the drying process. Most cut a top layer about four peats deep to the back of the bank, *druim a' phuill*, before beginning to dig downwards. The best are the blackest, high in carbon and most dense, they burn hottest and longest.

After a few weeks, the cutters return to stack the peats. Dwelly lists '*rudhan*, the small heap in which peats are built to dry after being cut for a month, consisting of three peats with one on top'. Depending on the wind and the rain, the peats are generally picked up by tractor and trailer to be taken away and stacked in a *cruach* outside houses. It takes skill to build one that is weatherproof. Peats must be laid on the slant, never flat. Large ones are set on the outside like small paving stones stacked side by side so that the rain runs off. Most *cruachan* are about six to seven feet tall and broadly rectangular in shape. Winter rains will soak the outside but winter winds will dry it.

*

In the summer of 1259, a very unusual wedding gift sailed into Galway Bay in the west of Ireland and disembarked at Dun Gaillimhe, what was to become the city of Galway. When the birlinns tied up at the quays, 160 Highland warriors came onshore with their servants. They had been sent as a dowry for his daughter's marriage by King Dubhgall macRuari of Argyll, a direct descendant of Somerled. She became the wife of Aed O'Connor, King of Connaught, and her dowry would help him drive back the Normans who had invaded Ireland in the twelfth century. The arrival of these men in Galway was the earliest recorded appearance of the gallowglasses. Much feared, highly disciplined, their name derived from *gall-óglaigh*, meaning 'foreign warriors'. The *gall* prefix did not mean that these Gaelic speakers seemed foreign to the native Irish of Connaught, but rather that they were identified with the descendants of the Gall-Gaidheil, the Stranger-Gaels, the Norse Gaels.

Aed O'Connor's ancestor, Rory O'Connor, was the last High King of Ireland and in the late twelfth century, he drove the Normans back east, to their base at Dublin and the coastal towns. They created the Pale, a secure and defended area (the name derives from the Latin *palus*, a stake or a fence post, and there was indeed a wide perimeter around the town with a bank, ditch and fence) around Dublin and it is probably the origin of the phrase 'beyond the pale'. That means that the first people to be described as uncivilised savages on the other side of the fence were Gaelic speakers.

Aed's wife's dowry was valuable because gallowglasses could put up the first sustained and reliable resistance to the charge of armoured cavalry, the Normans' great strategic advantage. These Hebridean warriors held formation, were fiercely disciplined and they had the confidence to stand their ground as heavy cavalry thundered towards them with their lances couched and levelled. But horses, even the half-wild stallions known as *destriers*, will instinctively wheel away from what they think is immovable, a well-organised, steady formation bristling with spears and great swords. A much later observer, Sir Anthony St Leger, was much impressed with the flinty fighting qualities of the regiments of gallowglasses he saw in Ireland: '. . . these sort of men be those that do not lightly abandon the field, but bide the brunt to the death'.

A series of remarkable sculptures at Saddell Abbey in Kintyre, not far from Campbeltown, show what these warriors looked like. As Alasdair Crotach MacLeod did, they wore conical steel helmets and what were known as jacks. These were long, thickly quilted garments belted at the waist that reached below the knee. Some had short lengths of bone or metal sewn into them to deflect or soften blows and others had long, padded arms and with gaps at the armpit to allow free movement. On their feet, gallowglasses wore long jackboots, a term that acquired other connotations in the twentieth century. A shorter version, to enable wearers to ride horses, gave the English language another widely used word – mounted warriors wore jackets. And those who could afford them had jacks and jackets made from chain mail.

The Saddell Abbey effigies carry long swords grasped at the hilt in one hand. These were the original *claidheamh mòr* – the claymore – the big sword, two-handed and much longer and heavier than the basket-hilted swords swung by clansmen at Culloden. Charging cavalry faced formations of gallowglasses thrusting forward a version of a poleaxe. About four to five feet long, it had a razor-sharp axehead at the business end and sometimes a spear-like spike above the axe. Unlike the very long spears with the butt-end planted in the ground and the point raised up at an angle to discourage the oncoming knights on horseback, poleaxes could be effective in close-quarter fighting. Gallowglasses could hook men and pull them out of the saddle, or cut their reins so that they lost control of their horses or slash at the animal's legs in an attempt to hamstring it and bring it down. Shorter, double-headed axes were also swung to devastating effect in battle.

Clans of MacSweens or MacSweeneys, men with a Norse name-father from the Outer Hebrides, eventually settled in Ireland, having accepted land as payment for their services as gallowglasses. When Irish kings sought to enlist them, they made sure that these mercenaries were properly equipped and that they were getting what they were paying for. Here is a no-nonsense record from the fourteenth century:

This is how the levy was made: two gallowglasses for each quarter of land, and two cows for each gallowglass deficient [i.e. not supplied], that is, one cow for the man himself and one for his equipment. And Clan Sweeney say they are responsible for these as follows, that for each man equipped with a coat of mail and a breastplate, another should have a jack and a helmet: that there should be no forfeit for a helmet deficient except the gallowglass' brain (dashed out for the want of it).

William Shakespeare had heard of the fearsome reputation of these Hebridean warriors, as seen in this very intriguing passage from *Macbeth*, Act I, Scene II:

> The merciless Macdonald
> (Worthy to be a rebel, for to that
> The multiplying villainies of nature
> Do swarm upon him) from the Western Isles
> Of kerns and galloglasses is supplied;
> And Fortune, on his damned quarry smiling,
> Showed like a rebel's whore. But all's too weak;
> For brave Macbeth (well he deserves that name),
> Disdaining Fortune, with his brandished steel,
> Which smoked with bloody execution,
> Like valour's minion, carved out his passage
> Till he faced the slave,
> Which ne'er shook hands, nor bade farewell to him,
> Till he unseamed him from the nave to th' chops,
> And fixed his head upon our battlements.

The point of this report to King Duncan is to emphasise Macbeth's initial loyalty and courage, but unlike the rest of the play, it might also contain the seeds of genuine history. In 1263, four years after he sent gallowglasses to Ireland, Dubhgall macRuari supported Haakon IV's attempts to assert Norwegian overlordship in the Hebrides – because he had recognised Dubhgall himself as a king in his own right. When Haakon was crowned King of Norway in 1247, Dubhgall had sailed to Norway to cement relations and to have his own rights in the islands confirmed. The descendants of Somerled often preferred the suzerainty of the more distant Norwegians to that of the Scots king. The 'merciless Macdonald' may well be a garbled reference to Dubhgall's support for Haakon and that he was willing to lead gallowglasses east from the western isles into Scotland, making him a rebel.

Towards the end of the thirteenth century, regional rivalries began to bubble up once more in the Hebrides. Clann Dubhghaill, or Clan MacDougall, supported Edward I against John I Balliol in the later 1290s, as did their neighbours to the north, Clann Domhnaill, Clan Donald. This alignment was unsatisfactory since these two branches of Somerled's descendants were normally bitter rivals. And so, when Robert Bruce had himself crowned in 1306, Clan Donald switched their allegiance to him, while Clan MacDougall supported his rival, John Comyn of Badenoch. After Comyn was stabbed to death in the Greyfriars Church in Dumfries by Bruce in 1306, Clan Donald and Clan MacDougall became deadly enemies. One could prosper in the west, but not both. The scene was slowly being set for what may have been the gallowglasses' greatest victory.

8

There Is No Joy without Clan Donald

1306–1492

On the night of Sunday 23 June 1314, the shadows lengthened as the summer dim crept across the Forth valley and thousands of campfires twinkled in the half-darkness. Somewhere in the woods of the New Park, in a clearing where an awning could be guyed, King Robert of Scotland summoned his captains. In the circle of firelight sat Sir Thomas Randolph, Earl of Moray, Sir James Douglas, Edward Bruce, the king's brother, Sir Robert Keith, Walter the Steward and Aonghus Og macDomhnaill. The soldiers were joined by Abbot Bernard of Arbroath and by something precious, something talismanic. The old priest had brought the Brecbennach, an ancient house-shaped metal box made in the eighth century to keep safe the relics of St Columba. Aonghus Og and his Islesmen will have been especially comforted to have the sacred power of the great saint of the west at their backs.

As the fire crackled, so did debate. No doubt his commanders rebuked the king for his reckless bravery in confronting and killing Sir Henry de Bohun that day – all could have been lost in a moment – and perhaps they thanked God and Columba for the skirmish won by Sir Thomas Randolph when his division was attacked by mounted knights and men-at-arms. But what must have dominated discussion was a simple choice: fight or flight. The English army was far larger. They had 2,500 armoured knights and the Scots had none. The English and Welsh archers could decide the outcome by themselves even before the armies engaged. Victory for the Scots seemed a highly unlikely outcome.

At the same time as Bruce and his captains debated, a man slipped out of the English camp under cover of darkness. As he made his way quietly across no-man's-land, he knew he would be challenged by Scottish pickets, but he trusted that his accent, his name and his nationality would get him through. He needed urgently to speak with the King of Scotland. Written forty years after the battle at Bannockburn, the *Scalachronica* takes up the story. It was an account written by Sir Thomas Grey, whose father had fought in the English army:

> . . . when Sir Alexander de Seton, who was in the service of England and had come thither with the king, secretly left the English army, went to Robert de Brus in the wood and said to him: 'Sir, this is the time if you ever undertake to reconquer Scotland. The English have lost heart and are discouraged, and expect nothing but a sudden, open attack.' Then he described their condition, and pledged his head, on pain of being hanged and drawn, that if he [Bruce] would attack them on the morrow he would defeat them easily without [much] loss.

It was a little before 'the third hour', about 8 a.m. to 9 a.m., when the Scottish army emerged from the woods of the New Park to form up in battle order. As the spear-points glinted in the morning sun, the captains and their lieutenants roared their men into position, into tight infantry formations known as schiltrons (a word probably deriving from Norse). Sir Thomas Grey wrote: 'They had axes at their sides and lances in their hands. They advanced like a thick-set hedge and such a phalanx could not easily be broken.'

It is tempting to see the experienced hand of Aonghus Og at work here. It is inconceivable that he had not brought many of his gallowglasses with him from the Hebrides. No lightly armed and relatively undisciplined infantry could withstand the charge of Edward II's armoured knights as they could and had. A year later, gallowglasses are explicitly named in the army Edward Bruce led in his ultimately ill-fated invasion of Ireland.

King Robert had chosen his killing ground well. It was a narrow strip of land. The 'dryfield of Balquhiderock' lay between the Pelstream Burn and the Bannockburn, neither of them broad but both with steep banks. Bruce hoped he could limit the involvement of the huge English army by presenting such a narrow battle front. And he wanted to attack immediately, before the English archers could rain death from the skies. If he could engage with Edward's army quickly, they would not fire for fear of injuring their own men.

Three divisions of the Scottish army advanced down the slope of the dryfield, keeping their formation tight. The king commanded the fourth division, the rearguard, and kept it in reserve. With him stood Aonghus Og and his Islesmen, the grim, disciplined ranks of gallowglasses under their banners of the black birlinns of Clan Donald.

The English cavalry charges began, even before Edward II had ordered a general advance. It turned out to be chaotic, uncoordinated. The Earl of Gloucester led 500 knights thundering across the grass, hooves kicking up clods into the air, and the clash and splintering of spears was deafening as *destriers* were impaled on them and their heavily armoured riders thrown. Men screamed and horses squealed their death agonies. But most of the Scottish line held as the scrummages of fighting men surged back and forth. Only Sir James Douglas' division seemed to take heavy casualties. Seeing that his army might be outflanked, King Robert moved to commit his division. 'My hope is in thee,' said the king to Aonghus Og. The Islesmen raised their banners, their chief roared the war cries of his ancestors and on either side of him, the mail-clad, grim, jackbooted gallowglasses advanced, their poleaxes and axes glinting in the midsummer sun.

Swinging their razor-sharp weapons, the Islesmen began to bring down knights, hooking them out of the saddle with poleaxes, slicing through horses' hamstrings with their axes. And then, it seemed in a moment, the battle was decided. A shudder rippled along the battle front, something born of a hundred incidents of hand-to-hand

fights where many Scots prevailed. Englishmen were suddenly sur-
rendering, throwing down their weapons. A cry went up from the
advancing Scots as the enemy line buckled; 'On them! On them!
They fail.'

And they did. They failed. Even though he fought courageously
in the ruck, mud and chaos of Bannockburn, Edward II was forcibly
led away by Sir Aymer de Valence and Sir Giles d'Argentan. When
the Scots saw the English king's banner leave the field, they knew the
day was theirs. When the English soldiers turned and saw it, they
knew all was lost. That was when the slaughter began, and as always
in war more were killed in the flight than the fight.

It was also the moment when the kingdom of Scotland survived
and also when Somerled's kingdom of the Isles was reborn.

*

In the wake of Bannockburn, King Robert rewarded his allies and
punished his enemies. Clan MacDougall had fought against Bruce
in the Battle of the Pass of Brander in Argyll and again at Dalrigh
near Tyndrum in 1306. John MacDougall of Argyll had fought for
Edward II and was made admiral of the English royal fleet. King
Robert did not hesitate and all of their lands in Lorne and Argyll
passed into the possession of Aonghus Og and Clan Donald.

In 1346, the old sea kingdom expanded once more when the last
chief of the MacRuaris died childless and all of the lands of Garmoran
were left to his sister, Amie. She was the wife of John I MacDonald of
Islay, Aonghus Og's heir and the first to style himself as 'Lord of the
Isles'. He and his descendants would rule in the west for a century
and a half.

Finlaggan was a curious choice to become the administrative
centre of the Lordship of the Isles. Named for Findlugan, a sixth-
century contemporary of Columba, it was the place where he probably established a *diseart* on the island of Eilean Mòr in this inland
loch. It lies a few miles south-west of Port Askaig and is a curious
choice because it was not on the coast, but instead the inland capital
of a sea kingdom.

Excavations in the 1990s revealed that beyond Eilean Mòr, 'the Great Island', the smaller Eilean na Comhairle, 'the Council Island', was in fact artificial, made from building rubble resting on wooden piles. The Great Island could be reached by a causeway from the shore, and the Council Island from another whose stones are still visible just under the waters of the loch. Archaeologists found that the Great Island had been encircled by a ditch and a turf bank faced with stone, more of a perimeter than a defence. Inside it were the founds of twenty or so houses connected by cobbled roadways and pends. There was a chapel, the most upstanding of the ruins with its gables having survived 600 winters, and a graveyard around it. The grandest building was a hall. It was more than sixty feet in length, large enough to accommodate great feasts and celebrations. It was probably where a new Lord of the Isles was inaugurated. By tradition, he entered clothed all in white, holding a white wand for honesty and justice, and a sword as a less metaphorical symbol of power. Just as Dál Riatan kings had done on the rock at Dunadd, south of Kilmartin Glen, the new Righ Innse Gall, 'the King of the Islands of the Strangers', placed his foot on a square slab of stone where a footprint had been carved.

Birlinns sailed the length of the Lordship to come to an inauguration on Finlaggan and the great magnates of the Hebrides, men who were in the process of becoming recognisable clan chiefs, joined in the celebrations. Writing in the sixteenth century, Dean Monro of Lismore left a record of the structure of the governance of the Isles. On Eilean na Comhairle, matters of state were discussed by a high council of four great princes of the blood royal of Clan Donald: Clanranald, MacDonald of Kintyre, MacIain of Ardnamurchan and MacDonald of Keppoch. Four others joined them in the hall: Maclean of Duart, Maclean of Lochbuie, MacLeod of Harris and MacLeod of Lewis. Four more had the right of attendance and presumably the right to be heard: MacNeil of Barra, MacNeil of Gigha, Mackinnon and one other by rotation. The word of God and his Church was heard from two final representatives, the Abbot of Iona and the Bishop of the Isles.

The frequency of council meetings is not known but the discussions can be guessed at. Disputes will no doubt have dominated, matters of rights to land, and also what might be called foreign affairs, what was happening to the east. During much of the life of the Lordship, the rest of Scotland was governed by a succession of weak kings and overbearing regents. After the death of Robert Bruce in 1329, the crown passed to his son, David II. He was only five years old and so the kingdom was governed in his name by a series of guardians, and rocked by invasions led by Edward III of England in support of Edward Balliol, son of the deposed John I. David was succeeded by his nephew, Robert II, the first in a long line of Stewart kings. His unhappy reign was characterised by feuding, and, in 1384, Robert was deposed and replaced by his son as regent, John, Earl of Carrick. Perhaps the fact that the old king had attracted the nickname of 'Auld Bleary' is eloquent. Carrick in turn was rendered ineffective by a kick from a horse that crippled him. He staggered on, eventually becoming Robert III in 1390, although by that time government was in the hands of his brother.

In 1396 a remarkable event took place on the river island in the Tay at Perth known as the North Inch. Grandstands were built and pavilions pitched so that guests could enjoy what was billed as The Battle of the Clans.

The origins of what took place are obscure, as is the identity of the clans who took part. It appears that there had been a long-running dispute over territory between, possibly, men from Clan Cameron and Clan Chattan. It had been decided, or perhaps suggested, that this should be resolved by judicial trial by combat. And so, thirty men from each clan faced each other on the North Inch as the crowd of courtiers, the king and foreign guests grew hushed, anticipating slaughter. For slaughter was guaranteed. No man was allowed to wear armour or carry a shield. Each had a claymore or a Lochaber axe, a dirk and a crossbow with three bolts apiece.

At an agreed signal, perhaps trumpets from the royal heralds, each band of clansmen fired three volleys of crossbow bolts. Many hit their mark, piercing unprotected flesh, and as the crowded gasped, roared and bayed for blood, men fell from terrible wounds, groaning and screaming their death agonies. Those still standing charged, and vicious hand-to-hand fighting followed. Wounded men were hacked at where they lay, and more and more blood spattered onto the grass.

When the trumpets sounded once more to end the contest, ten men of Clan Chattan were still standing, most of them wounded, but only two of Clan Cameron had survived the carnage. Thirty-eight Highlanders had died in a frenzy of butchery that would not have looked out of place in Rome's Colosseum. It was a gory, grim exemplification of the hardening of attitudes that would endure until modern times. The Lowlanders who screamed for blood from the grandstands saw themselves as civilised while the babbling, Gaelic-speaking savages who cut each other to pieces for their entertainment were lesser beings, to use a term from another time – they were *Untermenschen*.

A divide in Scotland was opening, and it was crystalised by the observations of a contemporary French chronicler Jean Froissart:

> The manners and the customs of the Scots vary with the diversity of their speech. For two languages are spoken amongst them, the Scottish [Gaelic] and the Teutonic [Scots]: the latter of which is the language of those who occupy the seaboard and the plains, while the race of the Scottish speech inhabits the Highlands and the outlying islands. The people of the coast are of domestic and civilized habits . . . The Highlanders and the people of the islands . . . are a savage and untamed race, rude [rustic rather than cheeky] and independent.

Apart from the last word, the cultural and political realities could not have been more at variance with Froissart's judgements. The independent Lords of the Isles imposed order in the west. The well-developed habit of young warriors sailing to Ireland each spring to fight as mercenary gallowglasses discouraged disorder as the potential for it was helpfully exported. Through judges known as brieves, a Celtic law code was enforced that preferred reparation rather than judicial revenge in the shape of punishment, or even obscene spectacles like the madness on the North Inch. Fines were far more likely to be imposed by brieves than heads or hands cut off. The political chaos of mainland Scotland contrasts starkly with the settled continuity of the Lordship of the Isles.

There were of course anomalies, and none were more stark than the story of Alasdair Mór, the warrior known as the Wolf of Badenoch. He married Euphemia, Countess of Ross, but fathered no children on her. Instead, he had a large family, including seven sons, with his lover, Mairead nic Eachainn, and held wide lands in Speyside and across Moray, much of the coveted earldom of Ross. Alasdair Mór underpinned his authority with a warband, men described as *caterans*, a Gaelic term that described a warrior, but later came to mean a bandit. The raiding and intimidation committed by these men created conflict with Bishop Bur of Moray, but the Crown was ineffective in its support, John of Carrick having taken over from Robert II in 1384. And so the bishop turned to the bible for help. Marital law was the prerogative of the Church and Bur ordered Alasdair Mór to abandon his mistress and return to his lawful wedded wife, Euphemia. More than propriety was at stake. Marriage to Euphemia was what gave Alasdair Mór title to the great earldom of Ross.

The reconciliation, however, was short-lived, the allure of Mairead nic Eachainn too great. Bishop Bur began to help Euphemia through the complex process of divorce in a Church that did not allow it. The annulment of a marriage, a technical dodge that asserted it never took place, was something only a pope could grant. Alasdair Mór was enraged at the bishop's meddling and was bent on vengeance. In May and June of 1390, he and his large band of caterans ran amok in the Moray coastlands, behaving like the savage, bloodthirsty Highlanders that they were, or were thought to be. The town of Forres, the ancient capital of the old kingdom, was destroyed, and in an infamous atrocity, Elgin Cathedral was burned, as well as the monastery of Greyfriars, St Giles parish church and the hospital at Maison Dieu. It was sacrilege, and shock waves rippled through

Lowland Scotland as yet another rabble of savages howled out of the mountains to attack Jean Froissart's people of domestic and civilised habits.

But all was not what it seemed. Alasdair Mór's full name in Gaelic was Alasdair Mór mac an Rígh – Great Alasdair, son of the king, son of King Robert II. He was also known as Alexander Stewart, a Lowlander hiding behind the chilling nickname of the Wolf of Badenoch. He had self-consciously styled himself as a Highland chief with a Highland mistress, and with many sons, behaving in a way a Lowlander thought such people did. The reality was that Alexander Stewart was an uncontrollable, reckless thug who, by his death in 1394, had lost almost everything.

*

What no regime could control was the weather. In the decades after Bannockburn and throughout the centuries that followed, it began to deteriorate markedly, affecting lives profoundly. The Little Ice Age was beginning.

In the summer of 1315, Robert Bruce invaded England and laid siege to Carlisle Castle. As soon as the Scots assaulted its walls, it began to rain, and it did not stop for weeks. Siege engines became hopelessly bogged down, the River Eden burst its banks and flooded so widely that the castle almost became an island. Eventually the Scots king was forced to abandon his expedition and retreat back north. The climate was changing, and changing rapidly.

In the second half of the thirteenth century, a massive volcanic eruption in what is now Indonesia may have triggered meteorological processes that led to the Little Ice Age. A vast volume of ejecta, about ten cubic miles, was hurled into the atmosphere as Mount Samalas blew itself apart. It was the stimulus for a long series of consequences that led to five centuries of sustained periods of very cold and wet weather. By screening the sun, the eruption may have caused the intrusion of warm water into the North Atlantic, which had, paradoxically, a cooling effect over several decades. It led to the calving of glaciers: bits broke off and drifted south like giant ice cubes and they made the ocean's water much colder. The vast shoals of cod and herring so common off Scotland's coasts migrated south to seek warmth.

Temperatures dropped, there were many more storms, more rain and Highlanders began to notice that the snow stayed on the mountain tops all year round. Permanent snowfields and a small glacier formed on the Cairngorm plateau. Growing seasons shortened and after repeated harvest failures, communities turned away from arable to more dependable pastoral farming. From the fourteenth century onwards, cattle-rearing became a staple of the Highland and Island economy.

Storms had dramatic and permanent effects. One of the most fertile valleys on mainland Shetland completely disappeared later in the Little Ice Age. Sandstorms repeatedly whipped over the township of Broo at Dunrossness, and by 1700 the farms had been abandoned. Instead of green grass and fertile fields, the valley had become the largest dune field in Shetland.

The Little Ice Age also changed attitudes, and was probably the prompt for the loaded and enduring phrase 'Highland weather', usually followed by raised eyebrows. But in fact meteorologists have a surprising tale to tell. Most people would not be surprised to learn that the West Highlands is one of the wettest places in Europe with an annual rainfall of 180 inches. The contrast between west and east is staggering. The little island of Inchkeith in the Firth of Forth sees only twenty-one inches of rain each year, and eastern Scotland as a whole only thirty-four inches.

But the coastal weather is warmer in the west thanks to the Gulf Stream and the fact that the waters of the North Sea are significantly colder than the Atlantic. Dundee and Aberdeen may be the sunniest cities in Scotland, but the record for the most sustained period of sunshine is held by Tiree. In the month of May in 1946, the island saw 329 hours of sun, and the skies were cloudless for more than ten hours for thirty-one consecutive days. By contrast, Cape Wrath holds a much grimmer record. During the whole of January in 1983 there were precisely thirty-six minutes of sunshine. These factors produce all sorts of surprises, but perhaps one will suffice. In the nineteenth century, Osgood Mackenzie could not have created a lush and subtropical garden like Inverewe on the east coast of Scotland. The weather is simply not good enough.

Edward Dwelly's dictionary lists a vast Gaelic vocabulary for different sorts of rain, wind, mist and sunshine; words and phrases too numerous to list. But one elemental effect of the Highland and Island climate is worth a moment's pause. Gaelic has an immense, nuanced lexicon of light and the weather that affects it, but not because the language is naturally poetic (although it is), but because it was necessary.

A purely rural society that lived by crofting, fishing and whatever else might be productive needed precision when it came to describing the weather, especially during the long centuries of the Little Ice Age. It was simply not enough to say it was sunny or raining. This was also a community that paid less attention to time as it is measured on watches or clocks, and more to the nature of the day, the quality of the light and the annual transit of the seasons.

Gaelic has more than twenty words or expressions that deal with different sorts of twilight. It can last a long time in northern latitudes, often more than an hour and so phrases like *liath-fheasgair*, literally a grey evening, were important at the end of a day working outside. Or *breac-sholas*, 'breaking' or 'broken evening light'. And there are technical phrases that were useful, like *aomadh na greine*, which refers to the oblique descent or setting of the sun and where it might or might not meet horizon clouds. Others are poetic and do not readily translate. *Glasadh* is 'a paling', 'a growing dim'. *Gealach a' bhruic* is literally 'the badger's moon', the time when the animals gather dry grass for their setts, but it was used to mean the full moon in October, often the turning moon of a waning year. Precision rather than poetry was also handy. *Ceoban* is small, drizzling rain with mist and *sgothachan* is the shade caused by a cloud momentarily obscuring the sun.

Gaelic understands land-light, sea-light, sunlight, dawn-light, twilight, moonlight, snow-light and cloud-light more clearly than

English. As its speakers have left the land behind and flocked to the large towns and cities in the last two centuries, language was also left behind, or no longer understood or needed in streets and factories.

*

In Gaelic, Tain is known as Baile Dhubhthaich, the Town of St Duthac. He was originally associated with Armagh, where St Patrick founded a church in the fifth century. It is now the ecclesiastical capital of Ireland for both Roman Catholics and the Church of Ireland. Dates are hazy but it seems likely that Duthac was active in the Highlands in the eighth century, about the same time as Maelrubha founded his community at Applecross, and, like him and the other Irish holy men, Duthac left his name on the map, at Loch Duich, Kilduthie, Arduthie and dedications in Forres, Aberdeen and as far north as Orkney.

Tain appears to have been Duthac's most important foundation and its status as a sanctuary was confirmed in a royal charter granted in 1066 by King Malcolm III 'Canmore'. The town is the oldest royal burgh in Scotland but its status was more than legal or mercantile. Tain was once one of the holiest, most revered places in the kingdom, a status now almost forgotten.

The bounds of sacred precincts around holy places were clearly marked, usually by crosses placed at the side of tracks that led to the church or chapel, and the graveyard around it. At Tain there were four crosses to the landward side, with the sea-coast defining the northern boundary. St Katherine's Cross stood on the north bank of Loch Eye, another was on a now-vanished mound on the Dornoch Firth coast and the remaining two lay to the west. That perimeter divided the spiritual world from the temporal world beyond it.

St Duthac's may also have been an actual place of physical refuge known as a 'girth'. But it was not always respected. After his defeat at the Battle of Methven in 1306, King Robert Bruce sent his wife, Queen Elizabeth, and his daughter by his first marriage, Marjorie, to Kildrummy Castle in Aberdeenshire. From there they fled further north to the safety of St Duthac's church at Tain. But supporters of

Edward of England ignored the sanctuary given by the saint and they captured Queen Elizabeth and her step-daughter. The queen spent eight years imprisoned in England and was only exchanged after Bannockburn.

What made the desecration particularly shocking was the presence of St Duthac's holy relics. In 1253 his head, breastbone, shirt, cup and bell were brought from Armagh, where the saint had died centuries before. This greatly enhanced the importance of Tain and made it a focus of pilgrimage. Relics mattered because they were tangible, physical links with sanctity and prayers in their presence were thought more powerful, more likely to be heard, with the implied intercession of the saint with God.

Duthac was attractive for another reason. He was often described as 'Chief Soul-Friend of Ireland and Scotland' and 'The Confessor of Alba'. The first is a literal translation of *anam-cara*, a term of affection and kindness that also carried a further sense of a confessor, someone to whom innermost thoughts might be confided and from whom forgiveness might be sought. Duthac had that particular reputation and it may be the reason for a remarkable royal connection. Every year between 1493 and his death at Flodden in 1513, King James IV made the long pilgrimage north to his shrine to pray. It was said that James saw himself as complicit in the murder of his father and sought Duthac as a soul-friend and his posthumous blessing and forgiveness. In penance, the king wore during Lent a solid iron belt next to his skin, known as a cilice, and it was said that with each passing year he added a weight to make the burden of guilt heavier, which seems to imply more than just complicity in patricide.

Duthac was an especially beloved saint in the Highlands, and it may be that on the evening of 23 July 1411, many men prayed to him, commending their immortal souls into his care, for, a hundred miles to the east of Tain, near Inverurie, the Lord of the Isles had massed his army. Having mustered at Ardtornish, the Islesmen cut a deadly swathe through the north, defeating Clan MacKay at Dingwall and marching east through Moray. Lord Donald had come to claim what was rightfully his, the earldom of Ross. Robert Stewart, Duke of

Albany and regent for King James I, who had been imprisoned in England, had seized it, and the valuable Moray coastlands and fertile Aberdeenshire were in the hands of lords loyal to the Crown.

When the two armies caught sight of each other, the preliminaries were eloquent. What may be called the Lowland army was led by Alexander Stewart, Earl of Mar, and it was arrayed in schiltrons, just as Bruce had done at Bannockburn. Armoured knights and other cavalry were held in reserve, and in front of the lines was set a small detachment of men-at-arms. Perhaps Mar had placed them there to disrupt the charge he knew was coming. Priests walked up and down the ranks, blessing the soldiers, assuring them that the hand of God would guide them and that a righteous victory would be theirs.

The Islesmen did something very different. Instead of prayer, they closed their eyes to summon memory, to remember the ancient courage of their ancestors. Lachlan Mór MacMhuirich, *seannachie* of the Lords of the Isles, walked out in front of the great crescent-shaped lines of the clans and turned to face them. His voice ringing through the summer morning air, the bard recited the *sloinneadh*, the naming of the names, the glorious genealogy of the Lords and Clan Donald. 'Sons of Conn of the Hundred Battles, remember hardihood in time of strife!' The name of a High King of Ireland whose prowess hovered on the edges of myth-history was invoked as an incitement to fight, to do battle against Lowlanders, cowherds and foreigners, men with no ancestry to speak of.

Known as 'Red Harlaw', because so much blood was spilled, the battle turned out to be indecisive. Donald of the Isles retreated through the evening gloaming, marched his battered army west and waited to fight another day. But what eventually restored the earldom to Clan Donald was not the shedding of more blood but the convoluted workings of dynastic politics. When James I was finally released from his English prison in 1424, he quickly removed Murdoch Stewart, Robert's son, from the regency and put him on trial. On the ominously named 'Heading Hill' in front of Stirling Castle, he was publicly beheaded. The earldom of Ross was restored to the Lords of the Isles.

But harmony was short-lived. Donald was succeeded by his son, Alexander, and he was summoned to Inverness to meet with the king. Instead of royal hospitality, the Lord of the Isles and his party were immediately seized and imprisoned in the castle tower. It was an insufferable indignity that was never forgotten or forgiven. In 1431 at Inverlochy, just outside Fort William, Donald Balloch, Alexander's cousin, fought a brutal, vengeful and victorious battle with the royalist earls of Mar and Caithness, scattering their army on the plain at the foot of Ben Nevis.

In the advances and reverses of the intermittent war between the Lordship and the Crown in the early fifteenth century, Inverlochy was one of several battles fought, won and lost. But it was enduringly significant in another way. In the midst of the fighting, a piper is said to have composed a slow air, possibly a lament, one whose music has survived. It was entitled 'Ceann na Drochaid Mhoridh', 'The End of the Great Bridge', and on the earliest printed sheet music, its composition in the heat of battle was confirmed.

*

The slow air established a long tradition that continued to associate the great Highland bagpipes with war for more than five centuries. On the evening of Monday 5 June 1944, 5,000 ships stood off the south coast of England waiting for the order to steam across the Channel to the Normandy beaches. Ignoring War Office directives, Simon Fraser, Lord Lovat and Chief of Clan Fraser, insisted on bringing his piper. On the chief's orders, Bill Millin began to play the old air, 'The Road to the Isles' as the great armada moved off into open water. The ship's tannoy was set up so that the pipe music echoed across the sea and was heard by many others in the invasion fleet. It broke the tension as well as the silence. Men cheered, two Royal Navy destroyers played 'A-Hunting We Will Go' and the Free French ships played the 'Marseillaise'.

When the landing craft reached Queen sector of Sword Beach, Fraser ordered his piper to play 'Highland Laddie' and 'The Blue Bonnets Are Over the Border' as men splashed ashore under heavy fire. All the time the battle for the beach raged. Millin marched up and down the tideline, playing continuously. Miraculously he was not hit. The only member of the D-Day invasion force to wear a kilt, the Clan Cameron tartan, and unarmed, the piper's weapon was his music.

Bagpipes are not unique to the Highlands and Islands. In medieval art there are representations of pipers in sculpture and engravings from all over Europe. Geoffrey Chaucer wrote in *The Canterbury Tales* that the pilgrims were piped on their way. The Battle of Pinkie in 1547, the last pitched battle between Scots and English armies before the union of the crowns, is the earliest known date that Highland bagpipes are mentioned. They appear to have been used for signalling, like bugles or horns. Pipers sounded charges, halts and, rarely, retreats – they even took up arms themselves. When confusion threatened to overtake the Jacobite army at Falkirk in 1746, its pipers gave their instruments to their servants before going in with their claymores.

Few of the achievements of the Lordship of the Isles survived so impressively or for so long as the 'Great Music'. First coming on written record in 1580, the piping college of the MacCrimmons had been established much earlier. *An Ceol Mor*, the Great Music of the Highland bagpipes, has endured as a classical canon of about 300 pieces. These are stately melodies, laments, gatherings or salutes, and they contrast with *An Ceol Beag*, literally 'the Little Music', the lesser music of slow airs, jigs and marches.

Bagpipes are not like other wind instruments. Their music is best heard out-of-doors and they are mouth-blown through a reed that thrives on being dampened by saliva and played almost every day to keep its condition stable. For this reason, pipers practice a great deal and some, like the great Allan MacDonald, are consummate musicians, virtuosos. Because the chanter, which allows notes to be played, is fixed below the bag, there can be no loud/soft variations, and this calls for singular skills from players and composers like MacDonald. Through the single bass drone and the two tenor drones, there is a continuous sound as the piper squeezes the bag with their elbow. To bring these into harmony, good players often play a series of informal preludes before they begin *An Ceol Mor.*

Composers use a classical structure developed by the Mac-Crimmons. First an *ùrlar*, literally a 'ground', is laid down and then followed by a string of variations. The climax of the piece is *an crun-lath*, where the melody is restated and then hung with grace notes, often played quickly and with great skill. Perhaps the most readily available sense of what this structure sounds like can be heard in a famous hymn. 'Amazing Grace' is set to a simple pipe tune and it grows more complex and beautiful as grace notes are added.

There is no music so stirring as pipe music, be it a lone piper on the battlements of Edinburgh Castle or a band marching at a Highland Games. When the instrument is played well, Gaelic speakers talk of *seinn air a' phìob* – 'singing on the pipes'.

Perhaps laments were played on the battlements of Ardtornish Castle after 1492 and the fall of the Lordship of the Isles. They should have been, because the institution was a great loss to the stability and prosperity of the Highlands and Islands. John of Islay's grandson, Donald Dubh, rebelled between 1501 and 1506, and after a long imprisonment, he again tried to rally Clan Donald and others. Both uprisings were decisively crushed, and the sixteenth century saw disorder begin to flare almost everywhere in the old Lordship. There is an elegiac poem that might serve as a sad farewell to the kingdom of the Islands of the Strangers:

It is no joy without Clan Donald,
It is no strength to be without them,
The best race in the round world,
To them belongs every goodly man . . .
Brilliant pillars of green Alba,
A race the hardiest that received baptism,
A race that won fight in every land,
Hawks of Islay for valour,
A race with arrogance, without injustice,

Who seized naught save spoil of war,
Whose nobles were men of spirit,
And whose common men were most steadfast,

Chaneil aoibhneas gun Chlann Dhomhnaill.
It is no joy without Clan Donald.

9

Kingdom Come

1492–1609

Gaelic was, and is, just, still spoken in the Highlands and Islands of the Atlantic littoral, continuing to describe and define a distinctive culture. The place names and early institutions of the Northern Isles had very different origins.

Had it not been for a cash-strapped Danish king urgently needing to raise money, Walter Sutherland may not have been the last native speaker of Norn. He died in 1850 at Skaw on the Shetland island of Unst, the most northerly settlement in Britain. Not only was Skaw closer to Bergen than Inverness on the map, it was much closer to Norway in culture and language than it was to Scotland. Norn was the dialect of Norse established by the Vikings from the ninth century onwards on Shetland and Orkney, and it was still spoken widely six centuries later. In 1468 Christian I of Denmark was forced to pawn the Northern Isles to the King of Scotland in return for much-needed cash. There was a clause in the contract that allowed him to redeem the pledge for a very large amount of gold or silver, but the Danish king showed no sign of ever being able to do that. And so, in 1472, the Northern Isles were formally annexed to Scotland and Norn began to rapidly decline, retreating further and further north until it disappeared into history with Walter Sutherland's death at Skaw.

Despite surviving until the middle of the nineteenth century, and the fact that fragments, poems and sayings were still being repeated well into the twentieth century, Norn is almost a lost language. Like Gaelic, it was spoken by country people, almost all of whom were not able to write it down, and when they died, the language expired with them. Very little was recorded. Norn was cognate to western dialects of Norwegian, the homeland of many who settled in the Northern Isles after the Viking takeover in the ninth century. After the death of Jon Haraldsson and the passing of the earldom of Orkney to Scottish lords, the use of Norn began to decline significantly as settlers moved north from the mainland. People became bilingual, but it is thought that by the middle of the seventeenth century it was still a first language for the majority. A hundred years later, it was dying quickly.

In 1958, Dodie Isbister from Foula, an island twenty miles west of Shetland Mainland and something of a last redoubt for the old language, could recite a verse of the 'Eagle Song':

Ante pedu, sat a growla,
Sat a growla festa,
Pirla moga, hench a boga,
Settar alla nesta.

Having read these attractive lines, I set about trawling through the internet for an English translation. After two hours I had found it recorded in slightly different spelling, some of it phonetic, but nothing to tell me what it meant. So that some colour and understanding can be found, here is the first verse of the Lord's Prayer in Norn:

Fa vor i ri i chimrie,
Helleur ir i nam thite,
Gilla cosdum thite cumma,
Veya thine mota vara gort,
O yurn sinna gort i chimrie
Ga vus da on da dalight brow vora
Firgive vus sinne vora
Sin vee Firgive sindara mutha vus,
Lyv vus ye i tumtation
Min delivera vus fro old ilt,
Amen

Cornish and Manx were last heard as spoken vernaculars on the decks of fishing boats, and the same seems to have been true for Norn. Fishermen are known to be very superstitious, not surprising given how chancy and dangerous their work is, and bits and pieces of the language have survived as a cover tongue. The English words for fish are often translated: cod is *drolti*, halibut is *da glyed*, and mussels *knoklins*. Ministers and churches were thought to be unlucky and so neither is ever mentioned on board. They become *upstaar* and *munger-hoose*.

One of the last surviving documents to be written in Norn was a mortgage issued in 1597 for a property belonging to Else, the sister of Anna Throndsen. A wealthy aristocrat and known as the *Skottefruen*, she married the notorious James Hepburn, Earl of Bothwell, who appears to have ignored that relationship. He married Mary, Queen of Scots after he had almost certainly arranged the murder of her husband, Lord Darnley. Anna managed later to have him imprisoned in Bergen and she reclaimed at least part of her dowry. The document issued to her sister in Shetland also had the force of law in Norway because it was framed according to the precepts of Udal law. It is a fascinating and tenacious historical relic from the centuries of Norse influence in the Northern Isles.

In essence, Udal law applies to land ownership in a pre-literate society. Udallers have absolute ownership of their property, with no superior and with no title deed needed. Their rights derive solely from continuity, from holding the land for a number of generations. Inheritance law is also different. The eldest son is bequeathed the father's main residence but the other siblings divide the remainder between them. Daughters receive only half of what younger sons are entitled to.

Udal is still in force and has been important in the huge expansion of North Sea oil and gas since the 1970s. Unlike in the rest of Britain, where land ownership on the coast extends to the high-tide line, and the Crown owns the foreshore, Udallers own it in Orkney and Shetland. Their rights extend to the low-tide line. This made for interesting and occasionally fraught negotiations on the siting of onshore pipelines.

The Vikings left another legacy on the land of the Northern Isles, one, like Norn, that was also fading in the nineteenth century. Boundaries of holdings were a constant concern to rural communities all over Scotland, but on Shetland the necessary precision and continuity was marked more emphatically, in all senses.

At intervals of two or three years Shetland crofters would 'ride the *hagri*' at midsummer. On their shaggy, tough little ponies, with the rider's legs dangling well below their mounts' bellies, they would ride around the boundaries of their common, the communal grazing for their cows and sheep. It was vital to check that there had been no movement of the *hagmets*, the boundary stones, and to make sure that their locations were well remembered by future generations, a young boy would get 'a sair treshin sae as he soud mind weel whaur da hagmets stude'. Different boys were beaten at each stone so that memory was indelible. No doubt to the great relief of many young lads, this harsh Norse tradition, 'the whipping custom', died out in the nineteenth century.

On the Shetland island of Fetlar, perhaps the most fertile in the archipelago, there is a very long boundary dyke known as the Funzie Girt. About three feet wide and now very ruinous, and even invisible in places, it runs north to south, bisecting the island. Its origins are thought to be ancient, perhaps prehistoric, and its building was certainly a great labour, more evidence of how enduring the importance of clear and undisputed boundaries was.

These were also important in the protection of rights to moorland, the source of essential supplies of turf, or peat. When the peats had been cut and dried (the phrase derives not from hairdressing but from the process of gathering fuel, both peat and firewood), they were taken off the moor in carts. And these were pulled by Shetland ponies, perhaps Scotland's most famous breed of horse. They are small, tough, highly intelligent and long-lived. What enabled these little horses to survive in the harsh winters of wind-driven rain in the Northern Isles was a remarkable evolutionary adaptation. Their thick coats are two-ply, which means that the growth of the hair of the undercoat runs one way and the overcoat at another. This prevents a thorough and potentially fatal soaking out on the exposed and treeless pasture.

The carting strength of these ponies is prodigious, and it condemned many thousands of them to miserable lives. Their smallness and their neat feet made Shetlands perfect pit ponies, used to haul heavy bogies of cut coal uphill to the pitheads. Many never saw the light of day and lived short and brutally hard lives.

Good grazing was at a premium in the Northern Isles and boundaries and dykes protected it. On North Ronaldsay, the northernmost island of the Orkney archipelago, a breed of mainly dark-brown coated sheep has evolved that can survive almost exclusively on a diet of seaweed. Dykes confine them to the foreshore except when they are herded into grass paddocks known as *punds* to be sheared, or to lamb, or to be taken away for slaughter. Like the Shelties, North Ronaldsay sheep have two-ply coats and their undercoat wool is very fine, suitable for making garments worn next to the skin. And like Orkney voles, these shoreline sheep are genetically singular, much smaller and very different from British sheep. DNA derived from the bones of a sheep found at the prehistoric village at Skara Brae is a very close match to the seaweed munching North Ronaldsay sheep, its descendants.

*

Not all of the Highlanders who fought for Bruce at Bannockburn were under the command of Aonghus Og MacDonald. Sir Niall Campbell had attended the coronation at Scone in 1306 and before then had married Mary Bruce, the new king's sister. She was one of the party of royal refugees who sought sanctuary at St Duthac's at Tain and was captured by the Earl of Ross, a supporter of Edward I. With characteristic cruelty, the English king ordered that Mary Bruce be held in a cage that was suspended from the walls of Roxburgh Castle, near Kelso. Exposed to all the elements and to the mockery of public view, like a captive animal, Mary endured this terrible treatment for four long years before being imprisoned indoors. Like Queen Elizabeth, she had to wait until the victory at Bannockburn in 1314 for release.

Meanwhile, King Robert was rewarding Clan Campbell for their steadfast support with lands confiscated from the defeated MacDougalls, and also the Earl of Atholl, who had supported Edward II. The grant of the latter's holdings was the foundation of the Campbell lordship in Argyll. After Sir Niall's death in 1316, his eldest son, Sir Colin Og Campbell, became Baron of Lochawe and Dubhgall. Like all of the Campbell clan chiefs, he took the Gaelic patronymic of MacCailean Mór, the son of Great Colin, who had died in battle against the MacDougalls in 1296.

Clan Campbell's origins could hardly be seen as less dramatic than the clan who would become their great rivals in the west, the MacDonalds, and yet they were. In reality they were very surprising. It seems that the first Campbell to come on record was not a Highlander but a Lowlander, Gillespie of Menstrie and Sauchie in Clackmannanshire. Some genealogies inconveniently trace him back to the Old Welsh-speaking Britons of the Clyde, Forth and Tweed and his possessions were in the ancient kingdom of Manau, a name preserved in Clackmannanshire, its heir, and long before that the territory of the Maeatae. And yet a royal charter of 1263 names him as Gilascoppe Cambell. The first name was often written as Archibald and the last seems as if might be retrospective.

It was Gillespie's son who first ventured into the Highlands. Cailean married a wealthy heiress (what would become something of a Campbell tradition), who brought him the lands of Clan O'Duine in Argyll. His wife's clan's Irish connections probably persuaded Cailean to claim descent from Diarmaid, a mythic hero as famous for his good looks and kindness as his fighting qualities. From that time on, Clan Campbell began to style themselves Siol Diarmaid, probably seen as a necessary rewiring of family history for a Lowlander coming to the Gaelic-speaking Highlands. Genealogies were run up by the *seannachies* to fit the adopted identity. Clan Campbell was nothing if not flexible, ready to adopt whatever interpretation of history would advance its interests. The name Campbell itself, from *caim-beul*, means 'twisted mouth' and it may be a reference to the likelihood that Cailean Mór, as he was called, was not a native speaker.

When the Lordship of the Isles fell in 1492, no clan chief was better placed to step into the power vacuum in the Highlands and Islands than Lord Colin Campbell. His support for James III had brought him a noble title, Earl of Argyll, and an astute marriage had made him more than a Highland aristocrat. The dowry of Isabella Stewart, the daughter of the wealthy Lord John Stewart, made him the owner of the wonderfully named Castle Gloom. It glowers over a hillside above the town of Dollar in Clackmannanshire (the name may derive from *doilleir*, a Gaelic word for dark and gloomy) and it brought Colin Campbell close to where the fortunes of his ancestors began to prosper in the thirteenth century. Castle Gloom was quickly renamed Castle Campbell and its location made MacCailean Mór a substantial Lowland landowner and placed him much closer to the royal court, the fount of political power, than Argyll ever could.

In 1460 Clan Campbell began to usurp the policing role of the Lords of the Isles in the Hebrides. The Earl of Argyll sailed his birlinns into Oban Bay to settle a dispute between branches of the MacDougall family who had managed to hang on to remnants of their clan's great patrimony. In 1474 MacCailean Mór was granted a royal charter to do something no clan chief had ever done before. He wanted to build a town. The original site of Inverary was immediately to the south of the existing castle, and it was constituted as a burgh of barony. This status allowed the agents of the Earl of Argyll to institute a weekly market, and create a means of stimulating economic activity that would generate toll revenue for them.

In 1483 MacCailean Mór achieved high office, a position of pivotal influence, when James III appointed him Lord Chancellor of Scotland. He was made Keeper of the Great Seal, whereby he impressed the wax attached to important documents giving them the force of law, and, in effect, the Earl of Argyll acted as the king's first minister and his closest advisor. But all was not well at court. For reasons that remain unclear, James III began to favour his second son, and created him Duke of Ross. Prince James, the heir apparent, rose in reluctant rebellion and MacCailean Mór supported him. Matters came to a bloody conclusion at the Battle of Sauchieburn, not far from Stirling, in 1488 when James III was killed in mysterious circumstances.

The Campbells found themselves on the right side of history, and their political judgements were usually, but not always, astute and advanced the interests of their clan. After the battle, MacCailean Mór was restored to the office of Lord Chancellor and the Campbells were once again in receipt of royal rewards when the valuable lands of Rosneath in Dunbartonshire were granted to them.

Piety and contrition for his role in his father's death at Sauchieburn were not the sole motives behind James IV's annual pilgrimage to the shrine and sanctuary of St Duthac in Tain. He liked to stop off on the way north at Darnaway Castle near Forres. In 1497 the king ordered that its hall be re-roofed and the living quarters refurbished. This was done not only for his own comfort but also because James was having a royal bower built. Sometime after the work was completed, Janet Kennedy came to live at Darnaway with her children and her companion, Katrine Douglas. The sole condition of her tenure was that she lived there 'without husband or other man'. King James came north to the Highlands to pray for forgiveness at St Duthac's, but also to spend time with his mistress.

It seems from the increasingly detailed written records of expenditure by the royal household that they had a nice time. At the king's request, the 'maidens of Forres' came to the castle on 20 November 1501, to give a concert. In the great hall, they sang for James and Janet. Even when the king was not present, he made sure that his lover was entertained. In 1502 he sent a lutenist, Adam Dickson, to play for his second family. Music seems to have been a constant theme, for in October 1504 the king brought with him four Italian minstrels and a fascinating accompanist, an African drummer. Known in the records as the More Taubronar (the Moorish/African drummer), his name may have been something like Cloffies or Clovis. Treasury records show that this man, whose appearance must have been close to a sensation at Darnaway, was well paid and well dressed. His quarterly fee was £4 7s 6d, and he was given clothes made from satin and a coat of camel hair woven with black and red thread. Clearly more than a mere drummer, Clovis looked theatrical because he was. He seems to have been a producer of masques, a form of courtly entertainment that included dancing, singing, music, mime and the acting out of short scenes. It is almost certain that masques were performed in the candlelight of the hall at Darnaway in front of the king and his mistress. Perhaps their children were allowed to stay up and watch. There were also other entertainments.

On 13 October 1505, new rushes were strewn on the floor of the royal bedchamber. Servants used to mix them with meadowsweet and other perfumed herbs and dried flowers to keep the air fresh as the fire crackled in the grate. James IV wished to play cards, almost certainly with Janet Kennedy and probably other courtiers. The Treasury accounts recorded the bringing of other delights, including 'ane flacat [flask] of aqua vite to the king'.

This is not quite the first historical notice of Scotch whisky. That was in 1494 when Friar John Cor was supplied with a great deal of malted barley to distill what must have been a lot. But it is the first time anyone is recorded drinking a dram. 'Aqua vite to the king' is noted elsewhere and it seems that James IV was fond of the 'cratur'.

Scotch whisky, and in particular Scotch malt whisky, has been explicitly associated exclusively with the Highlands and Islands of Scotland for half a millennium, but 'aqua vite' and its variations were no doubt distilled for a long time before that and also in many more places beyond the north of Scotland. Nevertheless, the two are inextricably linked and the threadbare adjective of 'iconic' is for once apposite. And, since the word whisky is derived from *uisge beatha*, Gaelic for aqua vita, the water of life, then iconic to the Highlands and Islands it shall be.

After the best part of a lifetime's research, what I would define as 'pot still Highland malt Scotch whisky' is unique and impossible to imitate successfully. All the necessary ingredients are to hand in the Highlands and Islands: pure, clear water tumbling from the mountains, good barley grown along the Moray coastlands, and plenty of peat to dry and heat the resulting mixture. Malt whisky may be seen as the quintessential product, taking its ingredients, and indeed its development, from every part of the region, highland and lowland.

Once again geography made history, and never more so than in the late eighteenth and early nineteenth centuries. Across approximately seventy years, thousands of unlicensed distilleries grew up in the Highlands and Islands. During a crackdown in 1782, more than a thousand stills were shut down, which only goes to show how many there were in total, no doubt many thousands. Stills also existed in the Lowlands, but it was much more difficult for them to operate undetected and to avoid paying the excise duty on malted barley. Two other factors helped Highland distillers flourish. Magistrates tended to be local landowners, some of them clan chiefs, many no doubt partial to the odd dram, and they tended to be lenient with the few illicit distillers who were caught. But it was quality that kept production high. The water, the barley and the peat were pure and the alchemy between them better understood in the north than in the Lowlands. Even though it was made illegally, King George IV insisted on drinking only Glenlivet on his royal visit to Scotland in 1822.

A year later a new Excise Act eased the restrictions and made licensing a distillery more attractive and affordable. George Smith applied for a licence and the famous Glenlivet distillery was founded in 1824. Its product has never varied in its quality since then – the Glenlivet is simply sublime. The Irish distiller, Aeneas Coffey, invented a new still that he patented in 1830 and it revolutionised the production of grain whisky in the Lowlands. Like vodka and gin, the raw spirit is clear and apart from sharpness and high alcoholic content, it has little character. The producers of malt whisky, the vast majority in the Highlands and Islands, sold their product, which had been given colour and taste by its maturation in oak barrels of various sorts, to flavour the Lowland grain. These blended whiskies can be good, occasionally, and now they make up the bulk of the market.

Happenstance propelled the distilling of Scotch whisky onto a world stage. A blight known as phylloxera devastated the European vineyards in the 1880s, stocks of wine crashed and so, more importantly, did the supply of brandy. The drink of choice amongst those who could afford it in Victorian Britain was brandy and soda. Whisky was seen as an acceptable substitute, Queen Victoria and Prince Albert had fallen in love with the Highlands and drank the stuff, and the distilleries have never looked back.

Highland malt remains the most complex, most satisfying and mouth-filling form of whisky. Leaving aside the eighteen single malt distilleries in the Lowlands, some of their products perfectly acceptable, there are five different sorts of malt: Campbeltown, Highland, Island, Islay and Speyside. The last is consistently excellent with the Glenlivet, Macallan and Glenfarclas all superb, mixed with the right amount of water (I am blessed to have a well, but bottled Highland Spring will do just as well, so to speak) to release the flavour. Malt must never be drunk neat. Never. But the greatest whisky I ever tasted was not from Speyside. It was a thirty-one-year-old Springbank from Campbeltown. Black-dark and a little viscous, it was magical, with the nose, the scent of it, almost as good as the taste, and in 1994, affordable. Then, I paid the same amount as the whisky's age, but checking on the internet, I see that a bottle now costs £3,000. Oh dear. We shall never see its like again.

*

For Ranald Gallda, chickens came home to roost. Sometime after 1540 he was installed as chief of Clanranald after John of Moidart had been imprisoned by James V while on a punitive expedition to the Highlands. At Ranald's inauguration, perhaps at Castle Tioram, cattle were being slaughtered in preparation for the great feast that was traditional at such moments of change. Clan chiefs were expected to be open-handed, extravagantly generous, a river to their people, particularly at the outset of their leadership. When Ranald Gallda arrived (significantly his nickname made him Ranald the Stranger) and saw the oxen being butchered, he is said to have remarked that chickens would have done just as well. It was a fatal blunder. Forever after he was known as Ranald nan Cearcan, 'Ranald of the Chickens'. In a world where authority stemmed from strength and military prowess, the demeaning nickname meant that even before he had been inaugurated, Ranald was diminished.

Gallda was a reference to the new chief's upbringing. He had been fostered with Hugh Fraser, Lord Lovat and Chief of Clan Fraser whose lands lay at the north-eastern end of the Great Glen. *Altrum,* or fosterage, was common amongst the families of Highland chiefs because it was a means of strengthening bonds and making alliances. The word also carries connotations of nurture and education; some fostered children developed very close relationships with their adopted families. That meant that Ranald the Stranger could call on the support of Clan Fraser in his attempt to install himself as chief of Clanranald, still a powerful force in the west even after the dissolution of the MacDonald Lordship of the Isles.

In 1543 the ambitions of Ranald of the Chickens began to unravel when John of Moidart escaped from prison. So shaky was his hold on power that Ranald immediately fled back up the Great Glen to seek support from the Frasers, his foster-family. Moidart ordered the fiery cross to be lit. This is an early notice of how the clans were mustered. *Na daoine uaisle,* the tacksmen, who were often closely related to the chief's family, were responsible for raising the fiery cross. Known as *crann tara,* made of wood soaked with pitch and sometimes with a bloody rag attached, it was set up somewhere conspicuous as a signal for clansmen to sharpen their dirks and swords. The fiery cross was last raised in 1812 in Canada, to summon the exiled Glengarry Highlanders to oppose a force of invading Americans. After that, the cross was seen once more across the southern states of the USA when the most infamous clan of all, the Ku Klux Klan, planted it wherever they wished to intimidate those who might resist their foul prejudices.

When John of Moidart's tacksmen had mustered his clansmen, perhaps 300 men, he moved quickly. With his allies from Clan Cameron, the MacDonalds of Glengarry, Keppoch and Ardnamurchan, Moidart raided Fraser and Clan Grant lands around Inverness and took Castle Urquhart. Before their enemies could retaliate, the MacDonalds retreated down the Great Glen with their plunder and disappeared into the Rough Bounds. Wild and inaccessible, the lands of Knoydart, Morar and Moidart were a familiar and safe refuge, and the Frasers and their allies, the Gordons, did not dare pursue any further in country they did not know and in whose passes and defiles they might easily have been ambushed. Hugh Fraser and George Gordon, whose clan had joined the hunt for Clanranald, decided to divide their forces and withdraw, believing that Moidart's small army was no longer a threat.

While the Gordons marched eastwards through Glen Spean, back to their own territory, Hugh Fraser led his men, maybe 300–400, up the Great Glen. Which was exactly what John of Moidart expected him to do. When his scouts reported that his enemies had divided, the Clanranald chief acted quickly and decisively. Threading their way through the mountain paths to the north-west, unseen by the Frasers, Moidart's men raced ahead to where the Inverness road crosses the glen between Loch Lochy and Loch Oich. And there they waited.

The fight was vicious, murderous, and many men were killed on what became known as the Blar na Leine, the Field of the Shirts. It was 15 July 1544, and the midsummer heat persuaded many to pull off their jacks of mail or thick, quilted tunics, and two forces of gallowglasses faced each other in only their linen sarks. Volleys of arrows hit their marks, just as in front of the grandstands on the North Inch at Perth, and many fell. Unprotected by armour, the clans charged each other and men were stabbed, slashed at and eviscerated. Those who fell, brought to their knees by grievous wounds, were hacked to death, repeatedly dirked and cut by razor-sharp weapons. Hundreds died on the Field of the Shirts, including Hugh Fraser and Ranald Gallda. By evening more of Clan Ranald were left standing, bloodied and exhausted, and John of Moidart was hailed as undisputed chief.

Blar na Leine may have been apposite, since it is likely that men threw off their armour in the heat, but it is probably a mistranslation. It should have been remembered as Blar na Leana, which Dwelly translates as 'a swampy plain', still a good description of the meadow between the two lochs before modern drainage dried it up. As with much of what went on in the Highlands and Islands in the sixteenth century, documentary evidence is patchy, but most sources agree that great slaughter took place and much blood was spilled amongst the lush, green grass.

The battle was one of many violent incidents that characterised the sixteenth century as Linn nan Creach. Disorder and feud crackled through the glens and across the islands like wildfire, and the Gaelic name of 'the Age of the Forays' was apposite. It was a direct consequence of the fall of the Lordship of the Isles after 1492, when the authority of the MacDonald princes was not replaced by firm royal government and a vacuum opened. And it was by no means unique in Scotland. Weak kings, scheming regents and the lack of coherent policy saw the growth of a similarly criminal society in the south of Scotland and northern England, the riding times, the age of the Border reivers. But there was a difference. The exploits of the Bold Buccleuch and Kinmont Willie Armstrong had the aura of daring, buckles were swashed and even a rough-hewn romance swirled around them, but the Highlanders were seen as other, different, half-dressed bands of babbling savages who spoke a foreign language and cut each other to pieces without hesitation.

Few crossed that cultural divide, but the sixteenth century saw a fascinating exception. According to the historian Keith Brown, George Buchanan was 'the most profound intellect sixteenth-century Scotland produced'. Hailed as the greatest writer in Latin of the European renaissance, composing prose and verse as though 'it was his mother tongue', and the author of a magisterial *History of Scotland* that was intended, he wrote, 'to purge it of English lies and Scottish vanity', this great scholar was certain that his work 'would content few and displease many'. His stellar career and great achievements should have surprised many Lowland Scots, for George Buchanan's mother tongue was Gaelic. He was a native speaker, a Highlander born in 1506 on a farm near Killearn, not far from the shores of Loch Lomond and in the centre of the lands of Clan Buchanan. They were closely linked to the cattle-thieving MacGregors, and like many others, the Buchanans feuded, especially with Clan MacLaren, and they also raided their neighbours during the bloody century of Linn nan Creach.

After his father's early death, George was raised in poverty and his prospects must have seemed bleak had it not been for his mother's family connections. She was Agnes Heriot, and her cousin, George, was a wealthy goldsmith whose son would go on to endow George Heriot's School in Edinburgh. As a child, Buchanan must have been bilingual, but little is known of his early education until his uncle, James Heriot, paid for the boy to go to the University of Paris in 1520. The family was clearly one that believed in the importance of schooling. The experience was transformative and even though he was only fourteen when he matriculated, George appears to have flourished in what might have been a difficult transition from a farm on the fringe of the Highlands to Europe's most populous city.

By 1523 the young student had returned to Scotland and found himself, by an unknown process, in the Scottish army at the siege of Wark Castle on the Tweed. It is not clear how and when this period of soldiering ended, but George then went to St Andrews University where he graduated in 1525. After studying on the windy shores of the North Sea, he returned to Paris as a teacher. Buchanan spent the following fifteen or so years lecturing and writing in various European universities.

The world was changing, and the young man found himself in the midst of turmoil, both intellectual and theological. Martin Luther had published his itemised disapproval of the Catholic Church in 1517 and others had followed him. But, like the great Dutch philosopher Erasmus, Buchanan did not overtly reject the teachings of the Church but was critical of how its bishops and priests behaved. In 1537, at the age of thirty-one, he joined the household of the Earl of Cassillis, who had been one of his students at both St Andrews and Paris. He too found himself moving closer to the views of the reformers. In Scotland, Cardinal Beaton led a reaction and, despite his connections, Buchanan was arrested, but was not detained for long. Having managed to escape, he spent ten years at European universities in France and Portugal.

In 1559 the Scottish Reformation exploded into life and events began to unfold very quickly. John Knox returned to Scotland and the houses of the friars, most of them in towns, the Franciscans, Dominicans and Carthusians, were attacked. Scone Abbey was destroyed, and when the regent, the Catholic Mary of Guise, died in June 1560 and the French troops who had supported her and suppressed dissent abandoned Scotland, parliament was taken over by the Protestant Lords of the Congregation and Knox was installed as minister of St Giles', the nation's most important kirk. The Scottish Parliament acted so quickly to substitute the Catholic Church with a Protestant national Church that the English ambassador, Thomas Randolph, was moved to remark that he 'never saw so many important matters sooner despatched'.

When George Buchanan arrived in Edinburgh, he was appointed tutor to Mary, Queen of Scots in 1562. Four years later he became principal of St Leonard's College at St Andrews University, where Church ministers were trained. A year later, Buchanan was elected Moderator of the General Assembly of the Church of Scotland, even though he was a layman. After 1570 he was appointed tutor to the young James VI, subjecting the boy to regular beatings as he attempted to convert him into a God-fearing Protestant king who understood that royal power was limited.

Old for the times, George was seventy-three when he appeared to retire from public life. It was then that he had time to complete his *History of Scotland*, and also something even more enduring and influential, *De Jure Regni apud Scotos*. Loosely translated, something that might have earned a beating from Buchanan, it dealt with the Rights of Kings in Scotland. Its central thesis was ultimately very influential. Power, he argued, comes from the people (by whom he meant the barons, burgesses and the Kirk), kingship is essentially conditional and not an absolute right granted by God, and that it is lawful to resist tyrants.

All of these precepts were lost on the Stuarts. Their anachronistic and unwavering belief in an absolute monarchy proved to be their dynasty's downfall. Even though *De Jure Regni apud Scotos* was condemned by the Scottish Parliament in 1584 and again in 1664, and in 1683 copies were burned by the University of Oxford, Buchanan's ideas laid important foundations in the creation of the idea of a constitutional monarchy. Keith Brown has argued that the deposing of James VII in Scotland in 1688 was an example of the power of Buchanan's thinking. His influence was profound but his career surprising – for a Highlander, a clansman who was raised speaking a barbarous language.

It is difficult to chart the ripple of Reformation across the Highlands and Islands. Honesty could involve jeopardy. Those who wished to remain Catholics might have said or done otherwise publicly in order to avoid persecution while remaining privately loyal to the Church of Rome. There were no doubts about the faith of Clan Campbell. Even before the upheavals of the mid sixteenth century, the Campbells of Ayrshire had been associated with Lollardy, an earlier version of some of the ideas that drove the Reformation. When John Knox returned to Scotland and embarked on a preaching tour in 1555 and 1556, he was guarded by contingents of Campbell clansmen often under the leadership of Cailean Liath, the Lord of Glenorchy, so called because of his white hair and long, flowing Old Testament white beard. Grey Colin and his kinsman, the Earl of Argyll, were amongst the leaders of the Lords of the Congregation, and their military muscle did much to advance the cause of Reformation in the Lowlands and across their own clanlands. But conversion to the reformed faith was by no means total and there is a striking, enduring divide in the Outer Hebrides.

South of the causeway that crosses from Benbecula to South Uist, there is a monumental sign that marks another crossing, that of an invisible cultural frontier. Thirty feet tall and made to seem even taller by its position on the western slopes of the hill of Ruabhal is Bana Thighearna nan Eilean, Our Lady of the Isles. A crowned Virgin Mary holds up the Christ-child by her right shoulder, and he is turned to the south as he raises his hand to make the sign of a blessing. The great sculpture was the creation of Hew Lorimer and the initiative of Canon John Morrison, the local parish priest. Christ is blessing South Uist because it was under great threat. The statue was raised and dedicated in 1958 as a protest against plans advanced by the Ministry of Defence to build a large missile testing base and an extensive military town that would have covered and cordoned off much of the island. An entire way of life would have been destroyed, argued the protesters. The blessing of the Lord Jesus Christ proved powerful and the plans were quietly shelved.

The sculpture was also intended as a statement that South Uist was different, and perhaps the most striking difference is to be seen by the side of the A865 as it snakes down the western side of the island. Many wayside shrines, often dedicated to the Virgin Mary, have been built. In contrast to the ascetic Presbyterianism of Lewis, Harris and North Uist, the southern islands of the Outer Hebrides are all predominantly Catholic. Recent statistics show that 91 per cent of the population of South Uist are, and 84 per cent on Barra. Some historians see this difference as a relic, the islands retaining their original faith, being places the Reformation never reached, but that is just a lazy example of back-of-beyondery. As ever, the reality is more interesting, and more instructive.

After the convulsions of the 1560s in the Lowlands, the pace of change was much slower and more difficult to trace in the Highlands and Islands beyond the territories of Clan Campbell, and their allies. Many clansmen and women followed whatever example their chief set, but not always. MacNeil of Barra became a Protestant, but many of his people did not follow suit. Instead, the cult of St Finnbarr remained powerful a thousand years after his exemplary life. He was an Irish holy man of the sixth century who may have founded a *diseart* on Pabbay, a significant place name. W. J. Watson explains that it means 'the Island of the Papar', an Old Irish word for a priest. There are the remains of a graveyard and a Pictish carved stone. And on the main island, the chapel at Cille Bharra is dedicated to St Barr, clearly the same man, and also the deriva-tion of Barra's name. The main chapel is now a roofless ruin but it was almost certainly a focus for pilgrimage. In the upper grave-yard is the tomb of Sir Compton Mackenzie, the author of *Whisky*

Galore, who lived on Barra, who loved the island and wrote about its Catholicism.

The enduring power of St Finnbarr, or St Barr, may have been the reason for the reluctance of the men and women of Clan MacNeil to follow the lead of their chief. In 1625 a mission of Irish Franciscans, who spoke enough Gaelic to be understood, arrived on Barra and baptised many, people who had probably been without a priest for some time. And by 1632, Roderick MacNeil, their chief, had converted to Catholicism.

Elsewhere, and especially on the mainland, the picture is blurry. As happened on Barra, when priests died they could not be easily replaced by a Church outlawed by the state. But Presbyterian ministers were also in short supply in the second half of the sixteenth century. Some scattered surviving records confirm that Clan Donald remained Catholic. In a letter from the chief of Clanranald sent in 1625 to Pope Urban VII, the message is unclear and garbled, but the sentiments are not:

> . . . the darkness I mean of error, which the turbulent, detested followers of the accursed faithless Calvin had introduced, through the violence and tyranny of the Council of Scotland [parliament], through lying pseudo-bishops and fraudulent ministers . . . It is certain and evident (since it is already known in the Council of Scotland that we have received the true faith) that we shall be compelled to the renunciation of it or to the loss of temporal goods and life, or both, as has frequently happened, not only to Scots but also to many Irish . . . our country and islands . . . are far removed from the incursions and outrages of the English to whom we have never at all given obedience. All the Gaelic-speaking Scots and the greater part of the Irish chieftains joined to us by ties of friendship . . .

Here is another series of observations made in 1669, quoted by Sir Compton Mackenzie in his book on Catholicism in Scotland, published in 1936:

[Highlanders] cease not, however, to cherish a great esteem for the Catholics, as it appears in many things. If a priest visits him, they show him more respect and honour him more than their own ministers. In fact the heretics amongst the Highlanders surpass in reverence for our priests the very Catholics of the Lowlands. They moreover retain many Catholic usages, such as making the sign of the Cross, the invocation of Saints and sprinkling themselves with Holy Water; which they anxiously ask from their Catholic neighbours. In sickness they make pilgrimages to the ruins of the old churches and chapels which yet remain, as of the most noble monastery of Iona, where St Columba was Abbot: also of the chapels of Ghierlock [Gairloch] and Applecrosse and Glengarry which were once dedicated to the saints. They also visit the holy springs which yet retain the names of the saints to whom they were dedicated and it has often pleased the Most High to restore to their health those who visited these ruins or drank at these springs invoking the aid of those saints.

This elegiac, if partial, memory of the slow disappearance of a sacred landscape and the enduring power of the saints to enable minor miracles is unusual and emblematic of a society, it seems to me, having changed reluctantly from the old ways. It is also striking that Maelrubha of Applecross was still revered as late as the mid seventeenth century, and that the ruins of the ancient Chapel of Sand of Udrigil, near Gairloch, still stands and it may have been dedicated to St Donan.

The saint would have been profoundly shocked by events that took place on Eigg, the island where he founded a community and where he himself was cruelly martyred. Irish records contain the following: 'Donnan, of Ega, Abbot. Ega is the name of an island in which he was, after his coming from Ireland. And there came robbers of the sea on a certain time to the island when he was celebrating Mass. He requested of them not to kill him until he should have the Mass said, and they gave him this respite; and he was afterwards beheaded and fifty-two of his monks along with him . . . AD 616.'

Nine centuries later, there occurred another, even more deadly, massacre on the little island. This time the perpetrators were not pirates but neighbours.

Visitors to Eigg were exploring Uamh Fhraing, 'the Cave of [St] Francis', in the autumn of 2017 when they came across bones, many of them, about fifty human bones. The police were called, and indeed, murder had been done. But no one was surprised that archaeologists rather than detectives were involved in the investigation. At Historic Environment Scotland, they dated the remains to the late sixteenth century. Since then, the cave had acquired another name. In 1577 perhaps as many as 400 islanders were killed in what became known as the Massacre Cave.

Clan MacLeod of Dunvegan on Skye pursued a long-running feud with Clanranald. Versions of events vary but the gist of the matter was that a raiding party of MacLeods sailed from Skye to Eigg bent on vengeance for cruel injuries inflicted on the chief's son. Their birlinns were seen by a lookout and the islanders fled to Francis' cave to hide. The narrow entrance was concealed behind a waterfall, and at first the ruse worked. Unable to find the hiding place, the MacLeods had to content themselves with burning the houses of the Clanranald families, but as they sailed away, one of the crew spotted a lookout on the shore. Someone had emerged from the cave to see if the raiders had gone.

They had not. MacLeod of Dunvegan had his men divert the waterfall, block up the narrow entrance to the cave with heather, kindling and green wood. Once it was set alight, smoke filled the interior and asphyxiated all of the men, women and children inside. One can only imagine the horror as the whole population of the island choked to death in the smoky darkness.

News of the massacre crackled across Scotland like wildfire, further confirmation of the barbarity of the Highland clans and their blood-spattered rivalries. Walter Scott visited the cave in 1814 and was so appalled and moved by what he saw that he raised money for the Christian burial of the skeletons he found strewn on the floor. He wrote: 'The cave is often visited by strangers and I myself have seen the place, where the bones of the murdered MacDonalds still remain, lying as thick at the door of the cave as in the charnel house of a church.'

*

Despite, or perhaps because of, the regular beatings he received from George Buchanan, James VI of Scotland despised Highlanders. *Basilikon Doron* is the Greek title of a book written by the king in the 1590s, when he was attempting to demonstrate to the English nobility how suitable an heir he would be to the childless Elizabeth I. The title means 'A Royal Gift', and it was in essence a manifesto, initially intended as guidance to his eldest son, Henry (who died in 1612), on how to be a good and effective king. Amongst the many clichés and commonplaces, James VI placed a divine right to rule at the centre of his brand of kingship, completely rejecting Buchanan's concept of constitutional monarchy, storing up a great deal of trouble for the future.

In the book, James made his views of the Highlands and Highlanders very plain, and there is a hint of a reference to the massacre on Eigg: '[Those] dwelleth in our mainland, that are barbarous for the most part, and yet mixed with some show of civility, the other, dwelleth in the Isles, and are utterly barbarous, without any show of civility.'

The king was determined to enforce the rule of law in the north, but he did not have the resources to police it. Instead, he relied on Clan Campbell and others to act as his proxies. But he also deployed his own and his advisors' knowledge of the clans and their culture. Perhaps he had paid some attention to George Buchanan after all.

On 20 January 1604, Alasdair MacGregor of Glenstrae shivered in his linen sark. With five of his fellow clansmen, he had been led out of the Tolbooth in Edinburgh's High Street to the insults and spittle of a jeering crowd. They had gathered for a gala day, the term deriving from a 'gallows day', what was seen in those days as an entertainment. With his hands tied behind his back, Alasdair stood at the foot of the gallows while a ladder was made ready. Unable to steady themselves on its rungs, he and his men were dragged up onto the scaffold. When the chief of Clan Gregor looked up at the beam, he saw that one of the nooses was higher than the others. It would be his, a macabre mark of his rank. And the cruel punishment for calling himself by his right name.

Clansmen were nothing without their names. Much more than labels, they were also addresses, pinning those with the same name to the map of the Highlands and Islands, to their clanlands, their own straths and glens, the kindred ground, what was central to their sense of themselves, to their *dùthchas*. King James and his council understood this well and in 1603 they disnamed Clan Gregor. Exasperated with their raiding and lawlessness, James made it a capital crime to use the name of MacGregor. Any who defied the king could be hunted down, robbed and killed without fear of any penalty or recrimination. The MacGregors became outlaws, beyond the protection of the law. Many changed their name, calling themselves Drummond, Gregory, Murray and even Campbell. But Alasdair of Glenstrae was defiant and when the hangman put a noose around his neck and kicked away the stool, he knew as he slowly choked to death and the crowd jeered that he would die a MacGregor.

Commerce, colonisation and exploitation were also proposed as a means of subduing the barbarous Isles. Towns, markets, courts and a centralising of authority and economic activity might be a way of taming and civilising the Highlands and Islands. In 1597 the Scottish Parliament passed an Act enabling the foundation of three burghs in the west: one in Kintyre (Clan Campbell had made a start at Inverary), one in Lochaber and a third on Lewis, based at the sheltered harbour at Stornoway. In order to 'civilise' Lewis, a company was formed, one very much in the enterprising spirit of the times – after the defeat of the Spanish Armada in 1588 and the appropriation of their captured galleons, adventuring had begun. English sailors like Francis Drake and Walter Raleigh sailed to the east and brought back fabulously valuable cargoes of spices, or they simply preyed like pirates on Spanish and Portuguese shipping. The East India Company of Adventurers was founded and it began to establish depots, or 'factories', on the Molucca Islands, known as the Spice Islands, and on Java.

A similar spirit of adventure was, surprisingly, swirling around Fife. To found a town at Stornoway, investors came together to form a company, The Gentlemen Adventurers for the Conquering of the Isle of Lewis. It mattered not at all that the island was already in the possession of the clans who had lived there for centuries. No more attention was paid to their rights than those of the peoples of the East Indies or India or the Malay Peninsula. They were all foreigners who spoke unintelligible languages.

In the winter of 1597/8, the ships of the Fife Adventurers dropped anchor in Stornoway Bay, and the colonists proceeded to do exactly what those who had landed on the Atlantic coast of America did only a few years before. Just as at Roanoke and later at Jamestown, in what became Virginia, the settlers built a stockade to keep themselves safe from the savages who inhabited the island.

Not surprisingly, the savages took exception to the arrival of the Fife Adventurers, especially when it was discovered that the Crown had in effect granted them ownership of Lewis. Neil MacLeod led his clansmen in an attack on the Stornoway stockade and burned the wooden houses and huts of the settlement twice. As well as smoke, there was also more than a little disappointment in the island air. The Fife Adventurers had led settlers to believe that Lewis was fertile, its lush pastures waiting to be grazed by herds of cattle, the sea around its shores crowded with shoals of fish waiting to be netted. When they looked over the parapet of their stockade at the eastern edge of bleak Barvas Moor, they must have wondered.

By the winter of 1600/01, the situation for the Adventurers had become desperate. Unable to source supplies in a hostile countryside, they were forced to depend on the stores they had brought with them and what could be supplied by sea. When James Learmouth sailed out of the harbour bound for the mainland, Neil MacLeod's brother, Murdo, pursued him in his birlinns, boarded the ship and slaughtered all on board. It was an unnecessary act of savagery, more apparent proof of barbarity, and it provoked an act of betrayal. Neil

MacLeod handed his brother over to the authorities, no doubt hoping for leniency for himself, and Murdo was hanged and his head set on a spike above the Netherbow Port in Edinburgh.

In 1601 matters came to a head. The settlers marched out of the stockade to hunt down the MacLeods and kill them. Instead, they were ambushed and at least sixty died in the fight that followed. A few months later, the clansmen stormed the stockade, and in return for being spared, the Fife Adventurers agreed to quit the island, giving up hostages to Neil MacLeod as a guarantee that promises would be kept. But, in the end, there was no victory. Legally, the Adventurers were still the owners of Lewis, and they sold it to Clan MacKenzie. Under the ruthless leadership of Roderick, known as the Tutor of Kintail, they defeated the MacLeods, and soon afterwards Neil MacLeod discovered that the betrayal of his brother had bought him no credit.

On a scaffold in Edinburgh, one of the executioners shouted at MacLeod: 'Come on, *bòdach*! We haven't got all bloody day!'

Neil understood no English and all he heard was the Gaelic word. *bodach*, 'old man'. Full of indignation, he turned and roared: 'Nam bithin air deck luinge far am bu duilich do thear seasamh, stiuireadh na mara gu tric, cha bhodach dhuit mis' a mhacain!' ('If I was on the deck of a ship, steering over the billows, trying to stand steady, you would not call me an old man!')

With his hands tied behind his back. MacLeod headbutted the young hangman and knocked him down on the scaffold. The huge crowd gasped for a moment, and then began to hurl insults, shouting, baying at the uncomprehending MacLeod that he would soon dance a jig as he squirmed at the end of a rope, pissing himself like a bairn.

James VI did not hesitate to use the full force of the law to pursue his relentless policy of 'daunting the clans'. In August 1609, the Statutes of Iona were enacted. Nine new laws were agreed by a group of compliant Highland chiefs that in essence began the formal dismantling of Gaelic culture. The eldest sons of chiefs were bound to attend Lowland schools until they were fluent in English. *Seannachies*, clan bards who were the guardians of history and tradition, were no longer to be entertained and the Protestant religion was to be actively promoted. The MacDonalds and MacLeans ignored much of this, but many dared not. The world was changing once more, and the old ways were passing.

10

Moments When Nothing Seemed Impossible

1609–1689

On my first visit to Lewis, more than thirty years ago, I had important meetings with a new organisation set up to administer the Gaelic
Television Fund. The Conservative government had unexpectedly
made available £8 million, later £9 million, for the production of
programmes in Gaelic to be broadcast on Scottish Television and
Grampian Television. As Director of Programmes, I thought it vital
to meet the executives running the fund so that we could work out
a strategy that might change perceptions of the language across
Scotland. It was also vital that I had time to walk out to Ropework
Park on the northern edge of Stornoway to meet Charlie Barley.

MacLeod is still the most common surname on Lewis and many
who bear it are known by patronymics or nicknames. But Charles
MacLeod's was puzzling. It should have been something like Charlie
Coirce, 'Charlie Oats', but perhaps the attraction of the alliteration of
Barley was too tempting and more memorable. Oats are an essential
ingredient in Charlie Barley's most famous product. At his excellent
butcher's shop in Ropework Park, his employees make the world-
renowned *marag dubh*, the unique Stornoway black pudding. And I
wanted to buy one, a whole one.

A smiling, welcoming man, he chatted to me on the pavement
outside his shop, having insisted on making a gift of his wonderful
product. Without giving away any culinary secrets, he explained
that of all the ingredients (beef suet, onions, blood – usually that of
cows, sheep or pigs – oatmeal, salt and pepper) oatmeal was the most

important. Also made by MacLeod & MacLeod of Stornoway, a different company, the black pudding is unlike any other. After I grilled it, turning it over often, following Charlie's advice, there was a slight crunch as well as the rich taste of blood and suet, and surprisingly little fat. *Marag dubh* has been hailed by the *Guardian* newspaper, no less, as the best sausage made in Britain. And they are right.

But it needed protecting. In 2009 an application was made to the European Union by the four authentic Stornoway producers of black pudding for Protected Geographical Indication of Origin, the same status as Parma ham or Stilton cheese enjoyed. Imposters not based on Lewis were marketing puddings that claimed to be something they were not. After four years of bureaucratic back-and-forth PGIO was granted and Charlie Barley's business flourished.

Oats are crucial to the distinctive quality of the puddings and indeed are and were a staple of Highland and Island life since a time out of mind. Oats are significantly more tolerant of rain and need less sun to ripen than either wheat or barley, something that was important during the bad weather of the Little Ice Age. And they are good for you, despite Samuel Johnson's entry in his dictionary: 'Oats. A grain, which in England is generally given to horses, but in Scotland supports the people.'

The great, and tragically short-lived, Scottish poet of the mid-eighteenth century, Robert Fergusson, wrote of Scotland as the 'Land of Cakes', and so did Robert Burns. They were not referring to Victoria sponges or Battenbergs, but oatcakes in all their forms. The recipe could not be simpler. Mix oatmeal with water, leave it for a while so that the water is absorbed, forming a porridge-like mixture. Then heat a griddle or even a flat stone in a campfire and spread out the mixture. The cakes cook in minutes. When clansmen were campaigning or driving cattle some distance, oatmeal made into cakes in this way was a mainstay. As was porridge oats heated in a crock by a fire. Since the clans were usually out in the summer, wild berries or nuts could be added, as well as butter or cream if it could be found.

When oats were harvested, Highlanders often preferred to use a sickle rather than a scythe. Swinging the latter could knock off precious ears and not all could be retrieved by gleaners. Women working in groups would grasp a handful of stalks and cut them at the bottom, keeping hold of the seedheads. The scythe also used to leave stalks in heaps that needed sorting so that the seedheads were all lying the same way. Once the sheaves were stooked and tied with straw ropes, a real skill, the wind dried them quickly. Oat straw also makes much better bedding than that of other cereals because it is much less dusty.

When the ears were dry and had been milled into oatmeal, nothing was wasted. The oat husks, which still had tiny bits of kernel attached, were made into *subhan*, or sowens, what was also known in Shetland as *virpa* – it is a Highland version of yoghurt.

The Orcadian author F. Marian McNeill, included in her definitive *Scots Kitchen* an ancient recipe for sowens. A wooden bucket known as a sowen-bowie was to be found in most blackhouses and farm cottages. The husks, or what we might call the bran, were tipped in and then covered with water. After the mixture had fermented (like live yoghurt) for four or five days, it was sieved. The husks were fed to chickens or pigs and the liquid poured back into the bowie. It soon separated with a sour-tasting but palatable white and watery liquid on top and a sediment of paste on the bottom. The sowans kept for a long time and could be eaten as it was or mixed with water to make a version of porridge. Scones and bannocks could also be made with it.

Oats were the basis of all these simple recipes, and being the food of subsistence farmers, nothing was ever wasted. When on rare occasions an animal was killed, every part of it, from horns to hooves, was used. Haggis is a testament to that cultural habit of waste-not want-not.

Robert Burns's 'Great Chieftain o' the Puddin-race' is often cited as the quintessence of traditional Scottish cuisine. A sheep's pluck or offal, that is, the heart, liver and lungs, is minced up with oatmeal, onion, suet, salt and some boiled stock made from bones, and then stuffed into a sheep's stomach before being cooked. It tastes wonderful, reluctantly lauded by the French *Larousse Gastronomique* thus: 'Although its description is not immediately appealing, haggis has an excellent nutty texture and a delicious savoury flavour.' It has become Scotland's national dish. But it is not Scottish.

The name, *hagws* or *hagese* is first recorded in England, but perhaps it did not originate there. The cook and writer Clarissa Dickson Wright believed that the recipe travelled in the Viking dragon ships from Norway. Others think haggis was invented in Lancashire. The historical reality is that it was probably a universal dish, the food of poor people who could afford to waste nothing.

Oats were and are the staple ingredient of almost all of the food traditionally associated with the Highlands and Islands, and indeed Scotland generally: black pudding, white or mealy pudding, oatcakes, bannocks, porridge and haggis. And they, or it, were nutritious. Recruiters for the growing Glasgow police force in the early twentieth century preferred to have Highlanders in their ranks, 'meal mountains, big, steady lads' who could impose themselves if need be.

*

James Gregory was a genius. Born in 1638 at Drumoak in Aberdeenshire, the son of Reverend John Gregory, he was a sickly child who was home-schooled by his mother. Nevertheless, after matriculating at Aberdeen University, and from the University of Padua, he was appointed the first Regius Professor of Mathematics at St Andrews in 1668, the chair having been endowed by King Charles II.

Gregory's immense talents were wide-ranging. In 1673 he laid the first prime meridian line on the floor of his laboratory, defining longitude at 0 degrees and measuring time on either side of it. He did this 200 years before Greenwich and so St Andrews can fairly claim to be the place where worldwide time began. In 2014, Gregory's pioneering work was marked by a solid brass line that follows the original meridian, as it runs across the pavement in South Street, below where his laboratory once was.

Astronomy and measurement fascinated the young man. With Isaac Newton and Gottfried Leibniz, he was one of the founders of calculus, the mathematical study of change, and wrote its first textbook. The subject was taught at St Andrews a century before it appeared on the curriculum at Cambridge University. Using a bird's feather, he demonstrated diffraction to his students, showing how sunlight split into its component colours. And he invented the Gregorian telescope, which is still in use. All of this and more was achieved in the span of a brief life. Tragically, James Gregory died of a stroke when he was only thirty-six.

He was also part of an intellectual dynasty. His cousin, David Gregory, produced an efficient and highly destructive new design for a cannon; Duncan Gregory developed algebraic theory while William Gregory was a chemist, the first to derive morphine and codeine from opium and isoprene from rubber. Another James Gregory was Professor of Medicine at Edinburgh University and invented Gregory's Mixture, a famously reliable laxative.

None of these brilliant men, however, used their right name. The Reverend John Gregory, James' father, was in reality a MacGregor, a descendant of the MacGregors of Glenlyon and Roro, and with other clan families, from whom all of these scholars came, he established himself in Aberdeenshire. After the Disarming Act of 1617, many of the clansmen scattered and were forced to take other names: Drummond, Murray, Grant, Gregory, and even Campbell. The most famous MacGregor of all, Rob Roy, even called himself Campbell, and despite his reputation as a cattle thief, he too went to university, matriculating at Glasgow. In 1774 the proscription of the name was finally lifted.

*

Charles I wanted to be crowned King of Scotland in London. But the Scottish Parliament pressed the royal court again and again, saying that his coronation had to take place in Edinburgh (Scone Abbey having been destroyed by John Knox's zealots) in order to confirm him as the rightful successor to James VI. When Charles I did, reluctantly, make his way north, many will have wished that parliament had not been so persistent.

It was one of the most lavish and extravagant royal tours ever undertaken. In the summer of 1633, the king progressed up through his realm with a retinue of 3,000, including a detachment of 350 fully armed soldiers, the entire royal household of servants and office holders, and 200 carts of luggage pulled by a thousand horses. Some of the noble families who hosted the king on his way north were bankrupted by the costs of hospitality.

It was decided that the coronation should be held in the Chapel Royal of Holyrood Abbey. It had been badly damaged in the upheavals of the Reformation but still had its roof. Much expense was incurred when the fabric was restored. The date was set for 18 June.

On the appointed day, the citizens of Edinburgh who lined the Royal Mile were treated to a sumptuous spectacle, something unprecedented. The gates of Edinburgh Castle opened and the king rode out near the head of a long procession that passed bunting, portraits of Charles I by Anthony van Dyck and under several ornamental gateways. Wine flowed freely for the crowds as bishops in gorgeously decorated copes processed downhill behind the king. During the ceremony itself there was a great deal of kneeling before the high altar. Ancient rites were being enacted, but a clear political statement was also being made.

To many watching, it must have seemed that a return to Catholicism or at least High Anglicanism was in the air. The day before the coronation, the devoutly Catholic Queen Henrietta had a Mass said for her in the Chapel Royal. At best, this ruinously expensive ceremony was insensitive in an overwhelmingly Protestant Scotland, and at worst, it may have seemed to those watching that the Church of Scotland was to be united with the Anglican Church of England.

A stool flew through the air on the morning of Sunday 23 July 1637, at the High Kirk of St Giles in Edinburgh. It was aimed at James Hannay, the Dean of Edinburgh, who had begun to read from the new *Book of Common Prayer*. It had been compiled by Charles I's close counsellor, Archbishop Laud, in an attempt to do exactly what those watching the coronation had feared. Laud had no authority in Scotland and no Church of Scotland minister had been consulted. It was a characteristically high-handed measure designed by Charles I to bring the Kirk into conformity with the Church of England, and Jenny Geddes would have none of it. After she had hurled the stool, she shouted 'Daur ye say Mass in my lug!' at the dean as he ducked. A riot followed and the first steps were taken down a path that would lead to the building of a scaffold in Whitehall on 30 January 1649, and the execution of the king.

After the rioters had dispersed, a moderate minister, Robert Baillie, feared for his country and himself: 'The whole people think Popery is at the doors. I think our people are possessed with a bloody devil . . . I think I may be killed and my house burnt over my head.'

But instead of more violence, a remarkable document was compiled that leaned heavily on the thinking of George Buchanan. The National Covenant protested loyalty to Charles I but insisted that his kingship was conditional on the maintenance of Presbyterianism in Scotland, and that, as Buchanan had written, a king who did not agree to this could be removed. Copies of the Covenant were sent all over Scotland and thousands of signatures were quickly attached. Only in the Highlands and the North-east was there resistance.

The creation of the National Covenant was the spark that ignited the War of the Three Kingdoms, often miscalled the English Civil War. In late 1638 ships carrying companies of battle-hardened Scottish mercenaries who had been fighting for the Protestant king of Sweden docked at Leith. At their head was a tough and gifted commander, General Alexander Leslie. The Church of Scotland had banned Laud's liturgy and deposed all bishops. Scotland was arming, and on a collision course with Charles I.

At the end of August 1640, Leslie led an enormous army across the Tweed and into England. More than 20,000 Scots were opposed by 3,500 Royalist troops at the bridge across the Tyne at Newburn, upriver from Newcastle. A young officer distinguished himself as the king's soldiers were swept aside. James Graham had signed the National Covenant and was fiercely opposed to bishops in the Kirk. Before Newburn, he had proposed to General Leslie that the Scots wear blue bonnet ribbons and the officers blue sashes, what has been the colour of militant Protestantism ever since. But Graham was uneasy at the attacks on the secular powers of the king. Despite his gallantry, he was accused in May 1641 of plotting on behalf of Charles I and imprisoned. Less than a year later, as part of an amnesty, Graham was released, but his political views had hardened. He had become a Royalist.

At the same time political differences boiled over into rebellion in the north of Ireland. Plantations of Protestant settlers, an initiative of James VI and I, had heightened tensions in the previous forty years and there had been regular outbreaks of violence. Ulster was Gaelic-speaking, Catholic and rural. Settlement was made possible by the defeat of the native Irish forces who had risen against English rule between 1593 and 1603. Following their failure to assert their rights, Hugh O'Neill, Earl of Tyrone and Hugh Roe O'Donnell, Earl of Tyrconnell and a retinue of supporters abandoned Ireland and sailed into permanent exile in Europe. The Flight of the Earls was a turning point and it allowed the British Crown to confiscate their lands and plant Protestant settlers in Ulster, mainly emigrants from southern Scotland and northern England. Centuries of bloody conflict would follow, and the war in Ireland continued.

In 1641 Irish Catholics rose once more in rebellion, attempting to seize power across Ireland and to halt and reverse the Plantations. Led by Felim O'Neill of Kinard, an army campaigned in the south with mixed success. Randall MacDonnell, the Marquis of Antrim, was one of the chiefs of Clan Donald and he raised forces that included his Highland and Island kinsmen. One of them was a man who would make history.

Alasdair mac Colla Chiotaich Mac Domhnuill, to give him his splendidly full name, was born around 1610 on the island of Colonsay. His father, known as Coll Ciotach (the nickname can mean 'left-handed' or 'devious') was a descendant of the branch of Clan Donald that had held Islay in the days of the Lordship. Its memory and hatred of Clan Campbell were strong and would be passed down from father to son.

Alasdair mac Colla joined the forces raised by the Marquis of Antrim and eventually found himself fighting alongside Felim

O'Neill and his Confederate Catholic army. On 11 February 1642, mac Colla and his men ambushed part of the garrison of the Protestant town of Coleraine while they were out foraging for supplies: '. . . having commanded his murderers [clearly a description written by an enemy] to lay down all their firearms . . . they [Alasdair's men] fell in amongst them (with swords and dirks and knives) in such a furious and irresistible manner that it was reported that not a man of them escaped of all the eight hundred'.

It seems that after mac Colla gave the order to charge the soldiers of the garrison, his men suddenly stopped, fired a single volley from their muskets or pistols at close quarters, dropped them, drew their swords and charged again. Great slaughter did indeed follow and only the Protestant commander, Archibald Stewart, and a handful of his men escaped.

Alasdair mac Colla had invented the Highland charge, what was at first known as the Irish charge. Much more than simply a shock tactic, it became a symbol, a greatly feared weapon, both military and psychological. Charging Highlanders were seen as crazed savages, their faces a rictus of rage, screaming war cries in a primitive language, racing half-naked across the heather to plunge into the thin red line that was all that stood between their slavering atavism and civilisation. An exaggeration? Not if you stood in the redcoat ranks of a government army watching a human wave of fury surging towards you.

Contrary to conventional belief, the Highland charge was in fact no mad, flailing rush followed by a disorganised melee. It was highly disciplined and required huge reserves of commitment and trust. Before the charge, safely beyond musket range, Highlanders often undressed for battle, taking off their plaids, knotting their linen sarks between their legs, casting off even their *brogan*, their shoes, so that they were physically unencumbered.

Since speed was of the essence, the ground had to be right, preferably downhill so that the clansmen would have *cothrom a' bhràighe*, the advantage of the brae. As one of Prince Charles's generals, Lord George Murray, later remarked, 'even a haggis can charge downhill'. And as he also said, in a much more serious tone, when he saw the boggy ground at Culloden Moor in 1746, that it was the wrong place for a successful charge. The terrain had to be firm and without obstacles like steep-sided burns or dykes with ditches.

Once the clans were ready, their chiefs, who led from the front, roared the *claideamh mòr* – the order to charge. This was the moment when discipline and raw courage were most needed. As the Highlanders sprinted across the heather towards their enemies' ranks, they were very vulnerable to musket volleys. And on a still day, faced by men who could stand steady and hold their fire until they were sure the Highlanders were in range, many would fall. Those who survived charged very close, within twenty or twenty-five yards of the enemy lines. And then they suddenly stopped. Those clansmen who had pistols or muskets fired them, sure that at that range they would hit something. And then, under the cover of clouds of acrid gunsmoke, their line broke up as they formed into small wedges of twelve or fourteen men. These were often relatives, fathers and sons, brothers, uncles and nephews. Gaels believed that courage flowed down the generations and the oldest and most experienced men were always set at the point of each wedge. Then the Highlanders dropped their firearms, drew their swords, pulled their small round shields onto a forearm and gripped a dirk with the same hand.

As the smoke cleared, opposing lines of soldiers saw these wedges charge towards them, heard them scream their war cries. Known as *a' dol sios*, 'going down', the Highlanders charged in a crouch to avoid another musket volley, and to get themselves into an attacking position. Their movement was always the same. When a wedge smashed into ranks of soldiers, they knocked up the points of bayonets or pikes with their targes, the small, parrying shields, before lunging and thrusting with their basket-hilted, razor-sharp swords. The shape of the wedge was vital, intended to break through the lines and turn them so that the battle would become a hand-to-hand melee, a style of fighting Highlanders excelled at.

Six months after the charge at Ballymoney in Ulster, war broke out. In August 1642, King Charles I raised the royal standard at Newark, and the Scots entered the War of the Three Kingdoms.

After a series of advances and reverses, Charles appointed James Graham as Lord Lieutenant in Scotland and made him Marquis of Montrose. But it was a hollow gesture, for Graham had no army to command, and indeed faced capture, humiliation and opposition from Clan Campbell and other clans he hoped to recruit. In August 1644, with two companions, the new marquis was hiding in the Methven Woods, west of Perth. There he unexpectedly came across a clansman carrying the *crann tara*, the fiery cross, a sign that the Perthshire clans should muster – but not for the king. An enemy was fast approaching from the north.

On 27 June 1644, Alasdair mac Colla sailed out of Waterford harbour on the south-east coast of Ireland with a small army of 2,000 men. The Marquis of Antrim and the Catholic leadership had decided that the best means of tipping the prosecution of the war in the king's favour was to foment rebellion in Scotland. And who better to do that than Alasdair mac Colla. Not only was he a Catholic Royalist, he was also a MacDonald who hated Clan Campbell, the Covenanting supporters of the English Parliamentarians. On board the ships were well-seasoned, well-armed, hardened soldiers led by captains they trusted and who understood the power of the Highland charge.

Montrose and his two companions rode north from Methven Woods to Blair Atholl to meet mac Colla and his men, but there was confusion, and potential conflict. The Robertsons and the Atholl clans had mustered at the appearance of the *crann tara* and they too were approaching Blair, but not to join mac Colla and his men, whom they saw as Irish raiders. When Montrose met Alasdair and announced himself as Lord Lieutenant, there was celebration. His coming had conferred political legitimacy on the Irish expedition and men threw their bonnets in the air. Some fired their muskets, a sound that nearly detonated a fight between mac Colla's men and the Perthshire clans who had come to oppose them. But the king's Lieutenant defused it, and also persuaded the Robertsons and the other chiefs to join him and mac Colla. Montrose was not a clansman, was therefore neutral and not beholden to anyone, as well as being an experienced soldier with the king's commission. No chief would have accepted another chief as their general, and so his leadership was immediately agreed.

On the morning of 1 September 1644, John Wemyss, Lord Elcho, led an army of Covenanters out of Perth and along the Old Gallows Road. About a mile away to the west, the Marquis of Montrose had arrayed his army near the hamlet of Tippermuir, and he rode up and down the lines of the clansmen and the Irish brigades under the command of Alasdair mac Colla. Montrose must have had Gaelic for he exhorted each company as he passed, promising them rich rewards as well as martial glory once they had defeated the Lowlanders. Here is an English translation of some lines he repeated to his men as they waited for battle: 'Be sparing of your powder, we have none to throw away. Let not a musket be fired except in the very face of the enemy. Give them but a single discharge and then at them with the claymores.'

It was a succinct precis of how the Irish charge should be executed.

The word of God was what the Covenanters heard. Ministers clutching their bibles walked up and down their ranks assuring them that it was God's work they would do and God's will that they would win. Banners fluttered above their heads with more words sewn into them. 'Death to the Enemies of the Covenant', and the grim and prophetic 'Jesus and No Quarter'. Might as well as right was on their side. Scouts from both sides will have been counting and they reported that the Covenanter army was much larger and had many more troops of cavalry.

Montrose's men had also looked closely at the ground on both sides of the Old Gallows Road and said it was firm and without obstacles, good ground to charge over. There was a slight incline but nothing to slow down the clansmen once the *claideamh mòr* had been roared out. And the day was bright, with no wind.

It may be that Lord Elcho suspected that the clans lacked powder and therefore firepower, for the opening action was a skirmish attack by his cavalry on Montrose's centre, where Alasdair mac Colla and his Irishmen stood. But even without the ability to fire musket volleys, these battle-hardened troops stood their ground and then drove back the Covenanter cavalry, causing confusion in the centre of their line. Montrose saw his chance and immediately ordered the *claideamh mòr*. When the wedges smashed into the enemy lines, the Covenanters buckled and then broke. Seeing his ranks penetrated in many places at once, Elcho may have suffered what modern soldiers call 'operational paralysis'. In those dithering moments of uncertainty, when no orders came, the Battle of Tippermuir was lost. As the Irishmen and the clansmen got behind the Covenanters, wide-eyed panic took hold and turned quickly into a headlong rout. As men fled back to Perth, throwing away their weapons, their only means of defence, a great slaughter began as the clansmen brought them down and hacked them to death, stripping their bodies for plunder. On 1 September 1644, the Irish charge became the Highland charge.

After their triumph at Tippermuir, Montrose and mac Colla fought a brilliant, stunning campaign in the north, winning five victories, always against the odds, using the new shock tactic of the highly disciplined charge. When the Royalist army reached Kilsyth in North Lanarkshire on 15 August 1645, their elan, their confidence, must have been sky-high. They were opposed by a large force of Covenanters augmented by new levies from Fife, but when these inexperienced men realised that they would have to face the Highland charge, many of them deserted. Some were rounded up by their officers and forced back to their camp.

The return of the reluctant levies made no difference. Even though many of the Irishmen had returned home, Montrose still had mac Colla and his own brigade. Highlanders now made up the bulk of the army and it was the charge of Clan MacLean that drove back the Covenanter cavalry. There is an early engraving of them fighting in their linen sarks against armoured troopers, but unfortunately the images of the great bravery of the charge are somewhat compromised by the fact that the artists made the clansmen look as though they were wearing flowing nightgowns. After Kilsyth, Montrose found himself master of Scotland, but the brilliant campaign and the immense achievement were fleeting. At the Battle of Naseby in

Northamptonshire, Charles I's army had been destroyed by Cromwell and Fairfax, and the Royalist cause in England lay in ruins. The bulk of the Scottish Covenanter forces had fought at Naseby with great distinction, and soon afterwards, they made their way north.

Montrose acted quickly, and marched south to try to rescue the situation, to come to the aid of the king. But the Highlanders would not go with him; their harvest needed to be ingathered and mac Colla went west to attack and raid Clan Campbell, the ancient enemies of Clan Donald. Only 500 Irishmen marched with Montrose to the Borders, but there were very few recruits to the cause in the south, and the small force, no longer an army, camped near Selkirk.

Hurrying north, at the head of 5,000 cavalry and with a thousand infantry, General David Leslie quickly reached Melrose, not far to the east of Selkirk, where he camped for the night. Scouts told him that Montrose and his men were at Philiphaugh, about a mile west of the town.

I know the ground well. On 13 September 1645, my little farm was in the midst of history. When General Leslie reached Selkirk early that morning, mist hung in scarves along the flanks of the Ettrick valley. He divided his forces and sent 2,000 cavalry troopers down the little valley where we live and work, while the remainder of the cavalry and the infantry moved towards Philiphaugh. Behind our farm rises Howden Hill and it would have hidden the horsemen from Montrose's lookouts. Or perhaps not, since some of the Covenanters rode through my fields. An expert metal detectorist has found a few mid-seventeenth-century coins, one of them a Charles I groat minted in 1645, and also some musket balls and a lump of the sort of lead that was melted down to make them. There may have been some sort of skirmish on the old track that marks our eastern boundary. In the seventeenth century it was the road from Selkirk to Hawick, and perhaps Montrose had sent out patrols.

Living as close to history as we do offers insight. Knowing the geography intimately, I understand why Leslie deployed his forces as he did. At the foot of our valley, his cavalry could turn east and outflank Montrose very quickly, which is exactly what happened.

But it's more than that, more than the coins and the musket balls. On autumn mornings when mist clings to the dense woods on either side of the road that snakes through our little valley, when there is a distant bleat of lambs from Howden Hill, I can hear the advance of Leslie's troopers, hear the low, drumming thunder of the horses' hooves, their whinnies and the whispered orders, the jingle of harness, the echoes of history.

At Philiphaugh there was slaughter. Overwhelmed by Leslie's army, Montrose cut himself out of the melee and escaped north into the hills. But the Irish Brigade suffered an appalling fate. Having fought bravely, most were killed in battle, but some surrendered on the promise of quarter, of being spared. Leslie granted it, but the firebrand Covenanter ministers disagreed. About a hundred soldiers and 300 camp followers, most of them women and children, were cruelly put to death. They were Catholics after all, seen as subhuman. It was a shocking, shameful episode, a permanent stain on Scotland's history.

Some years ago, I walked the ground near the battle site to look at a place that interested me. In 1810 excavations preparatory to the building of a school had uncovered many skeletal remains and it was said that skulls were washed down the Yarrow Water. Amongst the pine trees I found an unexpected stand of old yew trees and also a series of shallow pits. Yews are emblematic of graveyards, and perhaps it was more than tradition that named that place Slain Men's Lea.

The Highlanders who were absent at Philiphaugh had returned to their glens and straths to gather in the harvest and tend to their beasts. Just as the imaging of the charging clansman at Killiecrankie or Tippermuir is emblematic, there is another, much gentler icon that has come to symbolise life in the north, one that is recognised across the world.

*

He had his own Facebook page, a novel written about him, and when in 1996 his life was in danger, Hamish was rescued by a national campaign to save him – but no one seemed to call him by his right name. Hamish the Highland Cow was in fact a bull, the oldest bull ever to live in Britain, still munching grass and hay until he reached a venerable twenty-two. Having survived the threat of BSE, 'mad cow disease', he lived a contented life in fields next to the Trossachs Woollen Mill at Kilmahog, just north of Callander. Visitors stopped to look at him, petted him, took selfies with him because they all knew they were on the verge of elsewhere, about to move into the Highlands.

Hamish was emblematic. With his splendid horns, his shaggy, russet-coloured coat and his long fringe almost completely obscuring his eyes, the old bull was an image indelibly associated with the Highlands. Along with caber tossers, pipe bands and all things tartan, 'Hielan' Coos' appeared on thousands of biscuit tin lids, and on a sticky wrapper for toffee I was particularly fond of as a child who had not yet learned to care about his teeth. He was also a bovine version of *fàilte*, 'welcome', for Hamish grazed in fields that lie almost precisely on the Highland Boundary Fault. Immediately to the north-west, the A84 climbs up through the Pass of Leny, moving in a matter of minutes from one world into another, from Lowland to Highland. The mountains rise steeply, still capped with snow in May, and soon the road follows the shore of Loch Lubnaig before plunging into the Strathtyre Forest.

In the middle of the seventeenth century, when cattle droving from the Highlands to the Lowlands became an important business, thousands of cows travelled in the opposite direction – but they were not all like Hamish. Kyloes were smaller, black cattle that were bred in the Hebrides. Their name derives from *caol*, the Gaelic word for 'a narrow strait or sound', anglicised as kyle. In my lifetime, the breed was still seen in the Borders, known as 'kylie bullocks'. The little black cattle had to swim across these Hebridean stretches of water, something that can be difficult to imagine now. One of the most famous crossings was from Kylerhea on Skye to Glenelg on the mainland. It was an ancient journey, as shown in this relatively late record, from 1808:

All the cattle reared in the Isle of Skye, which are sent to the southern markets, pass from that island to the mainland by the ferry of Caol-rea [Kylerhea]. Their numbers are very considerable; by some supposed to be five thousand, but by others eight thousand, annually; and the method of ferrying them is not in boats . . . but they are forced to swim over Caol-rea. For this purpose the drovers purchase ropes, which are cut at the length of three feet, having a noose at one end. The noose is put round the under jaw of every cow, taking care to leave the tongue free. The reason given for leaving the tongue loose is, that the animal may be able to keep the salt water from going down its throat in such a quantity as to fill the cavities in the body, which would prevent the action of the lungs; for every beast is found dead, and said to be drowned at the landing place, to which this mark of attention has not been paid. Whenever the noose is put upon the jaw, all the beasts destined to be ferried together, are led by the ferryman into the water until they are afloat, which puts an end to their resistance. Then every cow is tied to the tail of the cow before [in front], until a string of six or eight be formed; a man in the stern of the boat holds the rope of the foremost cow. The rowers then ply their oars immediately. During the time of high water, or soon before or after full tide, is the most favourable passage, because the current is then least violent. The ferrymen are so dexterous, that very few beasts are lost.

These dangerous, remarkable and risky crossings were made because from the seventeenth century onwards, cattle production became the Highlands and Islands' most lucrative business, virtually the sole source of cash in a rural, largely barter economy. Since the beginning of the Little Ice Age in the fourteenth century, pastoral farming had become increasingly dominant north of the Highland Boundary Fault and Hamish's green fields.

Once across the straits, having swum against their strong currents, the cows were untied, they shook off their seawater and were herded together at Glenelg for the drove into the mountains. Ten years ago, I decided to follow them for part of the way if I could navigate these signless green roads through the glens and high valleys. Having parked at Glenelg and shouldered my pack under glowering, threatening skies, I walked up to the brochs at Dun Telve and Dun Troddan. They are massive fragments. Dun Telve's circular wall rises to more than thirty feet, only Mousa on Shetland is higher, but stone robbing to build barracks nearby at Bernera reduced Dun Troddan to only twenty feet or so. The brochs are wonderfully well preserved, and unusual, being only 500 yards from each other. An Glinne Bheag, 'the Little Glen', is steep-sided and seems to lean over these ancient towers standing sentinel by the single-track road to Balvraid.

There had been a smirr in the air, a fine rain of invisibly small droplets, what Edward Dwelly noted as *braon*, 'rain like dew'. I remember turning several times to look behind at the sky, having felt a freshening west wind blow up over the shore at Glenelg. The clouds were dark, gunmetal grey thunderheads billowing off the Atlantic to be pierced by the jagged Cuillin ridge as they rolled over Skye. In moments, the *braon* became a downpour, the gentle dewdrops followed by a drenching, slounging rainstorm. I ran to Dun Telve broch and crawled under the massive lintel of the entrance for shelter. I watched *dòirt*, the rain spill out of the sky, bucketing, splashing on the gravel on the floor of the broch. But the work of the drystane builders had worn well and their great stones kept me dry.

Just as suddenly as the downpour came, the sky cleared and the sun sparkled off the glistening trees and the well-washed grass. Keeping to the road to have dry feet for as long as possible, for even my good boots would not have kept out the wet from the saturated ground, I passed Balvraid Farm and followed a track that led to the pass between Beinn nan Caorach and the Saddle. Almost immediately I could see exactly where the drovers and their dogs had pushed on the cows to begin their journey through the mountains.

On the floor of the rising ground of the glen, I could make out something extraordinary, lit by the brilliant sun, clear traces of a trail that had not been followed for 150 years. The dull bracken and heather of the mountainsides seemed to stop abruptly at the edges of a series of lush and very green patches of grass, luminous after the morning rain. These oases are not botanical freaks, a species of lime-green grass that flourishes naturally. They are man-made, or rather, cattle-made. Each night, when the drovers halted the herd, they always halted in the same places. Not out of habit but because of necessity. To sustain them on the long journey the herds needed good overnight grazing, and it also helped to persuade them not to stray too far in the darkness. Because the cattle had halted in the same places for many decades, they dropped their muck and it fertilised the eaten-down grass shoots so that it would come away even more lush the following spring. Every ten or twelve miles on the drove roads through the mountain passes, these wide patches of grass are found, memories of the hundreds of thousands of animals that were taken south to market.

It was important for the drovers to keep their cows on grass or heather. The animals had been raised on summer and winter pasture and their feet were soft. Roads were to be avoided because a lame beast slowed the whole drove, and often it would have to be slaughtered. The herders would eat well for a few days, as would the dogs who gorged themselves on the offal, but the loss of a cow was a loss of income. Until the coming of the railways in the middle of the nineteenth century, all animals walked to market.

In the late summer of 1762, Robert Forbes, Episcopalian bishop of Ross and Caithness (who lived in Edinburgh most of the time), was travelling north to visit his own flock when he came across a herd moving south. Forbes was much impressed with the skill of the Highland drovers:

> They had four or five horses with provisions for themselves [pack horses] by the way, particularly blankets to wrap themselves in when sleeping in the open air, as they rest on the bleak mountains, the heathy moors, or the verdant glens, just as it happens, towards the evening. They tend their flocks [herds] by night and never move until about eight in the morning and then march the cattle at leisure that they may feed a little as they go along.

They rest awhile at midday to take some dinner and so let the cattle feed and rest as they please. The proprietor [owner] does not travel with the cattle but has one [man] for his deputy to command the whole and he goes to the place appointed against the day fixed for the fair [market]. When the flock is very large, as the present, they divide it, though belonging to one, into several droves that they may not hurt one another [with their horns] in narrow places, particularly on bridges many of which they go along. Each drove has a particular number of men with some boys to look after the cattle.

Once a stance had been reached and the cows began to graze the lush grass, the older men dismounted their shaggy ponies and set about making camp. They had done the drove many times and knew the best places to find kindling to make a fire, keeping it smoky to discourage the late summer midges. There would be a good, cool and clear stream nearby so that ponies, people and cows could drink. Pack saddles were pulled off the pack horses and laid beside the others around the fire for something to lean on when they sat down at last. Untacked ponies will have rolled in the grass to scratch and when they stood, they shook vigorously to fluff out their thick coats for the night chill. With long crooks to prod and whack the rumps of the cows, herd-laddies were sent out with the dogs around the edges of the herd to make sure none strayed too far or were tempted by the luxuriant grass that sometimes hid boggy ground. Men mixed oatmeal with water from the stream. When a flat stone in the fire was hot enough it would be raked out to one side. When the flat oatcakes were baked and hunks of hard cheese handed out with any berries or wild fruit that might have been foraged along the way, most of the drovers sat in the circle of firelight while the herd-laddies stayed out on point. Some sort of rotation of watches will have been set so that they too could eat and rest.

On calm, sunlit autumn evenings, droving will have seemed like a good life. As the dark shapes of the snuffling cows shifted around in the shadows of the stance behind them, some of them gently lowing, others grazing, some dozing, men and their boys might have looked out to the west in the mountains to gaze on the glories of a Highland sunset, its colours red-gold, its glow lighting the undersides of the horizon clouds, its warmth slowly sinking over the distant ocean.

It was a long time since wolves had howled in the glens, but there were other predators to worry about. Cattle on the move were easier to steal, but there is evidence of a system of safe passage through different clan lands being in force – at a price. Nevertheless, the drovers carried weapons – dirks, swords, pistols, even muskets – and in the Disarming Acts brought into force in the Highlands after the Jacobite risings of the eighteenth century, they were specifically exempted. The cattle trade was far too important to the business of supplying the British army and navy with salt beef.

Having settled hungry cows on the same stances for many decades, the older men knew where to bivouac out of the wind, and if there was night rain, places where a little shelter might be found. But the autumn weather in the mountains can often be dry and even warm until the darkness brings a chill air. In the circle of firelight stories were told, tales of former droves, of what sort of strange people the Lowlanders and the English dealers were, of the fun, the daftness and sometimes the dangers of moving cattle though wild country. And if the mood took them, some men could sing or recite the great epics, the exploits of Cúchulainn and Finn McCuil, the Irish warrior-heroes. Or tales could be told of prowess, of clan battles fought, won and lost. Gaelic speakers lived in an overwhelmingly oral culture where little was written down and much was remembered and could be called to mind. Ballads such as the one celebrating the exploits of Alasdair mac Colla had choruses that all around the campfire could sing. They gave the leading singer time to remember the next verse and the metre or rhythm, clapped or beaten, was also an aid to memory.

As the flames of the fire died away to the red glow of embers and the dogs came close to lie beside the men and warm them, the darkness fell at last and another day in the mountains waited for the drovers and their herds.

To the north of the Perthshire town of Crieff runs a green-crested track that leads down to Dalpatrick Ford across the River Earn. On the far side, the mountains rise steeply and seem to present an impenetrable barrier. On the narrow floodplain below them runs another green track known as the Highlandman's Loan. It leads north-east to the Sma' Glen and the course of the River Almond. When drovers reached the river, it was close to journey's end, the centre of a web of roads that patterned the landscape. The cattle were driven down to Crieff for the annual tryst held in October. The fields and hillsides surrounding the town must have been black with herds of grazing cows as about 30,000 were sold to dealers from the south. All of this activity made the little town a uniquely busy financial centre as more money was expended there than anywhere else in Scotland, more than in Edinburgh or Glasgow, as buyers and sellers hit hands as they struck a bargain.

As the British Empire began to form and expand, salted beef was needed in great quantities for soldiers and sailors, and demand mushroomed. Because it was nearer to England, the main tryst moved to Falkirk, and an account written in 1849, just before the coming of the railways changed everything, by Thomas Gisborne supplied a great deal of colourful detail about what had gone on for almost two centuries when Highland cattle were sold:

[At Falkirk, people] will there witness a scene to which certainly Great Britain, perhaps even the whole world, does not afford a parallel . . . here are three trysts every year – the first in August, the second in September, and the last and largest in October. The cattle stand in a field in the parish of Larbert at a distance of nearly three miles from Falkirk, at a place called Stenhousemuir. The field on which they assemble contains above two hundred acres, well-fenced and in every way adapted for the purpose. The scene, seen from horseback, from a cart, or some erection, is particularly imposing. All is animation, bustle, business and activity; servants running about shouting to the cattle, keeping them together in their particular lots and ever and anon cudgels are at work upon the horns and rumps of the restless animals that attempt to wander in search of grass or water.

The cattle dealers of all descriptions, chiefly on horseback, are scouring the field in search of the lots they require. The Scottish drovers are for the most part mounted on small, shaggy, spirited ponies that are obviously quite at home amongst the cattle; and they carry their riders through the throngest groups [of cattle] with astonishing alacrity. The English dealers have, in general, large, stout horses, and they pace the ground with more caution, surveying every lot carefully as they go along. When they discover the cattle they want, they enquire the price. A good deal of riggling [wonderful word for negotiating] takes place, and when the parties come to an agreement, the purchaser claps a penny of arles [a deposit] into the hand of the stockholder, observing at the same time 'It's a bargain'. Tar dishes are then got, and the purchaser's mark being put upon the cattle, they are driven from the field. Besides numbers of shows, from sixty to seventy tents are erected along the field for selling spirits and provisions . . . what an indescribable clamour prevails in most of these party-coloured abodes.

Far in the afternoon, when frequent calls have elevated the spirits and stimulated the colloquial powers of the visitors, a person hears the uncouth Cumberland jargon and the prevailing Gaelic, along with innumerable provincial dialects in their genuine purity, mingled in one astounding roar. All seem inclined to speak: and raising their voices to command attention, the whole of the orators are obliged to bellow as loudly as they can possibly roar. When the cattle dealers are in the way of their business, their conversation is full of animation, and their technical phrases are generally appropriate and highly amusing.

It sounds like an extraordinary and indeed amusing (what does 'technical phrases' mean exactly?) melee, the meeting of two different cultures animated by money and whisky.

The trysts were not the end of the line for the cattle. To be successfully salted only the beef of fat cattle will do (fat interacts with the salt to make an effective preservative), and so the herds were moved south to the lush, late autumn pastures of Lincolnshire and East Anglia before being taken down to Smithfield in London. Sometimes the Highland drovers were engaged to move the herds south. When they had been settled on good grass, the men often took ship back north, easily the fastest means of travel. But to save money and trouble, they left their dogs behind to find their own way home. And they did. Moving up through England and Lowland Scotland, retracing their steps, these faithful, intelligent animals returned to the mountains and glens. Packs of pastoral dogs were seen moving through English villages, and they would be recognised by landlords who had given the drovers lodging on the way down. These men fed the animals and let them sleep in stables, knowing they would be repaid the following year.

*

In 1631, Georg Coler, a German engraver, arrived at Stettin on the Baltic Sea coast of what is now Poland. One of the longest and most brutal ever fought in Europe, the Thirty Years War, was at its height. Primarily a conflict between the Protestant forces of Sweden, Denmark and Holland, with French support, and the great Catholic Habsburg Empire in Germany and Spain, it caused the deaths of 5–8 million people, both soldiers and civilians. One of the leading protagonists was King Gustavus Adolphus of Sweden and his army laid siege to the important port of Stettin in the imperial duchy of Pomerania. Coler had heard that the Swedish king had hired 800 mercenary soldiers who looked very different from the rest of his army, and he wanted to draw them.

The resulting engraving is one of the very earliest to show what Highlanders looked like when they went to war. On a ridge above a battle scene with the buildings of a port (probably Stettin) beyond the ranks of marching soldiers and ships at anchor in the Baltic Sea, four men stand in a line, clearly posing for the artist. They are not stereotypes but portraits of individuals, for each face and physique is different. Three are wearing the great plaid, but each in different styles. The square-checked pattern is identical on each and it mimics the look of tartan as well as a monochrome engraving could.

The man on the farthest left wears his plaid belted at the waist and slung over his left shoulder. Like all the others, he has no sporran. Second left is a shorter man. The only one who is clean-shaven, he looks decidedly younger. He wears tartan trews that are baggy above the knee but caught up by garters so that on his lower legs, they are tight, like stockings. The man beside him wears his plaid over both shoulders, like a coat, and only his hands are visible through the fold at the front. He is also the only one who wears no shoes. Beside him the fourth man has belted his plaid and slung the rest of it over his right shoulder from where it hangs down his back like a cloak.

It is clear that Georg Coler asked these men how the plaid was worn, and they showed him. The young man's trews were simply another variation. In the background, between the two men on the right, a detachment of Highlanders wearing kilts can be seen, and although the detail is blurry, they seem to have their plaids tightly belted like the man on the farthest left in the foreground. They will have wanted no loose or flapping cloth to encumber them in battle. Perhaps all except the man in the trews cast off their plaids before they fought, although that seems unlikely.

These four portraits may be the earliest certain depiction of the kilt, what was known as *an fèileadh mor*, 'the big kilt'. It was worn, as Coler showed, in various styles but in essence it was a big blanket that could be used to keep the wearer warm as they bivouacked in the open. Edward Dwelly emphasises the meaning of *fèileadh* as a 'wrap'. *An fèileadh beag*, 'the small kilt', is a relatively recent invention, or evolution. An entertaining tale has Thomas Rawlinson, an Englishman, of all people, take a leading role when he came to the Highlands after the 1715 Jacobite Rising to set up an ironworks. Having noticed that the men who worked for him wore 'a cumbersome, unwieldy habit', the big kilt, he decided to invent the small kilt 'and make it handy and convenient'. Perhaps he did. Either way, it is true that a shorter piece of cloth was worn belted at the waist in the eighteenth century and after then. Now when men wish to wear something like *an fèileadh mòr*, they wear what is called a separate fly plaid secured on the shoulder with a large, very masculine, brooch. Incidentally, kilt as a verb, meaning to hitch up or gather up cloth, as in 'she kilted up her skirt', and was originally derived from a Norse word.

Two of the Highlanders at Stettin carry bows and quivers of arrows, and one has a short sword or more likely a long dirk in its scabbard belted at the waist. The younger man and the individual on the far right also have sheathed dirks but the latter holds a long rod in one hand with its tip resting on the ground. It is difficult to make out what it is; a long, thin sword or a staff. Perhaps he is an officer with an early version of a swagger stick.

Coler's headline above the figures is a surprisingly casual mistake. In German Gothic black letter, he calls them Irish soldiers. In fact they were part of a contingent of 800 Highlanders who fought as mercenaries for King Gustavus Adolphus in the Thirty Years War, and they were only a small proportion of the very large number who did. Between 1618 and 1648, when a peace treaty was at last brokered in Europe, the Scottish Privy Council sanctioned the recruitment of more than 50,000 young men, about a fifth of that demographic in Scotland, by European armies. Elizabeth, Queen of Bohemia, found herself in the midst of the hostilities and she was the daughter of King James VI and I. Her brother, Charles I, was much motivated to help, and the involvement and encouragement of Scottish, and English, mercenaries was one way of achieving that.

In 1626 Donald MacKay, Chief of Clan MacKay, raised a regiment of 3,000 soldiers, mainly from the eastern Highlands, and embarked with them at Cromarty, bound for Denmark to fight in the service of King Christian IV. Five years later, MacKay led a force of 800 to Stettin where four of his men were drawn by Georg Coler. Perhaps he is the man on the right with the swagger stick. The caption under the engraving is further testimony to the Highlanders' 'hardihood in time of strife' hymned by Lachlan Mór MacMhuirich before the Battle of Harlaw: 'They are a strong and hardy people who survive on little food. If they have no bread, they eat roots. When necessary, they can cover twenty German miles in a day's forced march. Besides muskets, they carry bows, quivers and long swords.'

Clan Munro was also very active in the armies of King Gustavus Adolphus. Remarkably, three Munros served the Swedish king as generals, eight as colonels, five as lieutenant colonels and thirty as captains. The chief of the clan, Major Robert Munro, sailed with MacKay's men in 1626. At the siege of Stralsund, another port on the Baltic coast of what is now Germany, he commanded a force of his own clansmen who distinguished themselves by their bravery and resolution. The great Habsburg general, Albrecht von Wallenstein, mounted a night attack on the city and was repulsed by the Munros despite being greatly outnumbered and eventually running out of ammunition and powder. Repeated charges with swords, pikes and musket butts forced Wallenstein to withdraw having lost a thousand men compared to only two hundred casualties for the Munros. After the siege, Major Munro became Lieutenant Colonel Munro.

An Englishman from Devon, George Monck, fought as a mercenary in the long-running struggle between the emerging Dutch Republic and the Habsburg Empire who claimed the Spanish Netherlands as a colony. At the outset of the War of the Three Kingdoms he was a Royalist, but, after Charles I surrendered in 1646, he transferred his allegiance to the Parliamentary cause. Oliver Cromwell appointed Monck as military commander in Scotland in 1652, but when the Lord Protector died six years later, and the authority of his son, Richard, quickly disintegrated, George realised that he was in a very powerful, pivotal position. In February 1660, he led his army to Coldstream on the border, where he raised the famous regiment of foot guards and marched south to London to enable the Restoration of Charles II to the Crown of Great Britain and Ireland. On this journey into the midst of history, General Monck had a surprising travelling companion.

In 1647, Ewen Cameron of Lochiel became the chief of the name, and six years later he joined the Glencairn rising, what may be seen as the first Jacobite rising. It was a shambolic, almost farcical affair. Although 5,000 rallied to the royal standard, there were festering

resentments between Highland clansmen and the Lowland noblemen and officers who attempted to command them. To make matters
worse, John Middleton, a veteran of the Battle of Worcester in 1651
when Charles II was defeated, arrived with the king's commission to
take over from the Earl of Glencairn. With him was George Munro,
the uncle of Robert, recently returned from Europe, and he insulted
Glencairn and his soldiers. The pair fought a duel and Munro was
wounded. The following day two more officers fought another duel.
One was killed and the other arrested and hanged. At Dalnaspidal,
near Loch Garry, General Monck's army attacked the squabbling
Jacobites in the summer of 1654 and scattered them.

Resentments continued to burn fiercely. When Ewen Cameron
came across a party of Parliamentary soldiers foraging for firewood in
his forest on the shores of Loch Eil, he immediately attacked them.
An English officer pinned Cameron to the ground, but the chief bit
the man's throat and did not let go until he had torn out his wind-
pipe. It was later said it was 'the sweetest bite he ever had'. Despite
all his fabled, feral savagery, Lochiel was warmly received in London
by Charles II on his arrival with Monck's army.

For once, Clan Campbell found themselves on the wrong side
of history. In February 1685, the openly Catholic James VII and II
succeeded his brother, Charles II. There was no legitimate heir, but
one of the dead king's illegitimate children, James Scott, Duke of
Monmouth, raised the standard of rebellion. Having landed at Lyme
Regis on the English Channel coast, he quickly gathered support,
but his largely untrained army was decisively defeated a month later
at Sedgemoor in Somerset. On 15 July, Monmouth was beheaded for
treason.

While in exile in Holland, the duke had been convinced by
Archibald Campbell, Earl of Argyll, that a coordinated invasion of
Britain would succeed, and that James VII and II could be deposed.
Even though he was an illegitimate child, the Protestant Monmouth
should be king. But, like him, Campbell failed to ignite meaningful
rebellion, even in the clanlands of Kintyre and Argyll. The earl was
captured at Inchinnan on the Clyde, and taken for questioning and

certain execution in Edinburgh. Campbell appears to have been genuinely rather than politically devout, facing his death on the maiden, a form of guillotine, with equanimity. In his short speech on the scaffold set up at the Mercat Cross, he joked that the falling blade would be his 'inlet to glory' and it was 'the sweetest maiden that he had ever kissed'.

Perhaps the most feckless of a feckless dynasty – only James VI and I seemed to have any grasp of the realities of politics – James VII and II was eventually deposed in 1688. William of Orange, the husband of James' daughter, Mary, was blown by a 'Protestant wind' along the Channel coast to Brixham where an invasion force landed. Unlike Monmouth, William and Mary were widely supported. James' authority began to crumble and then suddenly collapsed. In December 1688, he fled into an exile from which the Stuarts never returned.

On 18 March 1689, James Graham of Claverhouse, Viscount Dundee, climbed up the steep western face of Edinburgh Castle rock to talk to the Duke of Gordon, who was holding the great fortress for the exiled king. Earlier that day, Dundee had attended a meeting of the Convention of Estates, a version of the Scottish Parliament, to determine who should wear the crown of Scotland. The political philosophy of George Buchanan had laid down a clear framework for discussion, and it appeared to Dundee that the barons, burghs and the bishops were going to depose James VII and pass the crown to his daughter, Mary, and her husband, William of Orange.

With fifty loyal dragoons to ensure his safety, Dundee had left the meeting in the High Street and ridden out of the West Port. Halfway up the rock, at the foot of the castle walls, there is a black, cast-iron postern gate, and inside it the Duke of Gordon was waiting. Dundee exhorted him to hold the castle as long as he could. For his part, he would ride north to raise the clans in support of the rightful king, James VII and II. Not for the last time would Highlanders become centrally involved in the fate of the British state.

At Tippermuir no eyewitness had left a written testimony, but thirty-five years later, the first battle in the Jacobite rising of 1689 was well documented. Donald McBane had been bored at his work as a tobacco spinner in Inverness, and longed for a more eventful life. After volunteering as a private in the government militia known as the Highland companies, he got his wish when a government army mustered to oppose the Jacobites.

Having raised the clans, Dundee marched south to the Pass of Killiecrankie, a strategically vital artery that led from the mountains into lowland Perthshire. With him was Ewen Cameron, no doubt armed to the teeth, as well as MacDonalds, MacLeans and other western clans.

Watching the Highlanders advance and take up a dominating position above the government army so that they had *cothrom a' bhraigh*, was an unlikely chronicler of the drama that was about to burst over the meadow beyond the pass. Private Donald McBane's company marched with the army from Dunkeld to Killiecrankie, and as he waited for battle to be joined, he knew what was coming. Almost forty years later, in a memoir entitled *The Expert Sword-Man's Companion*, Private McBane set down what he saw on the braes of Killiecrankie: 'We gave them a shout, daring them, as it were, to advance, which they quickly did, to our great loss.' When the charging Highlanders ran within range, perhaps fifty to seventy metres, 'we could only fire three shots apiece'.

These volleys did great damage. Around 600 clansmen were killed or wounded in the charge, but the musket fire did not check them. McBane remembered why they came on when they did, 'the sun going down caused the Highlandmen to advance on us like mad men, without shoe or stocking, covering themselves from our fire with their targes . . . they drew their broad swords, advanced furiously upon us, and were in the middle of us'.

In his memoir, Ewen Cameron of Lochiel wrote of a strange, eerie pause in the midst of the battle when his men 'fell in pell-mell among the thick of them with the broadswords. After this, the noise seemed hushed; and the firing ceasing on both sides, nothing was heard for some moments but the sullen and hollow clashes of broadswords with the dismal groans and cries of dying and wounded men'.

The Highlanders swept the government army off the field and as ever many were cut down in the flight. But not Private McBane:

I fled to the baggage [train] and took a horse, in order to ride the water. There followed me a Highlandman with sword and targe, in order to take the horse and kill myself, you'd laugh to see how he and I scampered about; I kept always the horse between him and me. At length he drew his pistol and I fled, he fired after me; I went above the pass, where I met with another water [the River Garry as opposed to the Allt Girnaig], very deep, it was about eighteen feet over betwixt two rocks, I resolved to jump it, so I laid down my gun and hat, and jumped and lost one of my shoes on the jump . . . The enemy pursuing hard I made the best of my way to Dunkeld, where I stayed till what of our men was left came up.

One of the most popular viewpoints in the Pass of Killiecrankie is the Soldier's Leap. Across the gorge of the gushing River Garry, McBane did indeed jump a little over eighteen feet. In 1901, the world record long jump was made by Peter O'Connor of Ireland at twenty-five feet, and he landed in sand. How much further would he have jumped if he had been chased by a hairy Highlander?

Killiecrankie was a stunning victory for the clans and their much-feared charge, but it was a disaster for the Jacobite cause. As he rode around the field to places where some desultory fighting continued, Dundee was shot out of the saddle. To the disgust of Ewen Cameron, he was not made commander-in-chief, because as he well knew, the other chiefs would not accept another chief in that role.

Colonel Alexander Cannon led those Highlanders who remained to Dunkeld where they laid siege to the strategically pivotal town, but its narrow streets and the walls of the cathedral precinct prevented them from deploying the devastating Highland charge. They were forced to withdraw and the first serious Jacobite rising eventually fizzled out.

II

Na Seumasaich

1689–1745

'The James Men' is the literal translation of Na Seumasaich, but more commonly it means the Jacobites. Their aims and the armed struggle to achieve them were to dominate the story of the Highlands and Islands for generations after the fighting at Killiecrankie and Dunkeld.

The use of the name of James for seven kings is shot through with metaphor and even prophecy. It is a biblical name and two of Christ's apostles bore it: St James the Greater and St James the Lesser. They were not related and their involvement at the beginnings of Christianity seems to suggest the name was common at that time. James in turn derives from Jacob, rendered in the original Hebrew form as Ya'aqob. According to the Book of Genesis, the first Jacob was the twin brother of Esau, the second son of Isaac and the grandson of Abraham, the founding prophet who climbed Mount Sinai to receive the tablets of stone, the Ten Commandments, from God.

It was said that Jacob was born gripping the heel of his brother, Esau, who emerged first from his mother's womb, and was therefore firstborn and the eldest. It was as though Jacob was trying to pull his brother back so that he would be the first to be born. Resentment simmered and grew with age, and, in the Book of Genesis, Esau is said to have come from a day's hard work in the fields, tired and famished, to ask his brother for food. In return for 'a mess of pottage' Jacob demanded that Esau give up his birthright, that is, the right to be recognised as the firstborn. In Hebrew, Jacob's name means something like 'the replacement', 'the supplanter' or 'the one who follows'.

In the fourteenth century, stories from the Bible were very familiar to very many people whether they were literate or not, and when Queen Anabella, the wife of Robert III of Scotland, decided to christen her son as James, a name rare in Scotland before 1394, she may have intended the latter meaning. James I was Anabella's last child, born when she was forty-three or forty-four, and no one expected him to become king. But his older brothers, David and Robert, died young and the queen may have intended the name to carry the meanings it has in Hebrew. The third in line, the replacement of the replacement, succeeded to the throne of Scotland in 1406.

With its terminal 's', like Charles and Giles, James was originally an Old French name. Jacques more closely derives from the original Jacob, or Ya'aqob. James may have been given a French name as an acknowledgement of a Norman-French heritage on his mother's side. Her grandfather was Sir William de Montifex or Montefichet. More biblical resonances echoed when James I's queen, Joan, gave birth to twins in 1430. Alexander, the firstborn, died at birth and his brother, the second born, succeeded as James II. As much as continuity after five Jameses on the throne, all of that heritage, from her own family, her marriage to the King of France, and the Old Testament may have motivated Mary, Queen of Scots to name her son James in 1566. Even though the unmarried Elizabeth I had another thirty-seven years to reign in England, there was more than an outside chance that her cousin's son might succeed her, might be the replacement, the one who follows.

*

A series of fascinating engravings supply a very early scene-setter, showing clearly and in considerable detail what the landscape of the Highlands looked like, and what the Highlanders were fighting for.

John Slezer was an unlikely Jacobite. Born a Dutchman, he was appointed Surveyor of His Majesty's Stores and Magazines (of weapons and gunpowder) in 1669. This involved a good deal of travel around Scotland looking at fortifications. In 1688 Slezer was promoted to Captain of the Artillery Company but was almost immediately imprisoned as a supporter of James VII and II. Released a year later, he began work on his magnum opus, *Theatrum Scotiae. Containing the Prospects of Their Majesties Castles and Palaces: Together with those of the most considerable Towns and Colleges; The ruins of many Ancient Abbeys, Churches, Monasteries and Convents*. This splendid book of meticulously detailed engravings is one of the earliest snapshots of Scotland to survive, and what it shows is fascinating.

Slezer's 'Prospect of the Town of Dunkeld', exhibits no sign of the damage caused by the siege of 1689. Much of the town was burned but all the houses shown in Cathedral Street have roofs, and amidst leafy trees and against the background of the mountains, the place has a settled air. Intense fighting raged around a grand house, a residence of the Marquis of Atholl, but Slezer drew a very intact and substantial three-storied mansion with eight windows on each floor and a decorative lantern on the roof. Perhaps it was taken from an earlier drawing made on Slezer's travels around Scotland before 1689. His caption is '*Prospectus Civitatis Calidoniae*', an indication of some scholarship since it is a direct Latin translation of what might have been a Pictish place name – Dunkeld was 'the Dun', the fortress of the Caledonians. In the *Theatrum Scotiae*, there is also an engraving of Dunkeld Cathedral (oddly misspelled as 'Dunkell') that may have been made after the siege since the old church looks slightly different from the representation in the wider prospect and there are some signs of slight damage.

Another cathedral on the fringes of the Highlands shows very considerable and well-documented damage. The roofless ruins of Elgin Cathedral remember the attacks of the Wolf of Badenoch, Alexander Stewart, in the fourteenth century but the rest of the town looks prosperous and extensive. When Daniel Defoe, the author of *Robinson Crusoe* and part-time English spy in Edinburgh before the Union of 1707, was touring Scotland, he enjoyed his visit to Elgin:

As the country is rich and pleasant, so here are a great many rich inhabitants, and in the town of Elgin in particular; for the gentlemen, as if this was the Edinburgh, or the court, for this part of the island, leave their Highland habitations in the winter and come and live here for the diversion of the place and plenty of provisions; and there is, on this account, a great variety of gentlemen for society, and that of all parties, and of all opinions. This makes Elgin a very agreeable place to live in, notwithstanding its distance, being above 450 measured miles from London, and more, if we must go by Edinburgh.

Much of Slezer's engraving shows the farmland to the south of the town, with the River Lossie winding its way to the Moray Firth and the sea. But there are no fields. Instead, the gently undulating landscape is open, patterned with the long, unfenced, serpentine lines of runrig cultivation. All over the Highlands and Islands, from Shetland to Kintyre, fertile ground was ploughed and sown in the same way. Ox-teams of often six or eight beasts dragged the old Scots plough, almost all made from wood and very inefficient, to make long furrows in narrow strips. These were bordered by drainage ditches and in Slezer's engraving, these lead down to the banks of the River Lossie. The rigs or ridges were usually between eighteen and thirty-six feet wide, depending on the nature of the terrain. They were always mounded to make a crown so that rainwater ran off into the parallel ditches on either side. This shape was achieved by consistently having the furrow-slice of the plough face inwards to build up the crown. Women and children followed behind the ox-team to pull out weeds and bash down big clods of earth because the ploughshare was flat-sided and did not turn over the furrow-slice completely. What made the rigs outside Elgin s-shaped was the wide turn that the ox-teams needed to make when they reached the end of these long strips.

Once the rigs had been raked, or harrowed if one was to hand, to make a seed bed, the oats were cast (and also barley around Elgin) by a man scattering them in a consistent rhythm from side to side. It is the origin of the word 'broadcasting'. At harvest time, depending on the width of the rig, three or four shearers could work line abreast, always using sickles. Scythes were used mostly to cut hay. Behind the line of shearers, the bandsters followed, gathering up the cut stalks into sheaves before stooking them on the stubble to let the wind dry them. When the very last rig was sheared and stooked, there was celebration. In Scots it was 'hairst hame', or *deireadh buana* in Gaelic, 'harvest home' in English.

Slezer shows what might have been farm buildings on the edges of his engraving. One has a mill to grind the oats and barley, its wheel just visible over a mill lade cut upstream from the River Lossie. On the far bank of the river is the semicircle of a wide fish net set out in the current and a man in a rowing boat waits near it. In the foreground another man, who might be a shepherd, walks with his dog into the hills to the south of the town. It is a picture of a settled, productive life on the edge of the Highlands.

*

It was winter in Glencoe. In the half darkness of December 1691, Alasdair MacIain, twelfth Chief of the MacDonalds of Glencoe, was riding through the snow to the new fort named after King William. Known to his people as Alasdair Ruadh because of his red hair, he was said to have been a giant of a man, a warrior who had charged down the brae at Killiecrankie in the summer of 1689. But MacIain was old, perhaps seventy, perhaps more, and his red hair had long ago become a white mane.

The snow was deep, still falling and on a bitter morning the chief led his shaggy garron to the ferryboat at Ballachulish. Having coaxed the little horse onto the swaying boat, the chief pulled his plaid tight around his shoulders as the icy wind blew in off the waters of Loch Linnhe. No one with any sense would have strayed far from the warmth of their fireside on such a stormy December day, but MacIain had urgent business with his friend, Lieutenant Colonel John Hill, the commander of the government garrison at Fort William.

In a society based not on pieces of paper but on trust, honesty and interlocking obligations, oaths mattered. King William of Orange rightly believed that if the western chiefs would swear an oath of allegiance to him after the rising of 1689, it would matter, and would have some purchase on them. An oath sworn to the king would also have the effect of granting them formal pardons for their parts in the rising, and a substantial cash payment to each might help to smooth the process.

The difficulty for MacIain, Ewen Cameron of Lochiel, Donald MacDonald of Glengarry and the others, was that they had already sworn oaths of allegiance to another king, James VII and II. And a deadline had been set by John Dalrymple, the Master of Stair and William III's secretary of state for Scotland. Oaths had to be sworn in front of a magistrate before 1 January 1692. The chiefs sent urgent word to the exiled Stuart court at St Germain-en-Laye near Paris, to seek release from their sworn allegiance. But, as usual, there was fecklessness and dithering. As days and weeks passed, and autumn gave way to winter, no word came back from France. It was not until mid-December, when the weather was closing in around the mountains and the sea lochs, that a messenger arrived with a grant of permission for the chiefs. They could swear allegiance to King William III, the usurper.

When MacIain at last reached Fort William, Lieutenant Colonel Hill could not help. To be valid, the oath had to be sworn before a magistrate, a sheriff of the Crown and no one else. Hill was sorry but MacIain would have to ride to Inverary, a very long way to the south. What neither man knew was that other plans had been laid.

Hill gave the old chief a letter of protection and also some reassurance. If the weather prevented him from reaching Inverary before 1 January, then no punitive action would be taken against the MacDonalds of Glencoe without MacIain having the opportunity to plead his case before the Privy Council, acting on behalf of the king. Hill had no idea then that the Privy Council and the Master of Stair had already decided the fate of the clan.

Blizzards swept in off the sea lochs as MacIain urged his pony on through the snowdrifts. On his way to Inverary he was detained by Captain Thomas Drummond of the Argyll Regiment, in what looks like a deliberate attempt at delay, to have the old man arrive too late. When MacIain at last reached the town and the shores of Loch Fyne, he had to wait another three days for Sir Colin Campbell, the sheriff of Argyll, to arrive.

Surviving correspondence from the Master of Stair is eloquent about attitudes and intentions. To the earls of Argyll and Breadalbane, he wondered if the use of 'fire and sword and all manner of hostility' against the clans who had not yet sworn should be put in hand. To the deputy commander of Fort William, he wrote, 'Let me hear from you whether you think this is the proper season to maul them in the cold, long nights.' Stair also believed that the MacDonalds of Glencoe should be made an example of because they were 'a Popish clan'. In fact, MacIain was an Episcopalian.

When at last Sir Colin Campbell came to Inverary, he reluctantly accepted the old chief's oath of loyalty to William III. Campbell had spent New Year with his family on the opposite shore of Loch Fyne, but instead of having his men row him across to meet MacIain, he preferred to have the old man wait so that he would be recorded as coming to swear after Dalrymple's deadline. When he mounted his garron for the long ride north to Glencoe, MacIain probably believed that he had discharged his duty. True, he was late, but only by a few days and other chiefs, like Glengarry, were yet to swear. That may be why, as events played out, MacIain was not suspicious of what happened a month later. For in the event, his arduous journey through the snow to Inverary mattered not at all.

The Master of Stair had already given orders that a detachment of soldiers should muster for the planned action in Glencoe. It would be commanded by Captain Robert Campbell of Glenlyon, sixty years old, a drunk and a gambler, and a man determined to have vengeance. On their way back from the failed siege of Dunkeld in 1689, the Glencoe and Glengarry MacDonalds had looted and burned Campbell's farms and impoverished him so much that at his age he had been forced to join the Argyll Regiment.

Sometime before (or perhaps even after) MacIain reached Inverary, the Master of Stair wrote directly to King William III: 'Glenco has not taken the oath [on time?], at which I rejoice . . . It will be a proper vindication of the public justice to extirpate that sept of thieves . . . It must be done quietly, otherwise they will all make shift for both men and cattle . . . Let it be secret and sudden.'

On 1 January 1692, the king signed a document explicitly ordering the massacre of the MacDonalds of Glencoe. Here is the full text of the orders passed to Campbell of Glenlyon from Robert Duncanson only hours before blood was spilled:

You are hereby ordered to fall upon the rebels, the MacDonalds of Glencoe, and put all to the sword under seventy. You are to have a special care that the old Fox and his sons do on no account escape your hands, you are to secure all the avenues that no man escape. This you are to put into execution at five of the clock precisely; and by that time, or very shortly after it, I'll strive to be at you with a stronger party: if I do not come to you at five, you are not to tarry for me, but to fall on. This is by the King's special command, for the good and safety of the country, that these miscreants be cut off root and branch. See that this be put in execution without feud or favour, else you may expect to be dealt with as one not true to King nor Government, nor a man fit to carry Commission in the King's service. Expecting that you will not fail in the fulfilling hereof, as you love yourself. I subscribe these with my hand at Ballachulish Feb: 12, 1692.

For their Majesties service
   [signed] Robert Duncanson
     To Capt. Robert Campbell of Glenlyon.

Sometime before these orders were passed to Glenlyon, he had led 120 men into Glencoe. They asked for, and received, what was known as free quarter; food and shelter in lieu of unpaid tax, something not unusual in an economy where exchange and barter were necessary in the absence of cash. The soldiers shared the warmth of the glowing peat fires of the blackhouses and such food as was available near the end of a snowy winter. On 12 February, the same Captain Thomas Drummond who had needlessly but deliberately detained MacIain on his weary and useless journey to Inverary arrived in Glencoe to hand Glenlyon his orders. Detachments of more soldiers were to be deployed at the mouth of Glencoe and where the road climbs up to Rannoch Moor at the eastern end. They were positioned there to block any escape, but it is not clear if those orders were carried out. Communications in the snow must have been chancy.

At dawn on 13 February 1692, a blizzard was howling up the glen. Lieutenant Lindsay, Ensign Lundie and several soldiers broke into MacIain's house at Polveig, and as the old man got out of bed to greet them, he was shot by a musket volley that must have catapulted him backwards. In the acrid gunsmoke, MacIain's wife was dragged out of bed, stripped naked and soldiers used their teeth to pull the rings off her bent and arthritic fingers before casting her out into the snow. Lindsay and Lundie went off in search of MacIain's sons as other detachments shot men at the townships of Achnacon and Achtriochtan. Although much muffled by the blizzard, the gunfire will have alerted some. Many fled into the high passes or climbed the mountainsides above the glen. Glenlyon drew up a firing squad at Inverrigan where nine men were lined up and shot. With a bayonet, Campbell stabbed to death those who had not been killed instantly. About forty men, women and children died in Glencoe on that awful morning, their blood spattered on the snow. But more will have perished in the blizzard in the mountains, shivering against the storm in their plaids, shocked at the slaughter taking place below them. There is some evidence that a few of Glenlyon's men were so appalled at their orders that they warned those whose firesides they had shared. Two junior officers, Lieutenants Farquhar and Kennedy, broke their swords rather than murder their hosts. They were immediately arrested and imprisoned.

At first, reaction to the massacre was muted, some even commenting that it was no more than the thieving MacDonalds deserved. Glenlyon appears to have been remorseful, or at least self-justifying. In Edinburgh taverns he showed any who were interested his explicit orders, and explained where they originated. Clamour for an enquiry began to build partly because under Scots law there was an abhorrence for 'murder under trust'. Eventually a parliamentary enquiry concluded: 'Though the command of superior officers be very absolute, yet no command against the laws of nature is binding; so that a soldier, retaining his commission, ought to refuse to execute any barbarity, as if a soldier should be commanded to shoot a man passing by inoffensively, upon the street, no such command would exempt him from the punishment of murder.'

The Master of Stair was forced to resign (although he was not long out of royal favour) as articles began to appear in journals, some of them reprinting Glenlyon's orders in full. Glencoe was widely reported and the events of February 1692 entered a national consciousness. Furthermore, it was a propaganda gift to the Jacobite movement, one that endured – in 1745 Prince Charles ordered that a pamphlet written by Charles Leslie that made clear King William's complicity should be reprinted.

The massacre of Glencoe was not the only, the last or the worst atrocity committed in the Highlands and Islands. Many more people were killed by the MacLeods on Eigg a century before, and the scale of killing, plundering and destruction after Culloden bordered on genocide. But Glencoe was emblematic. Well-publicised and often revisited, it was the beginning of a story of regret, of departure and abandonment, and the passing of an old order, of a world and a society that were rich and utterly distinctive. Glencoe became the Glen of Weeping. Red blood spattered in the snow is a powerful and brutally elegiac image, one that has never faded. The ruthless modernity of the new British state, one no longer ruled by a monarch who believed in the divine right of kings but increasingly by Parliament, had rolled over the ancient ties and traditions of the Highland clans, consigning them to history, and worse, to a cloying, tartan-wrapped romanticism that stripped them of their iconography and forgot their history. After Glencoe there was resistance, and there were moments of roaring defiance, even dignity, but the road would always lead to defeat and the destruction of a way of life, a unique way of understanding the Highlands and Islands.

*

Almost all of the houses burned by Glenlyon's men in Glencoe were *taighean-dubh*, or 'blackhouses'. They were probably so called to distinguish them from *taighean-geal*, 'white houses', built in the 1800s and since then, that had been rendered or harled on the outside walls better to keep out the weather. The original blackhouses were built from readily available materials; from stones picked up or quarried locally that could be used to make double drystone walls. For insulation, the gap was packed with rammed earth or peat. The roof was a thatch of heathery turf with straw or reeds overlaid to help with the runoff of rainwater. Old fishing nets were slung over the thatch and weighted with large stones to prevent high winds from damaging it. The smoked thatch was considered an excellent fertiliser and each year it was stripped off to be dug into the soil and replaced with fresh straw after harvest time.

These buildings were probably the descendants of Viking longhouses and could be said to reach back to Skara Brae and the building techniques used in prehistory. The earliest blackhouses had only a low door and no windows. In the centre of the living space a peat fire smouldered constantly for cooking and to keep the damp at bay, and instead of a chimney, the smoke seeped out through the roof. It must have sometimes been very murky in these houses on windless days when there was no draught to encourage the peat smoke to escape. Human beings shared their blackhouses with their cows and sometimes goats and other animals, often with only a penning fence or a low wall between them – the animals were too precious to be left outside in the worst of the winter weather and also at the mercy of whomever might want to steal them. They also added warmth, as well as agricultural odours. The blackhouses were occupied for a long time, well into the twentieth century.

In his classic account of the life and death of a Highland community, *Night Falls on Ardnamurchan*, Alasdair Maclean tells a story of an old neighbour. Ruined by the time of writing (in the years leading up to 1984), Murdo's blackhouse was old-fashioned. 'At one end', said Maclean in a later interview, 'lived Murdo, and at the other end lived his cow. And there was never a cross word between them.' As late as the 1970s, blackhouses were still occupied at Gearannan on the Isle of Lewis.

As in the rest of Scotland, the voices of the women who fed the peat fires, who baked the oatcakes on the hot stones of the hearth and milked the cow are silent in the historical record. That is true for most ordinary people, with Private Donald McBane a rare exception. But there is a voice from the Highlands and Islands in the seventeenth century that has come down to us, the words of an extraordinary woman.

Màiri nighean Alasdair Ruaidh, 'Mary, the daughter of Red Alasdair', is better known as Mary MacLeod. Dates vary, but it seems that she was born in 1615 and probably died in 1674 (though some sources have her living on into the eighteenth century). She is buried in the MacLeod church of St Clement's at Rodel, but no one knows where exactly her tomb is. Mary lived most of her life across the Minch at Dunvegan where at first she seems to have nursed the children of the MacLeod chiefs on Skye. Later, Mary appears to have become a bard and some of her poetry survives. Scholars of Gaelic literature write that she was the first to compose court poetry in the vernacular diction, by which they mean in language ordinary people spoke and not the heroic metrical modes of the past. Here is one of her praise-poems composed in thanks for a gift:

Tha mo chean air an Ruairidh,
  Gur luaimneach mu d' sgeula mi;
Fior bhoinne geal suairc thu,
  Am bheil uaisle na peucaige,
Air an d'fhàs an cùl dualach
  Is e 'na chuachagan teudbhuidhe;
Sin is urla ghlan shuairce:
Cha bu tuairisgeul breugach e.

My favour is with Ruairidh,
That you made my spirits leap with your news;
A true, bright, urbane drop you are,
With the nobility of the peacock,
On whom have grown tresses falling in locks
And with little curls string-golden;
That your aspect is clear and civil:
That would not be a lying, made-up report.

The translation is colloquial, if more than a little clunky. But it is refreshing to read the words of a woman, and they are distinctive. It may be that the poem was composed (and written down much later) on the occasion of Mary receiving the gift of a snuff mill from the chiefly family. Apparently she was also fond of a dram of whisky, and at one point Mary overstepped the mark with a poem satirising Ruairidh Mòr MacLeod, the chief at Dunvegan, or perhaps praising another chief too much, and she was dispatched into exile. Where she promptly composed another poem that persuaded the offended party to bring her back. And that is more less all that is known about one of the first Highland and Island women to come onto the historical record. It would not be until the nineteenth century that the voices of ordinary people would be heard.

*

The roar of rumbling thunder came from the earth not the sky. The ground shuddered and farmers looked up in horror as the fiery 'Gates of Hell' blew open. On 13 January 1693, without any warning signs, Mount Hekla erupted once more, hurling many cubic kilometres of tephra into the atmosphere, spilling burning rivers of lava down its flanks. Not a cone but a three-mile-long trench of bubbling, white-hot magma, the mountain devastated much of southern Iceland, covering the ground with a thick layer of ash, throwing huge boulders of solidifying lava into the air. The farmers whose lives and livelihoods were destroyed called the volcano the Gates of Hell, believing it was the prison of Judas and a place where Satan consorted with witches and devils.

The ocean winds carried the tephra to the coasts of Norway, 900 miles to the east. Records speak of dead salmon and trout floating to the surface of rivers and fjords, of poisoned farm animals and fields covered with a grey layer of ejecta. Modern sampling has shown that Hekla's tephra is particularly toxic if it is ingested.

Shetland, the Hebrides and the Atlantic shore are 200 miles closer to Hekla, but it may be that the prevailing winds did not carry as much tephra to the south-east. Or it may be that record-keeping in a non-literate society was much poorer. There was a tsunami after the volcano roared and great waves almost certainly reared up on western shores as a prelude to the coming darkness. The eruption went on for ten months and no fewer than fourteen craters along the length of the trench were active. Just as it had been in 1159 BC, Hekla's fatal thunder spelled disaster not only for Highlanders and Islanders, but for all Scots and many more who lived to the south. The period between 1693 and 1700 was known as the Seven Ill Years, another baleful biblical allusion, this time to the great famine in the Book of Genesis. Gaels called it Seachd Bliadhna Gorta, 'the Seven Years of Hunger'.

Tree-ring analysis of ancient woodland to the north of the Cairngorm plateau has yielded an extraordinary set of results. The 1690s in Scotland was the coldest decade in the last seven centuries. There were repeated failed harvests in 1695, 1696, 1698 and 1699. For not only did Hekla erupt, but two Indonesian volcanoes, at Serua in 1693 and Aboina in 1694, also sent vast tonnages of ejecta rocketing into the atmosphere. Scientists and palaeoclimatologists have described the 1690s as 'the volcanic cold pulse'. As in 1159 BC, the power of the eruption sent the tephra high into the atmosphere, into the stratosphere, too high to be washed out by rain. And so the sun was occluded for long periods, temperatures consequently dropped, growing seasons shortened, or did not happen, and crops simply failed to ripen. People starved all over Scotland. In the Seven Ill Years, it may be that between 10 and 15 per cent of the population perished. In some places, the losses were even greater. Aberdeenshire may have seen 25 per cent of its people die of hunger.

The famine caused great social dislocation. In 1698, the politician Andrew Fletcher of Saltoun, reckoned that about 200,000 Scots, a fifth of the entire population, had been forced to leave their homes to beg for food. Poor relief resources were overwhelmed. In the Highlands and Islands, there was extreme privation. Patrick Walker, a chapman who sold small items such as needles, pins and tobacco, saw the price of oatmeal treble in the communities, and the effects of the famine horrified him: 'Meal became so scarce . . . and many could not get it . . . I have seen women . . . clapping their hands, and tearing the cloths off their heads, crying, "How shall we go home and see our children die in hunger?" . . . deaths and burials were so many and so common, that the living were wearied in the burying of the dead.'

The weather changed dramatically. David Crawford, the secretary of the Duchess of Hamilton, observed 'cold weather, a [time of] grey frosts of which we had plenty in the first three weeks of July almost every night, [and] very rainy'. During the harvest in the autumn, he wrote that 'the wind [was] always in the east [and] somewhat cold and there was deep snow and an extraordinary great storm of frost and snow'.

David Scrymgeour, of Gartmore, near Stirling, described the winter of 1695/6 as severe with cold temperatures and snow until April, which delayed sowing. May too was cold, but July and August were strikingly hot and dry, hot enough so as to damage and scorch grasses and crops.

At the start of 1695, Daniel Hamilton reported from Kinneil that the farmers had endured 'a fortnight of most bitter cold weather of frost and snow', making it impossible to venture outside and preventing planting. Later that year, cattle had to be moved to other ground for want of pasture, as there was 'such a drought that it has destroyed both grass and cows whereby in all probability many of them [he must mean sheep] will not shear this season, as for our hay we have not a load where we used to have'. To make matters worse, the cut hay had started to rot because 'the rain is likely to be as excessive as the heat was'.

The terrible effects of the bad weather were compounded by

spectacularly bad judgement. In 1695 the Company of Scotland was established to operate what became known as the Darien Scheme. William Paterson, a wealthy merchant from Tinwald in Dumfriesshire, who had founded the Bank of England, saw an opportunity. If ports could be established on the Caribbean and Pacific shores of the Isthmus of Panama and cargoes transported over the narrow neck of land (where the canal now runs) then ships could avoid the long and dangerous voyage around Cape Horn. Paterson named the colony New Caledonia. It was a sound business proposal that depended on the operation of international trade and not the exploitation of natural resources, real or imagined.

The Company of Scotland raised a staggering sum from a nation in the grip of famine – £200,000 was about 20 per cent of all the disposable wealth in Scotland. But from the outset the enterprise was beset by poor planning and inadequate preparation. The same Captain Thomas Drummond who had ridden through the snow into Glencoe to give Glenlyon his orders, directed the siting and construction of Fort St Andrew on the Caribbean shore of the isthmus. It had no source of fresh water. There were also too few supplies, but William III ignored the fact that he was also William II of Scotland when he ordered English and Dutch merchants not to supply the beleaguered Scots colonists. By 1700 it was clear that Darien was a disaster. Following hard on the heels of seven years of famine, it rendered Scotland broke as well as hungry and set the scene for union with England, Wales and Ireland in 1707.

*

Asthmatic, widowed and childless, William III and II was not much mourned when he died in 1702, though for Highlanders much more attached to the House of Stuart than the rest of Great Britain, it was a consolation that Queen Anne succeeded. However, after the tragedy of no fewer than seventeen failed pregnancies and the death of her eleven-year-old son, the Duke of Gloucester, it was clear that the Stuart line of succession was going nowhere. The English Parliament legislated for the future. The Act of Settlement of 1701 excluded

Catholics, meaning the Stuarts, from the royal succession. After some rummaging around in the European genealogies and a great deal of negotiation, it was agreed that on Anne's death the thrones of England – and therefore Scotland – should be offered to the firmly Protestant Sophia, Electress of Hanover. She was the granddaughter of James VI and I and could therefore claim some, but not too much, descent from the Stuarts. As important, there were plenty of available Hanoverians, Sophia having six sons. The eldest was Georg Ludwig von Braunschweig-Lüneberg and it mattered not at all that he was notoriously foul-tempered, had got rid of his duchess and had imprisoned her for life in a castle. What mattered was that he too was immovably Protestant, had sons, and spoke not a syllable of English. As much as any legislation, that meant that the new dynasty (who continued to use German as a family language until the 1930s) would become subservient to Parliament in all practical senses, as well as constitutionally.

Another stage was set and parts were cast. The campaigns of Montrose and Dundee had shown how attached many Scots, and most Highlanders, were to the House of Stuart, no matter how hopeless they were. The Scottish Parliament appears not to have been consulted over the terms of the Act of Settlement and there was retaliation. In 1704 the Act of Security set out emphatically the right of Scots to decide their own monarch, and the Act anent Peace and War a year earlier reserved the right to go to war independently of England. In a game of legislative table tennis, the English Parliament passed the Alien Act in 1705, proposing a ban on all exports from Scotland to England, including the cattle droving trade. Negotiations began. The terms of the parliamentary union were hammered out, much lubricated by the Equivalent, a huge bribe to be distributed to the cash-strapped Scottish aristocracy and others. Conditions were agreed and a bill drawn up, and popular opposition mounted.

When the Scottish Parliament met in Edinburgh to consider what England had offered, there was rioting. In Glasgow the Provost was forced to go into hiding. Burghs sent petitions of objection and there were rumours of armed insurrection. English troops massed on the border, which further stoked unrest, but before a shot was fired, the terms were accepted. On 16 January 1707, the Scottish Parliament voted itself out of existence by 110 votes to 67. For Na Seumasaich, the Jacobites who still supported the Stuarts in Scotland, their moment had arrived.

The new kingdom and nation of Great Britain and Ireland was at war with Europe's largest and most wealthy country, France. And King Louis XIV needed cash to pay his armies and greatly wished to avoid the considerable cost of hosting the exiled Stuarts – it also made strategic sense to mobilise England's enemies within and foment rebellion.

George Lockhart managed to insert himself into the centre of this remarkable, pivotal passage of history. As a member of the Scottish Parliament, he opposed the union but paradoxically accepted a role as a commissioner in the negotiations of its terms. Lockhart was an Episcopalian, and a Jacobite. He could report back to the Stuart court in France on progress and on who would receive what. In discussion with his fellow commissioners and the English representatives, he could also divert attention and play down any threat of action from James VII and II. In fact, he reported to St Germain-en-Laye that between 30,000 and 40,000 sympathisers would rally if the Stuart standard was raised in Scotland, and he advised the exiled king to sign a manifesto that claimed only the throne of Scotland, that promised subservience to parliament and the independence of the Kirk. The union was so unpopular, Lockhart's estimates and his political insights were probably reasonable.

In February 1708, six French regiments and the Irish Brigade mustered to board an invasion fleet of five warships and twenty frigates at Dunkirk. Stowed in the holds were arms for 13,000 men who would join the rising. But, as usual, the Stuarts caused difficulties – James VII and II had the measles. Departure was delayed for three weeks while he recovered and the fleet ran into bad weather soon after they caught the tide on the morning of 17 March. Lacking clear leadership, the whole enterprise quickly developed into a fiasco. Having anchored off the fishing village of Crail in the Firth of Forth, the admiral of the French fleet appeared to panic when Admiral Byng sailed into view with a fleet of British warships. Instead of quickly putting the army of 6,000 hardened veterans ashore with all their weapons, the French admiral fled north and circumnavigated Britain before returning to France.

A mixture of measles, faltering resolve, poor planning and the usual fecklessness robbed the Stuarts of their best chance of a successful restoration, at least in Scotland. But it would not be their last chance.

*

Meanwhile, Scotland was changing, becoming more domesticated, and parts of the Highlands and Islands less of a wilderness. By the side of the A9, between Brora and Helmsdale, an inscribed stone reads: 'To mark the place near which the last wolf in Sutherland was killed by the hunter, Polson, in or about the year 1700.'

Polson came from Wester Helmsdale and, with his two sons, he tracked a wolf to its lair in a gully in Glen Loth. While the boys squeezed through the narrow entrance to kill the cubs inside, Polson kept watch. Suddenly the she-wolf appeared and dashed past him to get into the cave to rescue her young, but the hunter somehow managed to grab her tail. One of the boys shouted in Gaelic, 'Father, what is keeping the light from us?'

Polson shouted, 'If the root of this tail breaks, you will soon know that.'

One handed, he could not cock his musket and so Polson stabbed the wolf to death with his hunting knife. So the gory story goes.

The last element sounds highly dubious, and if the she-wolf was the last wolf in Sutherland, where was the father of the cubs? At the end of the seventeenth century, there are several similar and more or less apocryphal tales. Sir Ewen Cameron of Lochiel claimed to have killed the last wolf in Scotland in 1680 at Killiecrankie, while other stories insist on later dates in different places.

During the reign of James VI and I, wolves were considered a threat to travellers and roadside buildings known as spitals were apparently built for overnight safety. It seems, however, that wolves presented more of danger to the dead than the living. In Sutherland, which seems to have been the last redoubt of Highland wolfpacks, they dug up fresh graves so often that the people of Eddrachillis Bay in Assynt were forced to begin burying their dead on the island of Handa, as recorded in a poem from *A Book of Highland Minstrelsy*:

On Ederachillis' shore
   The grey wolf lies in wait, –
Woe to the broken door,
   Woe to the loosened gate,
And the groping wretch whom sleety fogs
   On the trackless moor belate.

The lean and hungry wolf,
   With his fangs so sharp and white,
His starveling body pinched
   By the frost of a northern night,
And his pitiless eyes that scare the dark
   With their green and threatening light.

He climbeth the guarding dyke,
   He leapeth the hurdle bars,
He steals the sheep from the pen,
   And the fish from the boat-house spars;
And he digs the dead from out the sod,
   And gnaws them under the stars.

Thus every grave we dug
   The hungry wolf uptore,
And every morn the sod
   Was strewn with bones and gore;
Our mother earth had denied us rest
   On Ederachillis' shore.

The eradication of wolves in the seventeenth century had an impact on the landscape as the ecology changed. In more remote and wilder places where human beings had yet to make a mark, these packs of apex predators had kept deer numbers down. But as wolves were hunted to extinction, the natural regeneration in the more far-flung parts of the Caledonian Forest began to decline. No longer kept moving by hunting packs, herds of deer behaved like locusts, grazing the young shoots of seedling trees down to the ground. Unmoored by the lack of tree roots and the underbrush of the forest, the soil eroded and the landscape grew barren and impoverished.

The dead may have stayed buried, but Polson's feral actions in Glen Loth had unintended consequences as the balance of nature was gradually upended.

*

When James VII and II fled to France in 1688, his cousin, Louis XIV, set him and his court up at the castle of St Germain-en-Laye near Paris. It was no grace-and-favour lodge, but a vast royal palace of hundreds of rooms organised into fifty-five opulent apartments. There was a large chapel, a banqueting hall and the castle came with a substantial town around it. But most of all, St Germain was set up as a royal court on a royal scale.

Underwritten by a subsidy of 50,000 livres a month, James' secretary of state oversaw the appointment of more than 300 officials and functionaries to the king's household, the queen's household, the princess' household and the stables. About a thousand Jacobite exiles were paid small pensions, and a network of agents in England and Scotland was maintained. Most striking was the existence of James VII and II's private army. The Irish Brigade of 'Wild Geese', soldiers who left Ireland after the Jacobite defeat, fought for France and were paid by Louis XIV, but the officers were commissioned by King James and they all owed allegiance to him. Two regiments of House Guards, two of cavalry, two of dragoons, eight infantry regiments and three independent companies made up an army of 14,000 men at its peak in the late seventeenth century. And at Brest in Brittany, nine ships were also under the exiled king's command. It was an extraordinary exception for Louis XIV to allow the existence of a nominally independent army on French soil, and so close to Versailles. The Irish Brigade overwintered at St Germain, and if so inclined could have threatened the French state rather than the British.

It may have been the court of a Pretender, an exile, but appearances mattered, were vital to credibility. What is even more surprising is how few Scots attended James VII and II. Scholarly analysis has found that the Jacobite court was 45 per cent English, 39 per cent Irish and only 3 per cent Scots. James Drummond, the Duke of Perth, was secretary of state, and a very rare Highlander. St Germain was a statelet waiting to become the real thing, but in the long, weary and vacant years of exile, it must also have been a febrile merry-go-round of gossip as men whispered behind their hands in the corridors and courtyards of the huge castle, and rumour and counter-rumour swirled around the walls. Behind the outward appearance of a royal court and all its formalities was the reality of absence, of powerlessness and of the bitter frustrations of dependency on others.

Seven hundred miles to the north-east, the Elector Georg Ludwig von Braunschweig-Lüneberg was also waiting. The Schloss Herrenhausen was a much more modest residence than St Germain-en-Laye, but it was home to prospects far greater and more concrete than the wishful intrigues of Jacobite pensioners and exiles who competed for the insubstantial favour of James VII and II.

Known as Gorgen, a diminutive of Georg and its hard Germanic 'g's, the Elector was said to be blunt, even uncouth. Having married Sophia Dorothea of Celle for dynastic reasons, he dutifully fathered two children on her before turning permanently to his mistress, Melusine von der Schulenburg. Painfully thin and known as 'the Scarecrow', she gave Georg three children and was openly his hostess at the Herrenhausen and his other palaces. When Sophia took a lover of her own, a Swedish nobleman, it is likely that the Elector had a hand in his murder and made sure his body was quietly disposed of. Following this, Georg's wife was forcibly removed from his court, separated forever from her children and imprisoned for the rest of her life, thirty years, in a castle in Celle. She was permitted to walk unaccompanied in its courtyard and to take occasional, heavily supervised carriage drives. Georg loathed his son, also Georg, and refused to speak to him unless it was absolutely unavoidable. The Hanoverians did not make an attractive picture, but appearances for them mattered much less than raw politics.

When Queen Anne at last died in 1714, Georg Ludwig became George I, Sophia was left in prison in Celle and Melusine became, in Robert Walpole's words, 'as much the Queen of England as anyone was'. Courtiers in London called her the Maypole, or the Goose. It seems that George also brought another woman, almost certainly another mistress. In contrast to the Goose, the more ample Baroness Sophia Charlotte von Kielmansegg was known as the Sow. By the time of his coronation, George I was fifty-seven, an old man, and he depended heavily on Walpole, his prime minister, even though it is likely that both at first were reliant on an interpreter. The king's manner was said to be abrupt, and perhaps a great deal was lost in translation. One of his earliest actions was to sack John Erskine, the Earl of Mar. He had been third secretary, the government minister in charge of Scottish affairs. Erskine went into a monumental huff and was so anxious to get back to Scotland that he took passage north on a collier, a coal ship. His dismissal was the spark that lit the first substantial Jacobite rising.

*

Cam ye o'er frae France? Cam ye down by Lunnon?
Saw ye Geordie Whelps, and his bonny woman?
Were ye at the place ca'd the Kittle Housie?
Saw ye Geordie's grace riding on a goosie?

Geordie, he's a man, there is little doubt o't;
He's done a' he can, wha can do without it?
Down there came a blade, linkin' like my lordie;
He wad drive a trade at the loom o' Geordie.

Though the claith were bad, blythly may we niffer;
Gin we get a wab, it makes little differ.
We hae tint our plaid, bannet, belt and swordie,
Ha's and mailins braid – but we hae a Geordie!

Jocky's gane to France, and Montgomery's lady;
There they'll learn to dance: Madam, are ye ready?
They'll be back believe, belted, brisk and lordly;
Brawly may they thrive to dance a jig wi' Geordie!

Hey for Sandy Don! Hey for Cockolorum!
Hey for Bobbing John, and his Highland quorum!
Mony a sword and lance swings at Highland hurdie;
How they'll skip and dance o'er the bum o' Geordie!

Recorded in modern times by Peggy Seeger, the Corries and Steeleye Span, 'Cam Ye O'er Frae France' is one of the most famous Jacobite songs, almost certainly written between 6 September 1715, when John Erskine (so called Bobbing John because he changed sides often) raised the royal standard at Braemar on behalf of Jocky, King James VIII and III, and the battle that was fought at Sheriffmuir on 13 November 1715. Music and popular song mattered a great deal in a time before mass media made the spread of information much easier and 'Cam Ye O'er Frae France' is as much a historical document as any chronicle, government record or Act of Parliament because it makes popular attitudes clear, and amusing.

When she introduced the song at a concert in 2006, Steeleye Span's Maddy Prior said it was incomprehensible. Perhaps that is because it was composed in early eighteenth-century Scots. In fact, the lyrics are very informative and show a clear understanding of politics, personalities and gossip – but they are also riddles. The sentiment of the song might be obvious, but words could be treasonous and it was better to use a little verbal disguise.

The first verse recounts a racy version of life at St James's Palace, the Kittle Housie, the residence of King Geordie and his 'bonny woman', a euphemism for a prostitute. The last line makes clear that's a reference to the Goose, Melusine von der Schulenberg. In the second verse the 'blade' is Sophia Dorothea's ill-fated Swedish lover who 'drives a trade', has sex with, Geordie's wife. 'Loom' is another word for vagina. Jocky and Montgomery's lady in France is James VIII and III, the Old Pretender, and his mother, Mary of Modena, who retained a great deal of influence at St Germain-en-Laye. 'Dance a jig wi' Geordie' means to do battle with his soldiers, and the final verse refers to the Jacobite leadership – Sandy Don is Major General Alexander Gordon of Auchintoul and Cockolorum is the Marquis of Huntly.

The jaunty, optimistic and surprisingly well-informed tone of the song must mean that it was written before the battle at Sheriffmuir and the eventual disintegration of the rebellion.

The rising began well and the omens were promising. Erskine used the traditional ruse of announcing a deer hunt as pretext for the muster of an army. With Gordon, Huntly and others, he planned to raise James VIII and III's standard on 6 September at Braemar. Word was sent out to potential supporters and 600 came to the castle to proclaim the cause of the rightful king. It may well be that Mar omitted to inform the rightful king of any of his plans because he had no commission to act for James VIII and III. For his part, the earl also had no idea that five days before the standard was planted on the Braes of Mar, his chances of success had diminished dramatically. After a long reign, Louis XIV died and the Regent of France, the Duke of Orléans, was much less enthusiastic in his support of the Jacobites. The exiled court had moved to Rome and although the rising had the backing of the Pope, it needed French regiments and French supplies and money to make success achievable.

Nevertheless, the unpopularity of George I, so well captured in 'Cam Ye O'er Frae France' and the union of 1707 with England and Wales brought many to join Mar. The eastern clans had come out, and also many Jacobite Lowlanders, especially from the north-east. By 22 October, Mar had received the king's commission and with the exception of Fort William, he controlled Scotland north of the

Forth. Perhaps as many as 20,000 recruits had joined him and his supporters across the north, far more than any of the other risings.

But Mar seemed paralysed by indecision and dithering. With 12,000 men he eventually took Perth, but then did nothing more for six weeks. Perhaps he was waiting for the arrival of King James, or word from his court in Rome, or for news of French involvement. With each week that passed, both momentum and men slipped away, clansmen and others deserting, anxious to be home before the winter set in. Eventually Mar was persuaded to act. Before it grew any smaller, he marched his army south-west to attack Stirling. News of this was passed to the Duke of Argyll and his government forces, and they advanced to meet the Jacobites at Sheriffmuir, near Dunblane.

It seemed to me an unlikely place to fight a pitched battle. Driving uphill out of Dunblane on a narrow minor road on a blustery autumn day, I quickly reached high moorland, barren but for extensive plantations of commercial forestry. I came across a tall roadside memorial erected at the instigation of the Clan MacRae Society to remember MacRaes who died at Sheriffmuir. A sign pointed to a path leading to the Gathering Stone, where part of Mar's army may have mustered, deployed or regrouped, but at first the dense plantations made it difficult to visualise what happened on 13 November 1715. Gradually the trees began to thin out and the path led to a wide area of heathery moorland that looked out over Strathallan to the foothills of the mountains. The shadows of clouds chased across the slopes and after a time sunshine lit the moor. There were stands of beautiful old Scots pines near the Gathering Stone, their bark rich russet and the needles of their upper limbs deep green. A faded information board told me it had once been a standing stone, now collapsed and covered with a protective ironwork grille. Perhaps it was a metaphor.

Sheriffmuir seemed to me an atmospheric place, rich with the memory of history, where the clash and roar of battle might be heard on the freshening breeze from the north. Hiding under the heather were tiny blaeberry bushes, their dark purple fruit ripe and sweet, the sort of thing foraging soldiers would have been glad of. I picked some and sat down on a bench to try to work out what happened, and where it happened.

Because of the undulating ground and the slope leading up from the roads on either side to the moorland plateau, it would have been difficult to see all of both armies. Mar had marched south-west down Strathallan while Argyll had moved up from Dunblane to meet him. When government troops were seen on the ridge above the road, Mar sent his left wing to challenge them, most of them Highlanders. But because of the terrain, they moved in long columns on the narrow paths. When Mar's men reached the plateau, Argyll saw his chance and charged them with the right wing of his army. Unable to deploy properly, the Highlanders were driven back down the slope.

Meanwhile, Mar led his right wing up to the western edge of the plateau, towards the Gathering Stone where I sat. There his men charged and scattered the left wing of the government army. It was a mid-November day, with fast fading daylight, making it difficult to see what had taken place, but in essence there were two battles at Sheriffmuir. Argyll's right wing defeated Mar's left, and in a separate action, Mar's right defeated Argyll's left. There was no clear victor.

However, what happened next was decisive. With far superior numbers, Mar could have pressed on towards Stirling. Instead he gave up the field and retreated to Perth, allowing Argyll to claim victory and making Sheriffmuir look like a defeat for the Jacobites. Which is precisely what it became.

In a dismal, characteristically half-hearted postscript that jarred with the jaunty optimism of 'Cam Ye O'er Frae France', James VIII and III did just that, but far too late and to little or no purpose. A few days before Christmas 1715, he disembarked at Peterhead and met Mar at Fetteresso near Stonehaven. Raised in the febrile, frustrated neverland of St Germain-en-Laye, the king seemed distant, cold and aloof, surrounded by clan chiefs and loyal noblemen he had never met and could barely understand, having made a winter journey through a country he had never visited. James appeared devoid of charisma or even enthusiasm, and could inspire no one around him. The plans for a coronation at Scone were quietly set aside. On 4 February, the king took ship at Montrose, shrouded in dismal failure, bound for Rome and exile.

*

As the fortunes of the Stuarts appeared to wane and their hopes of restoration faded, Highlanders enjoyed other forms of confrontation. Deer hunts were not the only pretext for gathering warriors, and the word 'shinty' was in common use by 1700. It probably derives from the Gaelic *sìnteag*, a 'leap' or a 'bound' (and good bounders are often good players), and it was played in the Highlands long before the beginning of the eighteenth century. The game's great antiquity was celebrated in 1881 in *The Book of the Club of True Highlanders* as

> undoubtedly the oldest known Keltic sport or pastime. The game is also called Cluich bhall, shinnie, shinty, bandy, hurling, hockey, and at one time was a universal and favourite game of the whole of Keltland . . . The origin of this game is lost in the midst of ages . . . indeed, it is said, and, no doubt, with great truth, that the game of Camanachd, or club playing, was introduced into the Green Isle [Ireland] by the immediate descendants of Noah. On such authority we may rationally conclude that it was played by Noah himself; and if by Noah, in all probability by Adam and his sons.

Of course it was. Shinty in the Garden of Eden. *Camanachd* as it is now known, may also have been imported from Ireland via the kingdom of Dál Riata, or perhaps later through the constant cultural contact across the North Channel. Or perhaps Noah brought it to Argyll in his Ark. In any event, the game was once played all over Britain but is now confined mainly to the Highlands and clubs founded in Glasgow and Edinburgh by exiles. Shinty may be seen as part of what makes the Highlands different from the rest of Scotland.

In 1700 games were probably played in fields vacated by the herds that had made the spring journey of transhumance up to the high pastures. Like early versions of rugby and football, the size of the teams was probably not limited, and the rules may have been both elastic and a matter for negotiation.

Nowadays shinty pitches are enormous. Here is a summary of the modern rules from the game's historian, Hugh Dan MacLennan:

The field of play is rectangular, not more than 170 yards nor less than 140 yards and its breadth not more than 80 yards nor less than 70 yards, with minimalist markings.

Scoring is by goals which consist of two upright posts, equidistant from the corner flags and 12 feet apart, joined by a horizontal cross-bar, 10 feet from the ground. The goal has a net attached to the uprights and cross-bars, as in Association Football.

The ball is spherical, made of cork and worsted inside, the outer cover of leather or some other approved material, not more than eight inches and not less than 7.5 inches in circumference. The weight of the ball at the start of the game should not be more than 3 ounces nor less than 2.5 ounces. In previous times balls have been made of India Rubber, wood, lemons, sheep droppings and sheep's vertebrae – basically anything which could be hit with a wide variety of curved sticks.

Players' equipment and apparel, apart from the obvious stick (known as a *caman*) is also minimal: shin guards and strips basically, safety being paramount. Helmets and face-guards are now more common, à la hurling and cricket, and helmets are compulsory for certain younger players.

The caman must conform to the following standard: the head must not be of a size larger than can pass through a ring with a diameter of 2.5 inches; no plates, screws, or metal in any form shall be attached to or form part of the caman. (The Irish game of hurling allows such attachments.) A player whose caman is broken during a game may play the ball before obtaining a replacement caman, providing the broken caman is not deemed dangerous to other players.

Like Rangers and Celtic in Scottish football, modern shinty has been dominated by two clubs, by Kingussie and Newtonmore, the 'big two'. In fact, Kingussie is reckoned by the *Guinness Book of Records* to be the most successful sporting team of all time, anywhere. In the early 1990s they were undefeated in a run of a hundred matches. They won twenty consecutive league titles. A recently retired Kingussie forward, Ronald Ross, is by far the game's highest ever scorer with more than a thousand goals. He was known as 'Ronaldo of the Glens'. Ross started playing when he was three years old and his father built a goal in the back garden to stop him breaking so many windows.

The principal competition has been the Camanachd Cup, a knockout format, and Kingussie's great rivals, Newtonmore, only four miles further up the Spey valley, have won it thirty-two times, a record unmatched by any other club. And since 2010 they have won the league seven times in a row.

*

The great players of Kingussie and Newtonmore were by no means the first Highlanders to become legends in their own lifetimes. Rob Roy MacGregor and his clansmen arrived at Sheriffmuir late in the day on 13 November 1715, and took no part in the battle. Rob Roy had fought at Killiecrankie at the age of eighteen before becoming a cattle dealer who also operated a protection scheme. In return for payment, he made sure that no other Highlanders stole the cattle of Lowland farmers to the south of the mountains. Life became difficult for him when an associate absconded with borrowed cash. MacGregor was pursued by the principal creditor, the Duke of Montrose, and was eventually imprisoned. With the threat of transportation to the colonies hanging over his head, Rob Roy was pardoned in 1727 by King George I. Seven years later, at the age of sixty-three, he died in his bed. In many ways, Rob Roy's life as a leader of clansmen was typical of the times and not especially noteworthy. Yet he became the most famous Highlander in history, and the story of how that happened is emblematic of the ways in which the Highlands had begun to change in the course of the eighteenth and nineteenth centuries.

Broadsides were the equivalent of today's tabloid newspapers. Single sheets printed on both sides, they were sold by pedlars and packmen for a penny or a halfpenny. They rarely carried actual news, but ballads, songs, poems and lurid stories such as the dastardly doings of murderers and thieves, or scaffold speeches, were all standard fare – the more shocking the better. The programme of mass literacy, the promise of a school in every parish, initiated by John Knox and the reformers after 1560 was beginning to achieve its aim of a literate society. Although the intention was to enable Scots to read the Bible and thereby become responsible for their own salvation, inevitably many enjoyed other sorts of, much less pious, stories. Because many more people could read, broadsides were particularly popular in Scotland and the Saltmarket in Glasgow became a busy centre of production, a detail that matters in the case of Rob Roy.

MacGregor's deeds and misdeeds took place not in the far north, the remote islands or the inaccessible glens of the central Highlands, but in the south, east of Loch Lomond for the most part, close to the Highland Line and the Lowlands. His story was clearly known to the composers of broadsides in Glasgow for Rob's name begins to appear in them. Mentions were incidental to other tales, but he began to be likened to Robin Hood, a Highlander oppressed by aristocrats and forced into outlawry and banditry. Sometimes he is even styled Robin Roy. Owing to his appearance in broadsides (and perhaps in more that have not survived) MacGregor's name and the barest outline of his story entered Lowland culture and consciousness.

In 1723 a biography was published in London. *The Highland Rogue* was probably written by Elias Brockett, the book 'impartially digested from the memorandums of an authentick Scotch MSS'. Which may be an allusion to the broadsides, or, more likely, to something that never existed. Brockett turned Rob into a Highland highwayman, wrote that he was of 'a gigantic size' with a foot-long beard and that his face and body were covered with red hair. The book refers to real incidents such as the dispute with the Duke of Montrose and MacGregor's life as a cattleman. Like Robin Hood, Rob was forced to become an outlaw and Brockett duly has him stealing from the rich and giving to the poor. A second edition published in 1743 carries a subtitle: *The Highland Rogue, being a General History of the Highlanders*, and also the assertion that MacGregor 'lived in the manner of the ancient Robin Hood of England'.

All of which was meat and drink to Walter Scott. In 1817 he published his best-selling *Rob Roy*, and its largely fictional account of the Highlander's life went through many editions as it embedded a romantic version of Gaelic-speaking culture in popular consciousness. The story of the eighteenth and nineteenth centuries became one of a radical shift from the clans as a threat to the stability of the British state, to a perception of a mist-strewn neverland amongst the bens and the glens peopled by noble savages swathed in tartan and entertained by the skirl of the pipes. It is a collection of clichés that has never faded, and it has obscured a richer, more surprising and more unlikely story, one that began to gather momentum in the early decades of the eighteenth century.

The 1719 Jacobite rising was the usual cocktail of confusion, bad luck and poor leadership, but at least Rob Roy turned up and did some of the fighting. It was the only time that Spain, rather than France, promised support for James VIII and III. The plan was to send 5,000 Spanish troops to land in south-west England where, it was believed, there might be some support for the Stuarts. At the same time another, much smaller, force would make landfall in the Western Isles, and from there move to raise the mainland clans. Almost none of it worked.

When 300 Spanish marines and a group of aristocratic exiles dropped anchor in Stornoway harbour in March 1719, they received news that bad weather had once again frustrated the landings in England. A severe storm off Cape Finisterre had sunk some ships and forced the others to run to Coruña for safety, where they stayed. But, as usual, the pitifully small army that had mustered in the Hebrides pressed on regardless. They sailed the Minch to Lochalsh where they set up a base at picturesque Eilean Donan Castle. Preparations were made to march up the Great Glen and capture Inverness. In 1718 unlikely help had been promised from Sweden, and it was hoped that perhaps it might still sail into the Moray Firth. More realistically, however, it was felt that some success might persuade further clans to come out for the Stuarts. Commanded by George Keith, the former Earl Marischal, around a thousand men made ready to move. There were 400 MacKenzies, 150 reliable and loyal Camerons led by Lochiel, as well as the Spanish marines and other smaller groups, including Rob Roy and his MacGregors.

On 5 June, General Joseph Wightman led a small army of about the same size down the Great Glen to prevent the march on Inverness. The Jacobites took up a position blocking Glen Shiel, and on 10 June battle was joined. Inexplicably, there was no Highland charge; perhaps the ground was not suitable. Peter Tillemans' near-contemporary painting is framed from the point of view of the government army, with Wightman posed on a prancing horse in the foreground, his drawn sword, oddly, pointing away from the battlefield beyond him. The main deployments, and most of the action (which Tillemans shows by puffs of gunsmoke) seem not to be on the floor of the glen, where the River Shiel runs, but up on the steep sides of Sgùrr an Lochain and Sgùrr na Ciste Duibhe. Apparently, the Spanish were in the centre of the Jacobite lines, presumably on the flatter ground on either side of the river, while the Highlanders on the mountainsides sheltered behind barricades and in trenches. For a fighting force that had as its sole tactic an all-out attack in the shape of the much-feared Highland charge, it is a surprising disposition.

Wightman had brought four mortars from Inverness. Known as Coehorn mortars after their Dutch inventor, they could launch volleys of 'plunging fire', throwing shells high in the air so that gravity added to their downward velocity. They appear to have been extremely effective, perhaps because the clansmen cowering behind their barricades had never seen anything like them. The government infantry marched uphill, covered by the Coehorns and their smoke, and threw grenades as well as firing musket volleys.

These government tactics were telling and as the light faded and the high mountains cast evening shadows over Glen Shiel, the Highlanders retreated into the welcome gloaming. The following morning the Spanish soldiers surrendered. Many leading Jacobites saw Glen Shiel as a full stop, a last, botched chance to restore James VIII and III. As George I established himself, and without significant, consistent support from either France or Spain, the Stuarts would remain exiles. Many Jacobite leaders accepted pardons or went into permanent exile, sometimes enlisting in European armies.

General George Wade was not so sure. 'More than half of the twenty-two thousand men capable of bearing arms in the Highlands and Islands were ready to create new troubles to favour the Pretender', he wrote in a report to the king. In July 1724, George I appointed Wade as Commander-in-Chief, North Britain, and this highly experienced and level-headed soldier saw immediately what needed to be done.

Thinking like a Roman rather than an eighteenth-century general, Wade proposed the building of a network of roads, bridges and barracks in the Highlands. Work began almost immediately. Four major routes were planned: from Fort William to Inverness, from Dunkeld to Inverness, from Crieff to Tummel Bridge and beyond, and from Dalwhinnie to Fort Augustus. Like the Roman roads, Wade's are uncompromising as they thread their way through the wild Highland landscape, climbing mountainsides in zigzags, crossing rushing rivers with solid, sturdy stone bridges and traversing soft and boggy ground.

Camps were set up at ten-mile intervals and the inns that were established there after the roads were completed were known as kingshouses. Perhaps the best known is on Rannoch Moor at the head of Glencoe, its apparent isolation a memory of all that digging, quarrying and sweat. Summer work parties of 100 soldiers were helped by masons and carpenters to lay down roads sixteen feet wide where the terrain allowed and ten feet where it was difficult. Gradients were dictated by the ability of horses to pull artillery up them. If the ascents and descents were too steep, then another route had to be found.

A new fort was built at Cille Chuimein at the south-west end of Loch Ness and named Fort Augustus after the third son of George

II, William Augustus, Duke of Cumberland, a man who would later gain great notoriety in the Highlands. The new road linked it with Fort William in the south-west and Fort George (then on the site of Inverness Castle) in the north-east. It was the first of what became known as the Wade Military Roads to be completed. Ruthven Barracks near Kingussie, its substantial ruins still visible from the A9, was at a crossroads. One new, and difficult, road was laid down west to Fort Augustus, and the other coming up from Dunkeld went north to Inverness.

Long stretches of Wade's roads are buried under modern tarmac and others, such as the route through the Corrieyairack Pass to Fort Augustus, are no longer used. But many of his bridges survive, and none are more splendid than the crossing of the Tay at Aberfeldy. Completed in 1734/5, it was expensive at £4,000, the equivalent of more than £1 million in today's values, and its five elegant arches were designed by William Adam, father of the more famous Robert.

General Wade, later promoted to marshal, never fought a battle against the clans, but the military importance of his work is recognised in the sixth verse of the British National Anthem. It is not often sung:

Lord, grant that Marshal Wade
May, by thy mighty aid,
Victory bring.
May he sedition hush,
Rebellious Scots to crush,
God save the King.

Overlooking the bridge at Aberfeldy and the river is the Black Watch Memorial. It remembers not only a famous regiment of the British army but also Wade's efforts to drain some of the Highland clans' military capability. He raised a militia known as the Highland Watches, men who would be paid to do just that, to police the glens and monitor any activity. Men were recruited from loyal Clan Campbell and later from the eastern clans, Frasers, Grants and Munros. By 1739 the regiment had become known as Am Freiceadan Dubh – the Black Guards or the Black Watch. When the Highlanders fought with great courage and steadfastness under the command of the Duke of Cumberland in 1745 at Fontenoy and at Tournai, they were described as 'the Black Watch of Battles, first to come and last to go'. In the same battle, in a rehearsal of what was to come, the regiment was repulsed by the Irish Brigade, the Jacobite 'Wild Geese', who fought in the army of the French king. Over three centuries of service, the Black Watch won 172 battle honours, more than any other regiment of foot and a unique achievement in the British army. Although now absorbed into the Royal Regiment of Scotland, the Black Watch is still headquartered at Fort George.

12

Defeat and Departure

1745–1753

The Reverend Thomas Bray was very worried about 'the growth in vice and immorality', which he believed arose from 'the gross ignorance of the principles of the Christian religion'. On 8 March 1698, in the wood-panelled chambers of Judge John Hooke at Lincoln's Inn in London, he met a small group of like-minded, worried friends. These included Colonel Maynard Colchester, the Commissioner for Superstitious Lands, a strange, more than faintly Orwellian role that disguised a ruthless political purpose. The 'Superstitious' were Catholics, and less than twenty years before the friends met, the fictitious conspiracy invented by Titus Oates known as the 'Popish Plot' had whipped up sectarian hysteria all over Britain.

Books were the cure. Bray and his friends raised money to found The Society for Promoting Christian Knowledge and its central role was to publish and distribute Christian, that is Anglican, literature throughout England and Wales, and also, very importantly, in the colonies in America and the Caribbean. Libraries were built – Bray is sometimes credited with the invention of the lending library – and schools were founded. Money was provided for teacher training.

One of England's most problematic colonies was Scotland, or more precisely, the Highlands and Islands of Scotland. Two years after the Union of the Parliaments in 1707, when there could be no legal or constitutional impediment, The Society in Scotland for Propagating Christian Knowledge (SSPCK) was founded by royal charter, a clear indication of the politics lurking behind the prayers.

Its principal purpose was the creation of schools 'where religion and virtue might be taught to young and old' in the Scottish Highlands, and any other 'uncivilised' places. Its clear purpose was to counter the twin threats of Irish Catholic missionaries, whose Gaelic would be widely understood, and the growth of Jacobitism. By 1711 five schools had been set up, and then more in Inverness, Glenelg, Lochearnhead, Glenartney on Arran, Callander and elsewhere, until by 1758 there were a staggering 176, most of them north of the Highland Line.

There was an emphatic, and ultimately self-defeating, insistence on the exclusive use of English in the classroom. From 1720, SSPCK rules were explicit: literacy and numeracy were taught 'but not any Latin or Irish [Gaelic]', both of these being attributes of popery and Jacobitism. Later, the society claimed that their missionary work in the northern colony had succeeded and 'that barbarity and the Irish language [both clearly and literally linked] are almost rooted out'. In 1753 children were specifically forbidden 'either in the schoolhouse or when playing about the doors thereof to speak Erse [Gaelic], under pain of being chastised [beaten]'.

It was largely pointless. Without a word of English, children rote-learned what they were taught, chanting the catechism and the times tables in class without understanding a word. But attitudes eventually softened a little. In 1741 the great Gaelic poet Alasdair macMhaighstir Alasdair, employed by the SSPCK as a teacher (apparently his employers were either ignorant of the fact that he had fought at Sheriffmuir in the MacDonald regiments, or chose to ignore it), compiled a short Gaelic to English glossary. In 1767 a version of the New Testament was published in Gaelic, with English facing pages.

Despite these concessions to common sense, the SSPCK led the assault on the language, taking it into the heart of communities, and although its attitudes moderated, they also persisted. Well into the twentieth century, Highland and Island children were still beaten if they slipped into their native language in the classroom or the playground.

Language mattered. It was and is a deeply embedded component of identity, a lexicon of experience in the glens and the straths, and when it came under sustained attack, ancient bonds were loosened, the glories of Gaelic demeaned and ignored, its dignity disrespected. To many, departure to the south or even further afield seemed more and more attractive. In the Northern Isles, history was taking a very different turn as Orcadians in particular began to look across the Atlantic for opportunity.

*

In 1659 two *coureurs des bois* ignored the orders of the governor of New France, Pierre de Voyer, Vicomte de Mouzay. Pierre-Esprit Radisson and Médard des Groseilliers were trappers who had heard from the Cree Indians of what is now northern Canada, that the best fur country lay to the north and west of Lake Superior. There was a frozen sea there around whose shores the beaver in particular were plentiful. But the Marquis d'Argenson was distracted – there was internal quarrelling amongst the French settlers and he was more concerned with repelling attacks from the Iroquois Confederacy on Quebec and Montreal, and on the farming land along the banks of the St Lawrence River, than he was with the business opportunities presented by the furs. He missed a great opportunity when he ordered the *coureurs des bois* not to explore the shores of Hudson Bay.

And so, Radisson and des Groseilliers travelled south to Boston, Massachusetts, to raise the capital for an expedition to the north, and were this time successful. However, in 1663 their ship became trapped in the frozen sea, its timbers groaning and cracking with the press of the pack ice in the Hudson Straits, the eastern entrance to Hudson Bay. Having returned safely to Boston, their undeterred investors sailed the two trappers across the Atlantic to raise more money. They met Prince Rupert, the dashing cavalry commander of the Royalist armies of the War of the Three Kingdoms. He was so impressed that he agreed to invest, and to introduce the Frenchmen to his cousin, King Charles II. More cash was duly raised, two ships were fitted out and after a long voyage, a fort was built on the shores of James Bay, the southernmost waters of Hudson Bay. It was to become the first of many 'factories' – places controlled by the company's agent, the factor.

The two *coureurs des bois* used all their skills and knowledge in the forests around the bay, enlisting native trappers to work with them. In the winter of 1688/9 one ship returned to England loaded with premium furs, mostly beaver pelts. The fashion for beaver fur hats had caused the extinction of the European beaver. The furs from New France were sold in London for high prices and on 2 May 1670, Charles II granted a royal charter incorporating 'The Governor and Company of Adventurers of England, trading into Hudson's Bay'. Prince Rupert was appointed the first governor, and the Hudson's Bay Company was born.

In the summer of 1702, a splendid new ship sailed into Stromness harbour on the western shore of Orkney Mainland. Its captain, Michael Grimington, had worked for the Hudson's Bay Company since its inception, crossing and recrossing the Atlantic many times, taking men and supplies out to the forts and factories around the bay and bringing back valuable cargoes of beaver pelts. However, he was having great difficulty recruiting men who would work hard and tolerate the harsh conditions of life in the long and bitter winters.

Many of the ships sailing up the east coast of Britain called in at Stromness to take on water and supplies before setting a course west over the ocean. The little port lay close to 60 degrees latitude north, the same as Hudson Bay, and the voyage across the North Atlantic was considerably shorter than that from London and the Channel ports to the British colonies in New England. It was also sensible to go north to Orkney in order to avoid the English Channel and risk becoming entangled with the warring navies of England, France, Spain and Holland. An inscribed stone marks Login's Well in the south end of Stromness, the place where seamen filled their ships' water barrels.

Captain Grimington began to recruit Orcadians for the Hudson's Bay Company, offering them far more money than they would ever earn in a lifetime as fishermen or farm workers. For periods of five to ten years, young men would go to the 'Nor' Wast' before coming home with the means to buy land to work for themselves and their family. With excellent seamanship skills learned from generations on the waters around the archipelago, Orcadians were much prized by the Hudson's Bay Company and they made up a large proportion of the workforce. They also had a reputation for reliability, hard work and patience, especially in their dealings with the native Canadian trappers. Several buildings in Stromness remember the recruitment. The Haven was a former Hudson's Bay Agency building, as was what is now the Pier Arts Centre.

When the company's ships were sighted sailing into the harbour in June, there was celebration and an old cannon was fired. Dances were held on the decks of the ships under awnings as the crews went about the business of gathering supplies, men and water before setting out on the Atlantic crossing. When the Hudson's Bay Company ships returned in November with Orcadians who had completed their terms of service, there was more celebration. Many brought back news of men in Rupert's Land, the vast territory covering most of Northern Canada that had been named after Prince Rupert. Shopping lists were also handed over from men who wanted clothing (thick, warm woollen stockings were knitted by their families, and that soon turned into a business in Stromness), books, sometimes musical instruments, sweets, even spectacles were to be sent out with the ships that would sail into Stromness the following June.

The names of the Orcadians who made up the majority of the Hudson's Bay Company workforce can easily be spotted on the ships' manifests and other records. Old surnames that descended through Viking ancestry could have come from nowhere else: the likes of Foubister, Isbister, Flett, Clouston, Linklater and others. Their origins and identity were clear. With the few Highlanders who went to the Nor'Wast, it is more difficult to work out exactly where they came from.

The ostensible reason was the fact that many men carried the same surname, particularly amongst the Campbells, the MacDonalds and the other major clans. Like many Anglicised names, most are simple patronymics, that is, a name taken from a father. In English, Johnson is an obvious example: the son of John. Campbell and Cameron are two major exceptions and both derive from nicknames. Campbell in Gaelic is *caimbeul* meaning 'twisted mouth' and may be linked to language rather than any deformity. Clann Caimbeul lands were close to the Old Welsh-speaking kingdom of Strathclyde and perhaps they spoke Old Welsh or their dialect of Gaelic was heavily influenced by the speech of their neighbours. Cameron is from *camshron*, for 'twisted (or broken) nose', perhaps a reference to their fabled martial prowess, their noses broken like an old boxer's.

Most of the other clan names come from name-fathers, distant ancestors whose descendants took their name. That is where confusions of identity can occur. Gaelic helps by adding a good deal to the simple formula of a given or Christian name and a surname. First of all, men call themselves MacDonald, for example, meaning the son of Donald, and it is rendered as MacDhomhnaill, the second element taking the genitive case. Women are styled NicDhomhnaill, where the first element is a conflation of *nighean* for girl and *mhic* being *mac*, also taking the genitive case, making it a patronymic at one remove, that is, daughter of the son of Donald.

In Keppoch, Glengarry, Morar, Ardnamurchan, Sleat and the other areas in the Highlands where there were many people with the name of MacDonald, more clarity was achieved in two main ways. A Donald MacDonald who was the son of James MacDonald and the grandson of Neil MacDonald might use that line of descent, whose combination of different elements might be fairly rare, to call himself Domhnall Sheumais Neill, or Neil's James's Donald, where the *mac* is dropped. If confusion persisted, a nickname might help. If Donald was hard of hearing, he might be Domhnall Bodhar, Deaf Donald. Others are conferred because of physical characteristics. As mentioned earlier, Rob Roy was originally known in Gaelic as Raibeart Ruadh – 'Red-haired Robert'.

In the case of Clan Gregor, names could be fatal. When James VI and I had the clan disnamed, those who bore it were fair game for anyone who wanted to rob, attack or even kill them. There would be no legal sanction. But in the case of Gregor Drummond and his cousin, James, a change of name did nothing to change their sense of themselves as proud Highland warriors.

As the last reigning British king to lead an army into battle, at Dettingen in 1743, George II was curious about the reputation of the fearsome Highland clans who had rebelled against the installation of his father as monarch in 1715. Sometime in the 1730s his agents made enquiries, and Gregor and James were summoned to a meeting in Perth. Both clansmen were suddenly seized, bundled into a stagecoach and, surrounded by a large escort of cavalry, were driven south to London.

MacGregors by blood, both had taken the name of Drummond after their clan had been disnamed once more for persistent lawlessness and seemingly endless raiding and feuding, not helped by the increasingly famous example of Rob Roy. Tall, strikingly good-looking, Gregor was known as Griogair Boidheach, 'Gregor the Beautiful', and he was reckoned the greatest swordsman in all the southern clans, while James Drummond, Seumas a' Ghlinne, 'James of the Glens', was not far short of his equal.

At St James's Palace these kilted warriors were taken under heavy guard into the central courtyard. While George II looked down from an upstairs window, each man was given a claymore, a basket-hilted sword that could be swung and thrust to devastating effect in battle. But then, to the surprise of everyone watching, Gregor and James laid down their weapons and in the middle of a ring of armed and watchful soldiers, they undressed, taking off their belts and heavy plaids and wearing only their linen sarks. They then put on a dazzling, glinting, clashing display of swordsmanship and sheer strength. And when the claymores were exchanged for the hooked pikes known as Lochaber axes, they swung and tossed them in the air like children's toys.

The king was impressed. But when Gregor and James were escorted into the royal presence, still under heavy guard, little was said, neither party having much English. After an embarrassing series of coughs and silences, George II signalled that each man should be given a golden guinea.

Insulted, affronted and very angry, Gregor and James looked at the coin in their hands, looked up at the king and said, 'Chaneil sinn 'a còmhrag 'son airgead, ach 'son urram' – 'We fight not for money, but only for honour.'

And as they stormed out of the stateroom, Gregor and James gave each of the amazed flunkeys at the door their golden guineas.

*

The patronymic of the author of the great epic poem *The Birlinn of Clanranald*, looks awkward at first sight. Alasdair macMhaighstir Alasdair macDhomhnaill is Alasdair, the son of Master Alasdair MacDonald, and is in fact very clear and specific. The Gaelic term of *Mhaighstir* derives from the Latin *magister* meaning 'master', but in the Highlands it was the title given to a minister or a priest, and is therefore better translated as Reverend.

Alasdair, the son of the Reverend Alasdair MacDonald, was born in 1698 and lived a long and very eventful, as well as creative, life until his death at Arisaig in 1770. Not only was he an immensely gifted poet – some say the greatest Gaelic poet until Sorley MacLean in the twentieth century, and perhaps greater even than MacLean – Alasdair was at the heart of politics in the eighteenth-century Highlands, and in important ways his verses caught and reflected the atmosphere of the times.

Born into the minor gentry, *na daoine uaisle*, of Clanranald, he was born and raised at Dalilea, a beautiful house that still stands in the green and undulating fields at the southern end of Loch Shiel. It seems that he was taught at home by his father, who introduced the boy to Greek, Roman and classic European literature. His later writing shows these influences clearly. Alasdair went on to matriculate at both Glasgow and Edinburgh universities but appears not to have taken a degree. It may be that life in either city was too expensive, forcing him to return home to Moidart.

In light of his Jacobite sympathies, Alasdair's eventual employment by the Society in Scotland for Propagating Christian Knowledge was not the only surprise, he was also well known for composing erotic poetry and declaiming it in public. The ministers of the Presbytery of Mull reported that Alasdair wandered through the countryside 'composing Galick songs stuffed with obscene language'. And so he did. 'In Praise of Morag', Alasdair's wife, does not mince its metaphors and her breasts are like *geal criostal*, 'white crystal', and lily of the valley, and he compares her kisses to cinnamon. 'Moladh air Deagh Bhod' translates as 'In Praise of a Good Prick' (although Edward Dwelly is very coy in his great dictionary: the entry, so to speak, for *bhod* is translated not into English but Latin, as *membrum virile*), and Alasdair's deeply poetic list of the surprising characteristics of a good prick are:

Iulach, feitheach, feadanach,
Laidir, seasmhach, buan.

Beckoning, sinewed, chanter-like,
Long-lasting, steadfast, strong.

Beckoning? And of course *feadan* in an obvious, entertaining metaphor, the chanter attached to the bag of bagpipes that allows the piper to play the notes of a melody.

Alasdair's poetry, profane and more serious, survived because he had the rare gift of being able to write in Gaelic. His *Leabhar a Theagasc Ainminnin*, literally 'The Book for Teaching Names', the glossary he compiled for the SSPCK, was not only the first secular book ever printed and published in Gaelic, but it also had a founding role in establishing the form and spelling of words, something that had never been necessary in an oral culture. Alasdair used early modern-Irish texts as a model for how the language might be read and written. To some extent that froze Gaelic orthography, and the written language has kept many silent letters and syllables, whereas the spelling of Irish was later made more phonetic and therefore easier to read.

In 1744, the SSPCK school at Kilchoan in Ardnamurchan appears to have lost its teacher. Officials wrote to Alasdair criticising him for sending his son, Ranald, to the school to teach the children in his place. They believed that he had 'deserted his post to help rally the Jacobite clans'. In fact, he had done much more than that. 'Oran Nuadh' ('New Song'), 'Oran nam Fineachan Gàidhealach' ('Song of the Highland Clans') and 'Oran don Phrionnsa' ('Song for the Prince'), had all been sent to Aeneas MacDonald, a banker who was an influential advisor to the Young Pretender, Prince Charles Edward Stuart. When Aeneas read translations of Alasdair's poems to the young man, it was said that their power played a key role in persuading him that another Jacobite rising might finally succeed.

Two events coincided in 1743 to translate Alasdair macMhaigh-stir Alasdair's poetry into action. Spain and France concluded the Treaty of Fontainebleau, making Louis XV and his uncle, Philip V, allies in the War of the Austrian Succession, essentially a territorial conflict in Central Europe that would ripple around the world as far as India and America. An important part of the treaty was a wish to destabilise Britain internally by becoming actively involved in the restoration of the Stuarts. The second event, which made that more likely to succeed, was James VIII and III's transfer of power to Prince Charles, his eldest son. He became the Young Pretender, in essence the prince regent, with the ability to act unilaterally on his father's behalf as king in all but name.

In February 1744, an army mustered at Dunkirk. Twelve thousand well-equipped soldiers, including the Irish Brigade, boarded ships at that Channel port because it was possible to sail from there to the Thames estuary on a single tide. At the same time, Admiral Roquefeuil's squadron moved out of the harbour at Brest in Brittany, in an attempt to lure the Royal Navy away from the mustered invasion force, but once again bad weather frustrated the invasion plans. Assailed by severe storms several French ships sank and others were badly damaged, making it impossible for their navy to protect the invasion fleet. A month later, Louis XV cancelled the expedition.

Prince Charles arrived in Paris in August to try to persuade the French to supply and support a landing in Scotland. Sir Hector Maclean, chief of the clan, had assured him that at least 5,000 men would join a Jacobite rising and others claimed that there was significant support in England for the return of the Stuarts. The French were not enthusiastic however, but the prince pressed ahead, certain that if he did land in Scotland and the clans rose, the French would be forced to support him. Having raised and borrowed a great deal of money with Aeneas MacDonald's help, Charles set sail in early July 1745, with only two ships, a handful of volunteers from the Irish Brigade and a store of weapons for those in the Highlands who might join him. One ship was attacked by a Royal Navy warship and was forced to turn back with the Irish and most of the weapons. The prince, though, was not deterred, and on 23 July, the *Du Teillay* dropped anchor off the little island of Eriskay in the Hebrides. Although he did not realise it at the time, one of the first people to meet him was Alasdair macMhaighstir Alasdair.

Robert Forbes, a Scottish Anglican bishop, compiled *The Lyon in Mourning*, a chronicle of the 1745 Jacobite rising that included interviews with men who took part, and a passage that describes the meeting on the *Du Teillay*:

> He did not then know that the Prince was among the passengers, who being in a very plain dress, Captain MacDonald made up to him without any manner of ceremony and conversed with him in a very familiar way, sitting close by the Prince and drinking a glass with him, till one of the name of MacDonald made him such a look that immediately he began to suspect that he was using too much freedom with one above his own rank. Upon this he soon withdrew, but still was in the dark as to what particular person the young gentleman he had been conversing with might be.

More than three weeks after this first encounter, Alasdair macMhaighstir Alasdair sailed up Loch Shiel from his house at Dalilea with Prince Charles and a handful of supporters. With Alasdair's help, letters had gone out to clan chiefs requesting that they do their loyal duty and bring their men to a muster at Glenfinnan at the north-eastern end of the loch. But when the prince's flotilla sailed close to the landing place, there was immense disappointment, as only about fifty men were waiting. So that no one could see his tears, Charles was escorted to a nearby barn by Colonel John O'Sullivan, his chief of staff. Even when Allan MacDonald of Morar came with 150 men, it was very far from an army, little more than an escort.

Sometime around the middle of the afternoon on 19 August, heads turned to the mountains to the north. Faintly at first, men could hear the sound that changed everything. Floating clear above the trees at the head of Glenfinnan, the war pipes rang out. Men knew the music. Thanks be to the Lord, Clan Cameron had come. Lines of clansmen were snaking down the paths on the flanks of the ridge of Sgùrr Thuilm, perhaps 700, perhaps more. Later in the day 300 MacDonalds of Keppoch came, and then the same number of MacDonnells of Glengarry. At last, an army had mustered. When the standard was raised and a proclamation read out, Alasdair macMhaighstir Alasdair sang his new composition 'Tearlach mac Sheumais' ('Charles, Son of James').

With General Wade's new roads allowing rapid movement through the mountains, Prince Charles's clansmen reached Edinburgh by 16 September and the following day a party of Camerons slipped into the city by the Netherbow Port. Without a fight, the Jacobites had captured the capital of Scotland, but soon afterwards, they would have to fight a battle.

Having failed to intercept the fast-moving Jacobite army on its way through the Highland glens, General John Cope had sailed his government forces to Dunbar. When word of their landing reached Edinburgh, Prince Charles ordered an immediate mobilisation. The armies got sight of each other near the village of Prestonpans. When Lord George Murray saw that Cope had deployed his army in a strong position, between walls and an embankment to protect their flanks, and with boggy ground at the foot of a slope to the south, he sent Colonel Harry Ker to reconnoitre. The details are revealed in a passage from John Home's *History of the Rebellion in the year 1745*:

He came down from the Highland Army, alone; he was mounted on a little white pony; and with the greatest deliberation rode between the two armies, looking at the ground on each hand of him. Several shots were fired at him as he went along. When he came to a dry stone dyke that was in his way, he dismounted, and, pulling down a piece of the dyke, led his horse over it. He then returned to Lord George Murray, and assured him that it was impossible to get through the morass, and attack the enemy in front, without receiving several fires.

By which he meant that if the clansmen were slowed by the boggy ground, Cope's redcoats would have time to reload, possibly more than once, and get off several volleys at men floundering in the marshy ground, sitting ducks. The Highland charge was the Jacobites' sole tactic, and if it was impeded and failed, they would be defeated. The ground had to be right. Despite this, Prince Charles wanted to attack immediately, and what followed was a fierce argument, the first of many. An able, experienced soldier, Lord George Murray had joined Prince Charles's army with the Atholl Brigade on their way south, and he and his commander-in-chief did not agree, but Murray managed eventually to persuade him to delay. Better ground needed to be found.

A local boy, Robert Anderson, was a keen wildfowler, and he knew the boggy terrain and its pools near Prestonpans well. Murray could see that the newly harvested cornfields to the east of Cope's position were far more suitable for the charge. Wishing to preserve as much of an element of surprise as possible, he asked Anderson to lead the army through the marsh in the grey hours before dawn by a path not easily visible to government pickets.

Just before the sun came up over the North Sea on 21 September 1745, the Highland clans were quietly deployed in the stubble fields. The Camerons and the Appin Stewarts were on the left wing, MacGregors and the Duke of Perth's men in the centre with Lord George Murray, and with the MacDonald regiments, Keppoch, Glengarry and Clanranald, in the place of honour on right, Captain

Alasdair macMhaighstir Alasdair waited with them for the order to advance. In the second line was the Atholl Brigade, Robertsons, McLachlans, Glencoe MacDonalds and Prince Charles on horseback protected by his Life Guards.

So that the clansmen could get as close as possible to General Cope's lines before being seen, Murray ordered his men to crawl through the stubble in the half-light before dawn. Like all the chiefs and the Duke of Perth, he led from the front.

And then it came. At Murray's signal, the army materialised as if out of nowhere, like spectres from the bowels of hell. Men stood up and their chiefs roared the order to charge. The war pipes played the battle rants, the war cries were shouted. Men raced across the stubble. After firing their weapons and forming wedges, Clan Cameron were first to hit, smashing into Cope's right. The lines of redcoats buckled immediately. On the right wing, Alasdair macMhaighstir Alasdair ran past Prince Charles, who shouted at him '*Gres-ort! Gres-ort!*' ('Hurry up! Hurry up!')

James Johnstone, a raw recruit who joined the army in Perth, later recorded in vivid detail what he saw. The MacGregor regiment in the centre charged into mounted dragoons, and some who did not own swords had lashed the long blades of scythes to poles to make primitive halberds, and they did terrible slaughter:

> They had been frequently enjoined to aim at the noses of the horses with their swords, without minding the riders; as the natural movement of a horse, wounded in the face, is to wheel round: and a few horses wounded in that manner, are sufficient to throw a whole squadron into such disorder, that it is impossible afterwards to rally it. They followed this advice most implicitly, and the English cavalry were instantly thrown into confusion.
>
> Macgregor's company did great execution with their scythes. They cut the legs of the horses in two, and their riders through the middle of their bodies.

Many redcoats panicked at the sight of the Highlanders coming on 'like a living torrent' and did not wait for the driving shudder of impact. James Johnstone again recounted:

> The panic-terror of the English surpasses all imagination. They threw down their arms that they might run with more speed, thus depriving themselves by their fears of the only means of arresting the vengeance of the Highlanders. Of so many men in a condition, from their numbers, to preserve order in their retreat, not one thought of defending himself. Terror had taken entire possession of their minds.
>
> I saw a young Highlander, about fourteen years of age, scarcely formed, who was presented to the Prince as a prodigy, having killed, it was said, fourteen of the enemy. The Prince asked him if this was true? 'I do not know,' replied he, 'if I killed them; but I brought fourteen soldiers to the ground with my sword.' Another Highlander brought ten soldiers to the Prince, whom he had made prisoners, driving them before him like a flock of sheep.

After the shambles at Sheriffmuir, the Battle of Prestonpans was a profound shock that shook the government of George II to its core. The rout had lasted no longer than ten minutes as an army from the past, many with only bladed weapons and raw courage, had blown away soldiers equipped with musket and cannon. Prestonpans gave Scotland to Prince Charles as the government army was cut to pieces, suffering around 400 men killed and very many more wounded and captured. Only thirty-five clansmen fell on the blood-spattered cornfields. Prince Charles, Murray and the chiefs were jubilant. James Johnstone was horrified: 'The field of battle presented a spectacle of horror, being covered with heads, legs, arms and mutilated bodies: for the killed all fell by the sword.'

At about 11 a.m. on 4 December, a troop of horsemen clattered down the cobbles of Friar Gate into the centre of Derby. Watching from doorways and windows, the townspeople were surprised and relieved. Rumours had reached them that a pack of howling Highland wolves was about to descend on them, savages who had butchered a government army at Prestonpans two months before. When Prince Charles arrived with his blue-coated Life Guards and an escort of clan chiefs in all their finery, he turned out not to be a blood-spattered demon but a handsome young man with a regal bearing and dressed in some splendour. But despite this, the people of Derby must have thought this a very foreign invasion as they watched kilted warriors who spoke a language no one understood and who marched into the town as their pipers played *An Ceol Mor*, 'the Great music'. Anxious about desertions from the army on the long march down the west of England and the fact that only in Manchester had any significant number of recruits come forward, Lord George Murray had given orders that the clan regiments march into the town in contingents, to give the impression of a much larger army.

Derby is only 125 miles from London, no more than a five- or six-day march for the fast-moving Highlanders, unencumbered by artillery and able to forage. Murray knew that news of the Jacobites' arrival in the town would reach London very quickly and he wanted to give the impression of strength. Fearing that a vast horde of slavering savages might swarm down Whitehall, there was panic. Those who had somewhere else to go, went. Others withdrew cash from banks, and many Londoners were very anxious, waiting for news.

But appearances were deceptive. To encourage an invasion of England, Prince Charles had talked up potential support, saying that the influential Tory MP Sir Watkin Williams-Wynn, would meet them in Derby with news of French help, and that the Duke of Beaufort was on the point of taking the important port of Bristol. Neither materialised. Only 200–300 volunteers had joined the army in Manchester and there had been no support from elsewhere. Nothing had been forthcoming from the French.

In the oak-panelled dining room of Exeter House, a council of war was summoned. Prince Charles, Cameron of Lochiel and Colonel O'Sullivan argued for an advance on London. George II and his court would flee they said, France would come and the symbolism of taking the capital city would be immense. Led by Lord George

Murray, the rest of the chiefs believed they had come far enough, too far perhaps – better to retreat and consolidate Scotland. Murray held the view that the fighting could go on 'for several years' and drain the London government's will to maintain the union. The Stuarts would recover the throne of Scotland. Furthermore, government armies were approaching: the Duke of Cumberland from the south and Marshal Wade from Newcastle. News had also come from Lord John Drummond, Duke of Perth, that French ships had landed some supplies and money at Montrose. There were only 200 soldiers from the Irish Brigade and the Royal Ecossais (Drummond's regiment of exiled Jacobites), but Drummond believed thousands more would follow. The debate swayed very much in favour of a retreat, but before a final decision was made, the council adjourned.

On the morning of 6 December, a man who gave his name as Captain Oliver Williams rode into Derby. His real name was Dudley Bradstreet, and he was a government spy funded by the dukes of Cumberland and Newcastle. Much later, Bradstreet recorded what happened when he was first challenged by a sentry: 'I told the fellow that I was a man of quality come to serve the prince regent, and would be followed by all my friends if my usage was good, and desired to be brought to the prince's quarters directly. I heard them whisper that an English lord was come to join them.'

Somehow, Bradstreet gained access to the prince's reconvened council of war on the afternoon of 6 December. He spoke of government armies closing in on Derby and invented another that had reached Northampton, seventy miles away, and they were approaching fast. Whether or not these exaggerations and fictions finally clinched the argument in favour of retreat, it is impossible to know, but events moved quickly and on the morning of 7 December, the Highlanders began the long march back north to the sanctuary of Scotland.

At first it appeared that the correct strategic choice had been made. After conducting a brilliant fighting retreat, the Jacobite army reached Stirling and were met by reinforcements from Banffshire and Aberdeenshire, as well as some Irish and French regular soldiers.

They brought Prince Charles's strength to 8,000, the largest army he had yet commanded. On 17 January they defeated government forces under General Henry Hawley at Falkirk, but were forced to abandon a siege of Stirling Castle. Many clansmen began to drift away, anxious to return home after a long time away on campaign. As the Jacobites retreated north to Inverness, their numbers dwindled, and the Duke of Cumberland pursued them.

When lookouts from Clan Cameron and the Atholl Brigade peered into the sleeting rain that blew down from the dark heads of the mountains across Drumossie Moor, not far from Culloden House near Inverness, on 16 April 1746, they could make out the red coats of the government army marching towards the chosen ground. Silk standards snapping, soaked in the stiff breeze, drummers rattling out the paradiddle, the sergeant-majors roared for their regiments to draw up and dress the line. 'Look to your fronts! Stand fast!'

Five hundred yards away stood the clans. In family groups, fathers and sons, uncles and nephews, cousins and brothers, they waited for the *claideamh mòr*. Unlike the Duke of Cumberland on a grey horse, riding up and down behind the government lines with his generals, the chiefs would lead from the front and would be the first to clash with the bayonets and suffer the musket volleys. The oldest men, who knew what was coming, were always set in front of the wedges that would form, and the younger clansmen, some no more than boys and often poorly armed, would charge behind them, following them as they cut swathes and fought their way into the ruck of battle.

At first the redcoats thought the Highlanders were singing – psalms and prayers were often offered up before battle was joined. But in fact, the clans were doing something unique, something that sprang from love, from the past and a time out of mind, from the beloved kindred ground, their native places. They were summoning the Army of the Dead.

Before they roared their war cries, the names of their places, raised their swords and charged across the moor, many men recited their genealogy: 'Is mise mac Ruaridh, 'ic Iain, 'ic Sheumais' ('I am the son of Rory, the son of John, the son of James'). Many could go back beyond twenty generations, far back into the darkness of the past and its tales of heroes, honour and prowess. And when they remembered those men who had gone before them, they knew that the ghosts of their glorious past with all their ancient courage would race across the heather beside them.

The order to charge never properly came. Unable to tolerate the murderous cannonade that ploughed through their ranks, the Atholl Brigade broke into the charge on the Jacobite right. And when Clan Cameron and the Appin Stewarts saw they were away, they too roared their war cries and charged across the moor.

Culloden began with the Highlanders remembering who they were and why they had come to the moor to fight, and it ended in disaster, the beginning of a flood tide that would sweep the clans from their glens and straths and into the pages of history.

Having escaped the carnage at Culloden by catching a spooked horse, James Johnstone disguised himself as a pedlar and walked south, down the length of Britain. On 30 July he was at Kennington Common in London, hiding in plain sight as part of a huge crowd. Tens of thousands had come to cheer the death of traitors and watch a series of public executions. Colonel Francis Towneley and nine other members of the Manchester Regiment had been convicted of high treason and condemned to be hung, drawn and quartered. This hideous medieval punishment was somewhat mitigated by the executioner's discretion. Before their naked bodies were emasculated, eviscerated and butchered, the condemned were generally hanged by the neck until they were dead. As James Johnstone watched, his fellow officer, a man with whom he had marched to Derby and fought at Culloden, went to his death with dignity. Dressed in a black velvet suit, Towneley climbed the ladder to the scaffold with apparent calm. When the stool was kicked away, the dark clothes will have disguised the stains of urine on his legs and the voiding of his bowels.

Johnstone was fortunate to escape. After his victory at Culloden, the Duke of Cumberland encouraged and enabled a campaign of mass punishment, plunder, rape and killing right across the Highlands and Islands. It was a sadistic cocktail of ethnic cleansing and gratuitous savagery against a people who were seen as barbarians who babbled an incomprehensible language and were less than human, and therefore easier to kill. Highlanders called it Am Bliadhna nan Creach, 'the Year of Pillaging'.

After the headlong flight of Prince Charles and the retreat of almost 1,500 men under the command of Lord George Murray, Culloden was the landscape of hell. Hundreds of badly wounded men lay in the heather, the blood loss from terrible injuries from grapeshot and musket ball causing them to pass in and out of consciousness. Supervised by General Henry Hawley on horseback, execution squads prowled. To save money on powder and ammunition, he ordered his men to bayonet or bludgeon clansmen to death with the butts of their muskets. A government officer, sickened by what he witnessed, later wrote: 'The moor was covered in blood and our men, what with killing the enemy, dabbling their feet in the blood, and splashing it about one another, looked like so many butchers rather than Christian soldiers.'

The assault on Highland society was economic as well as military. The commanders of the garrisons of the three Great Glen forts sent out raiding parties to steal all the livestock they could find grazing on the straths. In the summer after Culloden, one raid brought back 8,000 head of black cattle to Fort Augustus where they grazed the new grass to its roots. It did not matter to the government commanders that many of the clans they robbed had not supported the prince. They were all the same. The herds were sold on to Lowland cattle dealers at derisory prices, but that did not matter to Cumberland. Destruction of the pastoral economy and the beggaring of the people of the glens was his priority, but it was not his sole policy. The duke wrote to George II's prime minister, the Duke of Newcastle: 'I mean the transporting of particular clans, such as the entire Clan of the Camerons and almost all the tribes of the MacDonalds (excepting some of those of the Isles) and several other lesser clans, of which an exact list may easily be made.'

Owing to their nature, atrocities are often not recorded. Despite this, there are notices of several taking place across the Highlands and Islands, almost certainly only a fraction of the terrible vengeance taken by the British state on the clans.

In the summer of 1746, Major James Lockhart, a Lowland Scot, led a detachment of Cholmondeley's Regiment, which had fought at Culloden, out of Fort Augustus. When they marched west into Glen Moriston, Clan Grant country, they immediately made their intentions clear. When they saw three clansmen on the road, they shot them without warning or hesitation before rounding up their cattle. The herd belonged to Grant of Dundreggan and when the old man appeared with a letter of indemnity stating that he had not joined the prince, Major Lockhart ignored it. When Grant objected, he ordered his men to strip him naked, and when his wife protested they stripped her, humiliated the old woman and tried to cut the rings from her fingers. Lockhart gave orders that Grant be hanged, but when soldiers dragged him to the tree where the three dead clansmen had been strung up, an officer objected. His name was also Grant but he had fought in the government army at Culloden. He threatened to draw his sword to protect the old couple. It was one occasion when brutality backed down and the Grants were let go.

There was more outrage. At a township in Moidart, the clachan houses had their thatched roofs burned, and as the children scattered, the soldiers laid hands on their mothers. Women were raped outside their front doors. As her husband watched from the mountainside heather, Isobel MacDonald was held down and repeatedly raped by five soldiers. In the days after the battle, around Inverness, obscene acts were committed. A witness wrote of 'carnage made on both sexes'. A dead woman had been 'laid in a very undecent postour'. Many corpses of men had been stripped naked, some with 'their privites placed in their hands'.

The Islands did not escape the summer of terror either. Under the command of Captain John Ferguson of Aberdeen, HMS *Furnace* dropped anchor and soldiers rowed ashore to kill, burn and rape. The sailors raped a blind woman on the islet of Rona off Skye, and when they captured a fleeing French officer, Ferguson ordered him to be flogged. A young lieutenant of the Royal Scots Fusiliers objected, saying the man was not a rebel but a prisoner of war. Despite the prevention of this minor act of cruelty, more dreadful atrocities were carried out until the autumn.

A campaign medal was struck to honour the soldiers who had fought so bravely at Culloden. On one face was the profile of the portly Duke of Cumberland and on the other the image of the Greek god Apollo, pointing to a wounded dragon. The ominous inscription read *Actum Est Ilicet Periit,* and the date, *AP XVI MDCCXLVI.* 'The deed is done. It is all over. He has perished. April 16 1746'.

And as terrible deeds were done and many Highlanders perished, perhaps thousands, it was indeed almost all over. The economy was in ruins and never again would the clans play a role in the politics of the British state. Before long, there was departure as the glens began to empty and the time of the great emigrations began.

At first reluctant, Cluny Macpherson, the chief of the name, became in Lord George Murray's words an 'indefatigable' Jacobite. He did not join the prince's army after the muster at Glenfinnan, but instead helped General Cope in August 1745 raise more troops in the Highlands. After which Cluny was 'captured' and taken to Perth where he was quickly promoted from prisoner to become a colonel in the clan army. Macpherson fought at Prestonpans and Falkirk, but not at Culloden. Nevertheless, he was forced into hiding and a reward was offered for his head. For nine years, Cluny hid in the mountains of Badenoch, evading all attempts at capture. A government report stated that he 'haunts the houses of his kindred and his wife's in the day time, and he has proper places of retirement in the night time, to which he repairs by turns, according to the danger he [fears] he is in, from the different motions of the troops'.

It must have been a harsh life, especially in winter. In September 1746, Cluny and his fellow fugitives spent a week with Prince Charles, himself keenly hunted with a huge price on his head, in a cave on the rocky flanks of Ben Alder. It was known as the Cage: '[It] was no larger than to contain six or seven persons, four of which number were frequently employed playing at cards, one idly looking on, one baking [making dough] and another firing bread and cooking.'

The brutal realities of defeat and the destruction of Highland society and their direct and baleful influence on his family and his kinsmen had a curious effect on James Macpherson. A nephew of Cluny, he was born in October 1736, at Ruthven, in the heart of his clan's lands. As a boy, he saw government soldiers plunder and burn Cluny House and his family lose all their estates. It must have seemed a dark and ugly world, and James's reaction was to invent a better one.

While a student at King's College and Marischal College, both in Aberdeen and at the time separate universities, and later at Edinburgh, James claimed to have written 4,000 lines of verses. Some made their way into *The Highlander*, an epic poem published in 1758. It is hard going, a portentous and continuing fanfare of names and places that seem like a long introduction to a very short story. Macpherson himself later became similarly unimpressed and he tried hard to suppress it sometime after publication.

After university, the young man met the Reverend John Home, the author of *Douglas*, an enormously successful tragedy written in blank verse. It is the story of Norval, a lost child who became a soldier. Despite most of the characters dying by the end of the play, including Norval, it was immensely popular and was performed for decades. When he was with Home in the spa town of Moffat, Macpherson recited, and presumably translated, Gaelic verse from memory, and showed him manuscripts, presumably also translated, of poetry he said he had collected in the Hebrides. The great man was impressed, and Macpherson was impressed that he was impressed. An idea began to form, one that may have been inspired by the success of *Douglas*.

By 1760, Macpherson had compiled and published *Fragments of Ancient Poetry: Collected in the Highlands of Scotland and Translated from the Gaelic or Erse language*. It was a sensation, an immediate success, especially in Europe and North America. A year later, Macpherson apparently came across other manuscripts, the stories in them all narrated by the blind Gaelic bard, Ossian, and located in a distant, misty, heroic past. *Fingal* was published in 1761, and then more poetic tales of a similar sort in *Temora* in 1763.

Thomas Jefferson, later to become president of the United States, believed Ossian to be 'the greatest poet that has ever existed'. Napoleon Bonaparte, Denis Diderot and Voltaire were all ardent admirers. But at a distance of two centuries, it is difficult to understand what they saw in Fingal, as seen here in the opening, with a very necessary explanatory preface:

CATH-LODA — DUAN I.

ARGUMENT

Fingal, when very young, making a voyage to the Orkney Islands, was driven, by stress of weather, into a bay of Scandinavia, near the residence of Starno, king of Lochlin. Starno invites Fingal to a feast. Fingal, doubting the faith of the king, and mindful of a former breach of hospitality, refuses to go. – Starno gathers together his tribes; Fingal resolves to defend himself. – Night coming on, Duth-maruno proposes to Fingal to observe the motions of the enemy. – The king himself undertakes the watch. Advancing towards the enemy, he accidentally comes to the cave of Turthor, where Starno had confined Conban-cârgla, the captive daughter of a neighbouring chief. – Her story is imperfect, a part of the original being lost. – Fingal comes to a place of worship, where Starno, and his son Swaran, consulted the spirit of Loda concerning the issue of the war. – The encounter of Fingal and Swaran. – Duan first concludes with a description of the airy hall of Cruth-loda, supposed to be the Odin of Scandinavia.

A TALE of the times of old!

Why, thou wanderer unseen! thou bender of the thistle of Lora; why, thou breeze of the valley, hast thou left mine ear? I hear no distant roar of streams! No sound of the harp from the rock! Come, thou huntress of Lutha, Malvina, call back his soul to the bard. I look forward to Lochlin of lakes, to the dark billowy bay of U-thorno, where Fingal descends from ocean, from the roar of winds. Few are the heroes of Morven in a land unknown!

Challenging stuff. But then so is most literature from the eighteenth, nineteenth and even the early twentieth centuries. Daniel Defoe's *Robinson Crusoe* is a clunky read, Walter Scott's interminable novels with their lengthy introductions take an age to get moving and even something that moves fast like John Buchan's *The Thirty-Nine Steps* seems now mechanical and implausible. As I ploughed on through James Macpherson's 'Ossian', grasping at the threads of a narrative when they occasionally appeared, I realised I'd never get close to understanding what Thomas Jefferson or Napoleon Bonaparte saw in this tale. Stanzas that were intended to sound like a clash of cymbals must have struck them as moments of high drama or soaring expressions of noble sentiments, but to my ear, they were jerky jump-cuts from one windy and vague scene to another as the action, such as it was, moved between mountain tops and caves. I confess to a lack of stamina and even cross-eyed confusion after a morning reading 'Ossian' in an online version.

While Macpherson's *Fragments of Ancient Poetry* and Ossian were widely admired, they were also deeply suspected. From the beginning, he was accused of fakery. Instead of discovering or being given ancient manuscripts (from an oral culture?), Samuel Johnson and others accused the author of making it all up, convinced that Macpherson was 'a mountebank, a liar, and a fraud, and that the poems were forgeries'. When he was asked, 'Do you really believe that any man today could write such poetry?' Johnson said, 'Yes. Many men. Many women. And many children'.

Leaving aside a whiff of that quote itself having been manufactured, there were many in Britain who questioned the authenticity of the poems, and it must be significant that Macpherson never produced the original manuscripts he said he had found. When Gaelic versions finally appeared in 1801, after the author's death, they looked suspiciously like Gaelic back-translations of the original English.

Irish language scholars and antiquaries were also dismissive, saying that the style and the language were not convincing. There is even some anecdotal evidence that Macpherson's own command of Scots Gaelic was itself patchy. The genuine Fenian Cycle of Irish epic poetry, written down only in the medieval period, is indeed on a different plane. Here is a short extract that describes the hero of the *Táin Bó Cúailnge*, 'The Great Cattle Raid of Cooley'. This is how Cúchulainn prepared himself as he rode out to defend Ulster against the army of the King of Connaught:

The rage-fit was upon him. He shook like a bullrush in the stream. His sinews stretched and bunched, and every huge, immeasurable, vast ball of them was as big as the head of a month-old child. His face as a red bowl, fearsomely distorted, one eye sucked in so far that the beak of a wild crane could scarcely reach it, the other eye bulged out of his cheek. Teeth and jawbone strained through peeled-back lips. Lungs and liver pulsed in his throat. Flecks of fire streamed from his mouth. The booming of his heart was like the deep baying of bloodhounds, or the growl of lions attacking bears.

Now that is truly stirring stuff, clearly the exaggerated, overblown stuff of legend, but the use of language even in translation is stunning, original, memorable by comparison with Macpherson's Ossian. The lost manuscript device, a well-worked literary trope, excuses all sorts of difficulties and swerves around credibility as the story, such as it is, totters under its own weight. In the introduction above, the sentence; 'Her story is imperfect, a part of the original being lost' made me smile. Macpherson made a great deal of effort with the names he invented, correctly assuming that they matter very much in the creation of a credible imaginary world. The name of Fiona, meaning the White One, was coined by him and it has featured in baby name lists ever since they were first compiled. J. R. R. Tolkien understood the power of names and Sauron, Aragorn and Galadriel are only three in hundreds of convincing inventions in *The Lord of the Rings*. More recent scholarship on the work of Macpherson from Professor Derick Thomson, a native Gaelic speaker, concluded that the author did indeed collect some genuine material, employing scribes to record what had been held only in memory, but that he added a great deal that was his own invention. A generous assessment.

More important than their authenticity was the influence of the *Fragments of Ancient Poetry*, *Fingal* and *Temora*. They created a historical image of Homeric heroes in the Highlands and Islands that was very different from the harsh realities of the second half of the eighteenth century. In the aftermath of Culloden and Am Bliadhna nan Creach, the suppression of the clans was made formal with the removal of the heritable jurisdiction of the chiefs and the Act of Proscription of 1746. It became illegal in the Highlands for anyone to have 'in his or their custody, use, or bear, broadsword, poignard [a long knife], whinger [a short sword] or durk [dirk], side pistol, gun or other warlike weapon'. As previously mentioned, drovers were excluded from these prohibitions because the security of their supply of beef for the British army was too important to prejudice.

At Highland Games, formal dance competitions hold unlikely memories of the dismantling of cultural difference. The Seann Triubhas, 'the Old Trousers', is a celebration of the repeal of the Proscription Act that also banned the wearing of the kilt, or more correctly the plaid, in 1746. Clansmen were forced to wear trousers or trews, and when the dancer on the competition stage deliberately shakes each leg during the performance, it symbolises the shedding of the hated trousers. In the second part, the dancer claps their hands and the piper increases the tempo. As the pleats swing and flick up, the joy of the return to the beautiful, elegant kilt is unmistakable.

The suppression of the Gaelic language had begun well before Culloden with the establishment of the SSPCK schools, and in important ways James Macpherson's construction of a Celtic Never-Never Land contributed to the decline of the language by making its supposed myths and legends accessible in English. From near-universal currency across the Highlands and Islands, Gaelic became a secret cover-tongue, what lay behind the fanfares and the tinkling of the harp in *Fingal* and *Temora*. They were stories conceived and told in English but accepted as versions of Gaelic culture. The reality was shoved even further into the shadows offstage as Macpherson's heroes and heroines floated above the misty mountains and their echoing caves, and flitted through the twilit woods. Inauthenticity was more colourful than the grim realities of living in a badly damaged economy peopled by speakers of a language that was beginning to die, and was already sufficiently decrepit for Macpherson to get away with his inventions.

In 1788 a real Gaelic bard, Uilleam Ros, or William Ross, composed a lament. 'Soraidh bhuan do'n t-Suaithneas Bhàn' means 'Farewell to the White Cockade', and it mourns the death of Prince Charles. It is perhaps the last genuine Jacobite song ever composed in the Highlands. Ross fell passionately in love with Lady Marion Ross, but as the son of a pedlar, it was always an unlikely match and for the rest of his brief life, he never ceased to pine for her. His song, 'Cuachag nan Craobh' ('Cuckoo in the Woods'), is one of several eloquently tear-stained expressions of regret. The Gaelic lyrics faded, but Ross' tune survived and was adapted by an English songwriter, Sir Harold Boulton, in the 1880s with new words, and a new sentiment.

'The Skye Boat Song', sometimes also known as 'Over the Sea to Skye', is a remarkable, double-sided cultural artefact. It combines real events with invented romance and a dubious provenance to make something emblematic in its dripping nostalgia. It begins with a chorus that repeats between the verses, and it is worth quoting in full:

Speed, bonnie boat, like a bird on the wing,
Onward! the sailors cry;
Carry the lad that's born to be king,
Over the sea to Skye.

Loud the winds howl, loud the waves roar,
Thunderclaps rend the air;
Baffled, our foes stand by the shore,
Follow they will not dare.

Many's the lad, fought on that day
Well the claymore did wield;

When the night came, silently lay
Dead on Culloden's field.

Though the waves leap, soft shall ye sleep,
Ocean's a royal bed.
Rocked in the deep, Flora will keep
Watch by your weary head.

Burned are their homes, exile and death
Scatter the loyal men;
Yet ere the sword cool in the sheath
Charlie will come again.

Anne Campbell MacLeod was a nineteenth-century collector of folk songs and tales. On a short voyage across Loch Coruisk on Skye, the oarsmen began to sing William Ross' 'Cuachag nan Craobh', its rhythms working well as a rowing song and MacLeod immediately made notes. With Sir Harold Boulton's lyrics, based on Flora MacDonald and Prince Charles's escape to Skye in 1746, the song was published in a collection, *The Songs of the North*. It was very popular indeed, going into more than twenty editions, and the 'Skye Boat Song' became both famous and emblematic. So famous that its pro-Jacobite lyrics were widely believed to have been translated from the original Gaelic. The song is a remarkable mix of remembering and forgetting, of authenticity and inauthenticity, and perhaps the most appropriate symbol of how a cultural history was rewritten not for those who had lived it but for those who wanted to wallow in the tear-stained romance of its departure. The reality of course is that the lad who was born to be king represented a backward-looking, unwelcome return to a past that was already fading in the Highlands and Islands. Most of those who sway at the song's cadences, who enjoy the wistfulness and the idea that over the sea was a simpler, more innocent set of certainties, would have marched onto Culloden Moor in the ranks of the government army. It is surely beyond irony that of all the artists, from

Rod Stewart and the Corries to Nana Mouskouri, the most affecting version is sung in Gaelic by Griogair Labhruidh. He decorates the melody and its lyrics with grace notes and great feeling, but it is nevertheless every bit as fake as Ossian, *Temora* and the *Fragments of Ancient Poetry*.

*

Plate 108 is perhaps the most striking of all. Nowhere is the dominance of the mountains, the sea and sea-lochs made more spectacularly obvious. Plate 108 of the 'Great Map', the military survey of Scotland made between 1747 and 1755 by William Roy shows Ben Nevis, Loch Linnhe, Loch Eil and tiny Fort William at the mouth of the River Lochy. On almost every plate, geography dwarfs history in the Great Map. Paul Sandby, the artist who helped draw and paint it, used colour to dramatic effect. The lower slopes of Ben Nevis are pale grey where they begin to rise from sea level. Then they grow a gradually darker shade of charcoal before becoming black close to the summit. As if the westering sun is on the great mountain, the eastern slopes are darkest of all. Sandby has picked out Ben Nevis's summit in white; perhaps there was snow on it when he looked up. The flatlands at the south-western end of the Great Glen are streaked in light brown ochre and the famous and still extensive woods of Lochaber are indicated by dense patches of green dots. The blue of the rivers and lochs is a deep contrast. Loch Yeal (how the surveyors heard the pronunciation of Loch Eil by Gaelic speakers) is only blue on its shores and left white for much of its surface. Last, and smallest, are the marks of human habitation. Tiny specks of carmine red show the clusters of farms and townships in what was Clan Cameron country. A magnifying glass is needed to make them out around the foot of Ben Nevis, by the lochsides and along the banks of rivers and streams. There are scores of settlements, and near some of them the hatching that denoted open runrig fields. On a spit of land where Loch Linnhe turns west into Loch Eil is the outline of the bastions of Fort William, part of the reason why the Great Map was made.

It was a stunning achievement, for not only is it a powerful statement of how geography formed history in the Highlands, but it is also much more accurate than anything that had been drawn before it was made. And it had to be.

After Culloden and the Year of Pillaging, it can be tempting to read history backwards, arrive at a full stop and assume that the flight of the prince in his bonnie boat was the end of Jacobitism. The London government, King George II and the Duke of Cumberland did not believe that the threat of the Stuarts and their Highland and European supporters had departed in September 1746, when the prince sailed from Loch nan Uamh for Italy and exile. The clanlands would be policed and controlled but to do both effectively, good maps were needed.

In the summer of 1746, one of the government officers charged with patrolling the glens remarked to the Duke of Cumberland's secretary that 'by the map of the country [meaning the map he had], it appears very easy and a shortcut to cross over from Appin by the end of Lismore to Strontian. I have had it viewed and it is impractical in every respect.' When Cumberland appealed to his father for resources, 'the inconvenience was perceived and the resolution taken for making a complete and accurate survey of Scotland, of the coasts, creek, rivers, islands thereof'.

Lieutenant Colonel David Watson was commissioned to plan and execute this arduous and complex undertaking and he was fortunate to include on his staff a brilliant young man. William Roy was a Lowlander, born in Carluke in 1726. Educated at Lanark Grammar School, he seems to have found early employment at Edinburgh Castle as a very young trainee surveyor and draughtsman at the office of the Board of Ordnance. At the age of twenty, in 1746, Roy went north to Culloden to make a map. The marks of battle must still have been evident when the young man surveyed the site, but all he showed was the artillery track, a rutted line where the government ordnance had been brought forward. Roy's draughtsmanship and precision brought him to the notice of Lieutenant Colonel Watson and he joined the staff 'to begin, and afterwards to have a considerable share in, the execution of the map', according to the *Dictionary of National Biography*.

It was an enormously detailed and physically taxing commission to execute, but it was done very quickly. By the end of 1751, the survey of the Highlands (but not the Islands) was largely complete. With a team of six, Roy himself had walked and surveyed the entire coastline of the mainland, and at its height in the early 1750s, the project involved more than sixty people, most of them soldiers.

Based at Edinburgh Castle, survey parties would spend the summer, from April to October, out in the field and over the winter, they would work in the city, combining their measurements, their notes and drawings as the Great Map quickly took shape. William Roy began the inland survey at Fort Augustus. Each party generally comprised a surveyor, a non-commissioned officer and five or six soldiers. Paul Sandby, later to become a celebrated painter, often accompanied parties as he sketched 'the face of the country'. There is a watercolour by Sandby of a party at work at the south end of Loch Rannoch in 1749. It almost certainly shows William Roy looking through an instrument on a tripod called a circumferentor, a surveying compass used to measure angles between landmarks or poles held up at a distance by soldiers. In the distance, Sandby has painted two men, probably soldiers, and it is likely that they are using a measuring chain about forty to fifty feet long. These measured traverses were made along important features such as rivers, roads or shorelines. The features on either side, such as woodland or settlements, or mountains or hills, were sketched by Sandby and others, or taken from pre-existing local maps. The traverses and their plotting concentrate on information of military importance, what would help soldiers and artillery move through the landscape, or locate where trouble might lie. William Roy's own estimate was that the map was 'in an unfinished state . . . and is to be considered as a magnificent military sketch rather than a very accurate map of a country'. Even so, it was a quantum improvement on everything that had gone before.

Sandby's watercolour at Loch Rannoch shows three ponies: one has panniers on either side of a pack saddle, another appears also to have been used as a pack horse (the long iron chain must have been heavy) and only one has stirrups visible below its belly. Perhaps Roy was allowed the luxury of riding, but most of the time he and his men walked through the Highlands and they either camped, or were billeted with local people, or they stayed at the kingshouses built by the side of Marshal Wade's roads.

The Great Map was used to plot outposts for patrols in the glens and in the straths by the lochs and on the Atlantic shore. Usually companies of sixty soldiers were posted, often to remote places, sometimes to existing castles that had been forfeited by clan chiefs who had fought for the prince, such as Castle Duart on Mull and Braemar on Deeside. Each company's officers almost certainly had copies of the relevant section of Roy's map with them as they patrolled the countryside. At the same time, the road network in the Highlands was extended, with 900 miles completed between 1740 and 1767. Clansmen and their chiefs could be in no doubt that the London government was determined to stifle any hint of rebellion at its source.

The making of the Great Map was interrupted by the outbreak of the Seven Years War, and surveyors and engineers were diverted to campaigns in Europe and elsewhere. When the war ended in 1763, William Roy returned to London where he remained for the rest of his life. He became much interested in and involved with the development of more precise instruments for surveying. Roy's dream of a national survey for the whole of Great Britain was brought closer to a reality by work on triangulation and the correct measurement of longitude and latitude. In concert with colleagues at the Greenwich Observatory and the Paris Observatory, he completed a very accurate survey between the two points, using triangulation. Roy's methods laid the foundations of the Ordnance Survey that began in 1791, a year after his death, and forty-four years after he began the Great Map of the Highlands.

Roy's map was much more than a sketch, it was also valedictory, a snapshot taken over a short period of a landscape that was changing.

The tiny carmine red dots of clustered settlements were beginning to shrink, and even disappear. As patrols of redcoat soldiers moved through the glens, they were beginning to empty. The centuries of emigration, the time of departure, was beginning.

13

*The Tears of the Emigrant,
the Tongue of the Gael*

1753–1854

In the pale half-light before dawn, the Highland army moved quietly through the trees towards the river. A morning mist was floating over the water, making it difficult to see what was happening on the opposite bank. When the clansmen came near to the bridge, which appeared to have been broken down, a sentry on the opposite bank noticed movement in the woods, perhaps the glint of steel, and he shouted a challenge. Captain Alexander MacLean roared back in Gaelic, and, hearing no response, ordered his men to open fire. The replying gunsmoke revealed the enemy on the far side of the bridge, firing from what looked like a semicircular earthwork. Colonel Donald MacLeod and Captain John Campbell quickly mustered a group of thirty Highlanders, good swordsmen all of them. The piper skirled out a battle rant and before they reached the bridge, MacLeod shouted: 'Claideamh mòr! 'Son an Righ Seoras!'

Enemy officers ordered their men to hold their fire. Then, when the Highlanders were over the deliberately broken-down bridge and were no more than thirty paces away, the order was given. Lying on their bellies on the earthwork, scores of soldiers fired a devastating volley and artillery fire began. All of the Highlanders fell, Colonel MacLeod hit by more than twenty musket balls and pellets. When the clansmen waiting back on the other side of the river saw their commander and thirty men fall, they turned and scattered through the woods. Pursued by their enemies, others were shot and hundreds taken prisoner. The battle had lasted less than thirty minutes.

It was the last Highland charge. It took place on the morning of 27 February 1776 at Moore's Creek in North Carolina. Donald MacLeod and many of the Highlanders in his small army had fought for Prince Charles thirty years before, but life had moved on. The war cry of 'Claideamh mòr! 'Son an Righ Seoras!' showed how far politics had also moved on. It translates as 'King George and broadswords!' Colonel MacLeod's commanding officer was General Donald MacDonald, and he had charged with the MacDonald regiments on the left of the Jacobite lines at Culloden. Sixty-five years old in 1776, the march to Moore's Creek had exhausted him and he took no part in the battle. But that morning, many former Jacobites fought for the Hanoverians.

More historical ironies echoed through the trees beyond the river to the little town of Cross Creek. Tradition holds that when the royal standard, not the one that fluttered over Glenfinnan, but the standard of George III, was raised in the public square, the muster of Highlanders listened to a *brosnachadh-catha*, an incitement to battle. It was given in Gaelic by none other than Flora MacDonald, the Jacobite heroine who had brought Prince Charles to safety in her bonnie boat. With her husband, Allan MacDonald of Kingsburgh, she had emigrated to America three years before the battle.

Listening to Flora MacDonald's words was a man who appreciated their power. Iain mac Mhurchaidh was a bard from Kintail who composed war poetry to encourage soldiers loyal to George III. His son, Murdo, was mortally wounded at Moore's Creek. Three years before, while still in Kintail, Iain had received a letter from the Reverend John Bethune, an earlier immigrant to North Carolina and also present at the battle. He urged Iain to follow him by telling him how good the hunting was in the forests of America. Apparently, new landlords in the Highlands were attempting to restrict traditional rights and this had annoyed the great bard very much. Bethune himself had in turn been encouraged to emigrate by Allan MacDonald of Kingsburgh.

Once he had arrived in North Carolina, Iain mac Mhurchaidh composed poetry extolling the abundance and freedoms of his new home, although his enthusiasm did fluctuate with circumstances. Having been captured and imprisoned after Moore's Creek, he began to deeply regret his departure from Kintail, as seen in 'Tha Mì Sgith 'n Fhògar Seo' ('I am Weary of this Exile'). However, on his escape or release from prison, the poet once again joined troops loyal to George III and fought at the Battle of King's Mountain in South Carolina in 1780. There were Gaelic speakers on both sides, just as at Culloden, and it was said that Iain invoked the ancient custom of immunity for bards. He walked up and down between the opposing lines singing 'Nam faighte làmh-an-uachdar air luchd nan còta ruadha' ('Even if the upper hand were gained against the redcoats'), presumably meaning that even if this battle were lost, the war could not be won.

After the end of the War of American Independence, John Bethune and many other Highlanders fled north to British Canada, but Gaelic continued to be spoken in several areas of the Carolinas until the American Civil War devastated communities in the south. The Grandfather Mountain Highland Games remember these eighteenth-century links. Each year in a spectacular setting, thousands of kilt-wearing Americans come to celebrate a version of their heritage.

What is more puzzling was the support for the Hanoverians from the early emigrants. Nevertheless, it should be borne in mind that some Highland clans remained loyal to George II in 1745, and most were neutral. In addition, many men took their lead from Allan MacDonald and other minor gentry. They were instinctively not inclined to support rebellion in America, or anything that might prejudice the grants of land many had received. Revolution threatened stability and prosperity.

What is known as chain migration seemed to bring more and more men and women halfway across the world from the Highlands to North America and elsewhere. Letters home from men like the Reverend John Bethune encouraged them to follow. On arrival, many immigrants could expect help and shelter from relatives and fellow clansmen to allow them to establish themselves. And if they did not speak English, those links were even more important. After Culloden and the Year of Pillaging, when some lost everything they had, many people left the Highlands never to return. Between 1750 and 1815, more than 30,000 former clansmen and women emigrated to North America, about 10 per cent of the population.

When in 1773 Samuel Johnson and James Boswell visited Skye, they witnessed something surprising: 'In the evening the company danced as usual. We performed, with much activity, a dance which, I suppose, the emigration from Skye has occasioned. They call it "America". Each of the couples, after the common involutions and evolutions, successively whirls around in a circle, till all are in motion; and the dance seems intended to show how emigration catches, till a whole neighbourhood is set afloat.'

Emigrants are often very nostalgic. As they make new lives in foreign parts far from home, their sense of themselves clings to the past, and in some cases a past that became further and further distant from reality. The Highlanders of North Carolina or Ontario kept their Gaelic for a generation or two as they and their children became Americans or Canadians. Here is a verse from the 'Canadian Boat Song', probably composed around the end of the eighteenth century, in English:

From the lone shieling of the misty island
Mountains divide us, and the waste of the seas –
Yet still the blood is strong, the heart is Highland,
And we in dreams behold the Hebrides.

Despite the cliché of the first line, this is powerful writing and often quoted. For some, the pain of separation was hard to bear. More than homesickness, it is best expressed by a Gaelic word, *ionndrainn*, which carries the sense of something missing, the piece of the heart that will forever be Highland. Much later, this was very poignantly expressed in a diary extract from the middle of the nineteenth century.

In November 1852, 830 crofters were cleared off the land and forcibly evicted from Skye, Harris and South Uist. They boarded the emigrant ship *Hercules*, bound for the other side of the world, for South Australia and Adelaide. They knew that they would never return, and would behold the Hebrides only in their dreams: 'The Cuillin mountains were in sight for several hours of our passage; but when we rounded Ardnamurchan Point, the emigrants saw the sun for the last time glitter upon their splintered peaks, and one prolonged and dismal wail rose from all parts of the vessel; the fathers and mothers held up their infant children to take a last view of the mountains of their fatherland which in a few minutes faded from their view forever.'

Many emigrants took more than their longing and their language across the Atlantic. Some of the soldiers at Moore's Creek wore plaids and other exiled Highlanders continued to wear tartan. It is perhaps the most powerful emblem of the culture of the clans. In Britain and in Europe, no other men dressed in what looked like a skirt and that is probably why Georg Coler came to Stettin in 1631 to draw the four soldiers from the Highland companies. In the emigrants' dreams of the Hebrides, their people will all have worn the tartan, but in fact the political and legal realities were very different after Culloden. The setts of plaids, coats and kilts were the colours of Jacobitism and what is sometimes called the Dress Act of 1746 was very specific. It was 'An act for restraining the use of the Highland dress', and it was forbidden 'to wear or put on Highland clothes', including the kilt or plaid, and 'that no tartan or party-coloured plaid or stuff shall be used for greatcoats or upper coats'.

The terms of the Act are very clear, but what is meant by tartan can be confusing. In North America plaid is interchangeable, but in fact it really refers only to the garment. *Plaide* in Gaelic means a 'blanket', and tartan describes the pattern and the colours of a Highlander's plaid. Tartan is not a Gaelic term and probably derives from Old French *tartarin*, meaning the sort of cloth worn by Tartars or Tatars, a suitable cultural link, some might say, between the horse-riding hordes of the Steppes and the hordes of screaming Highlanders who charged across the stubble fields of Prestonpans.

Breacan is how tartan is described in Gaelic and it means speckled or chequered, and refers not only to the various colours but also the weave of the pattern, which is known as the sett. On the loom, each thread in the warp crosses the threads of the weft at right angles. When the crossing threads are the same colour, they combine to make a solid area of green, blue, red or whatever is needed. But when they are of different colours, they have the effect of producing a third shade. Setts or patterns were important, and weavers in the Highlands took great trouble to get them right. Each kept a *maide*, a pattern stick with colours etched on it, and threads or yarn were dyed accordingly to produce the desired sett.

Women dyed yarn and from the sixteenth century there is a record of a weaver creating a sett 'after his own fashion', and not using the colours his client prescribed, which led to complaints. Full-length tartan or self-coloured dresses were worn by women, because they appear not to have been banned by the Dress Act, often with another tartan mantle or shawl over their shoulders, a *tonnag*. On their heads they had what Edward Dwelly calls a 'mutch-cap', a white linen *currac*, sometimes fringed with lace or frills. Their long, often pleated, dresses were fastened by a brooch at their breast and caught up around the waist with a belt.

In the 1980s a piece of fabric was found preserved in the anaerobic conditions of a peat bog in Glen Affric. Measuring twenty inches by seventeen, it had been woven with different colours, definitely green and brown and possibly red and yellow, and made in the classic style of tartan with the warp and weft of different colours at right angles. In 2023, the Scottish Tartan Authority commissioned tests that confirmed that it is more than 400 years old, making it the oldest piece of true tartan yet discovered in Scotland. It was probably worn as an 'outdoor working garment', part of a much larger plaid. Glen Affric was Clan Chisholm country and the design of the sett may be characteristic. Their modern tartan contains green, brown and red, but it may bear no relation for reasons that will become clear, or not.

Written records are scant, but in 1538 James V was said to have worn tartan while out hunting and the find in Glen Affric may offer a clue as to what it looked like. On his wedding day in 1662, Charles II had a ribbon of tartan on his coat. The first helpful written source for the story of tartan appeared at the beginning of the eighteenth century. Martainn macGhille Mhartainn was a native Gaelic speaker who compiled *A Description of the Western Islands of Scotland*, published in 1703. Better known as Martin Martin, he was the first to suggest that different setts of tartan were worn by the people of different areas. The inhabitants of the islands and parts of the western mainland did not all dress alike, and it seems that their particular native places could be identified by the nature of the sett of their plaids. Which makes sense. The palette of plant and mineral dyes will have varied and the weavers' pattern sticks will have reflected that. Uncharacteristically, Edward Dwelly's entry for *breacan* is full of entertaining, Ossianic fantasy, as well as respect for Martin Martin:

> Highland plaid. 2 Tartan. Parti-coloured cloth was used by the Celts from the earliest times but the variety of colours in the *breacan* was greater or less, according to the rank of the wearer. That of the ancient kings had seven colours, that of the druids six, and that of the nobles four. In the days of Martin [Martin], the tartans seemed to be used to distinguish the inhabitants of different districts, and not the members of different families [clans] as at present . . . it would appear that such a distinction is a modern one, and taken from the ancient custom of a tartan for each district, the family or clan originally most numerous in each part eventually adopting it as their distinctive clan tartan . . . Martin's information was not obtained on hearsay. He was born in Skye and reared in the midst of Highland customs.

That latter passage is a very plausible analysis and probably contains a great deal of truth, something rare in the story of tartan.

The prohibitions of the Dress Act were very specific in that they banned the wearing of Highland dress in the Highlands, and by extension its manufacture in the north. In 1765, the enterprising

William Wilson set up weaving sheds at the village of Bannockburn, south of the Highland Line, safe from legal sanction, and he began to produce tartan in bulk. His main clients were the regiments of the British army. Highland regiments had fought with distinction in Canada against the French. At the Battle of the Plains of Abraham, near Quebec, the 78th (Fraser's) Highlanders drew their swords, roared their war cries and charged the retreating enemy in 1759, and the Black Watch had already distinguished themselves in Europe in the 1740s. These regiments were exempted from the restrictions of the Dress Act and Wilson's weavers turned out a great deal of what was known as 'government tartan'. This further encouraged the notion of different setts as marks of identity. At first, William Wilson simply attached numbers to these patterns but as his business expanded, agents were sent north to find samples of different tartans so that he could weave 'perfectly genuine patterns'. Setts began to acquire clan names, place names or those of the Highland nobility, and in the *Key Pattern Book* of 1819, these were illustrated and recorded.

In 1778, well-to-do emigrants formed the Highland Society of London and they quickly transformed their nostalgia into political action. Only four years after the formation of the club, influential Highlanders persuaded the government to repeal the Disarming Act and the Dress Act. The looms at Bannockburn rattled and clacked as business boomed and tartan was sold all over Scotland.

Perhaps as a symptom of the nineteenth-century's obsession with taxonomy, Colonel Alasdair MacDonell of Glengarry wrote to the Highland chiefs in 1815 asking them to send a piece of their clan tartan, authenticated by their seal, to the Highland Society in London for their collection. Most chiefs had no idea there was any such thing. The chief of Clan Donnachie, the Robertsons, rode around his Atholl estates asking old clansmen what their tartan was. None of them could agree. So, he sent to London a sample of a sett used for the kilts of the Clan Donnachie Volunteers, a version of the Home Guard, founded in 1803. Which meant that the ancient tartan of the Robertsons was precisely twelve years old. Duncan Macpherson, chief of the name, had no idea of any standard sett so he went to

Bannockburn to ask Wilson's advice. They supplied him with a tartan from their *Key Pattern Book* known as No. 43, Kidd or Caledonia. It had originally been made to the specifications of a Lowlander called Mr Kidd and was then sold to a Mr Macpherson who lived in the West Indies. It was the best they could do. No 43 was as close as Wilson could get to a Macpherson sett, and so the chief attached his seal and sent it to London.

Business in Bannockburn really began to boom in 1822. At a royal levee at Holyrood Palace, King George IV made a spectacular entrance. Swathed from head to foot in tartan, wearing two belts (to restrain his belly – he tipped the scales at twenty stone), dirks and a bonnet, his kilt sat well above the knee over flesh-coloured tights, essential to hide his varicose veins. On the first state visit since the Jacobite Rebellion in 1745, he was in Edinburgh for only a week. Watching his entrance was Lady Dalrymple, who, after hearing criticism of the king's short kilt, wittily sniffed, 'Since he is here for such a short time, it is as well we see so much of him.' The 'King's Jaunt' was stage-managed by Sir Walter Scott, and it saw the beginning of the wholesale adoption of Highland iconography by all Scots.

Twenty years after this remarkable royal visit, more fakery was added to the colourful history of tartan. The pioneering Edinburgh photographer David Octavius Hill took portraits of two brothers who claimed to be the grandsons of Prince Charles Edward Stuart. John Carter Allen and Charles Manning Allen took the names of John Sobieski Stuart and Charles Edward Stuart, moved to Scotland, converted to Roman Catholicism and claimed that their father, Thomas Allen, had been born in Italy, the only legitimate child of the Young Pretender and his wife, Princess Louise of Stolberg-Gedern. And therefore he, not Queen Victoria, was the rightful monarch, the king of Great Britain and Ireland.

Hill's photographs show two sinister-looking, shifty con men. Cadaverous, with wild dark hair and dressed in a faintly military uniform, John Sobieski Stuart claimed that he and his brother had 'a body of supporters ready to push their claims to the utmost'. Looking a little less menacing, Charles Edward Stuart lounges on a stone bench in full military fig, a huge, hairy sporran draped over his kilt and a hat with a white cockade by his side. Both look as mad as a box of frogs, but were nevertheless supported and believed to an astonishing degree by a gaggle of credulous aristocrats. Alexander Fraser, Lord Lovat, built 'an antique shooting lodge' for them on Eilean Aigas, an islet in the River Beauly, where they held court from 1838 to 1845. The romantic, tear-stained, utterly bogus afterglow of the 1745 Rising still exerted tremendous power.

It is a remarkable, crazy story of delusion and obvious nonsense that had a further twist to it. Like most con men, the Sobieski Stuarts were constantly short of money, and so like James Macpherson, they came up with a lost manuscript wheeze. In 1843 they published the *Vestiarium Scoticum*, which my Latin dictionary translates as the 'Scottish Wardrobe', and it was priced at ten guineas a time. The book was allegedly based on an eighteenth-century copy of a six-teenth-century manuscript (a deliberate cut-out) containing patterns of tartan neatly assigned to sixty-six different clans, and, surprisingly, to a further nine Borders clans. The original manuscript was, of course, never produced. It was all bunkum, especially the nonsense about Borders tartan, but despite being completely and repeatedly discredited, the absurd *Vestiarium Scoticum* simply added to the pop-ularity of Highland iconography. Queen Victoria and Prince Albert had bought Balmoral Castle on Deeside, and the interior decoration must have been overwhelming. The carpets were all tartan – Royal Stewart, of course, and Dress Stewart for the curtains and the uphol-stery. To avoid a constant headache, visitors must have done a lot of staring out of the windows.

*

As Highlanders departed, crossing the ocean into exile, unexpected help and sustenance for those who remained had already travelled in the opposite direction. In the spring of 1743, Ranald MacDonald, Chief of Clanranald, sailed north with a surprising cargo. He had been visiting his kinsman, MacDonnell of Antrim, and was pleased to learn that the families of that branch of Clan Donald were well nourished. After its journey across the Atlantic in the later sixteenth century, the potato had flourished in Ireland. Resistant to bad weather, tolerant of poor soil and requiring little maintenance, it had become a staple of Clan MacDonnell's diet. Sacks of potatoes were stowed in MacDonald's birlinn and when he made landfall in South Uist, his tenants were summoned. To a man, they flatly refused to plant these strange roots from America, but after threats, and some of them even being imprisoned, the clansmen finally agreed to plant them. In the autumn, they duly dug up the potatoes and piled them up at the gates of Clanranald's house at Nunton on Benbecula. They might have agreed, under duress, to plant these things, but they would not be forced to eat them.

However much that tale has been embroidered, it does mark an important moment in the culture of the Highlands and Islands. By 1760, potatoes were widely grown and ten years later they had become a staple, the source of perhaps 50–75 per cent of calories for families. The dependence on oatmeal was much reduced for, compared to grain, the humble tattie was easy to grow and would not be flattened by wind and rainstorms blowing in off the Atlantic. On his visit to the Hebrides in 1773, Samuel Johnson, who was fond of his food, observed: 'Their gardens afford them no variety, but they always have some vegetables on the table. Potatoes, at least, are never wanting, which although they have not known them long, are now one of the principal parts of their food. They are not of the mealy, but the viscous kind.'

Oidhche buntàta 's sgadan is still popular in the Hebrides, evenings when only potatoes and herring are served (with wine and beer) to those who enjoy tradition. There is not a scrap of green to be seen on any plate of boiled, white spuds and fish, but these events remember that Clanranald's initiative filled many a hungry belly. His thoughtfulness for his people, something that became increasingly rare amongst clan chiefs as the eighteenth century wore on, is celebrated with a fiddle tune, 'Buntàta 's Sgadan' ('Tatties and Herring').

Traditional paternalists like Clanranald became rare, and indeed his refusal to exploit his people bankrupted him. Most chiefs began to see their traditional clan lands differently. Rather than a sense of collective ownership implied by the idea of *clann* as the children of a common name-father, and also of *dùthchas*, which involved, but never stated, a notion of a traditional ancestral home, chiefs began to see the land differently. *Oigreachd*, meaning 'inheritance', made chiefs think that they owned the clanlands outright and were in a position to dispose of them in whatever way they saw fit, or exploit them – and their people – for gain. Cash rents began to climb steeply, trebling on Skye between 1750 and 1775. In the same period, Cameron of Lochiel raised his rents by 56 per cent and MacDonnell of Glengarry increased his rental income from £732 in 1768 to £4,184 in 1803, a huge increase of 472 per cent in thirty-five years. The old Gaelic phrase *Is treasa tuath na Tighearna*, 'the kindred is mightier than the Lord', became meaningless.

Here is Dr Johnson again: 'There was perhaps never any change of national manners so quick, so great and so general as that which has operated in the Highlands by the late conquest [which is clearly how the aftermath of Culloden was understood] and subsequent laws . . . The clans retain little now of their original character. Their ferocity of temper is softened, their military ardour is extinguished, their contempt for government subdued and their reverence for their chiefs abated.'

The good doctor was not entirely correct. The military ardour of the Highlanders did not disappear; it was diverted. The Seven Years War that interrupted William Roy's mapping also established the outline of the British Empire, with huge territories won from the French in India, Canada and elsewhere. In need of troops, the prime minister, William Pitt, encouraged the recruitment of two Highland regiments in 1757, only a little more than ten years after Culloden, and to justify his decision he wrote to the king: 'I sought for merit wherever it was to be found. It is my boast that I was the first minister who looked for it and found it in the mountains of the north. I called it forth and drew into your service a hardy and intrepid race of men . . . they served with fidelity as they fought with valour and conquered for you in every part of the world.'

Lest this paean on Highland bravery seem to represent the inclusion of Highlanders in the great imperial project, Pitt added a sour, even racist note of cynicism: 'The Highlanders are hardy, intrepid, accustomed to rough country, and it is no great mischief if they fall. How can you better employ a secret enemy than by making his end conducive to the common good?'

More regiments from the mountains of the north were brought into being as the drive for empire gained more and more momentum: the Cameron Highlanders, the Fraser Highlanders, the Seaforths and others, began their illustrious histories at the end of the eighteenth century. Between 1797 and 1837, the clans of Skye alone sent many men to serve in the British army, not all of them private soldiers: 21 lieutenant generals, 48 lieutenant colonels, 600 majors, captains and ensigns as well as more than a thousand regulars, and also a governor-general of India and four other colonial governors all came from the island. It is thought that a quarter of all men of military age in the Highlands served in the army between 1792 and 1815.

Unable to pay the increased rents demanded by their chiefs (who had developed expensive lifestyles in Edinburgh and London), many families walked south or east to the cities to find work and make a new life. By 1775, Aberdeen, Glasgow and Dundee had seen their population increase by 25 per cent in only twenty years. They were by no means all Highlanders. It is often forgotten that people were cleared off the land in the Lowlands as estates consolidated their smallholdings into larger farms. After 1785, the thriving village of Longnewton in the Borders simply disappeared, the Earl of Lothian wanting to combine a number of small tenancies into a big, and more productive, farm. John Younger recalled what happened: his father had fourteen acres with a house, but all the land was to be absorbed into the new farm. The dykes were thrown down and the land ploughed right up to the walls of the house, and even the hens were shot. In a very short time every one of the twenty houses of Longnewton was empty. All that remains of the settlement now is an isolated roadside graveyard sheltered by ancient yew and broadleaf trees.

Many Borderers migrated to the local towns where the textile industry was beginning to flourish, but for Highlanders, there were no towns apart from Inverness and it was the cities and their developing factories that attracted them. Many no doubt followed a domestic version of chain-migration as letters home were followed up and urban accommodation found with relatives. Edinburgh was the largest city in Scotland with 70,000 inhabitants by 1775. Although the building of the Georgian New Town was well underway, the focus of the city was still the High Street and its tottering rookeries of tenements and their warren of closes or alleyways. Edinburgh needed policing and the City Guard was recruiting. An early example of the tradition of 'big, steady lads' from the Highlands was Duncan Ban MacIntyre. He came from Glen Orchy and joined the City Guard, known as the 'Black Banditti', in 1767.

Duncan Ban was gifted. With Alasdair macMhaighstir Alasdair, Uilleam Ros and Iain Lom, he was part of what has been described as a golden age of Gaelic poetry. Like many bards, the Edinburgh policeman was completely illiterate, holding all of his compositions in memory, but other Gaels who had emigrated to the city wanted to write them down. Perhaps there was a sense of impermanence, the passing of an old culture whose poetry needed to be recorded before it vanished with the death of memory. James Stewart of Killin, a countryman of Duncan Ban, became his amanuensis, and arranged for the poems to be published. He had help and financial support from John Campbell, also from Glen Orchy, who was the principal cashier of the Royal Bank of Scotland. These men must have recognised that these poems were valedictory, an elegiac farewell to a way of life that was passing, the experience of men and women who were departing, leaving the glens and straths that were quickly emptying, people who had lived in the midst of the natural world, a world never better captured than in Duncan Ban's work.

Seen for a long time from the A82, Beinn Dorain is a singular, sweeping, majestic mountain, its mighty contours somehow enhanced by the railway line cut into its lower slopes. When he remembered it, Duncan Ban saw in his mind's eye the deer he loved so much and they are at the centre of perhaps his greatest poem, their description precise and timeless as the emptying land is reclaimed by its creatures. Here is part of a beautiful, elegant translation of 'Moladh Beinn Dobhrain' ('In Praise of Beinn Dorain'), made by Iain Crichton Smith:

> Pleasant to me rising
> At morning
> To see them the horizon
> adorning.
> Seeing them so clear,
> my simple-headed deer
> modestly appear
> in their joyousness.
> They freely exercise
> their sweet and level cries.
> From bodies trim and terse,
> hear their bellowing.

*

At a Highland wedding on 27 July 1792, a plot was hatched. Farmers from the townships of Strath Rusdale, inland from Alness on the Cromarty Firth, were very angry. Tenancies in the strath had been granted by Sir Hector Munro, the new owner, to two brothers, Allan and Alexander Cameron, sheep farmers from Lochaber. The local farmers found that the grazing for their black cattle was much reduced, their pasture cropped by *na caorach mora*, 'the big sheep'. These were Cheviots and Blackfaces originally bred in the Scottish Borders and Northumberland. Big and better wool and mutton producers than the hardy little Highland sheep, they offered more profit and allowed landlords like Munro to charge higher rents. In any event, the farmers of Strath Rusdale did not recognise Munro's right to rent their traditional pasture to others in this way and bad-tempered confrontations took place.

The coming of the big sheep badly disrupted the rhythm of the stock-rearing year when the black cattle were driven up to the high summer pasture and the grass in the straths was allowed to recover and the low-lying land could be cultivated. The Cheviots and the Blackface could summer on the high ground, but when autumn came, they needed to come down to the straths. There was simply not enough room for both, for the cattle and the big sheep, and indeed for the townships and their open, unfenced runrig fields.

William Roy's map, made only forty years earlier, shows a well-populated, busy landscape with at least eighteen townships in Strath Rusdale. There might have been more but my magnifying glass helped me count only those that were clear clusters of the characteristic carmine-red dots. Even fainter but still just legible is a wide area of runrig fields, especially at Inchlumpie, Strondrach and Taybrandrack, place names that read like poor transliterations of the Gaelic originals. It is particularly striking how far the runrig cultivation extends north-west up the strath, at higher altitudes, into the heart of the mountains. It is impossible to do more than guess, but if each dot in the townships represented a house, and allowing for some of these buildings to have been barns, perhaps 500 people lived in Strath Rusdale.

The details of the wedding plot were announced at several churches in Sutherland and Easter Ross on Sunday 29 July, and by the following Tuesday, 200 farmers and their dogs were droving 10,000 of the big sheep off the pastures of Strath Rusdale and elsewhere towards Inverness. Alarmed landlords sent urgent dispatches to Edinburgh, to Henry Dundas, Secretary of State for Scotland. Swift action followed. Three companies of the Black Watch marched out of their barracks in Inverness and the protest was quickly dispersed.

The date became grimly emblematic: 1792 was Am Bliadhna nan Caorach Mora, the Year of 'the Big Sheep', and in Sutherland in particular it set in train shocking events, some of the worst excesses of what became known as the Highland Clearances, a sustained period of forcible ethnic cleansing, a time when lives were shattered and a culture broken.

In the glens and the straths, the time of the townships, the small communities known as *na bailtean*, was coming to an end, and very quickly. In the districts of Assynt and Creich in western Sutherland, between 1790 and 1803, the numbers of black cattle fell from 5,140 head to 2,906, and in the same period the flocks of sheep multiplied dramatically from 7,480 head to about 21,000. The seasonal rhythms of the *bailtean* were the beating heart of Highland life and culture until the late eighteenth century. These were communities that cooperated in many activities, in the likes of peat digging, drying and carting, and most of all in the annual journeys of transhumance, the movement of stock to the high pasture, and the shepherding and care of the animals in the open hills. At Beltane, 1 May, the traditional moment when the herds and flocks were driven up the hill trails, families would prod their beasts to the sheilings. Mainly women and children would stay there, the men returning to what was known as the winter-town. The sheilings were the summer-towns and there were sometimes many small stone-built huts grouped together for shelter in bad weather. Much of the time was spent in the open air, summering out in the long evenings in the north, in what is known in the Northern Isles as the 'simmer dim', when darkness never really falls and the sun seems to dance along the horizon; what Pytheas saw when he came to Calanais 2,000 years before.

Cheese was made at the sheilings, for the cows and ewes could be milked once their calves and lambs had begun to wean, and the grass was sweet, full of nutritious herbage. Music was important around the fire in the summer-town and there is a famous song that captures what must have been an attractive atmosphere. 'Thug Mi n' Oidhche Raoir san Airidh' ('I Spent Last Night at the Sheiling'):

And cows are dripping milk
And night's dew is falling
On the maidens of the sheiling.

There is a beautiful version by Capercaillie, with Karen Matheson's haunting, crystal voice seeming to echo across the centuries as the song remembers:

Last night I was dreaming
Mary, the sheiling lass.

As the singing faded on the autumn winds and the sheilings tumbled and decayed, as the glens and the straths lost their people, a productive, busy landscape fell silent, degenerating into scenery.

Aristocrats, landlords and clan chiefs did not at first want to see their people board the emigrant ships or walk south and east to the cities. So long as it was the right sort of land, their presence on it would add value. As clansmen and their families were turned out of the *bailtean*, the crofting economy, such as it was, began to take shape. People were often moved out of the straths and glens to the coast, given a few acres that had often never before been worked, sometimes very rocky or boggy land. Most of the people of the long valley of Strathnaver were evicted from *na bailtean* and sent north to crofts along the jagged coastline of Torrisdale Bay on the North Atlantic shore. They were encouraged to become fishermen, a skill few who had lived in the inland glens possessed. But most could harvest kelp.

Kelp is a woody seaweed best collected in winter, when storms and heavy seas might tear it off its holdfasts and dump clumps of it onshore. Its value was in the primitive production of chemicals such as potassium, sodium and magnesium, essential ingredients in the manufacture of glass, candles, soap and other products. Gathering it in winter was grim, exhausting work. Kelp often had to be cut with saw-toothed sickles with hands submerged in chilly seawater for long periods, or from over the sides of rowing boats bobbing in rocky inlets. On shore, long coffin-shaped kilns were dug in the sandy ground and the dried kelp was burned for many hours. The resulting lumps of ash were very valuable. In peak years, between 15,000 and 20,000 tons of kelp was shipped south from Highland shores to factories in Scotland and England. At that time, the industry was worth a staggering sum, about £400,000 a year, but of course the kelpers were paid a pittance and landlords pocketed huge profits. Prices were high at the beginning of the nineteenth century, at about £20 a ton, because the Napoleonic Wars had cut off European supplies. But after Waterloo, the market was flooded and prices crashed.

At the same time, the first concerted clearances off the Sutherland estate began; 1814 became Am Bliadhna an Losgaidh, 'the Year of Burning'. It was an episode without precedent in British history, a time of heartbreak and of terrible cruelty as a vast swathe of the Highlands lost its people.

It appears from William Roy's map that there were many people living in the long straths. Even at the head of narrowing valleys far inland, on what must have high and more difficult ground, the landscape is speckled with the clusters of carmine-red dots marking townships. All of that settlement implies a detailed and intense knowledge of surroundings, not only cultivation of what would thrive and what would not, but also the secret places where wild harvests might be gathered. The amount of woodland marked on Roy's map of Strathbrora is surprising, dense in places, and it will have sheltered berry bushes, hazelnut bushes and trees as well as animals that might have been snared or hunted. Generations will have discovered the best places to fish for trout and even salmon in the River Brora, where birds' eggs might be found in the spring and where the sweetest blaeberries grew.

I counted at least nineteen townships in Strathbrora, all of them named. On the modern Ordnance Survey, near Balnacoil, a place name that has survived, there is a scatter of ruins. Some way inland from the little coastal village of Brora, beyond the loch of the same name, is Ascoilemore. It is still marked on the map, but no one lives there now.

In the afternoon of Thursday 31 May 1821, Donald Bannerman arrived with a party of men. He was a sheriff-officer and he had come to evict Jessie Ross and her young family. The township of Ascoilemore with its run-rug fields, dykes and houses was to be swept off the map to make way for the expansion of a neighbouring sheep farm. Jessie's husband, Gordon Ross, was not at home, and so when Bannerman arrived with between ten and twelve men, some of whom had been drinking the night before and that morning, she had to face them alone.

In the house at Ascoilemore were three very young children: Elizabeth was five years old, Katherine three and baby Roberta was asleep in her cradle. Having lost a baby twenty months before, Jessie Ross was not well, and neither was Katherine. It later became clear that the little girl and her older sister were both developing the symptoms of whooping cough. When Donald Bannerman barged into the house with his posse of men, he ordered the girls to leave, to get out of the house they had grown up in. It was a cold afternoon, a wind blowing down off the mountains from the north-east. Witnesses later said that the little girls 'looked cold' and were 'trembling', perhaps not just with the onset of illness. They must have been terrified.

Their mother refused to leave the house, not because she believed she could resist this group of men but because she wanted to make sure her furniture and her other belongings were taken out and not smashed up. They were all they had.

When William Stevenson picked up the cradle with baby Roberta asleep in it, he banged it against the doorframe. When the baby woke, startled, she began to cry. Stevenson was reported as being angry at Jessie's defiance, and probably drunk. Other families who had been evicted from their houses at Ascoilemore the day before had not yet left, and one woman, Mary Murray, was herself a nursing mother. She consoled the crying baby by 'giving the child a suck'. Once the men were in the house dismantling the likes of box beds and other furniture, Stevenson threw a plank of wood out through the door. It struck Elizabeth, the five-year-old girl, in the face, and she wept bitterly from the shock and the hurt for a long time. But these tears were nothing to those shed three weeks later when her sister, Katherine, died of whooping cough.

A good deal is known about the eviction of the Ross family from Ascoilemore because, in the Parish Register of Clyne, notes were made 'anent the Strathbrora Removings', and Gordon Ross, who was an SSPCK teacher, wrote to Lord Stafford, later the Duke of Sutherland. But many similar and perhaps worse episodes will have gone unrecorded as a wave of misery, humiliation and inhumanity washed over Sutherland in the early years of the nineteenth century. William Roy's map of the county counts many hundreds of carmine-red *bailtean* on the Stafford estates, and many acres of runrig around them that grew potatoes, oats and other good things to feed substantial communities. Within the span of only one generation Sutherland was emptied, generations of experience in one beloved place summarily removed at the behest of two enormously wealthy people in pursuit of even more money who were completely ruthless, the Marquis and Marchioness of Stafford. There is no equivocation possible. They may have, and indeed did, tut at some of the excesses of their estate commissioner James Loch and his gangs of thugs, and at his colleague, Patrick Sellar, calling the latter 'so exceedingly greedy and harsh with the people, there are heavy complaints against him from Strathnaver'. Perhaps, but these men were doing the exceedingly greedy Staffords' bidding and a word from them would have halted these disgraceful, cruel events in a moment. But that word never came, and the brutal treatment meted out to Jessie Ross and her little girls went on for several years, until the early 1820s.

In his superb account of the Sutherland Clearances, *Set Adrift Upon the World*, James Hunter begins with the evictions at Ascoilemore and then goes on to make a simple, but telling, and eloquent comparison. The average population density in England is 413 people per square kilometre. In Sutherland, about the same size as Norfolk or Northumberland, it is 2. And since most people live in coastal communities, like Brora, the interior is virtually empty. When the people go, only memories echo through the glens and straths, only sad music is heard.

The great Canadian writer Alistair MacLeod was a descendant of families cleared off the townships on the island of Eigg in the 1790s. He recalled an old lady remembering:

My grandmother gets up and goes for her violin which hangs on a peg inside her bedroom door. It is a very old violin and came from the Scotland of her ancestors, from the crumbled foundations that now dot and haunt Lochaber's shores. She plays two Gaelic airs – 'Gun Bhris Mo Chridh' On Dh' Fhalbh Thu' ('My Heart Is Broken since Thy Departure') and 'Cha Till Mi Tuille' ('Never More Shall I Return'). Her hands have suffered stiffness and the lonely laments waver and hesitate as do the trembling fingers on the four taut strings. She is very moved by the ancient music and there are tears within her eyes.

What became known as Fuadach nan Gàidheal, the 'Driving Out of the Gael', continued through the early part of the nineteenth century and with less force and more encouragement into the twentieth. By 1836 there were perhaps 22,000 Gaelic speakers living in the tenements of Glasgow, often clustered in districts such as Partick, or Partaig. Many travelled much further, and as he wrote these elegiac lines, a MacKenzie bard wept:

I see the hills, the valleys and the slopes,
But they do not lighten my sorrow.
I see the band departing on the white-sailed ships.
I see the Gael rising from his door.
I see the people going,
And there is no love for them in the north.

What the Clearances did was to fundamentally fracture an ancient, but unstated, agreement. It violated the principles of *dùthchas*, the right of clansmen, women and their families to live on and work the land so long as they in turn fulfilled their obligations to their clan chief. That this ancient agreement was so summarily and brutally broken left a sense of bafflement, something that even became clear to the perpetrators, as shown in the words of the Marchioness of Stafford: 'They argued that they had a prescriptive claim to the soil: that they did their lady justice if they farmed it as their fathers had done; and that, chieftainess though she were, she had no better title to eject them from their humble tenements than they had to drive her from her castle.'

*

For the rest of the nineteenth century and on into the twentieth, two very different narratives about the Highlands and Islands would run in parallel. In 1845, A. C. Fullarton of Edinburgh published a pretty picture book. *Scotland Illustrated in a Series of Eighty Views* looks as though it was an update of John Slezer's *Theatrum Scotiae* but it had an accompanying text by a Professor Wilson, and an introductory essay titled 'On the Scenery of the Highlands'. Here is a characteristic passage: 'There [in the Highlands] indeed all objects are on so vast a scale, that we are for a while astonished as we gaze on the gigantic; and all other emotions are sunk in an overwhelming sense of awe that prostrates the imagination. But on recovering from its subjection to the prodigious, that faculty every where recognizes in those mighty mountains of dark forests, glittering glaciers, and regions of eternal snow – infinite all – the power and dominion of the sublime.'

This is followed by fifty long, long pages in a similar vein. Amongst the most striking sentences is this: 'Look now at the Linnhe Loch. How it gladdens Argyle! Without it and the Sound of Mull, how sad would be the shadows of Morvern!'

Not until the last page of this essay is there any mention of Highlanders, of the people who gazed every day upon the gigantic. It begins with the enigmatic sentence, 'We love the people too well to praise them.' Whatever that may mean, there is no doubt about the sense of this: 'Severe as are the hardships of their condition, they are, in the main, contented with it.' The attitudes of Professor Wilson are not untypical. The eyes of breathless aesthetes like him lifted up to the Ossianic grandeur of the mountains and were wilfully blind to the realities of those who lived in the glens and straths at their foot, the natives in this magnificent landscape. Finer feelings and exclamation marks were reserved for the scenery and not extended to the fellow human beings who had named the mountains and the lochs and who were trying wring a living from the land. Theirs was a walk-on part, when they were not walking off and leaving for the cities, the quaysides and the emigrant ships.

One of the eighty illustrations in Wilson's book, however, is crowded with people. They are almost all performers in fancy dress, pretending to be something they no longer were while an audience watched the show. The first modern version of a Highland Games was held at St Fillans, at the east end of Loch Earn. Professor Wilson's extended (nothing he wrote was ever succinct, but at least what follows here is informative) caption for the engraving by Charles Joseph Hullmandel reads:

The St. Fillan's Highland Society, instituted in 1819, is, or rather was, an association of the gentlemen of the west of Perthshire, who held an annual meeting at St. Fillan's, about the latter end of August, for the encouragement and exhibition of Highland games and costume. On these occasions, a large square stage was erected on a level piece of haugh on the south side of the river, opposite the village, to which there is access by a timber bridge. Part of the ground surrounding this platform was railed in, and furnished with seats and awnings for the accommodation of the judges and visitors of rank. Behind these, a clear space was allowed as a promenade for the members of the society; and beyond the outer barriers, the mixed multitude of spectators found a convenient station on a semicircular sloping bank, from which they could easily see and hear the performances. On the opposite side of the ground, or that next the river, the carriages and other vehicles of the members were drawn up; and the whole being thus arranged in amphitheatrical order, and with a somewhat classical effect, the games were usually opened with a competition among the pibroch performers, for a handsomely mounted Highland bag-pipe. After this and some other minor prizes had been awarded, the competitors in reel and hornpipe dancing, and the ancient sword-dance claimed attention; afterwards followed putting the stone, – flinging the hammer, – leaping, – running, – wrestling,

– target-shooting, – boat-rowing, – and a variety of other manly and athletic exercises. Prizes were also awarded for the best exhibitions of full Highland costume. The amusements of the day terminated, the members of the association dined together in their hall, – a commodious building, capable of accommodating 140 guests, now the village-hostelry. We are not aware that the St. Fillan's society has had any gatherings of late years.

The engraving itself is fascinating. Inside a fenced area almost all the men are wearing kilts and plaids and most appear to be armed to the teeth. With dirks and pistols at their belts, some carry targes and muskets while the background bristles with long pikes and Lochaber axes. Watched by a row of seated ladies in bonnets and long dresses, and the occasional man in trousers, a hunky individual in his shirt-sleeves, who might be an actual Highlander, has what looks like a large stone in his right hand. He is on the point of putting the weight, the equivalent of putting the shot in modern athletics. Two men who might be judges look on. Behind them is a square-floored area laid on the grass, what was probably a surface used for Highland dancing competitions. In the top left of the small arena (where it looked to me that spectators might be in danger of having the weight putt in their laps) a man plays the bagpipes, while another piper, perhaps waiting his turn, stands in the foreground. Next to him is an odd figure: a kilted man with a fierce expression has a pistol in his belt, a targe in his left hand and a drawn sword in the other. The way in which Hullmandel has drawn him, it looks as though this chief has just shouted the *claideamh mòr*.

All of this is pure theatre, a series of vignettes of make-believe, remnants of a real military past that, little more than seventy years after Culloden, has become a show rather than a representation of reality. Quite who all these people gathered at St Fillans are, is difficult to work out. A boy standing near the swordsman about to charge is barefoot and so is a little girl next to him. But others are clearly the gentry of west Perthshire, dressed in tartan finery, their bonnets stuck with long feathers, and several are wearing what might be velvet tunics under their plaids. One has a plume rather than feathers in his hat. What they all thought they were celebrating is hard to parse. A spectacular amount of dressing-up was certainly going on and it is difficult to escape the conclusion that for Professor Wilson, all of the tartan and weapons supplied an appropriate sort of human set dressing, the sort of pageantry that fitted the scenery rather more pleasingly than the miserable wretches whom he believed to be, in the main, contented.

No doubt the gentlemen of west Perthshire would have thought differently. They were carrying on age-old traditions, preserving the history of the Highland clans and celebrating their manly prowess with putting the weight, their music with the pipers and their distinctive dress with their plaids. And yet the older men in all these rig-outs would have heard from survivors of the Atholl Brigade who charged into the murderous cannonade at Culloden, others who remembered Am Bliadhna nan Creach – the killings, the rapes and the destruction of a society and an economy. If they thought they were carrying on some sort of legacy, they were doing nothing of the kind. It was a parody of the past that gathered at the east end of Loch Earn at the end of August in 1819. They were dishonouring memory, not preserving it.

Perhaps one of the few scraps of authenticity to be seen at St Fillans was the big man putting the weight or the stone. Competitions to see who could putt it furthest were first noted in the fourteenth century and apparently King Henry VIII of England, who probably had the right physique, was a noted stone putter. At clan gatherings and deer hunts (when many men were needed for the drive and sett), small-scale versions of the Highland Games took place. An Invernesshire minister, the Reverend James Fraser, attended a hunt in 1666: 'The four days we tarried there [at the hunt] what is it that could cheer and recreate mens' spirits but was gone about, jumping, archery, shooting, throwing the barr [tossing the caber], the stone, and all manner of manly exercise imaginable.'

Feats of strength were popular, and part of a Highland sense of machismo. There was often to be found *an clach na feart*, the putting stone at the gates of a chief's residence and guests were invited to see how far they could putt it. There was also *an clach cuid fir*, 'the stone of manhood', and when a boy was strong enough to lift it, that was a sign that he had attained manhood. Perhaps the biological parallel was intended, for Edward Dwelly does note that *clach* could also mean testicle. The Inver Stone in Deeside is the best known of these and since it weighs 265 pounds, it might have induced a hernia rather than an introduction to maturity.

Four years after the inaugural St Fillans Highland Games, a tartan-swathed George IV made his unforgettable entrance to the levee at Holyrood Palace and ignited not only a royal fascination with all things Highland (except with what was actually going on in the Highlands) that reached full flower with Queen Victoria, Prince Albert and Balmoral. Highland Games began to spring up everywhere, and most followed the St Fillans format. There was piping, dancing, running, leaping, the three heavy events of putting the weight, throwing the hammer and tossing the caber (as well as some variations like putting the weight over the bar), marches of bands of clansmen, rifle shooting, best-dressed Highlander competitions, and very occasionally recitations in Gaelic. Too much authenticity could not be allowed to intrude.

Most emblematic is tossing the caber. The sight of a kilted man lifting the end of an impossibly long trunk of a tree (or more usually these days, a re-purposed telegraph pole), staggering forward and then tossing it in the air could only be associated with Highland Games. Many entertaining theories as to the origin of this event have been advanced, but as ever Edward Dwelly probably supplies the definitive answer. *Cabar* is a 'pole' or a 'rafter', most likely the ridge-pole set between the apexes of the gables of a blackhouse on which the roof timbers and then the thatch could be attached. These had to be lifted up and caber-tossing probably began as a bit of fun when men were roofing a house. At Highland Games, a good toss is when the caber is thrown so that it topples over when the top end lands and falls in a straight line, what is known as the twelve o'clock position.

The most famous of all the games is the Braemar Gathering. It takes place at the beginning of September and the first competitions were held in 1832. Queen Victoria and Prince Albert first came to Balmoral in 1848 and also attended the Gathering in the same summer. It was the beginning of a long tradition and since then each succeeding monarch has been appointed Chieftain of the Games. On a sunny day it can be spectacular, and the sound of the massed pipe bands is very stirring. In 1963 the hammer throwing competition was won by one of Scotland's greatest athletes. For thirty years he dominated the heavy events at Highland Games, winning eighteen Scottish championship titles as well as British, European, American, Canadian and World titles. Born in 1937 at Bucksburn near Aberdeen, Bill Anderson competed all over Scotland and abroad until the age of fifty. His success brought more spectators to the games circuit and his rivalry with Arthur Rowe, an Englishman who had been an Olympic shot putter, seemed to enhance the performances of both men as records were broken in their summer duels in the 1960s and 1970s.

In 1955 a remarkable film was released. *Geordie* told the story of a wee Highland boy and how he grew much bigger, having done a correspondence course in bodybuilding. At the surprising instigation of Henry Samson, the creator of the bodybuilding course, Geordie enters a hammer throwing competition at a local Highland games and at first does badly. But when he sees his 'best friend', Jean, run down a hillside waving and shouting encouragement to 'my wee Geordie', he produces a wonderful final throw to win the competition. The win quickly gets him into the British Olympic team for the 1956 Melbourne Games. After an argument about wearing a kilt in the opening ceremony and a dalliance with Helga, a blonde, buxom Danish shot putter, Geordie steps into the throwing circle and thinks of Jean (in a version of a cartoon thought bubble) and wins the gold medal before returning triumphant to the glens.

This preposterous nonsense was of course wildly popular at the box office despite the wince-making Scottish accents of Bill Travers (from Newcastle) as Geordie and Norah Gorsen (from Dorset) as

Jean, and the film picked up rhapsodic reviews and made Travers a star, for a while. What Bill Anderson made of it can only be imagined.

In 1842 Queen Victoria and Prince Albert caught their first sight of the Highlands when they were the guests of the Earl of Breadalbane at Drummond Castle in Perthshire, not far from St Fillans. Perhaps the earl was the man in the plumed hat in Hullmandel's engraving. Five years later, with the words of Walter Scott ringing in her ears, the queen and her husband cruised up the Atlantic coast in a yacht. It rained the whole time, and her doctor, anxious for his patient's health, suggested that Deeside was drier and the weather kinder.

History was turned inside out once more when the royal couple bought Balmoral Castle. It had belonged to the Farquharsons of Inverey, a clan that had fought for the prince at Culloden. Not far away were the Braes of Mar, where 'Bobbing' John Erskine had raised the standard of rebellion in 1715. Queen Victoria baffled her courtiers when she declared more than once that at heart she was a Jacobite. Nothing could stand in the way of the romance that swirled around what was in essence a catastrophe for the Highlands and its people.

The Farquharson's castle was demolished, deemed too small and pokey, and the familiar turrets and battlements of Balmoral were raised. After 1855 the queen arrived on Deeside to spend a few leisurely weeks in her beloved Highlands and it became an annual fixture in the royal year, and where the monarch led, everyone who mattered followed. Prime ministers, cabinet ministers, civil servants and the whole apparatus of the court were obliged to follow her into the glens. High society followed her example. Hunting lodges were built for the wealthy and the aristocratic. Many were keen deerstalkers (even inventing a hat made famous by Sherlock Holmes), including the royal family. On the Earl of Breadalbane's estate, Prince Albert had shot two stags and a trend was set. As more and more sophisticated rifles were produced, so-called sporting estates were established and by the outset of the twentieth century, several million acres of the Highlands were devoted to deer rather than people.

Behind all of these titled and rich people, those who could not run to guns, lodges and land also came north. Tourists began to arrive in the Highlands. The railway had enabled the royal family to get from London to Deeside much more easily and quickly, and trains reached Inverness by 1863 and Oban by 1880. Visitors to the Highlands were encouraged to follow the royal example by the enormous sales of *Leaves from the Journal of Our Life in the Highlands*. Published in 1868, this was a digest of Queen Victoria's diaries: 'I cannot describe all we saw. But we saw where the Dee rises between the mountains . . . and such magnificent wild rocks, precipices and corries, most splendid. It had a sublime and solemn effect; so solitary, so wild, so severe, no one but ourselves and our little party there.'

There is much more in this vein, similar stuff to the writings of Professor Wilson, and it neatly summed up the principal attraction of the Highlands for the last 150 years: a splendid, epic emptiness.

At the same time as Wilson published his book, there was famine in the north. The potato crop suffered repeatedly from blight, and although the effects were not nearly as severe as in Ireland, the winter of 1846/7 was very cold and too many died. But the government and the Free Church of Scotland acted promptly to mitigate the effects of the failure of crops, determined not to see starvation, and supplies of food arrived in sufficient quantity to stave off disaster. But people began once more to leave in large numbers. Between 1846 and 1857, more than 16,000 Highlanders emigrated to the Americas or to Australia, most of them from the islands. The Highlands and Islands Emigration Society was set up, and under the scheme a landlord could pay only £1 to nominate an emigrant and the Society made up the balance of the cost of a fare. A significant number bought their own passages. It is estimated that about one-third of the population of the western Highlands departed between 1841 and 1861. Many others walked to the cities to find work and food.

Despite the famine, not everyone wanted to leave. There were forced evictions in Barra, Lewis and the Uists, and sometimes men were tied up by the constables and forced to the quaysides and onto the ships. Catherine MacPhee witnessed what went on:

Many a thing I have seen in my own day . . . Many a thing, O Mary Mother . . . I have seen the townships swept, and the big holdings being made of them, the people being driven out of the countryside to the streets of Glasgow and the wilds of Canada, such of them as did not die of hunger and plague and smallpox while going across the ocean. I have seen the women putting the children in the carts which were being sent from Benbecula and Iochdar to Lochboisdale, while their husbands lay bound in the pen and were weeping beside them, without power to give them a helping hand, though the women themselves were crying aloud and their little children wailing like to break their hearts. I have seen the big, strong men, the champions of the countryside, the stalwarts of the world, being bound on Lochboisdale quay and cast into the ship as would be done to a batch of horses or cattle in the boat, the bailiffs and the ground officers and the constables and the policemen gathered behind them in pursuit of them. The God of Life, and He only knows all the loathsome work of men on that day.

To add to Catherine MacPhee's vivid memories, there are some photographs of what happened. Perhaps most poignant is one of a mother and her two children sitting on the wreckage of their house. On no more than a pile of stones and planks of wood and beams, the woman is looking down, her hand on her forehead while a boy, perhaps ten or twelve years old, and his younger sister, sit beside her. The little girl stares at the camera. Below them an old lady lies, apparently asleep, her eyes clearly closed and her hand on her stomach. It is a freeze-frame of misery and emblematic of a disgraceful and cruel series of episodes that stain the history of the Highlands with shame.

14

Resistance

Winter had not yet fled in the far north of Arctic Canada and on the shores of an icy bay, Aglooka and his men began to build a snow-house, a shelter from the biting wind and cold. First, they dug into the snow to form a circular hole with a wide terrace around it, and then, carefully cutting blocks of old, compressed snow, they made a dome with a low entrance at ground level. When the smoke hole was made, a welcome fire would be lit. But then Aglooka saw something that intrigued him. In the vast whiteness he and his band had seen no other people for some time, but while they were making the snowhouse, Aglooka noticed some human tracks. Mistegan, an Ojibwe from the south, and Ouligbuck, an Inuit, were sent to find the people who had walked that way. Eight hours later, they came back with a dozen Inuit men, women and children. They showed Aglooka the strange things they had found. He was very interested in a silver fork with initials scratched on the back of it and a spoon.

It was the spring of 1854. Aglooka was the Inuit name of Dr John Rae from Orkney. He had qualified as a surgeon at Edinburgh University and signed on at Stromness in 1833 to sail to the Nor'Wast with the Hudson's Bay Company. Twenty years later, Rae had joined one of the expeditions sent to search for the Arctic explorer, Sir John Franklin, and the crews of his ships, the *Erebus* and the *Terror*. In 1845, they had set out to find the fabled Northwest Passage around the north of Canada. Its discovery would have greatly enhanced trade and Britain's links with its empire since it would avoid the need to make the long and dangerous voyage around Cape Horn (the Panama Canal would not be completed until 1914). The *Erebus* and the *Terror* had been sighted by whaling ships in Baffin Bay on 20 July 1845, but nothing had been heard from them since. In 1848, the Admiralty finally decided to send out search parties, and one of them was led by Dr John Rae.

His survival skills were exemplary. Rae learned all he could from the native Inuit peoples, reasoning that they knew more about the hostile environment they lived in than any European. He understood that the compressed snow used to make snowhouses was full of trapped air that made excellent insulation and that the stone buildings made by other expeditions to the north were useless in extreme cold. Aglooka means 'Long Strider' and was a tribute to his ability to walk great distances in snowshoes. There exists an engraving of the Orcadian doctor that shows him in native clothes. He is wrapped in a long fur-trimmed coat made from what might have been deer pelts. On his head is a thick and elaborate fur headdress that looks as though its lower folds would wrap around his neck and chin. It has splendid wings on either side, and he has mittens attached to strings. Rae's leggings and a knapsack are beautifully decorated with beads. This is a Cree costume from a native people whose ancestral lands lay around the shores of Hudson Bay.

Rae had led the search party north to the Boothia Peninsula, and a few weeks after the Inuit had shown him what were probably relics from the ships of the Franklin expedition, he came across much more convincing evidence.

Sometime after Mistegan and Ouligbuck had tracked the first group of Inuit, Rae and his party moved on to Repulse Bay, about 160 miles to the south-east. When Inuit families came to the camp, they had a very persuasive story to tell, as well as undoubted relics that persuaded Rae the *Erebus* and the *Terror* had been lost, perhaps crushed in the pack ice, perhaps sunk beneath it. One man had found a silver plate engraved with Sir John Franklin's name, as well as other items. Talking to Rae through Ouligbuck, who acted as interpreter, the Inuit began to relate what they had seen and what they knew of the fate of the expedition. Four years earlier, in the autumn of 1850, hunters had seen a group of *kabloonas*, the Inuit name for white men, dragging a boat and some sledges across King William Island, to the west of the Boothia Peninsula. Through sign language, the *kabloonas* told the hunters that they were looking for deer, the caribou native to the Arctic. After bartering for some seal meat from the Inuit, the leader of the white men, a tall man with a telescope slung over his shoulder (who was probably Francis Crozier, captain of the *Terror*) moved off eastwards with his party. When the Inuit returned to the island the following spring, they found about thirty frozen bodies. Some of them had been butchered, clear evidence of cannibalism.

John Rae was in no doubt that the hunters were telling the truth, only relating what they had seen. Sir John Franklin's expedition, all 129 men, had perished in the storms of the Arctic winter and both their ships had been lost in the sea-ice, forcing them to abandon them and move overland. By the time he had spoken to the Inuit hunters, it was too late in the year for Rae to go north and see for himself. And that was his first mistake.

Lady Jane Franklin was very well connected and in London she had orchestrated a campaign to search for her husband's expedition, encouraging the Admiralty to put up a reward of £10,000 for any information that would lead to their rescue. Or their discovery. But as time went on, hope, even in Lady Franklin's heart, must have wavered. Nevertheless, she doggedly continued to campaign and the lost expedition became a great cause, regularly publicised, an example of British heroism and enterprise.

John Rae was certain that he had at last discovered what had happened to Franklin and his men, and he booked a passage across the Atlantic so that he could reveal his findings in person. On the voyage he wrote a report for the Admiralty that included what the Inuit had told him about the signs of cannibalism. Rae also wrote a letter to *The Times*, breaking the news, but careful to omit any mention of how members of the heroic expedition had attempted to survive by butchering the dead bodies of their comrades. Having docked in London, Rae went straight to the Admiralty to hand in his report and the relics, including the engraved silver plate, to Sir James Graham, the First Sea Lord. *The Times* had a sensational scoop, a solution to a mystery that had been in the public eye for many years and it published Rae's letter the following day. But for some reason, Graham also passed on the report to the newspaper, with its details of cannibalism, and that too was published.

There was immediate outrage. Rae was dismayed to see his confidential report in the newspaper, but Lady Franklin was furious. Her husband's heroism had been sullied by these allegations and they could not possibly be true, could not be allowed to stand. John Rae asked to see Lady Franklin and their meeting was brusque and brief. Immediately she set about having his story discredited. No less than Charles Dickens was persuaded to refute what Rae had asserted. The bodies must have been savaged by wild animals, the Inuit themselves were capable of murder since they were known to be 'covetous, treacherous and cruel', he wrote. The campaign of rebuttal succeeded. Sir John Franklin had a statue raised to him and a memorial set up in Westminster Abbey, and he was, wrongly, credited with the discovery of the Northwest Passage. Meanwhile, the Admiralty quietly accepted that Rae had found convincing evidence of the loss of the whole expedition and they gave him the £10,000 reward.

It was a travesty. Later searchers confirmed the evidence of cannibalism, preserved in the ice, but perhaps most galling was the fact that through his own mapping and expeditions in the Arctic, Rae had himself discovered the Northwest Passage, and not Franklin. But he never received the credit, no knighthood was bestowed, and, in 1893, Rae died in London in relative obscurity. Catherine Thompson, his widow, had her husband's body brought back home to Orkney to be buried at St Magnus Cathedral in Kirkwall.

Orkney and Shetland and the Highlands and the Hebrides also saw profound demographic change. The departure of men like John Rae and the thousands of others who sailed to the Nor'Wast, as well as emigrants from the mainland, forced and voluntary, meant that the fabric of life was both altered and diminished. The north began to look outwards and make distant links with communities across the world's oceans. As the landscape emptied, its people began to make distinctive marks. John Rae is only one heroic, spectacular example.

Many emigrants left historical legacies, many of them positive, some more stains than marks. The Ku Klux Klan not only borrowed the name, but also their symbol of terror, the fiery cross, derived from the *crann tara* of the clans. It was set up and set alight to make sure that black people remembered their place. William Wallace MacLeod was a slave owner whose plantation near Charleston in South Carolina grew sea-island cotton and indigo. Naming his grand mansion Inverness House, he remembered his Highland origins, and lining the drive up to the classical columns of its grand frontage were rows of slave cabins. Like garden sheds measuring about twenty feet by twelve feet, they housed a population of seventy-four slaves whose origins lay far to the east, across the Atlantic in the Gambia. MacLeod enlisted in the Confederate Army in 1860 at the outbreak of the American Civil War and died of pneumonia in 1865.

In 1781 the 71st Highland Regiment of Foot found itself in Charleston as the American War of Independence drew to a close. Lachlan Macquarie from Mull served as an officer. Between 1788 and 1800, he rose through the ranks, fighting in the British army in India, and in 1809 he was appointed governor of New South Wales. The penal colony was at that time controlled by the New South Wales Corps, a regiment notoriously corrupt and disobedient that conducted a lucrative trade in rum. With the help of regular troops who sailed to Australia with him, Macquarie restored order and began the transition from a penal colony to a civil society. His influence was all-pervasive, from laying out the street plan of Sydney to organising a currency for the colony. The governor bought 40,000 Spanish dollar coins and had a convicted forger, William Henshall, cut out their centres, stamp them with the seal of New South Wales and they were circulated with a modern value of about fifteen pence. The rim, known as the 'Holey Dollar', became a twenty-five pence piece. Macquarie also promoted the virtues of marriage and regular church attendance as well as banning the public consumption of alcohol. Just as Napoleon Bonaparte reordered the French Republic, this remarkable Highlander shaped the beginnings of Australia.

Another Highlander, James Matheson, became a taipan. Born near Lairg in Sutherland, he left to go to school and university in Edinburgh just as the clearances were gathering momentum in the early nineteenth century. Eventually he formed a partnership with William Jardine, another Scot, and they created the great conglomerate now known as Jardine Matheson Holdings. A taipan was the name given to a foreign entrepreneur working in China, and both men made fortunes, much of their wealth coming from the trade in opium. In 1844, Matheson paid half a million pounds for the Isle of Lewis, evicted more than 500 families and arranged for their emigration to Canada. In 1851, before the ships docked, he wrote a harsh and unfeeling note to the immigration authorities in Quebec saying that the Lewis people should not be allowed to remain in groups of neighbours or families and that they should be dispersed to different communities and places. This would be 'the best means of eradicating those habits of indolence and inertness to which their impoverished condition must in some measure be attributed'. It was an act of casual callousness.

*

In the autumn of 1834, the Reverend Robert Young climbed the steps up to the pulpit in the parish church at Auchterarder on the fringes of Highland Perthshire. His sermon did not go well. The ecclesiastical living at Auchterarder was vacant and Young had been a probationary candidate, but after hearing him preach, the congregation rejected him by an emphatic margin. Of the male heads of families in the parish who made up the electorate, 287 voted against Young and only two to accept him. But he got the job anyway.

In 1712, only five years after the Union of the Parliaments, the government passed the highly contentious Patronage Act, changing the constitution of the Church of Scotland. Instead of congregations deciding who their minister should be, the patron or the heritors (and often the Crown) were allowed to promote candidates and congregations had to accept them. There were substantial strings attached: patrons or heritors owned the churches, manses and parish schools but they had not only to pay for their upkeep but also the stipends of the minister and the schoolmaster. And if the church-door collections were insufficient to meet the outgoings of the poor relief fund, they had to make up the shortfall. Nevertheless, the British Parliament insisted on this system because it gave the government a degree of control. Few radical ministers were ever put forward and no administration encouraged criticism. Ecclesiastical patronage was also an extension of political patronage.

The quality of the Reverend Robert Young's preaching was not really the issue in Auchterarder. He had been the choice of the patron, Thomas Hay-Drummond, the 11th Earl of Kinnoull, and was, incidentally, a close relative of the estate factor. But perhaps more importantly, the earl was not a member of the Auchterarder congregation. Born in Bath, married in London and died in Torquay, it is unlikely that he was knowledgeable about local concerns. In addition, patrons and heritors were sometimes reluctant to do their financial duty and the upkeep of church, manse and school sometimes faltered.

The Church of Scotland had long been uncomfortable with the Patronage Act. It violated a founding principle, something the reformers of the sixteenth century and the Covenanters of the seventeenth had fought hard for. The Kirk was governed not by the state or any secular power, but by the Lord Jesus Christ. After 1712 a number of congregations formed the Secession Kirk, and it was the first of many fractures. After the Jacobite Rising of 1745, declarations of loyalty in Scotland were insisted upon and the Burgess Oath was mandatory from congregations. This caused further splits and the Burgher Secession Kirk came into being alongside the Anti-Burghers. More disagreement over the state's interference in the Church of Scotland caused the formation of the Auld Licht Anti-Burghers and the New Licht Anti-Burghers. The Auld Lichts wanted to continue the traditions of the Covenanters and the New Lichts were more concerned with personal salvation. Bewildering, even faintly ridiculous in a more secular age, these disagreements were on a small scale compared to what happened after the dispute in Auchterarder, but they are also evidence of fiercely held beliefs and a wish for spiritual independence, something that would continue in the Highlands and Islands until the present day.

The Patronage Act of 1712 had been tolerated in the Church of Scotland for more than a century because the Moderate, or conservative, party of ministers had been in a majority in the General Assembly, the governing body of the Kirk. But in the 1830s that changed, in part because of the beliefs and attitudes of Highland ministers and their congregations. Perhaps for historical reasons, they were less inclined to accept the influence of a patron or heritors. The party that became known as the Evangelicals was led by a very charismatic minister, the Reverend Thomas Chalmers, and its ideals and proposals for change were publicised by Hugh Miller, the stonemason and geologist from Cromarty. In 1840 he became editor of *The Witness*, a widely circulated newspaper based in Edinburgh that acted as a mouthpiece for the Evangelicals.

In May 1834, Thomas Chalmers introduced the Veto Act and it was passed by the General Assembly. It stated that if a majority of the male heads of families in a parish did not wish to accept a patron's nominee as their minister, they could reject him. This led directly to the ructions in Auchterarder, and from there to the General Assembly of 1843.

As other parishes, especially in the north, had followed Auchterarder's lead, momentum built quickly behind the radical notion of secession, a complete break with the Church of Scotland and the creation of a Free Church of Scotland. In November 1842, the Evangelicals began to organise, raising very substantial funds. 'The money has come in on us like a set rain of £1,000 a day,' wrote Chalmers. Four hundred local committees were set up to plan and prepare, many of them in the Highlands and Islands. In the Northern Isles, thirteen parishes looked as though they would secede, nineteen in Argyll, four on Lewis and four in Skye and Uist.

On the morning of 18 May 1843, crowds of many thousands gathered in Edinburgh's George Street and St Andrew Square outside St Andrew's Church, where the General Assembly was due to begin. Led by Dr David Welsh, the Moderator, 200 ministers walked out to found the Free Church of Scotland, a number that rose to 454 out a total of 1,129. It was a seismic moment. All of these men were giving up their manses, their churches and their stipends.

Chalmers, Miller and the others were prepared. Between 1843 and 1847, a staggering 730 new churches were built and 500 new schools. Some 650 teachers were appointed. A major difficulty was sites to build on. Landowners often refused to sell the land needed, and in many places the Free Church services were held out of doors, harking back to the field conventicles of the Covenanters. The people of Strontian were refused a site for their new church by Sir James Riddell, the landowner in Ardnamurchan. And so the congregation raised £1,400 and commissioned a floating church to be built in a Clyde shipyard. It was towed into Loch Sunart by tugs on 12 June 1846 and moored. Worshippers rowed out to hear the word of God, and no doubt Galilee was mentioned more than once. In Campbeltown a makeshift church was created in half a day in a local distillery. At Plockton an open-air church was built by the congregation pulling rocks from a hillside near the village to create a natural amphitheatre. More floating churches were proposed for Applecross and Lochcarron, but when the strength and determination of Highland Free Church communities became clear, landowners began to relent.

The traditions of religious independence and dissent did not abate in the Highlands and Islands, and the picture continued to change. In 1852 the Original Secession Church united with the Free Church of Scotland, and in 1900 both joined with the United Presbyterian Church, itself a union of the old Secession churches and the Relief Church, another breakaway from the eighteenth century. This did not meet with universal approval and the Free Church of Scotland came into being, made up from ministers and congregations who did not wish to join with the seceders. Known colloquially as the Wee Frees, the Church claims to be the true inheritors of the Free Church of Chalmers and Miller and it now has 105 congregations, many of them in the Highlands, and about 8,000 come regularly to services.

The process of schism continued into the twentieth century as more small groups broke away, again many of their congregations in the Highlands and Islands. The United Free Church came into being in 1900 and has fifty-one congregations. The Free Presbyterian Church of Scotland and the Free Church of Scotland (Continuing) both have twenty-nine and two more, the Associated Presbyterian Churches and the Reformed Presbyterian Church of Scotland, are tiny with only six and five congregations respectively. What unites them all is piety.

What used to unite more of them was a unique and wonderful music. At Queen Elizabeth II's lying at rest in the High Kirk of St Giles in September 2022, Karen Matheson sang Psalm 118, 'Chan Fhaigh Mi Bàs Ach Maiream Beò' ('I Shall Not Die But Live'). Her beautiful voice rang around the world as those who watched the ceremonies of the queen's funeral unfold heard the quintessential sound of Highland worship.

I first heard the Gaelic psalmody by accident when I was a boy and in the Highlands for the first time. Our school party was staying at Ratagan Youth Hostel on Loch Duich, and it was raining, ceaselessly. Clouds hid the Five Sisters of Kintail as a grey and wet Sunday wore on. It used to be an iron rule in youth hostels that all who stayed in them were turfed out after breakfast and not allowed to return until suppertime. Being in the healthy and invigorating open air was the point! In the unrelenting rain, most of my friends walked to the café at Shiel Bridge. It had rained all day on Saturday and we had eked out a single cup of coffee for a very long time before it was made clear that unless we ordered something else, we needed to leave. After an hour or two in a bus shelter, we wandered back through the puddles to the youth hostel where the warden took pity on us.

On the following Sunday morning, as the rain fell steadily, I decided that a return to the café was not for me, and so I walked by myself in the opposite direction, along the southern shore of the loch. Many cars began to pass me, and when I turned a corner,

I saw more parked by the side of the road. Opposite was a large, green corrugated iron hut that I realised must be a church. The sky was a leaden grey and the rain showed no sign of easing, so I decided to pretend to be a Christian.

The hut was almost full, and I noticed that no one had taken off their overcoats. I sat at the back and as I picked up a thick, black, leather-bound book marked *Am Biobull*, I heard the minister's sibilant, West Highland syllables welcoming a visitor and some of the congregation turned to nod to me and smile. That was the last thing I understood. The rest of the service was not in English.

But the little tin church was dry and as I listened, the minister looking directly at me occasionally as he spoke, knowing full well that I understood not one word, I began to feel a little drowsy. And then something remarkable happened to jolt me awake. After a prayer, I think, a tall, thin man was summoned. 'Air ceann na seinn,' said the minister. 'At the head of the singing', as I understood many years later, and the tall man stood forward, faced the congregation and opened his hymn book.

With no accompanying music, no ceremony and no warning, he sang a line of a psalm very loudly and without any conventional melody I could make out. It was more like a chant, an invocation. Then something extraordinary happened. The whole congregation, still seated, sang the line back to him very loudly, their voices swooping like flocks of birds over the lochs and mountains. I was stunned, and even as a boy, moved by the rumbling power and the swirl of the higher notes as the tall man sang each line and everyone except me responded.

Much later, I produced a film about this music like no other, and called it *I Shall Not Die But Live*, the name of the psalm sung by Karen Matheson in St Giles' Cathedral in 2022. The precentor begins by singing a line from whatever one of the Psalms of David is chosen and the congregation sing it back to him hung with grace notes, variations and other ornaments. Apparently no two renditions are ever the same. Illiteracy and a lack of psalm books in Gaelic may have helped this way of worshipping God in the Highlands and Islands. Until the American Civil War, the psalms were sung in exactly the same way in the Carolinas and for longer in Nova Scotia in Canada. The founding melodies for the psalmody came from the Lowlands and from England where precentors still sang the lines to congregations until the seventeenth and into the early eighteenth centuries. But now the old tunes are all but unrecognisable in their Gaelic forms. An echo of that heritage can be heard in the way in which 'Amazing Grace' is sung in America.

Twenty-five years after I first heard the psalms on a rainy Sunday at Letterfearn, I went with a film crew to a church in Stornoway. The minister and the congregation could not have been more welcoming, and when the precentor stood forward and the singing began, I remembered the awe, the wonder I'd felt as a boy. The swelling, soaring sound was transcendent, deeply moving, elemental and unique. These were not the voices of ordinary people. They sang like choirs of angels, the grace notes echoing across the vastness of eternity. The psalms are made to soar like eagles, to crash like breakers on the Atlantic shore, to sigh and rush like the mountain winds. They are amongst the purest, most compelling forms of worship in any church anywhere. And unique to the Highlands and Islands, an expression of faith like no other.

*

At the same time as the Free Church took shape in the Highlands, and its unique forms of worship developed, a revolution was taking place. Within only a few decades the north became suddenly and quickly accessible and the mountains, glens and islands ceased to be remote. The railways came.

In 2001, Roland Paxton of Heriot-Watt University returned to the famous viaduct at Loch nan Uamh to investigate a metaphor. The line from Fort William to Mallaig, under construction in 1898 and 1899, was the last major project in the Highland network. Not far from where Prince Charles boarded a ship for France in 1746, Paxton set up his equipment. For more than a hundred years there had been a persistent tale that a horse and cart had been entombed in one of the great concrete piers that carry the railway across the head of the loch. Paxton was nothing if not persistent himself.

In 1987, he used a tiny fisheye camera lowered into boreholes in the Glenfinnan viaduct only a few miles back up the line. Its scenic setting had been made world famous by the Harry Potter films, and Paxton wanted to investigate claims that the horse had fallen into one of its piers. He found nothing. But the rumours continued to be repeated, and local people insisted that the accident had definitely happened, but not at Glenfinnan. The horse and cart were inside the viaduct at Loch nan Uamh. So, in 2001 Paxton brought radar equipment and through nine feet of concrete, he saw something. Standing vertically against the east wall of one of the piers was the clear outline of a horse above the wreckage of a cart. One only hopes that the poor creature broke its neck as it fell, probably dragged backwards into the shuttered pier by a heavy load.

The metaphor had become a reality. As the railway made a last link through the glens of the Highlands to the Atlantic shore, old ways of travel and moving cargo became increasingly obsolete and the speed of travel increased enormously.

The British railway network had reached Inverness in 1855, Wick and Thurso in 1874, making a link with the ferries crossing the Pentland Firth to the Northern Isles. Oban Station opened in 1880, and Kyle of Lochalsh in 1897. In the space of less than fifty years, the remote, wild Highlands and Islands of Scotland were remote no longer and much more closely connected with the rest of Britain. The effects were far-reaching.

Droving gradually declined and the trysts at Crieff and Falkirk became obsolete. Innovative farmers in Aberdeenshire and elsewhere in the north saw an opportunity. With the creation of the Aberdeen Angus breed of polled cattle, without horns and bigger and much heavier than the black cattle of the Highlands, the market changed radically. Polled cattle, who would not damage each other, were bred and fattened in the north and could be loaded into cattle cars so that they arrived at Smithfield Market in London in a day. The long overland drives of the drovers, where the cows lost condition, were no longer necessary and the old green roads through the mountains faded into memory.

Travelling in the opposite direction, prompted by Queen Victoria's *Leaves from the Journal of Our Life in the Highlands* and romanced by the novels and long poems of Sir Walter Scott, tourists began to board trains to the north. Published in 1810, *The Lady of the Lake* had brought people to visit the Trossachs and Loch Katrine, a relatively accessible area of the southern Highlands before the trains opened up the north. Oban, though, became a hub in 1880 because it made a direct link between the rail network and the ferries of the western coast. The railway station is less than a minute's walk to the ferry terminal, where icons wait at the quayside.

The famous livery of the red funnel and the lion rampant, the white superstructure and the black hull of Caledonian MacBrayne ferries are unmistakable. From the coastal railheads at Mallaig and Kyle of Lochalsh, as well as Oban, passengers, goods and the post could be transferred to the ships and taken quickly to the islands. The most active of these carriers was David Hutcheson & Co., and in 1878 the company was taken over by a dynamic young business-man, David MacBrayne. Within twenty years he had built up a fleet of thirty ships plying the sea roads between the mainland and the islands, and between islands, and at its greatest extent, the network included sixty destinations. From the 1880s onwards, their arterial voyages were down the Clyde, calling at Dunoon, the islands of Bute, Cumbrae and Arran, through the Crinan Canal to Oban and up to Fort William, and thence up the Caledonian Canal to Inverness. The entire journey, along dramatic coastlines and up through the glories of the Great Glen, needed no land transport.

This tourist route turned out to be the saving of the canal. The great engineer Thomas Telford proposed a scheme that at the time seemed workable. Government money was promised and construc-tion began in 1804 on a project that was likely to be a great stimulus to the economy of the Highlands and Islands, because it would avoid the dangerous and time-consuming voyage from the ports of the east coast to the west through the Pentland Firth and around Cape Wrath.

But there were difficulties. Loch Oich had to be deepened and cost overruns forced the builders to reduce the draught from twenty feet to fifteen. This became a significant problem. Technological advances in shipbuilding, increasingly with iron instead of wooden hulls, meant that cargo vessels had become bigger, too big to use the canal.

Queen Victoria, however, came to the rescue. In 1873 she sailed along its length and, of course, tourists followed in her wake, booking passages on cruises through the canal's spectacular scenery. Perhaps some hoped to catch a glimpse of the most famous creature in the Highlands. Stories of a monster in Loch Ness began to circulate in the later nineteenth century – Donald Mackenzie from Balnain claimed to have seen a large object 'wriggling and churning up the water', and Alexander MacDonald said that 'a large, stubby-legged animal' surfaced not fifty yards from where he stood on the loch shore! When the railway came to Fort William and Inverness, the trains connected with the steamers that took visitors up and down the Great Glen. Now the canal attracts more than half a million visitors each year.

David MacBrayne's modern sea kingdom is a network of ferries that visit twenty-two islands and several mainland harbours such as Mallaig and Oban. The services are lifelines for communities, and, in 2018, 5.5 million tickets were bought. The busiest area remains the Firth of Clyde with services from Gourock (the headquarters of Caledonian MacBrayne, popularly known as Calmac) to Dunoon, Wemyss Bay to Bute, Largs to Cumbrae and Ardrossan to Arran and Kintyre. By comparison, the volume of traffic amongst the Hebrides is much lower, but absolutely vital. During the Covid pandemic, the timetables were much reduced, although essential goods and journeys always got through. When services from Armadale on Skye and Campbeltown in Kintyre were cancelled, it was because alternative land routes were possible, even though they were much longer.

At the beginning of the twentieth century, the Reverend Donald Lamont wrote in the Gaelic supplement of *Life and Work* (the magazine of the Church of Scotland) about how well loved the MacBrayne ferries were in those early years, and his article gives a pungent sense of how integral these ships and their resourceful crews were to Highland and Island life:

Although the *Claymore* was built to carry cargo, she was just as handsome as the *Columba*, and, although it is a big claim to make, her like has not been seen going up the Sound of Mull since she herself ceased to go there. The *Claymore* ran for many years between Glasgow and Stornoway, and I heard someone saying last year that old David MacBrayne was so fond of her that she never left the Clyde without his being on the quay, to see her off. It was said that she was wet in heavy seas, but she was strong and safe and robust in her construction. If she had not been, she would not have lasted as long as she did, fifty years, rounding the Mull of Kintyre in bad weather and up to Stornoway, where the sea was even worse, and where she received, on many a bad night, a battering and a twisting that only strong ribs and gear could withstand.

It was a fine sight to see the *Claymore* leaving Tobermory on a summer evening, resplendent in paint and every inch of her copper and brass polished as clean as a new shilling, and a row of English folk standing at her gunwale, with a telescope in the hand or at the eye of each one, gaping at the seagulls of the shoreline and other wonders which they came to see in the Highlands. But, although the English folk were profitable to MacBrayne in the summer, the *Claymore* was not built to carry Englishmen, but to convey the people of the Islands and the West Highlands to and from Glasgow, and to transport cargo to many a township and harbour which had no other way of obtaining goods.

If you have never seen one of MacBrayne's boats loading or unloading cargo, you have missed a spectacle as interesting as any in this world: bags of meal and boxes and baskets of bread, kebbucks of cheese and cement, wood and clay jars of whisky, calves and barrels of tar, all thrown on top of one another, and all the time pigs squealing so loudly and so angrily that men pushing them cannot hear their own bad language.

Like many businesses in the 1920s, MacBrayne's suffered badly as fewer tickets were bought and the costs of fuel soared. Governments realised that in order to keep these vital services running, subsidies were needed and these were duly forthcoming. Nevertheless, the transport links could sometimes be hair-raising. Having moved to Kirkcaldy from Ardnamurchan, where his parents were crofters, Alasdair Maclean's journey home could sometimes be eventful. Here is a passage from his elegiac and beautifully written memoir, *Night Falls on Ardnamurchan*:

For most of the [1950s], however, anyone bound for Ardnamurchan came via Oban rather than Fort William, boarding at Oban a steamer which took him through the Sound of Mull to Tobermory. Disembarking at Tobermory he took a ferry back across to the mainland – if mainland be the right word for Ardnamurchan – stepping ashore this time at Mingary Pier, Kilchoan.

The main potential trouble spot in this itinerary was the Tobermory–Kilchoan ferry, which was actually a small launch. If the Sound of Mull were at all stormy – and the Sound here is more or less at an end and has widened into open Atlantic – the launch crew generally refused to make the run. It did not matter if the crossing, though rough, was yet possible; if they did not feel like it they did not stir and there was nothing one could do about it. Though supposedly tied in with the national transport network, they had in practice a good deal of autonomy. Naturally too, the launch skipper had – or adopted – a sea captain's authority in regard to his vessel and claimed to be the sole arbiter in all decisions affecting her daily running and risk.

Once in a great while, on the other hand – I think when complaints became too loud and too prevalent even for those conveniently deaf to ignore – the same crew would display all the seafaring enterprise that one could wish, and perhaps a little more to boot. I have made the crossing on days when all was noise and welter, when the launch went from crest to trough like a bobsleigh and from trough to crest like a badly overloaded lift, when I had to wedge myself between bulkheads to avoid being hurled about the cabin and had to leap for my life when the vessel at last made a flying pass at Mingary Pier. But derring-do of that order was very much the exception rather than the rule . . .

When the ferry service was in its pomp, this verse of doggerel was composed, loosely based on Psalm 24:

The Earth belongs unto the Lord
And all that it contains
Except the Kyles and the Western Isles
And they are all MacBrayne's.

*

As often in the history of the Highlands and Islands after Culloden, two very different narratives were running in parallel. By the middle of the nineteenth century, attitudes amongst landlords had changed little since the Sutherland clearances. In the spring of 1851, in the wake of the devastation of the potato blight, the Duke of Argyll, MacCailean Mór and Chief of Clan Campbell, wrote to his chamberlain, 'I wish to send out [i.e. evict] those whom we would be obliged to feed if they stayed at home – to get rid of that class is <u>the object.</u>' Poverty and the drive to make profits from Highland estates were not the only factors that influenced landlords when it came to deciding who should be evicted and who should be allowed to stay. Argyll's chamberlain, John Campbell, issued 'removing notices' to those who had been 'selling whisky' or who had been guilty of 'unruly conduct' or 'extreme laziness and bad conduct', or had 'intemperate habits'. Duncan Henderson of Kilmory in Knapdale was said to be 'a clever man, a little too much so', and so he too had to go. It must have been akin to a reign of terror as these men made summary, even capricious, decisions that drastically affected thousands of lives.

While visitors scanned the surface of Loch Ness for monsters, the crofting community had suffered a series of poor summers and meagre harvests in the 1870s. Matters were made worse on Skye when crofters from the Braes, on the coast opposite Raasay, attempted to graze their animals on the slopes of Beinn Lì, land they considered to be common grazing. The proprietor, Lord MacDonald, refused to allow it, a highhanded decision that led to open conflict. There were rent strikes and on 7 April 1882, a sheriff officer was sent from Portree to serve eviction orders on several of MacDonald's tenants. He left an account of what happened when he reached Braes:

> . . . at that, Mairi nicFuilaidh suddenly cried, 'Men, make them burn the summonses.' At that they yelled, 'Put them down on the road.' I put them down on the road. And with stones in their hands ready to kill me if I disobeyed, they compelled me to make a heap of the summonses . . . a boy came running with a burning peat . . . never was an officer of the law so disgraced to come so far as to have burned them myself . . . that hurts me more than the stone or the clod.

Ten days later reinforcements arrived in Portree. Two sheriffs and a police superintendent led nine Invernesshire constables and forty-seven men brought up from Glasgow's police force. By arriving early in the morning, they surprised the crofters at Braes and they arrested five men who were seen as the ringleaders of the resistance, and of the rent strikes. It must be said that women also took a leading role in what happened. Word crackled around the crofts quickly and people rushed towards Allt nan Gobhlag, where the path back to Portree passes through a narrow gorge.

Not only was there vigorous resistance, rather than meek acceptance, the events that followed were witnessed by several journalists and what became known as the Battle of the Braes was widely reported. According to David Gow of the *Dundee Advertiser*, it was the women in the crowd of crofters at the gorge who urged an attack on the police. No doubt the local constables had enough Gaelic to understand what was being shouted, and when the police drew their truncheons and charged the crofters, Gow reported: 'Huge boulders darkened the horizon as they sped from the hands of the infuriated men and women. Large sticks and flails were brandished and brought down with crushing force upon the police. Many were struck and a number more or less injured.'

The police broke out of the melee at Allt nan Gobhlag but were again attacked at An Cumhang before finally arriving at Portree with their five prisoners. On their way to the prison, the constables were hissed at by bystanders, as recorded in *The Scotsman* of 20 April:

The feeling of the natives of Portree was strongly shown on the occasion, and the police received a perfect ovation of groans. The excitement throughout the town was intense, and expectation was on tip-toe, as it is confidently expected that an attempt at rescue would be made. During the melee twelve of the police were more or less injured. One had his eye severely cut, and it had been sewn up by Dr Ross, another was hurt across the nose and the rest suffered more or less from stones. Captain Donald was struck by a large stone near the knee, and is rather severely hurt. Sheriff Ivory and Sheriff-Substitute Spiers both bear marks of the encounter. On the other side one poor woman, said to be *enceinte*, was seriously hurt – cut terribly about the head with a stone or baton. She was left bleeding and fainting on the road side. Another old woman said to be about seventy years of age, was hurled down a steep hill and badly injured. Several men, not arrested, fought desperately.

The Sheriff-Principal of Invernesshire and Harris, William Ivory, appeared to panic and called for the immediate dispatch of a gunboat and marines to Skye. The police requisitioned the steamship, Lochiel, from MacBrayne's but the Highland captain and his crew refused to set sail. Eventually a force of more than 500 soldiers and more policemen were landed on Skye. Realising that more direct action would be futile, the crofters continued to resist passively, and the rent strikes went on.

But in fact a victory of sorts had already been secured. Widespread newspaper coverage exposed for the first time to the public and to

British politicians the iniquities and cruelties that had been going on for generations, and the atmosphere began to change. In 1883 the Napier Commission was set up 'to Inquire into the Condition of Crofters and Cottars in the Highlands and Islands', gather evidence and make recommendations. These were by no means all adopted, but the Napier report did prompt government to legislate and in 1886 the Crofters Holdings Act was passed into law. It guaranteed security of tenure in perpetuity and established the Crofters Commission to fix fair rents. But other grievances were left unaddressed and dissent rumbled on.

Within a very short period, the appalling behaviour of the Duke of Argyll and his factor would recede into the past (but would never be forgotten). In 1884 two related events gave voice to crofters and their concerns for the first time. Electoral reform had qualified many of them as voters and after an election a year later, there were six crofter MPs in Parliament. And based on an Irish model, the Highland Land League was formed to represent the crofting community and press for more reform. Its most famous slogan was 'Is treasa tuath na tighearna' ('the people are mightier than a lord').

Although the Crofters Commission had reduced rents, some by as much as 50 per cent, access to land for grazing and other purposes was still severely limited. Some of the Land League's objectives were adopted by the ruling Liberal Party and the Congested Districts Board was established in 1897 to help develop agriculture and fishing in the north. There was a slow, incremental improvement, but land raiding continued into the twentieth century. Perhaps one of the most vivid and celebrated raids took place in 1906, when landless crofters from Barra crossed the narrow sound to Vatersay. The lush, fertile little island had been run as a single farm but its owner, Lady Emily Gordon Cathcart, was the epitome of an absentee landlord. She had only visited once in fifty-four years. Immensely wealthy, she had inherited most of North and South Uist, Benbecula and Barra, and enthusiastically promoted mass evictions. Many islanders were forcibly re-settled in Regina and Wapella in Saskatchewan, probably because Lady Cathcart owned a block of shares in the Canadian

Pacific Railway and she wanted to see the west of the country become more populated. She took the ten lanc raiders on Vatersay to the Court of Session in Edinburgh where they were found guilty and imprisoned for two months, although the judges did rule that she had been negligent in her duties as a landlcrd. The raiders were released early.

Known as the Hebridean Princess (who never went to the Hebrides), Lady Cathcart died in Margate in 1932, and even after death, she continued to try to have people cleared off her land. In her will, she made provision for the Long Island (meaning the Western Isles) United States Emigration Fund. It was never set up because her trustees feared repercussions. The raiders though had the last word, for in 1909 the Congested Districts Board bought Vatersay and divided it into fifty-eight crofts.

Such were the sometimes brutal realities of life in the Highlands and Islands for ordinary people. For others, the Celtic edges of Britain could be a fount of fantasy. *The Gentleman's Magazine* of October 1792 reported strange goings-on in London on 23 September: 'This being the day on which the autumnal equinox occurred, some Welsh Bards, resident in London, assembled in congress on Primrose Hill, according to ancient usage . . . The wonted ceremonies were observed. A circle of stones formed, in the middle of which was the Maen Gorsedd, or Altar, on which a naked sword being placed, all the Bards assisted to sheath it.'

Since there was no great stone circle on Primrose Hill, Edward Williams had thoughtfully brought along some pebbles in his pockets and he laid them out on the grass. It was the first Gorsedd of the modern era, the first meeting of the bards, and Williams informed them: 'I am giving you the patriarchal religion and theology, the Divine Revelation given to Mankind and these have been retained in Wales until our own day.' By 'patriarchal' Williams meant ancient British or Druidical, and felt he was reviving a culture that had been suppressed since the coming of the Anglo-Saxons more than a thousand years before. In fact, it was mostly nonsense, brilliant, passionate, artful and confusing nonsense. Using his great knowledge of old Welsh manuscripts, Williams had invented most of the wonted ceremonies and Patriarchal rites.

Like James Macpherson with Ossian and his *Fragments of Ancient Poetry Collected in the Highlands of Scotland*, Williams had created a heroic past that was in reality a Celtic neverland, and because it was all in Welsh and not English, it escaped wider scrutiny. Williams also reinvented himself. Taking the name Iolo Morganwg, Iolo of Glamorgan, he claimed that the bards had somehow preserved the ancient wisdom of the Druids, whatever that was.

Local *eisteddfodau* were genuinely old and had survived all over Wales as poetry, music and dance competitions. In 1819, Iolo managed to persuade the organisers of the Carmarthen Eisteddfod to allow a Gorsedd of bards to be part of the festival. With another pocketful of pebbles, flowing Druidic costumes, mistletoe, strange headdresses and solemn invocations, this took place in the garden of the Ivy Bush Hotel. Its format gradually became the setting for the crowning of bards at *eisteddfodau* in a series of ceremonies in the Maen Gorsedd, in the centre of the circle of stones. When the first National Eisteddfod took place in 1861 in Aberdare, the Druids took the stage and have done so ever since. This huge event is now very popular, and profitable, supported by a large Welsh speech community, now 883,000 and rising, as well as those who do not have the language.

In the late nineteenth century, Gaelic was in a very different position. The 1872 Education Act had brought in compulsory schooling for five- to thirteen-year-olds. Existing Gaelic Society and Church schools were closed as the Scotch Education Department took over. Its offices were in London. There was no provision for teaching in Gaelic, and indeed children were punished if caught speaking the language in school or even in the playground. It was to be the death-knell of the monoglot speech community.

The Lorne Ossianic Society was established in the same year to promote Gaelic and it held Highland Games in Oban that included singing competitions. But, in the 1880s, it began to founder, and so some of its members formed the Highland Bardic Society. These were mostly aristocrats, no doubt encouraged by Queen Victoria's passion for all things Highland, as well as academics and clergymen. In 1891 the name changed to An Comunn Gàidhealach, the Gaelic Association, and it published a manifesto of goals. One of these was to hold an 'Annual Gathering at which competitions will take place, and prizes be awarded.' The example of the successful National Eisteddfod must have been encouraging, and influential. The manifesto ended with a ringing call to action:

Do Chlanna nan Gàidheil anns gach cearn.
Dùisgibh, ma ta, eirichibh agus cuiribh an gniomh. Rugaibh sibh
'n 'ur Gaidheil; 'n 'ur Gaidheil bitheadh sibh; agus togaibh bhur
cloinn gu bhi 'n an Gaidheil.

. To the children of the Gael in every region.
Awake, then, and put this strategy into action. You were born as
 Gaels, you continue to be Gaels, and you should raise your
 children to be Gaels.

The 1891 census was the first to count the number of Gaelic speakers in Scotland. There were 43,738 monoglots and 210,675 who were bilingual, very much smaller than the Welsh speech community. In the same year, the choir of St Columba's Church in Glasgow, established in 1770 specifically for the spiritual needs of Highlanders who had emigrated to the city, gave a Gaelic concert in Oban. It was attended by many Scottish aristocrats, and by Louise, the Princess Royal and Duchess of Fife, the eldest daughter of the Prince of Wales, later King Edward VII. No doubt encouraged by this sort of support, An Comunn Gàidhealach established the National Mòd and it was first held in Oban in 1892. The word simply means 'a meeting', or a court, which perhaps implies the judgements to be made in its various competitions.

In October 1981, I got off the train at Fort William. It was raining steadily. Ben Nevis was shrouded in cloud. A month before, I'd begun work at Scottish Television and the first documentary I was to present was about the National Mòd. Mostly it was held in towns in Grampian Television's transmission area, but by some quirk of broadcasting geography, TV sets in Fort William received STV. The documentary felt more like an obligation than an enthusiasm. The rain seemed mandatory.

At first I found it all baffling, impossible to make into a story. At Lochaber High School I watched singing competitions with twenty-four little boys and girls getting nervously up on stage to sing the same song, competing for the *Oban Times* gold medal in front of stone-faced judges. The 'Poetry Recitation, Fluent', had nine categories, all of them the recitation of a prescribed piece of poetry. No actions. That was the problem. It all seemed very static, suffocatingly formal, frozen in time, very Victorian. Except for the Highland dancing.

It was only when I realised what was behind the Mòd that the film began to acquire some shape. I did the opening piece to camera by the side of the A82, next to the sign for An Gearasdan, the Gaelic version of Fort William, 'the Garrison', an echo of history. The Mòd used to be virtually the only time that the language, or at least this somewhat stiff, Victorian version of Gaelic culture, made its way on to the stage of Scotland's national life. When the results of the competitions were listed in *The Scotsman*, *The Glasgow Herald*, *The Dundee Courier* and the Aberdeen *Press & Journal*, the language briefly emerged from the shadows.

I made the health and survival of Gaelic part of the narrative of the film and sadly it is not an encouraging story. Between 1891 and 2011, the number of speakers has collapsed, down from 254,415 to 57,602. In the nineteenth century, Canadian Gaelic was the third most widely spoken European language, but in the 2011 census there were only 1,275 speakers, almost all of them in Nova Scotia.

It is impossible to look back over the centuries after Culloden and see them as anything other than a story of decline and departure. Leaving aside the reams of romance, the wish-and-tell myth-history, there is no escaping a melancholy mist that seems to roll down the mountainsides. In the Highlands and Islands, change brought loss and only rarely renewal as the glens emptied, the dykes were tumbled, the blackhouses became roofless skeletons and the bracken and the marsh grass grew over the inbye fields.

Occasionally, the sad stories of emigration and loss could give rise to great and enduring art. On a bright summer Sunday afternoon in 1896, Donald Maciver flicked the reins, clicked his tongue as his pony pulled the trap out onto the track down the shore of Loch Roag, and began a long journey into the past. Beside him sat his uncle, Domhnall Ban Crosd. A few months before, Donald had received a letter from his uncle in Canada: the old man wished to come home, to see the place where he had been born and raised, before he died – when Sir James Matheson had bought the Isle of Lewis in 1844, many families were cleared off the land and more or less forced onto the emigrant ships.

Domhnall Ban Crosd's bynames hint at appearance and character. *Ban* means fair-headed and *crosd* is a Gaelic version of the English 'cross'. In his young days, Donald was a keen boxer, a feared 'pugilist', wrote his nephew. As the pony pulled the trap up over the rising ground at Miabhag and the vast panorama of the Atlantic Ocean opened before them, it may be that the old man set a characteristic stone-face when at last he gazed once more on the heartbreakingly beautiful, broad sands of the bay at Uig. A sight that had been bright in his mind's eye for more than fifty years.

Donald Maciver pulled on the reins, spoke softly to his pony, halted and braked the trap when they arrived at Carnais, his uncle's birthplace. There was almost nothing to see. A busy, living township of blackhouses, homes to the chatter of children, skittering hens and a lowing milker cow and the daily labour of growing potatoes, oats and tending to animals, was silent. The walls of the houses and the dykes around them had been thrown down, the place given over to the grazing of sheep.

As he stood in the breeze off the ocean, staring at the ruins of lives, of generations, the old man's face crumpled at last. He wept for all that experience in one place, all lost and gone. Turning to his nephew, Domhnall Ban said: 'Chaneil nith an seo mar a bha e, ach an ataireachd na mara' ('There is nothing here now as it was, except for the surge of the ocean').

Much moved and inspired by his uncle's sadness, Donald Maciver later wrote his great lyric, 'An Ataireachd Ard'. It won the gold medal at the 1908 Mòd at Rothesay:

An ataireachd bhuan,
Cluinn fuaim na h-ataireachd àrd,
Tha torunn a' chuain
Mar chualas leams' e' nam phaisd
Gun mhuthadh, gun truas,
A' sluaisreadh gainneimh na tragh'd
An ataireachd bhuan
Cluinn fuaim na h-ataireachd àrd.

The ceaseless surge,
Listen to the surge of the sea,
The thunder of the ocean
As I heard it when I was a child,
Without change, without pity,
Breaking on the sands of the shore,
The ceaseless surge,
Listen to the surge of the sea.

Set to music and in Ishbel MacAskill's rich and haunting voice, 'An Ataireachd Ard' is an elegy for the passing of a culture, and the departure of most of its people.

*

Through the deep winter darkness a thousand torches flare and sparks fly in the bitter January wind. A procession begins, two long parallel lines of torch-bearers snaking through the streets as music plays and songs are sung. Between the lines of marchers, a galley is dragged. Colourful round shields are attached to its gunwales, a mast carries a raven banner and on the prow is a dragon's head. Standing in the stern is a man wearing armour that glints in the torchlight and a splendid steel helmet with the wings of a great raven attached on either side. He is the Guizer Jarl, the principal in Europe's greatest fire festival, the Up Helly Aa, held on the last Tuesday in January in Lerwick, the capital of Shetland.

In an open space the galley halts and the long processions begins to wind itself around it in a wide circle as the music blares. Some of the torch-bearers are dressed in armour and steel helmets, and many others are in fancy dress. They are all guizers who will celebrate the fire festival long into the night in the halls across the town, performing sketches and skits, often on recent events.

When the Guizer Jarl comes down off the galley and the circle closes in, there is a fanfare. It is the signal for torches to be thrown into the boat. From all directions, they arc through the night air, sparks flying and a great conflagration flares as more and more pile up. When the mast catches fire and falls, the guizers sing 'The Norseman's Home'. The dragon's head on the prow is silhouetted against the yellow inferno blazing behind it, and when it falls, the fire ceremony is over.

Up Helly Aa came into being in the 1880s as both a winter fire festival and a celebration of Shetland's Viking heritage. After a day of marching through the town of Lerwick and visits to specific locations, the Guizer Jarl leads the Jarl Squad, the men in armour, at the head of the torchlight procession past many onlookers to the burning site at the King George V Playing Fields. There can be as many as 5,000 watching. The Lerwick street lights are switched off as the thousand torches are lit. Made from substantial poles with hessian sacking wrapped tight around one end and soaked in fuel, they burn long and bright into the January night. Up Helly Aa is also held in eleven other communities in Shetland and all are characterised by spectacle and good humour.

These celebrations are a stark contrast with the formalities of the Mòd (although a good deal of whisky is consumed at both events) but they share a sense of renewal. They were assertions of a separate identity after generations of corrosive change and oppression.

At Fethaland, on the northernmost tip of Shetland's Mainland, there was a busy haaf fishing station. In the local dialect, haaf meant the open sea, the Atlantic Ocean. From June to the end of August, fishermen came north to live in the wooden huts that had been built above the pebble beach. Perhaps as many as sixty men rowed out into the ocean in open boats known as sixerns, three pairs of oars. In the later eighteenth century and into the nineteenth these were rowed out into the Atlantic, sometimes more than fifty miles from Fethaland, well out of sight of the low Shetland hills. On the edge of the continental shelf, they fished for ling, catching them on long, baited lines. Even though catches could be good, the work was very dangerous and could be miserable. In an age before the availability of waterproofs, fishing out in the spray and rain of the haaf could see men soaked through for many hours as they rowed out and back to safe harbour. In heavy seas, their open boats were in danger of being swamped or becoming lost in fog and drifting even further out to sea. On the pebble beach below their wooden huts, the fishermen immediately gutted their catch and laid out the fish to dry in the breeze. How they kept the gulls at bay is a mystery, but the birds must have been a constant problem.

What compelled Shetlanders to undertake this dangerous, exhausting work in boats not suitable for it is not a mystery. Realising that there was good money to be made at haaf fishery, certainly much more than the rents paid by their tenants, landlords made an explicit threat. If crofters did not agree to go to the haaf for three months each summer, then their tenancies would immediately be terminated. And they were also forced to agree to sell their catches only to their landlords. Because of this and the threat of eviction, the fishermen risked their lives for a pittance. Even that was partly reclaimed because many landlords maintained stores that sold provisions to their tenants on credit and so crofters often ended up owing money. It was a vicious circle of servitude.

Elsewhere around the coasts of the Highlands and Islands, the fishing industry began to boom. At the beginning of the nineteenth century, Wick was a small village on the estuary of the little river of the same name. Within a very short period, it had become the fishing capital of Europe, and herring were the stimulus. By 1840 more than a thousand boats sailed in and out of a harbour designed by Thomas Telford (he also designed Pulteneytown, laying out the crescents of a new town for fishery workers) and around it cooperages and curing businesses were established.

In part it was the behaviour of the shoals of herring, known as draves, that led to the creation of a peculiarly peripatetic industry that, unusually, involved many women. The various species of herring in British waters mature at different times of the year, and the fishermen followed them. In May and June, the season began off the coasts of the Hebrides and when catches were landed, Na Clann Nighean an Sgadain, 'the Herring Lassess', took over. They gutted the fish and packed them in barrels with coarse salt that acted as a preservative. On the quaysides were farlans (troughs) into which the herring were tipped. The lasses wore long oilskin aprons over a skirt, cotton blouse and cardigan. On their feet were knee-length boots and on their heads were shawls tied under the chin. They worked in all weathers.

At the farlans were teams of three, two gutters and a packer, who was usually the tallest so that she could lean down into the barrel. Before starting, the lasses tied bandages around their fingers and hands to stop the fish from slipping as they slit them open and removed the guts. These 'clouts' also covered the many cuts from the sharp knives that were necessary. Experienced herring lasses could gut a fish in two seconds.

If the fishing was good and many boats came in, the hours could be long. Incoming catches had to be packed and salted within twenty-four hours. Starting at about 5.30 a.m., the lasses worked until 8.30 a.m. when they were given porridge, hunks of bread and hot, steaming tea. A hot lunch at midday was followed by more food at 6 p.m. All those necessary calories were burned as the hard work went on relentlessly. The money in the later nineteenth century was good, at eight pence a barrel for each team. As they moved around the coast to Wick and then down to Peterhead and eventually to Yarmouth and Lowestoft, each lass could earn £17–20 in a season.

To get into a rhythm as well as to relieve the monotony of filling countless barrels, they often sang. Here are two ditties that have survived and they give a sense of the working atmosphere on all those quaysides:

Never mind that old-fashioned mother of yours,
What about your old-fashioned father?
He wears no fine rich clothes
His socks are cotton and they've got no toes
Never mind that old-fashioned mother of yours
In the chorus that you bawl
If it wasn't for your old-fashioned father
She would never be your mother, at all!

And then,

Oh, Charlie take it away
Oh, Charlie, do what I say
It makes me feel so funny every time we cuddle and kiss
It makes me shiver,
It makes me quiver,
It fills me full with bliss
Oh, Charlie take it away
Oh, Charlie do what I say
It's the little bit of hair you wear upon your upper lip
It tickles me, Charlie do take it away.

*

Highlanders were hardy, used to working out of doors in all weathers, like the Herring Losses. Crofters also regularly braved the elements as the clouds scudded in across the North Atlantic, but some developed skills that brought them indoors and out of the wind and the rain. In the second half of the nineteenth century, two upper-class ladies became involved in the development of a particular kind of tweed that was to become world famous. In 1843, Lady Catherine Herbert inherited a vast 150,000-acre estate in North Harris after the death of her husband, Alexander Murray, the Earl of Dunmore. She knew that many crofters had looms and turned out rough homespun cloth that was part of the local barter economy. Known as *clò mòr*, the 'big cloth', these plaids and other stuffs were much valued. Thick and with enough lanolin from the fleece still in the yarn, they could keep out the worst of the weather in an age before waterproofs and ensure that the wearer was warm. And the colours of the *clò mòr* could be beautiful, imitating the moods and seasons of the land because they were derived from the traditional palette of plant and lichen dyes.

Lady Herbert wanted her late husband's clan tartan to be woven, perhaps to honour his memory, and the widow had heard of two sisters in Harris who had been trained in Paisley as weavers and so she contacted them. What they turned out was well made and it delighted Lady Herbert so much that she had enough cloth produced to make up working suits for all the ghillies and gamekeepers on her huge estate. It was an important decision, one that would have consequences. The weight and water-resistant qualities of the *clo mor* were welcomed by men who could be out on the moor and in the mountains in all winds and weathers. Other landowners copied this and, swept up in Queen Victoria's growing love of the Highlands and how that deeply influenced the aristocracy, the Harris weavers began to spend long hours in their loom sheds. Some estates asked for their own weave, their own colour and pattern of tweeds.

Another well-connected lady became involved. Fanny Beckett recognised the quality of what was becoming known as Harris Tweed and, realising its commercial potential, she sought outlets for it in Edinburgh. At the same time, working with Lady Herbert, she helped to organise the weavers' output and introduced a system of basic quality control. As more young women were sent to the mainland for training at Lady Herbert's expense, yarn production was improved and speeded up, and a company, Scottish Home Industries, was set up to manage sales.

Boosted by royal and aristocratic approval, business boomed – but overall quality declined. Attracted by the promise of jobs and profit, more weavers began to make tweed and turned out goods that were not up to standard. They used mill-spun and not homespun yarn and what they made came to be derided not as Harris Tweed but as 'Stornoway Tweed'.

In 1909 a trademark, the famous Orb, was granted and applied only to tweed whose yarn was hand spun, hand dyed and hand woven by 'crofters and cottars' in the Outer Hebrides, not just on Harris. Business boomed once more and production reached a peak of 7.6 million yards in 1966.

But then there followed a period of decline in the face of competition from cheaper synthetic fabrics and cotton, much of it produced in the Far East. In 1993, Harris Tweed became the only cloth to be protected by an Act of Parliament. A statutory body was formed and slowly the trade began to revive. In 2003 the sportswear company Nike placed a substantial order and since then several prestigious menswear brands have become customers. Harris Tweed is now used in footwear, handbags and interior decoration.

*

On 3 September 1893, a young woman sat down to write a letter. Having rented a large house on the banks of the River Tay, close to Dunkeld in Highland Perthshire, she and her family were coming to the end of a summer holiday. They had made the long rail journey from London to Birnam Station for eleven years and the young woman had fallen in love with the rivers, glens and mountains, and she had become a keen student of the natural world of the north. A skilled artist, she was fascinated by fungi and drew and painted the many varieties she came across, and often compared notes with Charlie McIntosh, the local postman, who was also an enthusiastic naturalist. One of the young woman's most atmospheric paintings is of a beech wood near Inver, not far from her holiday home.

When she picked up her pen and paper on that September morning, she knew it would be good to amuse the recipient of her letter.

The son of her former governess, Noel Moore was only five years old and often unwell.

My dear Noel,

I don't know what to write to you, so I shall tell you a story about four little rabbits whose names were – Flopsy, Mopsy, Cottontail and Peter.

Between the lines that followed, Beatrix Potter drew the four rabbits. Flopsy scratches an ear, Mopsy and Cottontail seem to be asleep, but Peter sits up, alert, his forepaws on the ground, looking straight out of the letter, waiting to be naughty, waiting to enter the childhood imaginations of millions. Behind Peter's exasperated mother, another drawing shows the bole of a great tree with the young rabbits lying at the entrances to two rabbit holes.

Eastwood House had been let to Rupert Potter and his family by Mr Atholl McGregor, and when Beatrix later turned her picture-letter into one of the most famous and successful children's books ever written, she entitled it 'The Tale of Peter Rabbit and Mr McGregor's Garden'. Perhaps a tale told in verse rather than prose might work better for Peter Rabbit:

Now Mr McGregor
Was down on his knees
Hard at work planting cabbage
Between his green peas
Up he jumped and he ran
And no dog could be fleeter
And furious he waved his rake,
Went for Peter;
And tho Peter was flurried
It is his belief
That Mr McGregor in Gaelic
Kept calling 'stop thief'.

Two days after she corresponded with Noel, she sat down once more to write to Eric Moore. She did not want Noel's little brother to feel left out and so she told him a tale about a frog, Mr Jeremy Fisher. Years afterwards, when Beatrix decided she would like to see her stories published, she had help and advice from a family friend, Canon Hardwicke Rawnsley.

Beatrix Potter lived for many years at New Sawrey in the Lake District where she preserved much of the land that now makes up the Lake District National Park. For the illustrations for her books, she often used real places; The Tower Bank Arms at Near Sawrey is recognisable in *The Tale of Jemima Puddleduck*, and the local shop appears in *The Tale of Ginger and Pickles*. But her letters to the Moore boys leave no doubt that the beginnings of her first, and perhaps most famous, story came to her on the banks of the Tay. Flopsy, Mopsy, Cottontail and Peter were Highland rabbits who prompted Mr McGregor to shout at them in Gaelic.

At the same time as *The Tale of Peter Rabbit* was being published, the geography of the Highlands supplied another, altogether different sort of inspiration. In 1904, thousands of men walked along the loch shores and over the mountain passes to Kinlochleven. Some climbed the Devil's Staircase from Glencoe and in the whipping winter winds and snow, a few died, their bodies lost in the blizzards. Others came from the north, walking from Fort William down the road by Loch Linnhe, many having come from the islands. All of these men sought work, employment in a huge undertaking, the building of the first hydroelectric scheme in the Highlands.

An Act of Parliament in 1904 saw the Loch Leven Water and Electric Power Company merge with the North British Aluminium Company. It was not an unlikely marriage but one based on clear mutual benefit. An enormously versatile metal used in the manufacture of cutlery, cars and many other products, aluminium is extracted from bauxite mined in Africa and Australia. But the process of smelting requires a vast amount of electricity, and cheap electricity could be supplied by the Loch Leven Company. In the mountains west of the village, at the head of the River Leven, they planned the largest dam ever built in Europe. It would create the eight-mile-long Blackwater Reservoir, fed by streams from the patchwork of lochs and lochans to the west of Rannoch Moor, and the water would rush down from the mountains to sea level and turn the turbines of the power station. To build the dam, between 2,000 and 3,000 navvies were needed, and most of them walked to Kinlochleven.

In an age before mechanical diggers and bulldozers, all of this back-breaking work would be done by hand. Picks, shovels and barrows would build the vast barrier and all of the huge volume of concrete needed would be mixed by hand. Below the dam, a covered conduit that snaked along the flanks of Meall Bad a' Bheithe, 'the Mountain of the Birch Woods', and Meall Ruigh a' Bhricleathaid, 'the Grey Mountain of the Sheiling', needed to be constructed. It would take the rushing water down a drop of almost a thousand feet to the power station at Kinlochleven. Gangers ran the work squads, and they had to be bilingual in Gaelic and English as well as good with their fists when necessary. The work was unrelenting, hard and difficult: hands chapped with hacks in the winter, and faces and arms bitten by clouds of midges in summer. With men swarming all over the dam site and on the course of the conduit, it must have looked like a Highland version of the building of the pyramids. But the job was done quickly, and in 1907 the first ingots of aluminium were smelted. A new, industrial small town was created almost overnight in the shadow of the mountains.

Based on the layout of planned villages, with crescents, gardens, open spaces, good local facilities and, above all, lit and powered by electricity (the first community in Britain to have street lights and every home lit and heated by electricity), Kinlochleven was a good place to live, a world away from the townships and the damp black-houses some had come from. The houses were all owned and well maintained by the company, the wages were good and business was booming – the smelter could not turn out ingots fast enough. Pride in the work and in the company was expressed in a series of medals struck with views of Loch Leven flanked by its steep mountains and ringed with a Gaelic motto – *De nach dean an t'uisge, 'nuair a rinn e mise?* 'What cannot water do when it made me?' (Meaning of course the aluminium that made the medal.) Perhaps industry would come to the Highlands, perhaps it would be celebrated in Gaelic.

The great dam at the Blackwater Reservoir was the first of many, and in 1929 a smelter opened at Fort William. It was powered by a huge hydroelectric scheme that had the lochs and rivers of the central Highlands feed into a fifteen-mile-long conduit that brought the water to the flanks of Ben Nevis. But all of that spectacular development had to wait. No doubt more schemes would have followed Kinlochleven more quickly if it had not been for the gathering shadows of war.

In 1897, Rear-Admiral Alfred von Tirpitz was appointed secretary of state in command of the German Imperial Naval Office by Kaiser Wilhelm II. His strategy was simple: parity of power, or better, with the Royal Navy. The immediate consequence was an intense and immensely expensive naval arms race. Von Tirpitz dramatically increased the construction of U-boats and also a new class of battleship. In 1906, HMS *Dreadnought* was launched and its design revolutionised naval warfare. The new Royal Navy ship carried armament that was 'all big-gun', that is, everything a calibre of 12 inches and no small guns at all. This assumed that Naval battles would be fought at considerable distances, and the need for close-up smaller weapons would disappear. HMS *Dreadnought* was propelled by steam turbines, and these made it faster and able to increase speed more quickly.

These new battleships not only accelerated the arms race between Britain and Germany, but they also redrew the strategic map. The main Royal Navy bases at Portsmouth and elsewhere in the south had grown up there in response to historic threats from Spain, France and the Dutch Republic. As Von Tirpitz expanded the German Imperial Navy and its bases at Wilhelmshaven on the North Sea coast and Kiel on the Baltic (but with access to the west through the Kiel Canal), British's strategic focus shifted. More northerly naval bases were needed and both Rosyth on the shore of the Firth of Forth and Invergordon on the Cromarty Firth were seriously considered. Naval exercises had used Scapa Flow, a very large bay south of

Orkney Mainland, to moor and shelter ships and as the naval arms race intensified and Europe seemed inexorably to be drawn into war, it was chosen as the Royal Navy's main wartime base.

Sheltered from the storms of the Atlantic by the islands of Hoy, Mainland, Graemsay, Burray and South Ronaldsay, Scapa Flow made a very large anchorage, more than 125 square miles. With a sandy, rather than a rocky, bottom, it is also deep enough for large ships (like the dreadnoughts), at 100 and 200 feet in places. Scapa Flow could comfortably accommodate several navies. In 1909 the combined Home and Atlantic fleets dropped anchor in the Flow, eighty-two ships in all, a splendid sight rapturously reported in *The Orcadian*. What also recommended the new base was its relative remoteness. German spies who wanted to observe ship movements would be quickly noticed on Orkney. Also, it was believed by naval high command that the entrances to the anchorage made U-boat attacks 'practically impossible'.

The immediate issue was to secure those entrances. Scapa Flow was to be defended by blocking most of them and closely guarding those that were to be used by the fleet. Coastal artillery batteries were installed, booms were laid across channels, submarine nets sunk and old merchant ships were scuttled as blockships to prevent access. Under the command of Admiral Sir John Jellicoe, the Grand Fleet, the main battlefleet of the Royal Navy, sailed into Scapa Flow in late July 1914. More than twenty dreadnoughts were the core of its immense firepower, twice as many as Tirpitz had, and in all there were 160 ships in the fleet. In the Royal Museum at Greenwich there is an aerial photograph of these magnificent – and menacing – battleships lying at anchor in the Flow. Ordered in ranks, there are almost forty in the foreground and they seem all to be capital ships, dreadnoughts and battle cruisers. Further in the distance, and the scale is difficult to work out, there are scores more anchored beyond the small islands. The photograph is a snapshot of a moment in British history: a potent, huge symbol of imperial power on the eve of its passing. Only a few days after the Grand Fleet sailed into Scapa Flow, on 4 August 1914, war with Germany was declared.

15

Recovering

In the bitter winter darkness of the evening of 31 December 1918, hundreds of demobbed men, most of them having served in the Royal Navy and all of them anxious to get home to the Isle of Lewis and to Harris, were milling around the railway station at Kyle of Lochalsh. It was two months after the guns of the western front had at last fallen silent and the Armistice had brought an end to the fighting and to the First World War. Many sailors had survived the brutal sea battles of the North Sea and, with their kitbags on their shoulders and gifts for families some had not seen for four years, they moved to the pier. The *Sheila*, the mailboat that plied between Kyle of Lochalsh and Stornoway, took on board as many men as it could before making way up the Inner Sound between Raasay and Applecross and out into the Minch. The 284 men left on the pier were told that HMY *Iolaire*, a large luxury yacht that had been requisitioned by the Admiralty, was on its way in the opposite direction, coming from Stornoway to pick them up.

However, the captain was said to have had misgivings. The *Iolaire* had only eighty lifejackets and two lifeboats, but it was New Year and men were desperate to get home to their families. Celebrations and the twinkling lights of a warm welcome were waiting on the other side of the Minch. This was the last leg of a long journey through four years of war. They needed to get home.

There was no moon that night, it may have been raining or even sleeting and the sea seemed unsettled in the Inner Sound. When the

Iolaire set a course to the north-west into open water, high winds whipped up the waves and spindrift spattered over the men crowded onto the decks of the yacht, but many had on their naval waterproofs and their sea-boots.

When the *Iolaire* had crossed the Minch and the crew reckoned they were no more than twelve miles off Stornoway harbour, things started to go wrong. A drifter, the *Budding Rose*, had been sent out to pilot the yacht home because the captain was uncertain about entering the narrow approaches. But the *Iolaire* could not make contact with the *Budding Rose*, and an hour later the crew of another fishing boat saw the lights of the yacht and realised it had set the wrong course, had gone north of Stornoway. In what had blown up into a gale, and in moonless darkness, the *Iolaire* was sailing full steam ahead down the coast of the Eye Peninsula and making straight for the Beasts of Holm. The rocky outcrop near the entrance to the harbour had a warning light set on it, but no lookout saw it. At 2 a.m. the yacht smashed into the Beasts, quickly foundered and began to break up. As men tried to launch them, both lifeboats were swamped. The stern of the *Iolaire* was at one point only twelve yards from the shore, but the seas were mountainous and it was black-dark.

With a line wrapped around his body, John Finlay MacLeod fought through the undertow and clawed and clambered his way onshore. Having dragged a hawser behind him, he managed to secure it to a rock and with the help of others, pulled forty men along it to safety. But, only an agonisingly short distance from the shore, 206 men were drowned. Having survived the most murderous war in history, they died within sight of the harbour lights of Stornoway. Some survivors were so traumatised that once onshore, soaked to the skin, they kept walking through the darkness, crossing the moors through the storm to get home to their families.

Donald MacPhail was a young boy in 1919 but he never forgot the events of that terrible night. Here is a translation of a radio interview he gave fifty years later, the tragedy still burned indelibly into his memory:

I was only a young lad at the time – I was seventeen – in the high school in Stornoway, and I remember well New Year's Day . . . A man in the next house, next door to me, he came home across the moor – how he got ashore I do not know – but he was like a man out of his mind. And those in the village who had lost men – the mothers and the wives – they were coming in to ask if he had seen any sight of Donald, or Angus, or John, but he could only look at them and the tears [were] coming down his cheeks; and he had two words, I remember that, he had two words that he said often: 'Good God – Good God . . . ' as though he caught on to those words on board and they had followed his mind, and he had no other words. It was a very sorrowful business for those who were waiting. As the bard said, 'home awaited them warm, and all was best prepared'. All had been got ready for those who were expected; friendship and warmth, the families at home; then the awful news that they would never come . . .

I left for Stornoway – I remember it was dawn – with a horse and cart, myself and two other boys, and the father of one of the lads who had been lost, and we went down to the Battery, where the bodies had been laid out for identification. I remember they had tickets on them . . . Leurbost . . . Shawbost . . . Tolsta . . . and the man from Shawbost who went over with us, his son was there and I remember he was so handsome that I would have said he was not dead at all. I remember the colour on his face. I remember that fine yet . . . His father went on his knees beside him and he began to take letters from his son's pockets, and there was money, I remember, silver and paper money, in the pockets of the trousers. And the father was reading a letter that he found and the tears were falling from him, splashing on the body of his son. I think it is the most heart-rending sight I have ever seen, and that was only one of many to be seen at the Battery that day – and for days afterwards.

The sinking of the *Iolaire* was a sickening, stunning blow. The census of 1911 counted a total population of 36,600 for Lewis and

Harris, and at the end of the war almost 1,500 men had been killed. In one black night, 206 families lost a father, a son or a brother. Close to an entire generation of young men had been lost as a result of the First World War. Recovery would be a long time coming.

Like most men who do come home from war, survivors only rarely leave much in the way of memoir. They want to put the experience behind them and get on with their peacetime lives. But one poem, that became a famous song, beautifully describes what that experience could be like for a Gaelic-speaking islander. Donald MacDonald of North Uist wrote the elegant and elegiac '*An Eala Bhàn*' ('White Swan'). This is its poignant and extraordinary moving final stanza:

Oidhche mhath leat fhéin, a rùin nad leabaidh chùbhraidh bhlàth
Cadal sàmhach air a chùl do dhùsgadh sunndach slàn
Tha mise 'seo 'san truinnsidh fhuair Nam chluaisean fuaim a bhàis
Gun dùil ri faighinn às le buaidh – tha 'n cuan cho buan ri shnàmh.

Goodnight to you, my love, in your warm, sweet-smelling bed;
May you have peaceful sleep and afterwards may you waken
   healthy and in good spirits
I am here in the cold trench with the clamour of death in my
   ears
With no hope of returning victorious – the sea is too wide to
   swim.

Six months after the tragedy of the *Iolaire*, more ships sank off the shores of the Highlands and Islands.

Moored in Scapa Flow, the great German battle cruiser, *Friedrich der Grosse*, suddenly listed to starboard on 21 June 1919, and began to sink. It was the flagship of the Imperial German Grand Fleet and forty minutes before, Admiral Ludwig von Reuter had sent a coded flag message to all seventy-four ships. It instructed their captains to sink their own ships, to scuttle them by opening seacocks, flood valves, smashing internal water pipes and loosening portholes, and leaving bulkhead doors open. All of this activity was invisible to the Royal Navy guard ships. After a short time, ship after ship began to go down as their crews abandoned them. When they sank, British sailors saw that each had run up the Imperial German Ensign on their mainmasts. It was a symbol of defiance. Of the seventy-four ships under von Reuter's command, fifty-two sank. And while the remainder were towed into shallow water by the Royal Navy, the entire German Grand Fleet was destroyed in little more than an hour.

By chance, a large party of schoolchildren were touring Scapa Flow on the morning von Reuter gave the order to sink an entire navy. Watching from an Admiralty tug, a fifteen-year-old James Taylor later recalled the remarkable events that took place:

Suddenly, without any warning and almost simultaneously, these huge vessels began to list over to port or to starboard; some heeled over and plunged headlong, their sterns lifted high out of the water and pointing skywards; others were rapidly settling down in the ocean with little more showing than their masts and funnels, while out of the vents rushed steam and oil and air with a dreadful roaring hiss, and vast clouds of white vapour rolled up from the sides of the ships. Sullen rumblings and crashing of chains increase the uproar as the great hulls slant giddily over and slide with horrible sucking and gurgling noises under the water. The proud vessels slowly disappear with a long-drawn-out sigh.

On the surface all that remains is a mighty whirlpool dotted with dark objects swirling round and round, many of them drawn inwards until they too sink from sight. Now the sea is turning into one vast stain of oil which spreads gradually outwards as if the life-blood of some ocean monster mortally wounded was oozing up from the seabed. And as we watched, awestruck and silent, the sea became littered for miles round with boats and hammocks, lifebelts and chests, spars and matchwood. And among it all hundreds of men struggling for their lives . . . Suddenly the air was rent by the lusty cheering of long lines of sailors drawn up on the deck of one of the largest German ships. They were bidding farewell to a sister-ship whose decks were now under water.

More than six months earlier, the German fleet had sailed into the Firth of Forth to formally surrender as a condition of the Armistice. From there they were escorted to Scapa Flow to be interned and their crews became prisoners of war. None were allowed ashore, conditions on board the fleet quickly deteriorated and mutiny was threatened. Through the winter of 1918/19 most sailors were gradually repatriated, and by June there were only skeleton crews.

At the same time, the terms of the Treaty of Versailles were being negotiated and the outcome greatly concerned the German admiral. The likely consequence would be that his fleet, which contained several dreadnoughts, would be divided between allied navies. That was something von Reuter could not contemplate. There was also a possibility that Germany would not accept the terms of the treaty and that war might break out once more. In which case, Germany's own navy could be used against Germany. There was only one honourable, patriotic alternative.

In May 1919, the admiral made plans to scuttle the entire fleet in Scapa Flow, rendering it useless in the event that war resumed. While the high command of the Royal Navy suspected that something might be afoot, they did nothing to prevent it. The redistribution of seventy-four battleships to other navies might make them a little too powerful, threatening the dominance of the Royal Navy. Noon on 21 June was the time and date fixed for the signature of the Treaty of Versailles, exactly the same time as the *Friedrich der Grosse* listed to starboard and the German fleet began to destroy itself.

As sailors took to their lifeboats, Royal Marines began to shoot at some of them – what they were doing was strictly forbidden. But when it became quickly clear that all the ships had been scuttled, the firing ceased. Nine German sailors were killed as Orkney saw the final casualties of the First World War.

No family in the Highlands and Islands was unaffected by the extraordinary casualty rate of the First World War. For all combatants, the overall death rate across Britain was 11 per cent, a huge, unprecedented proportion of the adult population. But in Scotland, the death rate was a staggering 26 per cent, more than double. A total of 142,000 Scotsmen enlisted in the armed forces before and during the course of the war, and a quarter of them did not come home. The casualty rate in the Highlands and Islands was even greater. The Black Watch and the Highland Light Infantry each lost more than 10,000 men, most of them from the north. The evidence of the scale of the slaughter can be seen on Highland roadsides every day, where war memorials in seemingly remote and sparsely populated areas list impossible numbers of dead. Even in a population centre like Fort William, where 2,000 people were counted in the 1911 census, the war memorial in the middle of the town lists 116 names, an enormous proportion of the men eligible to enlist. *Dileas gu Bàs*, says the Gaelic inscription, 'Faithful unto Death'.

These shocking numbers take no account of those maimed, blinded or gassed. Many of these men, including my grandfather who was gassed in a tunnel at Ypres, never recovered their health and often died young. But the place that suffered the most devastating casualty rate in Britain was the Isle of Lewis, and the losses of the young men in the trenches and on the *Iolaire* were soon augmented by the departure of more.

It must have seemed to some that there was a curse on the Highlands and Islands as parents and siblings crammed onto a Stornoway quayside to wave goodbye to the future. If such feelings were in the air above Lewis in the years after the First World War, it was nothing new, the continuation of a bitter heritage.

On 24 May 1845, almost all of the crofters of Glencalvie in Sutherland were cleared off their land. Eighteen families, ninety people in all, were evicted to make way for a sheep farm. Without a roof over their heads, they all came to Croick churchyard and against the wall of the church, they built a rough, lean-to shelter as they waited for their landlord's factor to pay them for the stock they had been forced to leave behind. In those black and hopeless days, someone left behind a message. On the glass of a church window, still legible, was scratched a testament of despair:

Glencalvie people was in the churchyard here, May 24th, 1845.
Glencalvie People, the wicked generation of Glencalvie.

That these wronged and brutally treated families could think that somehow sinfulness had brought down their grim fate on themselves is sad beyond words. But it may be that many Highlanders and Islanders believed that their homeland was indeed cursed and held no future for them.

On 21 April 1923, the ocean liner *Metagama* dropped anchor off Stornoway harbour. On board were 1,000 emigrants who had been picked up in Glasgow and were bound for Eastern Canada and the St Lawrence River. Waiting on the quay at Stornoway were 300 more who would be taken out to the liner by the *Hebridean*, a smaller, more manoeuvrable vessel. There were civic speeches and expressions of good wishes before embarkation and other bits and pieces of ceremony. Of those with their trunks and suitcases, a staggering number, 280, were young men. Their average age was only twenty-two. No one was forcing them to leave, unlike the Glencalvie people and countless others in the recent past, they could simply see no future for themselves on Lewis and Harris. And they were by no means alone. A month earlier, another liner had taken 300 emigrants from Lochboisdale on South Uist, many of them young. The future was leaving the islands, never to return, compounding the terrible losses of the First World War.

There is a famous photograph taken from the deck of the *Hebridean* not of the emigrants but of those they were leaving behind. In a very closely packed crowd teetering on the edge of the quay, most are men wearing the ubiquitous cloth cap: some are waving handkerchiefs, many are smiling and there is a general air of jollity. To watch the ship sail out of the harbour, others have climbed up onto the roof of an adjacent building. But at the front of the heaving crowd, where the quayside curves, stands a small woman. She is wearing what looks like a white linen mutch cap with a frilled border and a heavy overcoat. She picks at something in her hand without looking at it, perhaps a scarf or a handkerchief. The little woman neither waves nor smiles and seems to stare down at the water at the moment the camera shutter clicked. Beside her a young girl leans her head on the woman's shoulder. Perhaps her son is on the *Hebridean*, and if he is, she knows she will most likely never see him again.

*

Not all of the stories that came out of the Highlands and Islands were about struggle or spoke of decline and depopulation. Sometimes the sun shone and people smiled.

When readers of the *Glasgow Evening News* opened its pages on 16 January 1905, they were introduced to one of the most enduringly famous fictional Highlanders:

A short, thick-set man, with a red beard, a hard round felt hat, ridiculously out of harmony with a blue pilot jacket and trousers and a seaman's jersey, his hands immersed deeply in those pockets our fathers (and the heroes of Rabelais) used to wear behind a front flap, he would have attracted my notice even if he had not, unaware of my presence so close behind him, been humming to himself the chorus of a song that used to be very popular on gabbarts [inshore boats], but is now gone out of date, like 'The Captain with the Whiskers Took a Sly Glance at Me'. You may have heard it thirty years ago, before the steam puffer came in to sweep the sailing smack from all the seas that lie between Bowling [on the Firth of Clyde] and Stornoway. It runs –

'Young Munro he took a notion
For to sail across the sea,
And he left his true love weeping,
All alone on Greenock Quay,'

and by that sign, and by his red beard, and by a curious gesture he had, as if he were now and then going to scratch his ear and only determined not to do it when his hand was up, I knew he was one of the Macfarlanes. There were ten Macfarlanes, all men, except one, and he was a valet, but the family did their best to conceal the fact, and said he was away on the yachts, and making that much money he had not time to write a scrape home.

'I think I ought to know you,' I said to the vocalist with the hard hat. 'You are a Macfarlane: either the Beekan, or Kail, or the Nipper, or Keep Dark, or Para Handy – '

'As sure as daith,' said he, 'I'm chust Para Handy, and I ken your name fine, but I cannot chust mind your face.' He had turned round on the pawl [stone] he sat on, without taking his hands from his pockets, and looked up at me where I stood beside him, watching a river steamer being warped into the pier.

'My goodness!' he said about ten minutes later, when he had wormed my whole history out of me; 'and you'll be writing things for the papers? Cot bless me! and do you tell me you can be makin' a living off that? I'm not asking you, mind, hoo mich you'll be makin', don't tell me; not a cheep! not a cheep! But I'll wudger it's more than Maclean the munister. But och! I'm not saying: it iss not my business. The munister has two hundred in the year and a coo's gress [grazing]; he iss aye the big man up yonder, but it iss me would like to show him he wass not so big a man as yourself. Eh? But not a cheep! not a cheep! A Macfarlane would never put his nose into another man's oar.'

'And where have you been this long while?' I asked, having let it sink into his mind that there was no chance today of his learning my exact income, expenditure, and how much I had in the bank.

'Me!' said he; 'I am going up and down like yon fellow in the Scruptures – what wass his name? Sampson – seeking what I may devour. I am out of a chob. Chust that: out of a chob. You'll not be hearin' of anybody in your line that iss in want of a skipper?'

Skippers, I said, were in rare demand in my line of business. We hadn't used a skipper for years.

'Chust that! chust that! I only mention it in case. You are making things for newspapers, my Cot! what will they do now for the penny? Well, that is it; I am out of a chob; chust putting bye the time. I'm not vexed for myself, so mich as for poor Dougie. Dougie wass mate, and I wass skipper. I don't know if you kent the *Fital Spark*?'

The *Vital Spark*, I confessed, was well known to me as the most uncertain puffer that ever kept the Old New-Year in Upper Lochfyne.

Between 1905 and 1923, the *Vital Spark* and its crew became very well known indeed. Para Handy succeeded in getting a chob, was reunited with the *Vital Spark* as well as Dougie, his first mate. Macphail, the engineer and eventually Sunny Jim, the ship's cook. Together they sailed from the Clyde to the Hebrides summer and winter for almost twenty years, calling in at scores of quaysides to supply small communities with necessities. Coal, gravel, timber and other bulk goods were the staples of the Clyde puffers, but they would carry anything that would fetch a fee or help someone out. Loch Fyne was the centre of Para Handy's world with no fewer than seven piers on its long shores and other places where a small boat would come out to offload goods from the *Vital Spark*.

Before and after the First World War, the puffers, MacBrayne's ferries and other maritime traffic were busy as Glaswegians increasingly went 'doon the watter', down the Firth of Clyde to Rothesay, Troon, Largs, Millport, Brodick, Ayr and the other sea towns that were quickly developing into resorts. The Crinan Canal cut through Kintyre and took vessels up to the Dorus Mor, 'the Great Door', the narrows between Jura and the mainland, to the mouth of the Firth of Lorne, then to Mull and beyond. By the end of the nineteenth century, working people could afford trips aboard the passenger steamers, especially on the annual holiday of Glasgow's Fair Fortnight in the last two weeks of July. Here is an atmospheric description from one of the early Para Handy stories in the *Glasgow Evening News*:

The last passenger steamer to sail that day from Ardrishaig was a trip from Rothesay. It was Glasgow Fair Saturday and Ardrishaig

Quay was black with people. There was a marvelously stimulating odour of dulse, herring and shell-fish, for everybody carried away in a handkerchief a few samples of these marine products that are now the only sea-side souvenirs not made in Germany. The *Vital Spark* in ballast, Clydeward bound, lay inside the passenger steamer, ready to start when the latter had got under weigh, and Para Handy and his mate meanwhile sat on the fo'c'sle-head of 'the smertest boat in the tred [trade]' watching the frantic efforts of lady excursionists to get their husbands on the steamer before it was too late, and the deliberate efforts of the said husbands to slink away up the village again just for one more drink. Wildly the steamer hooted from her siren, fiercely clanged her bell, vociferously the captain roared on his bridge, people on board yelled eagerly to friends ashore to hurry up, and the people ashore as eagerly demanded to know what all the hurry was about, and where the bleezes was Wull. Women loudly defied the purser to let the ship go away without their John, for he had paid his money for his ticket, and though he was only a working-man his money was as good as anybody else's; and John, on the quay, with his hat thrust back on his head, his thumbs in the arm-hole of his waistcoat and a red handkerchief full of dulse at his feet, gave display of step-dancing that was responsible for a great deal of the congestion of traffic at the shore end of the gangway.

The Para Handy stories were the creation of Neil Munro (initially under the nom de plume of Hugh Foulis) and their popularity was immediate as well as enduring. The short stories from the *Glasgow Evening News* were collected and published in book form by Walter Blackie in 1906 and serially after then, the last of them appearing in 1923. The *Tales of Para Handy* have never been out of print and three sets of TV series based on the stories were made by BBC Scotland. Broadcast in 1959, the first starred Duncan Macrae as the skipper, and Roddy McMillan as Dougie, the mate. Macphail, the engineer, was played by John Grieve and Sunny Jim by Angus Lennie. The second outing for the *Vital Spark* saw Roddy McMillan cast as Para

Handy and shot in colour (although a good deal was filmed in a studio), showing the glories of the Highland landscape as the puffer sailed through it. Gregor Fisher played Para Handy in the most recent series and most of it was shot on location.

Born near Inverary in 1863, Neil Munro was the son of Annie Munro, a kitchen maid. The census of 1871 recorded the illegitimate child being raised in the household of his grandfather, Angus McArthur Munro, and his aunt, Agnes Munro. By the time Neil went to school, he was bilingual in Gaelic and English, and clearly a clever boy. By 1881 he had followed in the footsteps of many when he went to work in Glasgow in an ironmongery shop, before becoming a young reporter first at the *Greenock Advertiser* and then at the *Glasgow Evening News*. When he came to write the Para Handy stories, it was clear that his ear for dialogue was well attuned to the nuances of both languages. His rendering of Para Handy's Gaelicisation of Lowland Scots is pitch-perfect, the apparently eccentric word order often a precise translation and the emphases and cadences unfailingly correct. It read as though the skipper thought in Gaelic. Para Handy may have been a larger-than-life character bordering on caricature, but he always sounded like the real thing. It was one proposition for Lowlanders to poke fun at Gaels and imitate the quirks and sibilance of their accent, but quite another for a Gaelic speaker raised in the Highlands to do that. Affection was ever-present.

The name, Para Handy, might seem odd, but it comes from the Highland habit of using patronymics. To family and friends, it was important to distinguish the boy from his nine brothers and so he became known, in an unstated back story, as Padraig Shandaidh, Sandy's Peter, or Peter, son of Sandy. The first syllable of Shandaigh is pronounced 'Han-' and the last is truncated to '-dy'.

Neil Munro clearly had fun writing these stories, and it is no accident that many of them are set on Loch Fyne, where he grew up, and an attractive ribbon of nostalgia runs through them. But it was his novels that he really valued. In 1891, only twenty-seven, he published *John Splendid*. It was one of the first really authentic Highland novels, a story told from the inside of a culture Munro grew up in and understood. Like Griogair Boidheach, 'Gregor the Beautiful', Highland men could be comfortably so described and the title character of the novel, John Splendid, also a warrior, is a direct translation of *Iain Allain*. It tells the story of Montrose and Alasdair mac Colla's descent on Inverary in the winter of 1644/45, but from a Campbell point of view, not that of the more dashing, even romantic, Royalists. John Splendid's chief, Gillesbeg Gruamach, was a moderniser. He fought Montrose and all he and mac Colla stood for because he wanted to look to the future, beyond the ancient ties of clanship to a more peaceful and productive society governed not by warfare and the bonds of service but by the rule of law. Gruamach wanted to see a Highland society built on trade rather than the old staples of cattle rearing and droving. *John Splendid, Doom Castle* and *The New Road*, Munro's last completed novel, are half-forgotten masterpieces deserving of revival.

When Para Handy navigated the *Vital Spark* past the hamlet of Craigendoran, near Helensburgh, he might have sounded the ship's horn in salute. Not only was it where Neil Munro lived, but the village sits almost exactly on the Highland Boundary Fault. All sorts of symbolism is at work here. Not only did Para Handy regularly move from Lowland, urban Glasgow into Highland waters, but Munro himself bestrode the ancient divide and made wonderful stories out of his Janus-like ability to look both ways. In 1935, at the surprising initiative of An Comunn Gàidhealach, for a novelist who wrote in English, a memorial to Neil Munro was raised at Glen Ary, his birthplace. When he made a speech, the writer and political activist, R. B. Cunninghame Graham, missed the point when he hailed Munro as the 'successor to Walter Scott'. The latter was a Lowlander romanticising the Highlands, and the creator of *John Splendid, The New Road* and Para Handy was a Highlander who understood the Highlands.

What has kept the Para Handy stories from the obscurity that has enveloped Munro's novels is something simple and elemental. The *Vital Spark* sailed on through the majesty of the West Highland landscape on the sea-roads. Like the oarsmen of Somerled's birlinns and the curraghs of the *Senchus fer n-Alban*, the crew of the puffer

– and the reader – saw the land from the sea, and in so doing understood it in ancient, and different ways.

*

The shores of the Highlands and Islands Para Handy saw in the early twentieth century began to look very different after the First World War. The demand for timber for the armed forces saw many woods felled and produced a dramatic after-effect that changed the landscape.

On 24 October 1966, I went the wrong way round a forest. My school had entered a team in one of the first Scottish Orienteering Championships. A sport new to Scotland, imported from Scandinavia, it was a combination of cross-country running and map-reading. The idea, if you read the map correctly, was to run along the various rides through the densely planted forest to find a series of controls. These were stations where someone stamped your map before you set off to find the next one. There were about fifteen controls and whoever got round them fastest was the winner.

And that damp, autumn morning in the Highlands, it wasn't going to be me. Not really understanding how to take a bearing on my compass and relate it to my map, I went 180 degrees the wrong way. Instead of the first control, I found the last one, I think. And when the surprised person with the stamp sent me packing, I got completely lost. No idea where I was as I thrashed through the trees, being scratched, tripping and wiping off facefuls of spiders' webs. The competition was held near Aberfoyle in one of the vast Forestry Commission plantations to the west of the village. All the rides looked pretty much the same, all the trees were definitely the same, and I could find no geographical feature like a stream or a lochan that looked like anything that was on my map. No matter how many times I turned it upside down or on its side. In that forest, I felt as though I had entered the Scottish Disorienteering Championships.

When I finally found another control, it wasn't the first, perhaps the twelfth or thirteenth, but at least and at last I knew where I was. And so I simply ran in the opposite direction to all the other competitors, who did look a little quizzically at me, until I found the first control. Then I got my first stamp on my map and simply turned around and ran back the way I had come. It was getting dark when I reached the final control – the people there remembered me for some reason – and then jogged out into a field towards the finish. My teammates were all jumping up and down and yelling at me to run faster. It turned out that our school team was leading the competition, but to win, I had to finish and there were only a few minutes left. I just made it, absolutely knackered, and we did win. Even though I'd been around the course backwards. I still have the pennant to prove it.

These huge Forestry Commission plantations were perfect for orienteering because the trees, towering over the rides, hid the land very well, carpeting it in regiments of darkness, the trees so dense that it seemed no light penetrated. Short of climbing one, there was no way to see the general lie of the land. Once or twice, I'd strayed off the rides at Aberfoyle in search of short cuts and become quickly lost in the sterile silence, peering through the trees to find my way, eventually stumbling out into the light none the wiser.

These great forests were a direct legacy of the First World War. Britain's woodlands had been very severely depleted, almost 95 per cent felled to fulfil the needs of the armed forces and, in 1919, the Forestry Commission was set up. Funds were quickly found to buy up large parcels of land. The first chairman of the eight commissioners was Simon Fraser, Lord Lovat, a decorated soldier, Conservative politician, chief of the name and the owner of 180,000 acres, much of it the old clan lands. By 1939, the Forestry Commission was the largest landowner in Britain with more than 2 million acres, most of it covered with forest.

About 70 per cent of the Commission's land was in Scotland, and most of that in the Highlands. My ill-fated orienteering efforts took place in the Loch Ard forest, west of Aberfoyle, and, fifty years ago, it was mainly planted with Sitka spruce. It looked nothing like the old Caledonian Forest. The Sitka is a native of Alaska and was first introduced into Scotland in 1831 by David Douglas, the explorer and botanist, who gave his name to the Douglas fir. Very well suited to poor soil, fast growing (up to four feet a year) and happy in a wet climate, the Sitka was immediately adopted by the Forestry Commission as a staple planting and millions of saplings went into the ground.

While these huge forests provided a relatively rapid solution to timber shortages with the first harvests available after only forty years, the Sitka planting was not without problems, both ecological and aesthetic. As I'd found at Aberfoyle, the trees were so close together that nothing grew on the dark forest floor and so there was little bio-diversity, no undergrowth to provide habitat. And since these forests were all planted and replanted at the same time, they are generally clear-felled at the same time, leaving wide areas of ugly devastation on hillsides and lochsides. But attitudes and working practices are changing and new planting now has to include a significant per-centage of native trees, both conifers and hardwoods. The Forestry Commission in a devolved Scotland has been reorganised as Scottish Forestry, and Forest and Land Scotland.

Other, more dramatic changes are taking place in the landscape. In response to the increasing severity of the climate crisis and the mounting threat to native species of all sorts, from the insect popu-lation to golden eagles, the Highlands is beginning to rewild and the ghost of the old Caledonian Forest is stirring.

A glance at maps of the Highlands shows there are huge, wide-open places where roads do not penetrate far, long abandoned places from where people departed generations ago as the land was brutally cleared, where the silence is broken only by the wind. Between the A890 and the A832 from Loch Carron to Dingwall in the north and the A87 from the head of Loch Duich and the A867 to Invermoriston and the banks of Loch Ness, no roads run except for single, dead-end tracks to remote places, such as hunting lodges and tiny hamlets, like Monar Lodge and Mullardoch House.

In the southern part of this vast area, the Affric Project will begin. Over a staggering 500,000 acres stretching from the Kintail Mountains in the west to the Great Glen in the east and taking in much of Glen Affric, Glen Cannich, Glen Moriston and Glen Shiel, the beginnings of a renewed Caledonian Forest will be planted and an ancient wilderness will be reborn. And in the wake of the trees, the animals, large and small, will return.

Millions of native saplings will be planted: Scots pine, birch, alder, oak and other species once found in the ancient forest, and they will be protected in the early years of their growth. This is very important because the tender shoots of young trees are succulent and very attractive to herds of hungry deer and sheep in the long Highland winters. Hundreds of miles of high fences (an adult deer can jump six or seven feet) will keep the stags and hinds at bay for thirty years, enough time for saplings to have securely established themselves. River corridors will be enhanced, probably with more fencing, peat bogs will be restored by damming and dispensing with drainage, and environmentally friendly farming encouraged.

But the essence of the Affric Project is very straightforward. It is to allow nature to regenerate and recreate the sort of places that will attract pine martens, wildcats, red squirrels, capercaillie, eagles and all of the native fauna of the recent past. After these great tracts of forest have grown high and strong, the fences will be removed and the deer allowed in to complete the ecological balance. And then the people can come as trails are laid out and outdoor pursuits encouraged. Perhaps some will be the descendants of the departed.

*

Far out in the wastes of the Atlantic, the early twentieth century saw more departure and finally a complete abandonment. In April 2016, an old lady died in a care home in Clydebank, and with her passing, a precious link in the long chain of human history in the Highlands and Islands was broken. Eight years old in 1930, Rachel Gillies was one of thirty-six people to board HMS *Harebell* and abandon their homes on the archipelago of St Kilda. Forty miles west of North Uist, lashed by the waves of the mighty Atlantic, the jagged scatter of small islands and sea-stacks were all that remained of an ancient volcano. Its sea-cliffs rise sheer from the ocean, dangerous, dark and foreboding, the highest in Britain. They were also what sustained the population, 180 at its height, for the cliffs were home to thousands of seabirds: fulmars, gannets and puffins, whose eggs and flesh were staples of the islanders' diet. They were the last of the hunter-gatherers, and when thirteen men, ten women, eight young girls and five boys stood in the stern of the *Harebell*, they watched the sun set on four millennia of occupation, perhaps 200 generations of experience in one place.

After her death, Rachel's son, Ronnie, was interviewed: 'If you asked her about St Kilda now, she would look at you and smile. It was an important part of her life but she did not speak much about it. She was very private.'

In 1928 or 1929, a photograph was taken of all five boys and four of the young girls who sailed away on the navy ship. Rachel has a ribbon in her hair, but she is the only child not to look at the camera, her eyes are downcast and she is partly hidden by the little boy standing in front of her. The group was posed against the white wall of a house and on stony ground. Two of the girls and one of the boys are barefoot. In other, earlier photographs all of the children and some of the adults are also barefoot. Poverty and remoteness were not the main reason for that.

Rachel did tell her son something of her life on Hiort, the Gaelic name for the main and only inhabited island in the St Kilda archipelago. Having tied a rope around his waist and the other end around his daughter's, Rachel's father lowered her down the sheer sea-cliffs with a basket. Every spring, young children, who were of course much lighter, gathered the eggs of seabirds from their nests on cliff ledges. It was clearly very dangerous – sometimes the children were attacked by the birds – but also a necessary moment in the seasonal rhythms of the life of a community of hunter-gatherers. Later in the year, men and boys killed young birds using a similar means to get at them on the cliffs. In the middle of the nineteenth century, John Ross, a Gaelic-speaking schoolmaster from the mainland, found himself looking up from a boat at the foot of the high cliffs on the north-east coast of Hiort:

The first thing to attract our notice was one of the men and his little boy on a rugged but fairly level piece of ground rather down near the sea. One end of the rope was tied around the father's waist while the other was tied round the boy's waist, most probably lest he, being young, rash and inexperienced, might slip into the sea. There they were, all alone then, killing away at a terrible rate, for the boy was collecting while the father kept shaking and twisting.

The man removing himself from the rope shouldered a burden of dead fulmars, made for a cutting in the rock, too narrow one would think for a dog, and too slippery for a goat. Along this he crawled on hands and knees. A single slip in the middle would have hurled him at least 80 feet sheer down into the sea. But he landed his burden safely and returned to the boy. The rope was tied as before, but only about a yard was left between them and that brave little fellow of only ten summers fearlessly followed his father and reached safety without a hitch. This is how St Kildans train their young to the rock and what a dangerous life it is.

The islanders climbed down the cliffs in bare feet, and over the millennia they had been doing this, their ankles and toes had genetically modified. In order to stay secure and steady on the often slippery, wet surface of the rock, usually while doing something else, like wringing the necks of the young fulmar, the St Kildans' toes had become more widely spaced than those of any mainlander or Hebridean. They could spread their toes to grip a foothold just as most people can spread their fingers to hold on to a handrail or an edge. The St Kildans' ankles had also become tremendously strong and were half as thick again as most people's. The barefoot children in the photographs were in a real sense developing the ability of their feet to hold on to the ground as well as toughening them.

Along with other women and their daughters, Rachel and her mother hunted puffins. The work was much less dangerous since these birds live in burrows, but the means of catching them was, to our sensibilities, cruel. With horsehair snares, the women would catch a puffin and, careful to keep it alive, they plucked its feathers, except for those on the wings and tail. Curiosity killed its neighbours. When other puffins approached the plucked bird, wondering what it was, their clumsy, waddling feet quickly became tangled in the snares.

At their suggestion, HMS *Harebell* took the islanders to the Gaelic-speaking community of Lochaline on the mainland, not far from the Lord of the Isles' sea-castle at Ardtornish. Even though they had never seen a tree, some of the men went to work for the Forestry Commission, but others could not settle. For years St Kildans sailed out to the islands on the edge of the world to climb down the cliffs and go after the fulmar so that they could bring a few birds away for themselves. Rachel returned twice, once to be interviewed for a documentary film and again as a guest of the British army who had established a base on Hiort. Perhaps others went to climb up to the summit ridges of the Cuillin on Skye. Even though it lies eighty miles to the west, St Kilda and its cliffs can be seen on the far horizon.

The abandonment of settlements on the Highland mainland, especially in the farthest north, had obvious demographic effects as the landscape emptied. The severe depopulation also had a clear impact on the workings of democracy. The voices of those Highlanders who remained were not always heard by those elected to represent them.

In the immediate aftermath of the First World War, the political map of the Highlands and Islands began to change in at least two significant and enduring ways. A series of radical boundary changes intended to rationalise the relative populations of seats had the effect of creating vast new parliamentary constituencies in the north. After the clearances had all but emptied the hinterland, Caithness and Sutherland was combined, an immense area with long and difficult distances between its small population centres that made it difficult for an MP to relate in any meaningful way with the electorate. Some were more or less absentees. Between 1918 and 1922, the Liberal MP for Caithness and Sutherland was Sir Leicester Harmsworth from the Rothermere newspaper dynasty. He lived in London and seems to have remained there for most of his time as the representative of the people of Wick, Thurso and the other small communities in the farthest north of the British mainland.

On 6 February 1918, the Representation of the People Act extended the franchise to women aged over thirty and, ten years later, the Equal Franchise Act awarded the same rights as men. For much of the inter-war period, Highlanders and Islanders usually cast their votes for Liberal candidates, a tradition that continued throughout the twentieth century. Land reform had been part of party policy for some time and the Liberals had also laid the foundations of a welfare state in the decade before the First World War, bringing in pensions for the elderly, health insurance and unemployment insurance. Despite the post-war schisms that effectively killed the party's chances of ever again forming governments, there was a consistently loyal Liberal vote, especially when candidates with genuine Highland and Island connections stood. Sir Archibald Sinclair was born in Thurso and he took over the Caithness and Sutherland seat in 1922 and held it until 1945. In Ross and Cromarty, another enormous constituency, Ian Macpherson was the MP from 1911 to 1935. Sir Murdo MacDonald , born in Inverness, held the seat from 1922 to 1950 and the Northern Isles remained solidly Liberal territory. Highlanders and Islanders rarely followed national British electoral trends and tended to remain loyal to candidates. At the age of only twenty-two, Malcolm MacMillan won the newly created seat of the Western Isles for Labour and, with a break when he enlisted in the army in 1939, he held it for the following seven general elections, ultimately losing to Donald Stewart of the SNP in 1970.

*

Departure haunted the imagination of Gaelic's greatest bard, Sorley MacLean. Here are the first three stanzas of 'Hallaig', an extraordinary, talismanic poem that remembers the clearance of the township of the same name on the island of Raasay. At the same time, it is a love poem, a hymn to the beauties of the Highland and Island landscape and how its people were once in and of it:

'Tha tìm, am fiadh, an coille Hallaig'

Tha bùird is tàirnean air an uinneig
trom faca mi an Àird an Iar
's tha mo ghaol aig Allt Hallaig
'na craoibh bheithe, 's bha i riamh

eader an t-Inbhir 's Poll a' Bhainne,
thall 's a-bhos mu Bhaile-Chùirn:
tha i 'na beithe, 'na calltainn,
'na caorann dhìreach sheang ùir.

Ann an Sgreapadal mo chinnidh,
far robh Tarmad 's Eachunn Mòr,
tha 'n nigheanan 's am mic 'nan coille
a' gabhail suas ri taobh an lòin.

'Time, the deer, is in the wood of Hallaig'

The window is nailed and boarded
through which I saw the West
and my love is at the Burn of Hallaig,
a birch tree, and she has always been

between Inver and Milk Hollow,
here and there about Baile-chuirn:
she is a birch, a hazel,
a straight, slender young rowan.

In Screapadal of my people
where Norman and Big Hector were,
their daughters and sons are a wood
going up beside the stream.

In Edinburgh in the 1970s, perhaps at the festival, I heard the
author read this atmospheric, immensely powerful poem. It was a

strange experience, one that has stayed with me. Sorley MacLean explained that the English translation he was about to read first was not itself intended to be understood as a poem, it was only a translation. Then he read the original Gaelic in what sounded almost like a chant. Often his eyes were closed. Seamus Heaney, the great Irish poet, once wrote, 'MacLean's voice had a certain bardic weirdness that sounded both stricken and enraptured.' And hypnotic.

Much later, when I had learned a little Gaelic, I found I could not understand much of the original, but I could hear most of it in my mind's ear. That allowed a small, partial sense of the great power of MacLean's language, its fluidity and its beauty, enough to recognise the magical, transcendent nature of what he had written in *An Cànan Mor nan Gàidheal* (*The Mighty Language of the Gael*). 'Hallaig', *Dàin do Eimhir, An Cuilithionn* and other poems were part of a surprisingly small corpus of work that had a huge impact, eventually. Written and published between the mid-1930s and the early 1950s, MacLean's poems were recognised and celebrated by the Gaelic speech community, but it was not until the 1970s and 1980s when the excellent translations by Iain Crichton Smith and others were published that their greatness was understood more widely.

Somhairle MacGill-Eain was born in 1911 at Osgaig on Raasay. Until he went to school at the age of six, he had very little English. The boy was steeped in the oral musical traditions of Gaelic, especially influenced by his grandmother, Mary Matheson, and his aunt, Peigi, who both taught him songs. Though his family were communicants in the Free Presbyterian Church, MacLean did not share their faith and instead became interested in socialism, refusing to accept the notion of the elect, the few who would be saved, and the certainty that the great majority would be eternally damned. He later wrote, 'perhaps my obsession with the cause of the unhappy, the unsuccessful, comes from this'.

MacLean also believed that the Gaelic language was probably also doomed, but nevertheless he remembered that 'I was not one who could write poetry if it did not come to me in spite of myself, and if it did come, it had to come in Gaelic.' After graduation from

Edinburgh University, where he was fortunate to be taught by the great W. J. Watson, the young man trained as a teacher. In 1934 he returned to Skye to teach English at Portree High School, but when the Spanish Civil War broke out two years later, he wanted to volunteer, though the need to provide for his family (his mother was very ill and his father's business was not doing well) prevented MacLean from joining the International Brigade. He then spent a year teaching on Mull and family memories affected him greatly. His ancestors on both sides had all been evicted from their homes on the island and he later said, 'I believe Mull had much to do with my poetry: its physical beauty, so different from Skye's, with the terrible impact of the clearances on it, made it almost intolerable to be a Gael.'

Perhaps distance also affected MacLean's poetry. Between 1939 and 1941 he taught at Boroughmuir High School in Edinburgh and at Hawick High School in the Borders. It was during that period that he wrote the cycle of poems that would become *Dàin do Eimhir* and *An Cuilithionn*, the Cuillin, his great epic, of which this is just a small sample:

> *Thar bochdainn, caithimh, fiabhrais, àmhghair,*
> *thar anacothruim, eucoir, ainneirt, ànraidh,*
> *thar truaighe, eu-dòchais, gamhlais, cuilbheirt,*
> *thar ciont is truaillidheachd, gu furachair,*
> *gu treunmhor chithear an Cuillithionn*
> *'s e 'g èirigh air taobh eile duilghe.*

> Beyond poverty, consumption, fever, agony,
> beyond hardship, wrong, tyranny, distress,
> beyond misery, despair, hatred, treachery,
> beyond guilt and defilement, watchful,
> heroic, the Cuillinn is seen
> rising on the other side of sorrow.

In 1956 MacLean was appointed Head Teacher at Plockton High School in Wester Ross. From there he campaigned for Gaelic medium education and for learners to a have a separate higher examination. After retirement he was much in demand at poetry readings and travelled extensively, often to receive honorary degrees and awards. It was said that the Nobel Prize for Literature only eluded him because he chose to write in the language of a small and diminishing speech community. But his lasting achievement was to show that great, new art could be made from Gaelic, that it could be a language of the future as well as the past. And most of all, it had great power. Sorley MacLean's work inspired many.

In 1901 another great writer moved from a northern Arcadia to the tenements of industrial Glasgow. Born and raised on an Orkney farm, Edwin Muir would become one of Scotland's greatest poets and he never forgot the fertile fields of his homeland and how they were worked. Here are the first two verses of 'Horses', a crystal memory of ploughing, seen through the eyes of a child:

Those lumbering horses in the steady plough,
On the bare field – I wonder why, just now,
They seemed terrible, so wild and strange,
Like magic power on the stony grange.

Perhaps some childish hour has come again,
When I watched fearful, through the blackening rain,
Their hooves like pistons in an ancient mill
Move up and down, yet seem as standing still.

In 1934, Muir's friend and fellow Orcadian, Stanley Cursiter, a painter and Keeper of the National Galleries of Scotland, lent him his car. It was a convertible and temperamental 1921 Standard whose spark plugs were a constant source of concern. After the success of J. B. Priestley's *English Journey*, the publisher Victor Gollancz had commissioned Muir to write *Scottish Journey*. It is a brilliant snapshot. Starting in Edinburgh, Muir drove all over Scotland in Cursiter's unreliable car, rarely daring to travel faster than thirty miles an hour and, of course, he ended his journey in Orkney.

He clearly understood that there were many Scotlands, no single, tartan-swathed identity but instead a patchwork of cultural difference. When Muir reached the town of Beauly, west of Inverness, he reflected on the recent history of the Highlands in what is an excellent summary:

> The destruction of Highland life on a large scale began with the severities that followed Culloden. The second stage in it was the clearances. The third is still continuing, and its symbol may be found in the pictures of slaughtered animals that disfigure the walls of Highland hotels. [Walter] Scott and Queen Victoria were probably the two people most responsible for this last disastrous phase. Scott sent the tourist wandering over the Highland hills, and Queen Victoria built Balmoral. The net result of these two innocent actions was to turn the Highlands into a huge game preserve covered with fences and dotted with notices making the pedestrian a trespasser. Consequently a great part of the Highland population now depend for their living on their obsequious skill in rendering the slaughter of wild creatures more easy or convenient to the foreign owners of the shooting lodges, and in performing whatever other menial services these people may require. The Highlanders' numbers have been thinned, their mode of life degraded, by a series of objective calamities. They have kept through all these changes their courtesy, their dignity, and one may almost say their freedom, for that seems to exist independently of any service, however menial, which they may render. But these qualities are bought at the expense of the disdainful resignation which a proud people feels in acknowledging defeat, a resignation so profound that it can treat its conqueror with magnanimity, while keeping him at his distance. Whether that is a good quality or a bad one I do not know, but it is in any case an extraordinary one.

*

At the same time as Edwin Muir was making his halting way north to Orkney, George MacLeod was thinking about another Arcadia. In 1899 the Duke of Argyll gifted the site of Iona Abbey to a group of trustees drawn from the hierarchy of the Church of Scotland. An appeal for funds to restore the ruinous Benedictine abbey was launched and rebuilding began in 1904. By the following year, a service of dedication could be held in the reroofed east end of the abbey church. By 1910, the whole of the old church had been restored. For the following twenty years more work was done on the interior and services were held regularly, but the other conventual buildings remained in a poor state, ruinous and neglected. In 1933 it was proposed that a second appeal be launched, this time for £47,000, to make all the buildings whole again so they could be used as a retreat centre. The genius loci of Columba's island had not faded over fifteen centuries, but the trustees believed an appeal would not be successful: the world economy was still reeling, not yet recovered from the Great Depression.

In 1935, perspectives suddenly changed. The trustees received an unexpected approach from the American Iona Society who proposed to have the abbey completely restored at their own expense. Many members were emigrants from the Highlands who had been cleared off the land, some from Mull, and they wanted to do something to maintain their Gaelic-speaking heritage. A Celtic College should be founded on Iona. The trustees were both astonished and suspicious, but George MacLeod saw an opportunity.

At that time he was a parish minister in the district of Govan in Glasgow, and very concerned about the role the Church of Scotland might play in a society that was changing rapidly. Radical demographic shifts were taking place. Around Glasgow and Scotland's other cities large new housing developments were being built and communities decanted from the city centre tenement slums to the periphery. At Mosspark, Carntyne, Knightswood and Blackhill, the people of MacLeod's parish at Govan and other deprived areas were housed in new accommodation that at first seemed like a New Jerusalem. Inside and private toilets for each flat or house, sometimes gardens, reliable plumbing and heating all seemed like the ingredients of a better life. But George MacLeod was concerned that a real sense of community and social cohesion would be lost in these sprawling council estates (and ultimately, he was right) and he wondered if the Church of Scotland would or could adapt.

The traditional approach to ministry and indeed the attitudes of ministers would be challenged in this new environment. And would the role of the divinity colleges at Scotland's four ancient universities not have to change? Graduates from St Mary's College in comfortable, academic, old-fashioned St Andrews might struggle to understand the lives of those who lived in the likes of Edinburgh's Craigmillar, an estate built in the late 1920s to accommodate communities from the tenements of Gorgie and Leith. MacLeod feared that the old universities would not provide graduates with the right grounding to cope with these new circumstances – and if they did not, then the Kirk would quickly be seen as irrelevant.

Perhaps Iona might supply a solution. As the trustees mulled over the generous offer from the American Iona Society and worried about what a Celtic College might be, MacLeod proposed a radically different scheme. He wrote a long letter that outlined how young ministers might be helped, in practical ways, to cope with the challenges of dealing with the new configuration of communities in the council estates. Instead of a cultural initiative that might sustain interest in the Gàidhealtachd, might there be a return to a version of the communal life established on Iona by Columba in the sixth century that would help the Kirk cope with the twentieth? MacLeod suggested that each summer a group of young divinity graduates would come to the island to work on the restoration of the conventual buildings. Crucial was the notion that these young, licentiate ministers would roll up their sleeves and labour to a number of volunteer tradesmen, most of them masons and joiners, under the direction of an architect. All would live communally in temporary wooden huts on the abbey site and commit to work for two summers. MacLeod hoped that through working together, the middle-class, university-educated ministers and the tradesmen would learn to communicate, as well as understand something of each others' lives. Captain George MacLeod had served in the Argyll and Sutherland Highlanders in the First World War and he insisted on discipline and hard work as the backbone of what became known as the Iona Community. His style could border on the dictatorial and one young minister wrote that the group should be renamed 'I own a Community'.

The trustees accepted MacLeod's proposal and work began in the very wet summer of 1938. But it was not to last. Dark clouds were also gathering to the east. Adolf Hitler's Germany was rearming and beginning to assert itself, and in the same year the *Anschluss*, the forced union with Austria, took place, and Neville Chamberlain waved a worthless piece of paper on the steps of an aeroplane promising peace in our time. In the summer of 1939, the Royal Navy sailed north once more to Scapa Flow as a second world war loomed.

16

War, Peace and Renewal

1939 to the Present Day

The vivid green, gold and purple rays of the Northern Lights seemed to soar high into the night sky, showing its vastness, glowing in the very vaults of Heaven. East of Orkney Mainland, the sea shimmered as the colours backlit the dark heads of the hills. It was a night made for a hunter.

In the afternoon of 13 October 1939, only forty days after war with Germany was declared, Captain Günther Prien's U-boat lay submerged on the seabed off the coast of Mainland, waiting, hiding. Knowing that the sun would dip below the western horizon at 18.13 precisely, Prien decided to wait a little longer. At 19.00 he at last gave orders for U-47 to surface. Moments after the U-boat's bow emerged from the dark water, Prien, his First Officer, Bertl Endrass, and his Second Officer, Amelung von Varendorff, put on their oilskins and climbed up to the conning tower. Having been submerged for most of the day, they were expecting darkness, and were all amazed to see the Northern Lights blazing in the sky. 'By now our eyes had become accustomed to the night,' Prien recorded, 'and we could see everything clearly – almost too clearly.'

Von Varendorff was uneasy, 'Man, it's going to be a sticky night.'

Prien may have considered aborting the mission, but Endrass said, 'Well, sir, it is a good night for shooting.'

The captain gave orders: 'Both engines half speed ahead.'

German intelligence officers believed that Scapa Flow was not a safe anchorage and was vulnerable to U-boat attack, but only if navigation was faultless – and luck held. U-47 slowly made its way into Holm Sound and then turned north. The channel between the islets of Lamb's Holm and Gump Holm was too risky with at least four blockships sunk more or less in a line to present an impenetrable barrier. But to the north, there might be another way into Scapa Flow. Sitting on the sea floor of Kirk Sound, between Lamb's Holm and Mainland were three blockships, but they had not settled in a line.

Prien took his time. There was a strong tide running into the Flow, pushing at the U-boat. For four hours, the captain steadied it, moving very slowly. He had kept its tanks partially flooded to stay low in the water, be as inconspicuous as possible, but that meant the hull scraped over the steel hawsers strung between the blockships. As it reached the last line of them, the U-boat had to move hard to starboard and it ran aground on the seabed as it rose up towards the shore of Mainland. Anticipating this, Prien had the tanks emptied, the U-boat floated, and after midnight, it was through, sailing on into Scapa Flow.

Moments later, Prien's boat was suddenly lit up. The headlights of a car on the shore road shone directly on it. The officers on the bridge could see sentries and trucks, and they expected to be shot at, but nothing happened. No one was looking in their direction. The headlights belonged to a taxi that was making a U-turn, and the driver must have been concentrating, for he did not notice a U-boat only about a hundred yards away.

The hunter began to prowl. Prien knew that under the waters of Scapa Flow were the sunken wrecks of the German Imperial Fleet, and no doubt he planned vengeance. But from his conning tower, using his night binoculars, he could see very few ships. German intelligence had not picked up the movement of most of the Home Fleet out of the Flow. The Admiralty had been anxious not only about U-boat attacks but also German bombing raids. And so, a few days earlier, the fleet had sailed around Cape Wrath to the safer anchorage of Loch Ewe. Its wide waters were protected by a narrow entrance from the Atlantic but more important, the West Highland coast was thought to be beyond the range of Luftwaffe bombing raids, whereas Scapa Flow was not.

As U-47 sailed slowly up the coast of Mainland, searching for prey, von Varendorff thought he could, at last, make out the outline of a battleship. He reported that it was one of the Royal Oak class. As the U-boat crept closer, they realised that it was the *Royal Oak* itself. Prien ordered the torpedo tubes to be flooded, the doors to open – and U-47 began firing. Two of the first volley of torpedoes missed, but one hit the *Royal Oak*, appearing at first to do little damage. But having quickly reloaded, the captain fired again. Three torpedoes all smashed into the battleship's starboard side and exploded. 'Flames shot skywards, blue . . . yellow . . . red,' Prien wrote. 'Like huge birds, black shadows soared through the flames, fell hissing and splashing into the water . . . huge fragments of the mast and funnels.'

A drifter, *Daisy II*, had been moored to the stern of the *Royal Oak*, and as the huge battleship heeled over, it dragged the little boat up out of the water like a toy. The captain tried to have the lines cut – by the cook with a kitchen knife – but the immense weight tore the cleats off and the drifter slapped down free into the Flow. *Daisy II* managed to pick up 386 sailors from out of the oily water, but in the burning ship, 834 men died. The *Royal Oak* took only eight minutes to sink.

Meanwhile, U-47 fled, making for Kirk Sound. Prien wrote: 'At high speed I pass the southern blockship with nothing to spare. The helmsman does magnificently. High speed, ahead both [engines], finally three-quarter speed and full ahead out . . . and at 2.15am we are once more outside.'

When U-47 docked at Wilhelmshaven, all of the crew were awarded the Iron Cross, and with Karl Dönitz, the commander of the U-boat fleet, Prien and his men were flown immediately to Berlin. Hitler personally awarded the captain the Ritterkreuz, the Knight's Cross of the Iron Cross. Ever alert to the power of propaganda, Joseph Goebbels had the arrival of the crew filmed as huge crowds mobbed them on their way to the Reich Chancellery. For the cameras, Prien made a short speech describing what he and his men had done at Scapa Flow. Many of them were filmed in grinning close-up, looking like heroes. Their captain ended with: 'You can imagine the excitement and happiness we all felt about the fact that we managed to fulfil our mission and achieve such a huge victory for Germany.'

War had come quickly to Orkney, and geography ensured that the Northern Isles and the eastern Highlands were on the front line.

In the middle of October 1942, ten men walked up to Lunna House, a large and imposing mansion on the north-east coast of Shetland Mainland. They had sailed into Vidlin Voe in a converted fishing boat, the *Arthur*, and having reassured each other and their colleagues that all was ready, they knew they would have to wait and be patient. Five of the men were from the Royal Navy: Sub-Lieutenant William Brewster, Able-Seamen A. Brown, Billy Tebb, Malcolm Causer and Bob Evans. Sergeant Don Craig, also part of the team, was a soldier in the British army. Four others were all Norwegian: the engineer, Palmer Bjørnøy, deckhand Kohannes Kalve and radio operator Roald Strand. The fourth man was the most highly decorated naval officer of the Second World War. No other man, British or foreign, was awarded comparable military honours. The Victoria Cross can only be given to British nationals, and so Leif Larsen received the Distinguished Service Order, the Conspicuous Gallantry Medal, the Distinguished Service Cross and the Distinguished Service Medal and Bar. Known as 'Shetlands Larsen', he was the most famous and the most daring skipper of the Shetland Bus, a clandestine group who established a permanent seaborne link between Nazi-occupied Norway, its resistance fighters and Shetland. It was run by the Special Operations Executive, and the lonely manor house at Lunna was its headquarters.

In the late evening of 8 April 1940, Colonel Birger Eriksen received a series of alarming radio signals from the fortress at the mouth of the Oslo Fjord. Lookouts had seen the outlines of six ships steaming northwards. None showed any lights or responded to radio signals. When a warning shot was fired across the bow of the leading ship, it did not slow or turn. Norway was neutral, but Colonel Eriksen was

in little doubt. The Germans were invading, and the dark, unrespon-
sive ships were heading for Oslo. Urgent signals were radioed to the
capital and Eriksen made preparations. He was the commander of
the Oscarsborg Fortress. Set on a small island in the fjord, it guarded
the narrows of the Drøbak Sound and the colonel was determined to
use his land-based torpedo battery to buy time for the king and his
government to evacuate the capital and escape to the north.

When the German ships came into view, looming out of the
darkness, the tubes were flooded and the torpedo doors opened. The
leading vessel was large, perhaps a battleship, and when it came into
point-blank range in the narrows, Eriksen gave the order, saying:
'Either I will be decorated or I will be court-martialled. Fire!' The
leading battleship, the *Blücher*, was badly hit and quickly sank. King
Haakon and his government escaped from Oslo along with the
Norwegian gold reserves, the army held out in the north for another
few precious weeks, and after the war Colonel Birger Eriksen was
decorated.

The Nazi occupation of Norway was seen as strategically vital. It
gave Germany's war industries much more secure access to iron ore
from Sweden, the harbours of the western coasts also became bases
for naval operations against Allied shipping in the North Atlantic,
and in the words of the directive authorising the invasion, its other
purpose was 'to give our navy and air force a wider start-line against
Britain'. And if an armada of ships carrying an invasion force had
sailed west from ports like Bergen or Trondheim, their first landfall
would have been Shetland.

In the early summer of 1940, another, very different armada
crossed from Norway to Shetland. Mostly in fishing boats, sometimes even in rowing boats, a stream of refugees arrived, so many
that a herring station, and the huts used by the herring girls from
the Hebrides, were commandeered and adapted to house them. Kare
Iversen left a vivid record of his escape across the North Sea:

The first two days passed in perfect weather conditions. But at
3.10 on our third day trouble arrived. I was coming out of the

engine room when I saw through the wheelhouse door that a German flying boat was coming straight for us. At the time two of us were down in the engine room, two in the forward cabin. After the first burst of gunfire, I went out on deck and released all the halyards to let the sails drop to the deck, then went back down to the engine room. The Germans continued shooting at us for twenty minutes. Their gunfire riddled the wheelhouse and holed the boat just above the water line with their shelling. Whenever we rolled, a big rush of water now came in to the hold. The flying boat tried to land but the sea was too rough, so they gave up the attempt. *Vila* was just drifting.

We set course again for Shetland and I drove the engine to its maximum. I myself was in the engine room from four o'clock on Saturday afternoon until five o'clock on Sunday. At 6am on the Monday I was on top of the wheelhouse when I spotted land to the west of us. We knew that it was somewhere in Shetland but where? There was only one thing to do – put two of the boys ashore. They found an old rowing boat and came back to us. We had dropped anchor and stopped the engine, ready to go ashore and find out how far we were from Lerwick. We made the beach and pulled the boat clear from the water then began to walk up through some fields. We came to a farmhouse and the lady of the house told us that we were on an island called Fetlar and that our boat was at anchor at Sandwick.

In February 1941, Leif Larsen undertook a similar voyage in a fishing boat and he immediately joined the Shetland Bus, making an astonishing fifty-two trips back to Norway, sailing without lights in the darkness, always on the lookout for attack, continually risking his life. The old skipper returned to Shetland in 1985 and visited Lunna House. In excellent English, he gave a short radio interview about his wartime experiences. 'You almost got the *Tirpitz*,' said the interviewer.

'Yes,' said Larsen. 'Almost.'

The ten men who waited at Lunna House in October 1942 were

part of Operation Title. The prime minister, Winston Churchill, was very concerned about the German navy's ability to attack the Atlantic convoys from North America, and also the Arctic convoys (which usually assembled in Loch Ewe) that sailed up the Norwegian coast to supply the Russians through their port at Murmansk. The German battleship, *Tirpitz*, was based in the long Trondheim Fjord and was attacked several times by RAF bombers, but no damage was done, and so a different approach was adopted. In Loch a' Chàirn Bhàin on the Assynt coast, manned torpedo crews had been training – these men were not, however, the naval equivalent of kamikaze pilots. The torpedoes looked more like mini-submarines designed to travel on the surface, and they carried detachable warheads that, like limpet mines, could be attached to the hulls of ships and then detonated.

Operation Title involved the transport of two manned torpedoes and their crews on Leif Larsen's fishing boat, the *Arthur*, across the North Sea. The Norwegian resistance had supplied information about the sort of documentation Larsen would need to gain entry to Trondheim Fjord, and, once in, the torpedoes could be manned and the crews would approach the *Tirpitz* under cover of darkness to attach the warheads. In the chaos following the explosion, Larsen was to scuttle the *Arthur*, meet up with the torpedo crews and the Norwegian resistance would drive them to the Swedish border and safety.

It did not work out like that. Once in the Trondheim Fjord, the *Arthur* was badly buffeted when a severe storm blew up. The torpedoes had been attached to the hull below the waterline, but bad weather had pulled them off and they were lost. The operation was immediately aborted. Larsen managed to scuttle the *Arthur* in a secluded stretch of water and all ten men scrambled ashore. Split into two parties of five, they walked the fifty miles to the Swedish border. After an exchange of fire with a German military policeman and Norwegian collaborator near the border, Able Seaman Evans was badly wounded. Certain he would be treated as a prisoner of war since he was in uniform, Larsen's group left him behind. They and the other party of five reached Sweden and through the British Embassy in Stockholm, were quickly flown home. But Evans was taken to Oslo and shot as a saboteur by the Gestapo.

The brave men who operated the Shetland Bus helped sustain the Norwegian resistance throughout the war, making almost 200 crossings, taking 192 agents and 383 tons of arms and supplies. Some 373 refugees and 73 agents travelled in the opposite direction. This vital link was made possible by repeated acts of extraordinary courage, and also a fellow feeling that remembered a long-shared Scandinavian past as Norwegians once more sailed 'westoversea'.

*

Perhaps time has lent too much enchantment, but I have an indelible memory that the little plane, one with propellers, that I'd boarded in Glasgow, was going to fly straight into a sand dune. Or maybe the pilot was having a laugh. From what I could see from my window seat, we were heading for a grass-topped sand dune. Then the plane seemed to hop, skip and then land on a long beach of brilliant white sand. Whatever was or was not the case, landing on the Traigh Mhor on the island of Barra was unforgettable. It must be the only airport in the world that closes at high tide. Once we had reached the end of the beach, spraying seawater, I think, or maybe sand, the pilot turned the propeller plane towards the little control tower, and stopped the engines. I disembarked and saw that the arrivals hall was a small wooden hut and baggage reclaim was a bus shelter. It was wonderful. Why can't all airports be as simple – and as stunningly beautiful – as the Traigh Mhor?

I picked up my bag from the bus shelter and asked the taxi driver to take it to the Castlebay Hotel in Castlebay, the largest community on Barra (I nearly typed 'capital'). It was a lovely, warm, still, sunny West Highland morning and I had one more trip to make, in the opposite direction. I walked north to Eoligarry to catch the ferry to Eriskay. Once again my memory may be faulty, for this happened in the summer of 1989, but I clearly remember a small, passengers-only boat slowly making its way (with me as the only passenger) through a channel between rocky outcrops that were so close you could almost reach out and touch them. And then out into the Sound of Barra, where on another fine summer's day in 1745 Alasdair macMhaighstir Alasdair met Prince Charles on board the *Du Teillay* and did not know who the young man was. The ferry passed close to the rocky islet of Fuday, and I am sure the skipper was navigating by sight, lining up landmarks, sailing towards them before finding another one and changing course. Maybe beneath the crystal blue water, invisible danger was lurking. Beyond the skerries around Lingay, we came into the Sound of Eriskay to dock at Ludag on the shore of South Uist. 'Only a couple of minutes,' said the skipper. 'Post to pick up.'

I could see a scatter of white houses on Eriskay as we chugged between two more skerries and imagined that I was on board the *Vital Spark*. As the jetty came into view, it seemed that Para Handy was aiming off, lining the boat up too far to the east. But then he turned the wheel hard to starboard and smiled at me as I grabbed the gunwale rail. 'Sandbanks,' he said, and then we docked.

The landlord was waiting on the jetty. We walked up the hill to his new pub which, I am bound to say, looked more like a bungalow. But inside there was treasure, liquid gold.

'Now, don't add any water,' he said as he poured the smallest thimbleful of whisky into a crystal glass. 'And have a nose at it first.' I did. And then I tasted it. Terrible. Oily and bitter. But a droplet of history.

My friend's bungalow pub had been named Am Politician, the Politician, after a famous ship that ran aground in the rocky Sound of Eriskay, whose waters I'd just crossed. On the morning of 4 February 1941 it foundered. The SS *Politician* had 22,000 cases of whisky in its hold, 264,000 bottles, and I had just tasted some. The story of the foundered ship is famous and it inspired the bestselling novel, *Whisky Galore*, by Compton Mackenzie and the superb Ealing Comedy film of the same name. The title is an amusing, ironic play on words. Galore is one of the few borrowings from Gaelic into English – it comes from *gu leòr*, which means 'enough'.

On 2 February 1941, the splendidly named Captain Beaconsfield Worthington gave orders for the SS *Politician* to cast off from Liverpool docks. Bonded warehouses in Glasgow and Leith had been damaged by German bombing and a great deal of whisky could no longer be securely held. And so a government decision was made to transport 22,000 cases to the USA, where it would be sold to raise hard currency for the war effort. On board there was also a great deal of newly printed currency, £3 million in Jamaican banknotes. The *Politician* had crossed the Atlantic many times and plied the eastern coats of the United States as a general cargo ship. For safety, Captain Worthington had orders to rendezvous with an Atlantic convoy.

As the ship passed through the North Channel and on northwards, bad weather, heavy seas and poor visibility appear to have blown it off course. Somewhere in the narrow Sound of Eriskay, the *Politician* ran aground on submerged rocks between the island and South Uist, probably north of the islet of Calvay. Quite what the big cargo ship was doing in such dangerous waters might be explained by a series of radio signals. After Worthington's attempts to use his engines to free the *Politician* had failed, he ordered the crew to abandon ship. Heavy seas might break it up. The radio operator's first SOS message was: 'Abandon ship. Making water. Engine room flooded.' A second message sent at 8.22 a.m. may explain why the *Politician* had foundered: 'Ashore south of Barra island, pounding heavily.' In fact, Eriskay lies north-east of Barra. It looks as though in the foul weather, Captain Beaconsfield Worthington's navigation had gone disastrously wrong. The Barra lifeboat spent hours searching for the stricken ship in the wrong place.

In the grey morning light, fishermen on the north shore of Eriskay had seen that the *Politician* had run aground and they immediately put to sea to rescue the crew. A ship's lifeboat with twenty-six men on board had been launched but the heavy seas drove it onto rocks at Rubha Dubh on the shore of South Uist. Meanwhile, the Barra lifeboat had received a signal that a ship's siren could be heard in the Sound of Eriskay. When it finally arrived at the foundered *Politician*, the fishermen were already on board helping men to get off. By the time darkness fell, the whole crew had been safely rescued and they were taken in by the islanders to be warmed and fed in front of their peat fires.

That night, the sailors told their hosts that the *Politician* had a great deal of whisky in her hold. Whisky that might need rescuing.

By coincidence, an Eriskay man, Angus John Campbell, had served as boatswain on the *Politician* in the 1930s and as small boats rowed across the sound, usually under cover of darkness, he helped them navigate around the ship and pointed out where the holds were. Estimates vary wildly, for it was in no one's interest to supply accurate numbers, but a great deal of whisky was hooked out of the oil- and water-filled main cargo hold, and by no means all by Eriskay and Barra men. Once news got out, boats arrived from all over the Hebrides and the mainland. During the Second World War, whisky was often in short supply or very expensive. And here was a treasure trove, an answer to many prayers, perhaps even a gift from God. Cases and bottles from the hold of the wreck were hidden all over the islands, buried, pushed down rabbit holes, stored in caves, put under peat stacks, behind panelling. And some of it was forgotten. In 1991, the buyer of an old croft house on Eriskay found four bottles under the floorboards and more buried in the garden.

HM Customs and Excise took a dim view and thirty-two men were arrested for theft. Thirteen were either acquitted or fined, while nineteen went to prison for terms that ranged between twenty days and two months. There was a good deal of ill feeling and the local police seemed unwilling to cooperate with the Customs men. The Jamaican currency was of little interest, but some was removed from the ship. Island children were found playing with it and some damp banknotes turned up in Liverpool.

On Barra, a well-known writer watched at first hand what happened and no doubt began to make notes.

When I walked back from Eoligarry to the Traigh Mhor to find a taxi to take me to Castlebay, I passed a large, low, bungalow-like house. Named Suidheachan, it was built in the late 1930s for the great novelist, Compton Mackenzie. He was immensely prolific, the author of more than a hundred books that ranged right across the literary spectrum, from history through biography to a great deal of fiction. In 1913 he published *Sinister Street*, a novel that was not only an immediate bestseller but also a critical success, lavishly praised by George Orwell and John Betjeman. But it is his comic novels set in the Highlands and Islands that have kept Mackenzie's memory alive. *The Monarch of the Glen* was made into a successful TV series (although the plots had less and less relationship with the original) and as mentioned *Whisky Galore* into a superb film, directed by Alexander Mackendrick.

Although he was born in West Hartlepool, County Durham, in 1883, Compton Mackenzie enthusiastically embraced what he saw as his ancestral Highland identity, showing a deep attachment to Gaelic culture. In 1928 he was one of the co-founders of the National Party of Scotland, the forerunner of the SNP. A converted Catholic and an ardent Jacobite, the writer was the third governor-general of the Royal Stuart Society, one of whose somewhat vague and lukewarm aims was 'to uphold rightful Monarchy and oppose republicanism'. Despite this, Mackenzie was knighted in 1952 by Queen Elizabeth II of England and I of Scotland, presumably rightfully so.

He lived on Barra between 1933 and 1945, most of the time at Suidheachan, his new house at the Traigh Mhor, and became deeply involved in the affairs of the island community. When the SS *Politician* foundered in the Sound of Eriskay, Mackenzie was the officer commanding the Barra Home Guard, with the rank of captain, a role and a character who found his way onto the pages of *Whisky Galore*. When the author sat down at his desk in Suidheachan, he based the plot of the novel on the rescue of the whisky from the ship but simplified and expanded the story. The enemies of the islanders were not only HM Customs and Excise and the police, but also Captain Paul Waggett, a pompous Englishman who was commander of the Home Guard. Barra and Eriskay became Great Todday and Little Todday, and Mackenzie added some spice by making one a Protestant island and the other Catholic. Subplots involved two couples who planned to get married, and to add real flavour and authenticity, the author added some Gaelic to the West Highland English spoken by the islanders. There was a glossary at the back of the novel to explain meaning and aid pronunciation. *Whisky Galore* was a runaway bestseller, constantly reprinting, eventually selling hundreds of thousands of copies.

The film rights were quickly snapped up by Ealing Studios, and Mackenzie and Angus MacPhail, a very experienced screenwriter of Highland descent who had worked with Alfred Hitchcock, were commissioned to write a script. The result was a classic, beautifully shot and cut film that has stood the test of time, possibly the best ever to be set in the Highlands and Islands, the best because it had a palpable air of authenticity, great good humour and a magical atmosphere.

In 1948, Ealing Studios were very busy with films such as *Passport to Pimlico* and *Kind Hearts and Coronets*, both in production at the same time. Their studios in West London were full to capacity and so it was decided to do something very different, very unusual; to film *Whisky Galore!* on location on Barra. But almost as soon as Mackendrick and his crew arrived, it began to rain and throughout the shooting period, the schedule was constantly interrupted by bad weather and gales – in July. The Catholic chapel at Castlebay was converted into a studio so that interiors could be shot there no matter the weather. Barra had only one very small hotel and so cast and crew were billeted with local families. This had unplanned benefits. With the excruciating exception of Joan Greenwood, the actors were able to pick up decent Hebridean accents, and Gaelic and references to the language added a sense of difference, even of otherworldliness. When an English suitor asks Joan Greenwood's character to marry him, she tells him that if he does it in Gaelic, she might consider it. 'Tha gaol agam ort,' he says. 'I love you.' Macroon, the informal leader of the community, is a wonderfully sardonic character brilliantly played by Wylie Watson. When, in his best cut-glass accent, Captain Waggett mangles 'Good morning', *madainn mhath*, in Gaelic, the old man looks up, takes his pipe out of his mouth and says, 'Aye, Captain, ye have the Gaelic fine.'

Like Para Handy, Macroon and the other islanders were not free of parody, but what made *Whisky Galore!* different was that the Gaels of the Hebrides manage to triumph, for once, over external authority. More than that, a Gaelic identity had a smile on its face when it defeated the Anglo-Saxons. For once.

When the shooting was finally completed, five weeks and £20,000 over budget, and Mackendrick had produced a rough cut, there was great disappointment. The director himself though it 'amateurish' and the studio wanted to cut it down to an hour and release it as a B-feature. Charles Crichton shot some more material in the studio and re-edited the film so that it was closer to Compton Mackenzie and Angus MacPhail's script. When it was released, *Whisky Galore!* gathered excellent reviews and made money in the USA, the first Ealing Studios film to do so. It remains a glorious, hilarious black-and-white romp, its age having lent much enchantment.

*

Tom Johnston was a visionary, and also an effective, practical politician able to work behind the scenes to make deals, stave off opposition and smooth the path of legislation. His contribution to the development of the Highlands and Islands was immense, and it began to turn the relentless tide of emigration and decay. Johnston was also instrumental in the creation of the National Health Service.

During the First World War, there had been significant social unrest, objections to poor pay for workers in munitions and other essential industries as well as rent strikes. As MP for Stirling and Clackmannan West in 1922–4, Tom Johnston had formerly been closely associated with a parliamentary grouping known as the Red Clydesiders, and in 1909 had written *Our Scots Noble Families*, an attack on the landed aristocracy. When Winston Churchill came to power in 1940, he wisely appointed prominent Labour politicians to those ministries that were key to the home front. Herbert Morrison became home secretary, Ernest Bevan minister of labour and Tom Johnston secretary of state for Scotland. He drove a hard bargain with the prime minister, demanding wide powers to act independently. And he got them.

On the nights of 13 and 14 March 1941, the Luftwaffe launched devastating bombing raids on Clydebank. Their targets were the shipyards and factories but most of these survived unscathed. Instead, much of the town was destroyed, with only seven houses escaping damage. With 528 dead and 617 badly injured, the casualties were severe. In anticipation of further lethal bombing raids, Tom Johnston pushed through the Emergency Hospital Scheme. In rural locations, remote from the threat of bombing, new hospitals were built at Law in North Lanarkshire, Ballochmyle in Ayrshire, Peel in the Borders, Stracathro in Angus, Bridge of Earn in Perthshire, Killearn in Stirlingshire and at Raigmore near Inverness.

Like most of these hospitals, Raigmore was built very quickly with wards in separate, single-storey huts close to central services such as operating theatres. Rebuilding was a long time coming after the end of the war and Highland communities had to wait until 1970 before the huts began to be replaced.

Tom Johnston's fears of repeated bombing raids proved mercifully baseless, and there was nothing on the scale of Clydebank. When it seemed unlikely that the Luftwaffe would again darken Scotland's skies, he opened up the new hospitals to the long civilian waiting lists that had built up. By 1945, 33,000 patients had been treated free of charge, and what Johnston saw as a pilot scheme for the NHS was shown to work well. The Emergency Hospital Scheme had laid important, credible foundations for how a free health care service might work.

As secretary of state for Scotland, Johnston was very concerned about the economic health of the Highlands and Islands, and in parliament he spoke of the region 'rapidly bleeding to death' as a result of emigration. The wholesale expansion of the sort of hydro-electric scheme established at Kinlochleven was seen as providing many benefits: a reliable electricity supply for remote communities, a great deal of work for Highlanders and others as well as the ability to supply the national grid with cheap surplus power.

Opposition from the landowners Johnston attacked in his book, from sporting estates and the coal mining industry (who did not want the competition) and local faction-fighting had scuppered plans in the past. At one point, Inverness County Council had refused to allow water from the Spey to cross into Argyll.

Using his wide-ranging powers as secretary of state and all his formidable political skills, Johnston succeeded in pushing through the formation of a Committee on Hydro-Electric Development in Scotland. In a very short time it produced a detailed and wholly convincing case for the creation of a government-funded body to implement new schemes. In September 1943, five members were appointed to the new North of Scotland Hydro-Electric Board with Johnston as chairman. With the nationalisation of Britain's electricity supply industry in 1948, the board took over the private companies in Scotland. Johnston had left Parliament in 1945 to concentrate his efforts on the new board, and work went ahead at pace. By 1958 there were thirty-eight newly completed schemes in operation and many more in the pipeline.

Perhaps the most spectacular of all was the power station built at Ben Cruachan. Below the peak of the mountain is a small lochan and its existence prompted designers to conceive a simple idea. They drew plans for a great dam to create a reservoir. The first stages of the concept were conventional. Gravity would send the water behind the dam rushing down the steep mountain to turn four huge turbines that would harness the force of nature to create electricity. But what made the design elegant and simple was what happened next. The plan was to use off-peak electricity (generally at night and at the weekends) to pump the water back up to the reservoir near the top of the mountain.

In the great turbine hall, tunnelled deep into the heart of the mountain, the men who built the power station are commemorated. On one wall is a vast, monumental relief, forty-eight by twelve feet, made from inlaid wood. There are stylised electricity pylons, a huge Celtic cross and a tribute to fifteen men who died when the roof of the turbine hall collapsed. Very sadly, Tom Johnston died before this ingenious scheme began to generate electricity.

*

In the 1945 general election a young soldier narrowly failed to capture the seat of Orkney and Shetland, losing by only 329 votes to the Conservatives. Five years later, Jo Grimond won by a wide margin and launched what turned out to be a charismatic political career. The Liberal Party had dwindled dramatically from a party of government before and during the First World War to holding only six seats in 1955. After that year's general election, Clement Davies resigned as leader and Jo Grimond replaced him, embarking on a remarkable rescue mission. By force of personality as well as a refreshing political directness, he gave the party a voice out of all proportion to its numbers, both of MPs and voters. Their share had shrunk to only 2.5 per cent. At a by-election in Torrington, the Liberals made their first gain since 1928, and very gradually they began to become significant once more.

A gifted orator, Grimond led the party for eleven years and was also an excellent constituency MP, his national prominence helping the visibility of the Northern Isles. Another by-election was won at Orpington in 1962 and in 1965 he came to Roxburgh, Selkirk and Peebles to campaign on behalf of the young David Steel. I heard Jo Grimond speak in the assembly hall of my school in Kelso and it was a revelation. Without a note, or any hesitation, he outlined why the Liberals were different – and better than – either Labour or the Conservatives. Laced with unforced and, it seemed, unrehearsed humour and delivered with an impeccable patrician accent (Grimond has gone to school at Eton and university at Oxford), his speech seemed part of a genuine crusade to change fusty, grey, old-fashioned post-war Britain. I found it inspirational. And I do remember that he talked about his own constituency, saying it was rural, and distinctive, like the Borders. He also talked, long before any other party leader, about home rule for Scotland. David Steel famously won the seat with a substantial majority, and he was only twenty-six.

Jo Grimond stood down at the general election of 1983 just as a very young Highlander was setting out on his political career.

Twenty-three years old, not long out of university, Charles Kennedy stood as the Social Democratic Party candidate in Ross, Cromarty and Skye, and achieved a stunning victory over Hamish Gray, a Conservative minister. In 1999 Kennedy too became leader of a party, the merged Liberal Democrats, and his fluency and dynamism contributed to an excellent electoral showing, winning fifty-two seats in 2001. Four years later, the party did even better with sixty-two seats and 22 per cent of the popular vote. But concerns were raised about Kennedy's drinking and some subpar performances on television and at party conferences. Despite electoral success, he was eventually forced to resign. Charles Kennedy died, tragically young at fifty-five, in 2015, after losing his seat to the SNP in a bitterly fought campaign.

Joining Ramsay MacDonald, who was prime minister for a short time and led the Labour Party between the wars, Grimond and Kennedy were Highland and Island MPs who rose to national prominence, and also trailed in their wake a greater consciousness of the region, mitigating the notion that the north might be a political backwater. But other stereotypes clung on doggedly.

*

A year before Alexander Mackendrick and the crew and cast of *Whisky Galore!* arrived on Barra, another feature film was being made on the mainland, one that set an extraordinary and persistent cultural tone. At glorious, sunlit locations at Glenfinnan, Glencoe, Morar and elsewhere, *Bonnie Prince Charlie* was in production. Made by Alexander Korda's London Films, it was shot in rich technicolour, unlike black-and-white *Whisky Galore!*, and Robert Krasker, the Australian director of photography, framed the set-pieces with real flair. The raising of the royal standard and the entry of the Highland army into Edinburgh are masterly, and in 1949 Krasker won an Oscar for *The Third Man*, a classic film starring Orson Welles and Joseph Cotton.

But all that skill and experience was not enough to rescue *Bonnie Prince Charlie*. There was nothing classic about it, at least not in any positive sense. Almost as soon as it begins, the film collapses into muddled pastiche, and worse. Miscast as the prince, David Niven (minus his trademark moustache) arrives at Glenfinnan where Finlay Currie as the Marquis of Tullibardine, one of the few Scottish actors involved, reads out King James' proclamation. Like George IV in 1822, he wears a kilt well above the knee, but at least as a Scottish aristocrat, Currie sounds plausible even if he does look faintly ridiculous. Once the standard is raised, the clansmen raise up David Niven on their shields – a surprising, and unique, moment of authenticity – and he makes a supposedly rousing speech, inciting the clans to battle, which begins, 'Hello, Scotsmen!'.

In his cut-glass, English public school accent, wobbling a little on the shields, Prince Charlie goes on to note that 'This is a most joyful meeting between a man and his friends. Fellow countrymen, here is my sword.' At the moment when he reaches to draw it, Niven fumbles a little. And then with his hat in his other hand, he goes gamely on, 'I have flung away the scabbard!' He hadn't, it was still on his belt. 'Battle for me as I shall battle for you.' Then, somewhat uncertainly, he shouts, 'God defend Scotland!' Blue bonnets are thrown in the air and then the whole dismal plot unfolds, punctuated by eyewatering, unrelenting bad acting and woeful scripting. Jack Hawkins plays Lord George Murray and a blearing, tearful Margaret Leighton does a turn as Flora MacDonald.

The trailer for *Bonnie Prince Charlie* should have been enough of a warning. After the copperplate credits, Robert Krasker's cinematography sweeps across Glencoe, mixes very cleverly to the Old Man of Storr on Skye and pans over other scenic clichés. The landscapes are all entirely empty; not even any sheep, far less people, can be seen and the montage is accompanied by mournful choral music. No words can be made out. It might be Gaelic, or Croatian, but the wistful mood is unmistakable. The impeccably groomed Prince and his ragged followers triumph at first before Flora flees with Charlie through the heather (where there is a little, very chaste, love interest between them halfway up a mountain), and the last, elegiac shot in this extraordinary film is the stern of the French ship sailing into the mists of bad history on Loch nan Uamh.

Leaving aside the truly terrible script and the laughable acting, the importance of this film should not be underestimated. Defeated and empty, the Highlands and Islands were being fixed in the popular imagination as places full of regret and with no future, part only of the romantic past, not linked to the present, but somewhere apart from the modern world, forever moored to failure.

Three years after David Niven was saying hello to Scotsmen at Glenfinnan, the Walt Disney Company released *Rob Roy: The Highland Rogue*. Even though it was also beautifully shot in colour on location near Aberfoyle, the result was also execrable. As Rob Roy, Richard Todd was completely miscast and Glynis Johns' accent as his wife was like fingernails on a blackboard. As for the plot, the subtitle almost said it all and the *New York Times* described it as 'a fine lot of fighting in the hills'.

A year later, *Brigadoon* was released and although there was less fighting, the portrayal of the Highlands, even as a myth, was simply baffling. While what might have been a medieval village was clothed in tartan, even on the washing lines, it was not at all clear who these people were. There was a tremendous amount of dancing, with Gene Kelly looking very uncomfortable (unlike 'Singing in the Rain' which worked wonderfully well) and a series of set-pieces that showed the film's origins as a stage musical. A bit of sword and dirk play erupted now and then, with some of the warriors wearing what looked like colanders on their heads, but no one seemed to be hurt. Cyd Charisse as Fiona Campbell was unintentionally hilarious, and the film could have been set in the Swiss Alps, or the Himalayas. That might have spared us Cyd lip-synching 'Waitin' for My Dearie'.

American film producers might be forgiven for parodying the Highlands and Islands, but the makers of television programmes who lived and worked in Scotland had no excuse for being marooned in Brigadoon.

On 31 August 1957, Scottish Television began broadcasting over a wide transmission area that included all of Argyll and some of the western Highlands as far north as Skye. And at that time, it was the only ITV station in Scotland. The new service began with a live programme from the stage of the Theatre Royal in Glasgow. Entitled *This Is Scotland*, it was a strange ragbag of acts and items introduced by the actor James Robertson Justice, who had played the doctor in *Whisky Galore!* He knew his lines for that film, but they deserted him only a few moments into the programme and he read from a script or perhaps from cue cards just below the camera. After a brief poetic wander around Scotland's history and geography, the show returned to the theatre and the young Kenneth MacKellar stood on a high podium and began to sing while various figures jigged and reeled around the stage. They were intended to be somehow representative of the nation. One was dressed as a shepherd and another carried a shotgun. Perhaps some prayed he would use it. Ribboned through this whole sorry mess was tartan (or perhaps not, the programme was made in black and white and maybe it just looked like tartan) and Highland dress. It was also baffling, completely unrelated to the realities of post-war Scotland. Maybe fantasy, even badly conceived fantasy, was preferable to reality.

A year later the BBC weighed in with *The White Heather Club*, another travesty of Highland life and culture. The conceit was that the viewer was invited, at 6.20 p.m. every Wednesday, perhaps a little early, to a television version of a ceilidh. A commissionaire opened the door to what looked like a glass and concrete office block rather than Grannie's Hielan' Hame, saluted the invisible cameraman and by extension the viewer, who was then welcomed by the host, Andy Stewart:

Come in, come in, it's nice to see you,
How's yersel', ye're looking grand.

All the men appeared to be wearing kilts and the ladies were in white dresses swathed with tartan sashes. And although it was supposed to be a ceilidh, there was no sign of any drink. Dancing was heavily featured in what always seemed a very cramped studio space. The Dixie Ingram Dancers did well not to bump into the furniture. This cringe-making, nauseating mash-up of clichés ran for ten embarrassing years and was distressingly popular. It played all over Britain and regularly attracted more than ten million viewers in an era when only between 60 and 70 per cent had a television. The creaking format was carried by Andy Stewart, a very talented entertainer, a decent singer, a good mimic and sometimes funny, especially when he adlibbed. At the end of the show, he would sing:

Haste ye back, I love you dearly.
Call again, you're welcome here.

The White Heather Club was harking back to a Highland Never-Never Land, a past full of warmth and reassurance that was pure invention. Its appeal may well have been its misty distance from the bustle and racket of city life, of a week spent working in factories. The show was particularly attractive to Scots living in England. What the English, the Welsh and the Northern Irish made of it, goodness knows. The programme may be thought of as harmless kitsch, but it is not. When the culture of the Highlands is shown as a retreat into the cloying, parodic world of tartanry, Highlanders and Islanders are labelled as quaint, not forward-looking, and they are patronised, thought to be backward-looking – to a past that never existed.

*

But in the present, consciences were stirring, pushing politicians to act more positively. The adjective 'formidable' might have been coined to describe Willie Ross, Scotland's longest serving secretary of state. A less kind description was a 'stern-faced and authoritarian Presbyterian conservative who ran the country like a personal fiefdom for Harold Wilson'. Having served in the Highland Light Infantry in the Second World War, Major Ross stood as the Labour candidate in a by-election in Kilmarnock in 1946 and served the constituency until 1979. He was indeed seen as a conservative, a firm unionist who branded the SNP 'Tartan Tories' and opposed entry to the Common Market (as the EU was then known). And, in 1954, when the ITV franchise for Scotland was being considered, Ross wanted a ban on advertising on Sundays, Good Friday and Christmas Day.

Despite his headmasterly manner and a commanding, even intimidating deep bass voice, Willie Ross was in fact a sympathetic politician, often determined to do the decent and appropriate thing. In early 1965, he stood up in the House of Commons to introduce a bill to establish the Highlands and Islands Development Board (HIDB): 'For two hundred years, the Highlander has been the man on Scotland's conscience . . . No part of Scotland has been given a shabbier deal by history . . . Too often there has only been one way out of his troubles for the person born in the Highlands and Islands: emigration.'

He went on: 'If there is any bitterness in my voice, I can assure the House that there is bitterness in Scotland too, when we recollect the history of these areas. We have to put this aside, however, to do what we are all now determined must be done to redress history . . . We have nine million acres, where two hundred and seventy-five thousand people live, and we are short of land.'

Such awareness of history in the midst of the hurly-burly of politics and politicking is rare, and so is the notion of the rest of Scotland and Britain understanding that wrongs had indeed been done, and that the Highlands and Islands were owed help and economic stimulus after centuries of repression and loss. Although some, more radical commentators complained that there was no right of compulsory purchase of estates owned by absentee landlords to deal with the shortage of land for development, the new board was given far-reaching powers. Loans, grants and the purchase of shares were all deployed in the creation of new businesses, and the support and encouragement of those already existing that had ambitions to grow. A central plank of HIDB policy was the perception that the Highlands and Islands needed substantial industrial plants to be established in addition to the aluminium smelters at Kinlochleven, Fort William and at Foyers, near Loch Ness. Tom Johnston's Hydro-Electric Board was moving ahead at pace with schemes to provided cheap energy and at least some of it should be used where it originated.

There had already been movement in this policy direction. At Dounreay in Caithness, the United Kingdom Atomic Energy Authority had set up a fast-breeder reactor in 1954 and it had had a dramatic effect on the local economy. So many workers came north to build and operate the power station that the population of the nearest town, Thurso, trebled from 3,000 to 9,000 – that increase, and others, doubling the number who lived in Caithness. Good new housing was needed and four large estates, known locally as the Atomics, were quickly built: between 1955 and 1963, more than a thousand houses went up as well as new schools. Caithness' Norse heritage was acknowledged when Thorfinn Terrace, Sigurd Road and Sweyn Road became new addresses. By 1994 Dounreay had come to the end of its productive life and was closed, but the long process of decommissioning still employs many and will continue into the middle decades of the twenty-first century.

Other attempts to establish labour-intensive industries in the Highlands and Islands were less sustained and less successful. A huge aluminium smelter, much larger than the others, was opened at Invergordon on the Cromarty Firth in 1971 but it closed only ten years later with the loss of many jobs. A pulp-making mill at Corpach, near Fort William, closed in 1980. But despite these reverses, much of the work of the HIDB did begin to bear fruit and the local economies of Easter Ross, Inverness and Lochaber began to grow – after a very long period of recession.

Perhaps an overly crude and obvious indicator, but nevertheless very informative, the fluctuation of populations can be a solid way of measuring success. Increase is good, decline is unwelcome. Between 1983 and 2001, the number of people living in the Highlands and Islands increased overall by 2.2 per cent after centuries of decline. Highland Region saw the largest increase of 6.8 per cent with Inverness a major driver, the city's population growing by 0.5 per cent a year to reach almost 47,000. There was, however, severe decline in the Western Isles with a drop of 15.8 per cent. But between 2001 and 2018, a further and greater overall rise of 7.6 per cent saw the total for the Highlands and Islands reach 489,330. However, recent projections suggest that in the wake of Brexit, Covid and the economic downturn caused by both, this rate of growth will slow or even decline.

*

In September 1969, Amoco, the American Oil Company, was drilling in the North Sea from the *Sea Quest* rig. It lay about 150 miles east of Aberdeen. Secrecy was vital. All communications with exploration headquarters in Great Yarmouth, 400 miles to the south, were in code, using the names of American universities. But what the geologist Brendan McKeown had found was very important indeed. It needed to go with him, and a helicopter was summoned to take off from the submersible rig. Something very surprising had come up from the bed of the North Sea. When he arrived at HQ, McKeown handed a jar to Mitch Watt:

> I suspected from the information that was available on the logs that we would see good oil. The most significant thing was to see if the pressure and the flow would stabilize over a period of time. As soon as the valves opened, we knew we had a winner . . .
>
> None of us were prepared for oil. We thought we might find some gas or at the most watery oil traces, so I didn't have any stainless-steel containers. I had to clean out an empty pickle jar from the mess hall to collect the sample.
>
> It was what we call sweet oil with not a trace of hydrogen sulphide. Mitch then poured it into an ashtray on his desk and set it alight and it burned well. But unfortunately the heat caused the ashtray to crack and the bloody stuff spilled all over the floor.

The *Sea Quest* had discovered the Montrose oilfield. The companies had been prospecting for natural gas, but it became quickly clear that there was a great deal of oil under the bed of the North Sea. A year after McKeown flew to Great Yarmouth, the giant Forties Oil Field was discovered and, in 1971, Shell found the great Brent Field, due east of Shetland. Estimates fluctuated wildly at first but it was obvious that the licences granted by the British government to oil companies would become very lucrative, despite the challenges of drilling in such a hostile environment as the North Sea.

In the late 1960s a young accountant moved to Shetland. Not yet thirty, Ian Clark first became county treasurer and then county clerk to the old Zetland Council, based in Lerwick. He saw immediately what needed to be done. 'Shetland would have to acquire special powers from Parliament if the feared free-for-all with the oil business was to be avoided,' he later wrote. Urgent discussions took place between councillors and the local MP, the redoubtable Jo Grimond. In 1973, he introduced a Private Member's Bill to the House of Commons designed to allow what became Shetland Islands Council to negotiate directly with the oil companies over the key issue of onshore facilities. The bill became an Act and discussions began. Apparently, the oil companies later said that the Libyan dictator, Colonel Gaddafi, was easier to deal with than Ian Clark. And the whole process was given added piquancy by the 1973 oil crisis when the Arab producers who led the OPEC consortium reduced supply and tripled prices.

In essence, Shetland Islands Council agreed to fund and facilitate the construction of the huge oil terminal at Sullom Voe, as well as other infrastructure such as the necessary improvements at Sumburgh Airport. Ownership of these, and also of the tugboat fleet that piloted supertankers in and out of the Voe, allowed the council to charge for the use of all that had been built at their expense. In one year, these revenues could amount to £56 million. This made Shetland Islands Council the second richest in Britain, behind the City of London. All sorts of welcome facilities were built for community use: these included a large sports and leisure centre in Lerwick, and eight swimming pools with centres attached in the rest of the archipelago. Investment funds were also made available for the indigenous industries of fishing, fish processing and knitwear, and also for crofting. The Shetland economy boomed.

When the film-maker Bill Forsyth sat down to write the screenplay for *Local Hero*, a very successful film that starred Burt Lancaster,

Peter Riegert and Denis Lawson, he had the example of events on Shetland to draw on. In 1983, I made a documentary for ITV about the film, and Forsyth told me that he'd read the newspaper stories about the council and Ian Clark. The plot of *Local Hero* revolves around the efforts of Knox Oil and Gas, a Texan company run by Burt Lancaster's character, Felix Happer, to buy a beach near a village in the Highlands so that an oil refinery could be built. The Americans have to deal with a young, local accountant, Denis Lawson's character, Gordon Urquhart, and he turns out to be far from naïve. Perhaps because it was loosely based on recent and real events in the Islands, the film has an atmosphere of authenticity, as well as magic, like *Whisky Galore!* and none of the clunking, cliché-ridden nonsense of most other Hollywood efforts.

Elsewhere in the Highlands and Islands, the discovery of North Sea oil had a dramatic impact. At Nigg Bay in Easter Ross, not far from Invergordon and the ghost of the great smelter, the construction of oil rig platforms began. The damaged local economy quickly recovered and expanded with more than 5,000 employed at the yards, and more found work in oil-related businesses. Houses and schools were built as communities expanded dramatically. Around the coasts of the Highlands and Islands, more construction sites were set up at Kishorn in Wester Ross, Arnish near Stornoway and at Ardersier, close to Inverness. The changes were very positive. In 1961 the number of people in work in the region was 97,000, but by 1991 it had jumped to 134,000, a 40 per cent increase.

Not all of the new jobs were stimulated by the discovery of North Sea oil however. Tourism in the Highlands and Islands began to move out of the coach trip and bed-and-breakfast market. The ancient cliché of the Highland landlady – send your money and don't come – became less quoted. Lord Godfrey Macdonald, the High Chief of Clan Donald and formerly a widely landed aristocrat, and his talented wife, Claire, opened Kinloch Lodge as a hotel in 1972. For some time, it was a lonely beacon of excellent food and comfortable accommodation. But on Skye, the hotel was joined by The Three Chimneys when it opened at Colbost, and not far from Kinloch,

Eilean Iarmain began to offer good food and accommodation, as well as a stunning location, at Isleornsay.

Salmon farming emerged in the 1980s as a significant business, employing hundreds rather than thousands, but by its nature it brought jobs to more remote locations on the coasts of the Hebrides, the western Highlands and the Northern Isles. Associated jobs in processing were also created. What connected all of this economic activity was a sustained drive to improve infrastructure, much of it funded by the European Union. The forlorn little blue signs with their circle of stars can still be seen on roadsides, structures and buildings. Bridges crossed firths where either long detours or ferries were involved.

What is also striking are the initiatives taken locally to encourage business. Shetland Islands Council, the HIDB and other public bodies and charities like the Highland Fund, seemed collectively determined to reverse centuries of decline and exploitation. Perhaps some of these positive attitudes were fostered by a greater awareness of history and the dangers of repeating it. In 1974 a famous and effective warning was issued.

The Cheviot, the Stag and the Black, Black Oil, written by John McGrath and the cast of the 7:84 Theatre Company toured the village halls and community centres of the Highlands and Islands that summer. The show was also filmed and screened by the BBC as a Wednesday Play; a version is still available to view online. The plot and purpose of the play is encapsulated by its title. The Cheviot sheep were emblematic of the Clearances, the stag of the landlords and the creation of vast sporting estates, while the black, black oil might turn out to be another spasm of exploitation. The brilliant Billy Paterson played Texas Jim (as well as many other parts, including the Glasgow property developer, McChuckemup) and here is his song and his ominous warning:

Take your oilrigs by the score,
Drill a little well just a little off-shore,
Pipe that oil in from the sea,
Pipe those profits – home to me.

So leave your fishing, and leave your soil.
Come work for me, I want your oil.
Screw your landscape, screw your bays
I'll screw you in a hundred ways . . .

All you folks are off your head
I'm getting rich from your seabed
I'll go home when I see fit
And all I'll leave is a heap of shit.

*

In early 1972 Brian Wilson, Dave Scott and Gordon the printer drove a long way south to an industrial estate in Walthamstow on the north-east fringes of London. In *Exchange & Mart* they had spotted a bargain, a machine called a Vari-Typer and a small printing press. With Jim Wilkie and Jim Innes, all four of them friends from Dundee University, they had decided to set up a weekly newspaper in the Highlands and Islands. An advert in the *Oban Times* had found them premises in Kyleakin on Skye, a house close to the ferry owned by Kay and Flo Reid. The sisters were active in the Skye Labour Party and sympathetic to the left-leaning politics of the group of young men and their ambitions to give those views a voice in a Highland context. In stables behind the King's Arms Hotel, they installed the Vari-Typer and the small printing press. All was set for a launch in April. The newspaper was to be called *The West Highland Free Press*.

It very nearly never appeared. The Vari-Typer was very slow and erratic, and as the launch date loomed and all the advertisers and newspaper shops waited, it looked as though nothing would be ready on time. Jim Wilkie contacted printers in Inverness to see if they could cope with a rush job and one, Eccleslitho, agreed to take it on. The business was located in the church hall of the Free Presbyterian congregation and the twin brothers who ran it, Donald and George MacAskill, were also sympathetic to the new paper's aims. For the masthead, a slogan from the Highland Land League was adopted: *An Tìr, An Cànan, 'S na Daoine*, '[For] The Land, the Language and the

People'. A friend had invested £2,000 in the venture, some of which had paid for the dud Vari-Typer, but what really secured the *Free Press'* future was the arrangement agreed by the MacAskill brothers. The four partners would keep £100 a week from sales and advertising to live on, and the printers would keep most of the rest of the revenue as payment for the job.

Success was by no means assured. Brian Wilson had toured doubtful newspaper shops, and when he visited the offices of *The Stornoway Gazette* to tell them of his plans, Major Sam Longbotham, the managing director, said, 'If you start a paper on Skye, we shall fight you and we shall destroy you.' Advertisers were a little warmer and when what quickly became known as *Am Pàipear Beag*, 'The Little Paper' (a tabloid size as opposed to the broadsheets of the *Stornoway Gazette* and the *Oban Times*), finally launched, copies sold well, and weekly circulation eventually settled on 7,500. In his magisterial history of the Highlands and Islands, *Last of the Free*, James Hunter wrote:

And when, in 1972, there was launched in Skye the *West Highland Free Press*, the Highlands and Islands were presented with a newspaper which – in a way no other paper had done since John Murdoch's *Highlander* ceased publication – took up causes like land reform, Gaelic revivalism and the wider right of Highlands and Islands communities to determine their own futures. To those of us who had grown up in the West Highlands and Islands at a time when political protest had largely been confined to Free Church demonstrations against Sunday ferries, the *West Highland Free Press* was as startlingly iconoclastic as it was liberating. Some of us might have heard over and over again, from our own families, that the Highlands and Islands would be better rid of the landlords who had controlled so much of the area's life for so long. But to see such views in print was tremendously exciting.

Land reform was not the only cause espoused by *Am Pàipear Beag*. They fought to protect and promote the Gaelic language, for improvements in public services and against the interests of private landlords.

When Margaret Thatcher's Conservative government unexpectedly pledged almost £10 million a year for the production of TV programmes in Gaelic, initially to be broadcast only on Scottish Television and Grampian TV, Brian Wilson and the newspaper campaigned for a dedicated Gaelic TV channel. As director of programmes at Scottish Television, and responsible for the Gaelic output, I believed that that would create a broadcasting ghetto. The native speech community was clearly shrinking and survival seemed to me to depend on learners, and if Gaelic programmes were sprinkled through the schedule, more would come across them than would go to a dedicated channel. As the debate went on, I had the honour to be defamed twice in the columns of the *West Highland Free Press*, once in English, over which Scottish Television took legal action, and once in Gaelic, which I forgave, it was so well written. All good, knockabout stuff.

A circle of sorts was closed in 2015 when Brian Wilson, by that time a columnist in the paper, was sacked by the editor, Ian McCormack. He had defended a fellow columnist over a piece the latter had written about Muslim immigrants. Another columnist resigned in protest. In 2021, Brian Wilson found himself co-editing, and attempting to revive the ailing *Stornoway Gazette*. Whatever the opposing views and their merits, there can be no doubt that over more than fifty years *Am Pàipear Beag* has brought much needed energy and even passion to the cultural and political life of the Highlands and Islands.

In 1975 boundaries were redrawn and ancient identities were recognised – eventually. Despite frequently vociferous opposition, the old counties of Scotland were swept away and, in the Highlands and Islands, certain anomalies also disappeared. Lewis used to form part of Ross and Cromarty, while Harris, the Uists, Benbecula, Barra, Skye and the Small Isles were in Invernesshire. All of them lay a long way west of the county towns of Dingwall and Inverness. There was a land border between the two counties at Aird a' Mhulaidh, between Loch Shiphoirt and Loch Reasort rather than at the more logical and emphatic isthmus at Tarbert. Which made little sense. What was sensible about the reform of 1975 was the creation of the Western Isles Council, the Outer Hebrides, as a unitary authority. The same transition took place for Orkney and when Shetland Islands Council replaced Zetland Council, it was much easier for Ian Clark and his councillors to negotiate with the oil companies.

On the mainland, and in the Southern Hebrides, the changes of 1975 made less sense. Argyll, Islay, Jura, Mull and smaller islands like Lismore found themselves part of the vast Strathclyde region that was run from Glasgow. Almost half of Scotland's population, about 2,286,000, was in the new council area, the overwhelming majority living in the conurbation around Glasgow. The concerns and needs of southern Highlanders and Islanders would have to join a long queue and wait their turn behind more populous and politically significant areas. But in 1996, a further wave of reform moved local government closer. The island authorities were untouched (except that the Western Isles became formally known as Na h-Eileanan nan Iar, a straightforward Gaelic translation), but Argyll and Bute, along with the vast area of Highland Council to the north, became unitary authorities with headquarters at Lochgilphead and Inverness.

*

At 9 p.m. on 8 May 1990, the culture and history of the Highlands and Islands and the Gaelic language unexpectedly moved centre-stage for an hour as Scotland's sense of itself shifted. Over the opening titles of a documentary film on Scottish Television, the words of an anthem were heard:

Comhla rium
A tha thu an drasd
Mo shuilean duinte, mo chuimhne dan

At present
All you were is with me
My eyes closed, my memory confident

Based on the soaring cadences of the Gaelic psalmody, the song's climax is in its title: 'An Ubhal as Àirde' ('The Highest Apple'). There were no subtitles, even though only a tiny sample of the TV audience could understand the lyrics. But their beauty and their soulful music were compelling. After the title sequence, the film intercuts the early darkness of a winter's day in the waking city of Glasgow with a glowing, blue dawn in the islands of the Hebrides. As two fishermen get into a van and switch on the headlights, we hear, again without subtitles, the weather forecast in Gaelic before another song begins:

Tha am ball air fhuasgladh,
Is tha sinn a' gluasad,
Air a' chuan, air a' chuan,
Tha sinn a' seolladh.

The ball is unlocked,
And we are moving,
On the ocean, on the ocean,
We are sailing.

In their bright orange oilskins, two fishermen walk through a clutter of nets, creels, plastic floats and fish boxes to begin their day's work. The opening of the film sets up and informs all that follows, the contrast of the ocean and the huge Highland skies with the bustle and traffic of the city and the preparations for a concert at the Barrowland Ballroom. By chance, my wife had come across a cassette, *The Cutter and the Clan*, recorded by a band called Runrig. Knowing of my concern that Gaelic's obsession with the past would make it difficult to produce programmes that might appeal to a wider TV audience (I was at that time controller of features at Scottish Television with responsibility for Gaelic), she suggested I listen. The first track I played was 'An Ubhal as Àirde', and it immediately caught my attention. Other songs in English dealt with the past, with Highland history, but this band made the stories seem new and accessible, and, it occurred to me, perhaps a way to understand a future. 'The Cutter', the title song, was about a man called Johnny Morrison who had emigrated to Canada in the 1960s. He was known

to Calum and Rory Macdonald, the composers, and also the founders of the band. The lyrics and sentiment were based around the fact
that Johnny had prospered in Canada and had got into the habit of
ordering goods to be sent to his mother's croft: a fridge and other
conveniences might make the old lady's life easier. But she didn't
want them. If her son had money to spend, he should buy a plane
ticket each spring and come back to go up to the moor and cut her
peats:

And so, you hold your mother,
And you bless the air,
With the tears of the emigrant,
The tongue of the Gael.

The film we made with Runrig was called *City of Lights* and on
the morning after it was broadcast, my PA put the overnight ratings
on my desk. We had replaced a very popular ITV network drama
with the documentary film because it felt like the right thing to do,
no more than an instinct. And even though the company would
probably lose money, I pushed hard for the substitution. We knew
that the audience was likely to be well down on a normal Tuesday
evening, but when I looked at the ratings, I was astonished. More
than a million people had watched a programme that began in a language that almost none of them understood and celebrated a history
and a culture that few of them recognised. Gaelic and the Highlands
and Islands, for an hour, had been centre stage. It was a remarkable,
turning moment that no one predicted.

Runrig were an immensely talented group of musicians, and
Calum Macdonald's poetic lyrics, both in English and in Gaelic,
were memorable and, in the world of popular music, exceptional.
No artists from the Highlands and Islands had ever achieved such
widespread popularity. A year after *City of Lights*, the band played
to an audience of 50,000 at Balloch Country Park on the shores of
Loch Lomond. In the same year, 'Runrig on the Rock' were sell-out
concerts on Edinburgh Castle's esplanade with audiences of more

than 10,000. Before one of these began, the band invited Sorley MacLean onstage to read some of his poetry. It was another remarkable moment.

Runrig's beginnings were unremarkable. At Lochmaddy Hall in North Uist, in August 1973, the Run Rig Dance Band played their first concert. There were three members: Rory and Calum Macdonald and Blair Douglas. The singer, Donnie Munro, joined shortly afterwards. Runrig's first album came out in 1978. *Play Gaelic* did just that, offering a mixture of new and traditional songs, all in their native language. It was gentle, folksy, tentative and a little repetitive. But as the band grew more confident, the music became much more distinctive and emphatic, often dealing with important themes. One of Runrig's greatest successes was 'Dance Called America', the lyrics based on James Boswell's record of his visit to Skye in the later eighteenth century with Samuel Johnson and on the impact of the Clearances. Opening with huge attention-demanding chords and impressionistic, statement-making lyrics, the song then picks up the rhythm of dance music. 'Sìol Ghoraidh', 'The Seed of Godfrey', of Clan Donald, is a powerful version of a moment in history, a memory of a clan battle that took place in Sleat on Skye, and also a celebration of the importance of kinship.

Disbanded now, after forty-five years of performing and recording, Runrig were a true cultural phenomenon, succeeding in bringing the story of the Highlands and Islands to huge audiences in Scotland, Britain and Europe in a way no others had. Through them and other gifted performers, like the band Capercaillie, Gaelic became part of the present, of Scotland's sense of itself, not marginal and not something from the tear-stained past. And it mattered little that few understood its literal meaning, the sentiment was eloquent enough. In 2018, when Runrig had played their last concert, a music video was released with Donnie Munro singing 'An Ubhal as Àirde'.

Change was in the air throughout the Highlands and Islands. In 1999, the Scottish Parliament reconvened. Its MSPs would govern all Scotland, but power moved closer to all of its regions. A mixture of the old first-past-the-post system and proportional representation,

129 members were elected, fifteen of them from the eight constituencies of the Highlands and Islands. In crude terms, this boosted
representation proportionately from seven MPs out of 650 at
Westminster, or a little over 1 per cent, to fifteen MSPs out of 129 in
Edinburgh, or almost 12 per cent, a considerably louder voice.

Two native Gaelic speakers were elected in 1999, and in the
Labour/Liberal Democrat coalition led by Donald Dewar, Alasdair
Morrison held the Western Isles seat and was appointed minister for
Gaelic. In the huge Ross, Skye and Inverness West constituency, the
Liberal Democrat John Farquhar Munro narrowly defeated Donnie
Munro, the singer from Runrig. He had left the band in 1997 to
pursue a political career and was the Labour candidate. Overall, the
Highlands and Islands elected five Liberal Democrats, thereby maintaining long traditions, especially in the Northern Isles, four Labour
candidates, two Conservatives and four from the SNP. One of these
was the veteran MP Winnie Ewing, and as Mother of the House, it
fell to her to utter these memorable words when the new parliament
met in the Assembly Hall of the Church of Scotland in Edinburgh:
'The Scottish Parliament, adjourned on the 25th day of March, 1707,
is hereby reconvened.'

Three years earlier, a distinctive voice was stilled, one that had
seemed to bring Highland and Lowland Scotland closer together.
Norman MacCaig's mother was a Gaelic speaker from the little
island of Scalpay, off the eastern coast of Harris. In a long life his
poetic influence was immense, reaching across several generations
as well as between cultures. Amongst MacCaig's contemporaries was
Sorley MacLean, with whom he occasionally gave public readings.
As the Highlander stood up to read, looking at his text for what
seemed like a long time, MacCaig stage-whispered, 'I think you are
meant to read aloud, Sorley.'

A primary school teacher in Edinburgh for most of his working
life, MacCaig spent every long summer holiday in Assynt, on the
coast at Achmelvich, near Lochinver. Occasionally, he crossed the
Minch to visit relatives on Scalpay. Here are two verses from 'Return
to Scalpay':

While Hamish sketches, a crofter tells me that
The Scalpay folk,
Though very intelligent, are not Spinozas . . .
We walk the Out End road (no need to invoke
That troublemaker, Memory, she's everywhere)
To Laggandoan, greeted all the way –
My city eyeballs prickle; it's hard to bear
With such affection and such gaiety.

Scalpay revisited? – more than Scalpay. I
Have no defence,
For half my thought and half my blood is Scalpay,
Against that pure, hardheaded innocence
That shows love without shame, weeps without shame,
Whose every thought is hospitality –
Edinburgh, Edinburgh, you're dark years away.

MacCaig's poetic voice was singular, fresh and clear, and somehow redolent of the big skies, the wide vistas and the rich detail of
Highland and Island landscapes. The last verse of 'Praise of a Man'
might stand as an elegy for the poet himself, a man who wrote so
beautifully in English about Gaelic Scotland:

The beneficent lights dim
but don't vanish. The razory edges
dull but still cut. He's gone: but you can see
his tracks still, in the snow of the world.

*

With campuses in Lerwick and Scalloway in the north, and also 400
miles to the south at Dunoon, and more dotted at several points
between, the University of the Highlands and Islands (UHI) may
fairly claim to be one of the very largest universities in the world.
There are twelve campuses or colleges and each teaches subjects as
diverse as aquaculture and Nordic studies to approximately 31,000

students scattered over a vast area. Modern communications technology (its development greatly accelerated by the Covid pandemic) links all these campuses and their students. Other centres offer tuition where communities are. On Benbecula, a centre runs full-time courses in Music and Archaeology, part-time Gaelic conversation and has access to much else. At Thurso, the Environmental Research Institute was set up near the Flow Country. On the islands of Barra and Islay are more centres fully equipped with PCs and video conferencing to enable distance learning. Long gone are the days when school leavers had to leave their communities to take a degree or train in tertiary education.

In 1992 the University of the Highlands and Islands Project was set up. From the beginning it was conceived not as a centre but as a wide network, a partnership of twelve colleges and research institutions across the north and west. In 2005 it became Scotland's newest university when the Privy Council granted UHI the autonomous power to confer degrees. Six years later, official university status was granted and the following year the Princess Royal became the first chancellor.

A barn in the Sleat Peninsula of Skye was, for me, emblematic of what could be achieved in further education in the Highlands and Islands, and it was crucial in the establishment of the UHI.

Early candles of educational and economic revival were lit on the island of Skye by an unlikely hand. In 1972, Iain Noble, a merchant banker and a Gaelic learner, bought an estate in the Sleat peninsula from Lord Godfrey Macdonald that included a farm steading at Ostaig, not far from the ferry terminal at Armadale. He planned to convert the derelict buildings into a cultural centre for the language. The project turned out to be much more than a metaphor. Noble had visited the Faroe Islands and been much struck by how important culture and language were in stimulating business and creating jobs:

When I asked the Faroese, I was amazed when they all replied that things began to happen when they decided to be Faroese and stop being Danish. This sparked the whole thing off. It gave them a sort of self-respect . . . I am convinced that through the revival of the language there came a pride in identity and all else followed. We mustn't be frightened of being a small community. Instead we must create our own internal binding factors. People here have never believed that things are possible. But there is virtually nothing that could not be achieved in the Highlands.

At first a library was established in the refurbished buildings of the old farm steading at Ostaig and the barn made into a meeting space. Through donations, it quickly grew into the largest public collection of Gaelic texts in the Highlands. But Noble was not satisfied. More metaphor described his ambition: 'a library by itself is like mustard without beef. It would have to be open to the public and should become a centre for students. Teachers and an academic ambience were the logical extensions of the new theme.'

The library needed to acquire students. In 1973 Sabhal Mòr Ostaig, 'the Big Barn at Ostaig', became a charitable trust devoted to the creation of a college that would teach courses through the medium of the Gaelic language. Summer courses were also held for learners, a lecture series was established, as was a Gaelic playgroup, and a writer in residence and a director were appointed.

Progress was slow and in the 1980s only ten full-time students a year took courses at the college. What transformed the pace of development was the startling announcement in 1989 from Malcolm Rifkind, Secretary of State for Scotland, of government funding for Gaelic television.

Norman Gillies, the visionary director of Sabhal Mòr Ostaig, saw an opportunity and having secured funding from STV, Grampian TV, the Scottish Office, and Highlands and Islands Enterprise, he launched a diploma course in Gaelic broadcasting. I was closely involved with this since I needed, as a matter of urgency, Gaelic speakers to work on the range of new programmes for the STV schedule. Looking at our output as a whole, it was clear to me that Gaelic programmes would not thrive as versions of what was already broadcast in English. What was the point of making a current affairs programme or creating a news service for a community that was bilingual and already served with news and current affairs (although these were eventually created)? Instead, we decided that since there was no Scottish cookery series in English, no DIY series, no comedy for young people, we would do these in Gaelic with subtitles. That way, two constituencies of interest could be engaged, those who were keen on cooking or DIY and also Gaelic speakers and learners. But I had far too few people to write, produce and present them, and when we created *Machair*, a soap opera set in the Hebrides, I had to use English speakers as directors, producers, authors and show runners, and then have what they did translated. Despite the continuing logistical difficulties, the shows were made and were very popular.

At the same time, the college expanded dramatically with student accommodation and a new campus at Àrainn Chaluim Chille. Instead of its annual appearance on the pages of the national papers at the time of the National Mòd, suddenly Gaelic found itself regularly part of the mainstream of Scottish cultural life as the language was heard, often for the first time, on TV screens across the country. The Runrig film was no longer a lonely exception. And as important, and for the first time, the ability to speak and write Gaelic became valuable and highly marketable.

*

One of Norman MacCaig's most atmospheric and sensual poems is 'A man in Assynt', the corner of the North-west Highlands he returned to each summer, and which he loved with a passion – despite the apparent playfulness of what follows. Here are the first two verses:

Glaciers, grinding West, gouged out
these valleys, rasping the brown sandstone,
 and left, on the hard rock below –
ruffled foreland –
this frieze of mountains, filed
on the blue air – Stac Polly,
Cul Beag, Cul Mor, Suilven,

Canisp – a frieze and
a litany.

Who owns this landscape?
Has owning anything to do with love?
For it and I have a love-affair, so nearly human
we even have quarrels. –
When I intrude too confidently
it rebuffs me with a wind like a hand
or puts in my way
a quaking bog or a loch
where no loch should be. Or I turn stonily
away, refusing to notice
the rouged rocks, the mascara
under a dripping ledge, even
the tossed, the stony limbs waiting.

Allan MacRae might not have agreed with MacCaig's notions on
ownership, although he would have recognised all the metaphor as
well as the characteristically precise use of language to describe the
place both men loved. MacRae was himself a writer, a stonemason, an
occasional athlete, but above all a crofter with a keen sense of history
and how it could be made to turn. In front of more than a hundred
people in Stoer Primary School on the evening of 8 December 1992,
he stood up to make a short, emotional speech: 'Well, ladies and
gentlemen, it seems we have won our land. It is certainly a moment
to savour. There is no doubt about that . . . My immediate thoughts
are to wish that some of our forebears could be here to share this
moment with us . . . Assynt crofters have struck a historic blow.'

The North Assynt Estate had been sold to a Scandinavian property
developer whose business had gone bankrupt, and the liquidators
planned to break it up and sell it off in seven lots. The crofting tenants
were not consulted or even contacted, it being none of their business,
the fate of the land they lived and worked on. On 6 June 1992, a
meeting of the Assynt branch of the Crofters Union was called and

a radical proposal discussed. Led by Allan MacRae, Bill Ritche and others, a bid to buy the land would be made, the money raised by a trust that would quickly be constituted. And the money was indeed raised, £300,000 to buy the 21,000-acre estate. Approximately half came from public donations, from many people who had ancestral links with Assynt, and the rest from public funds. After months of frustration and negotiation, and faced with the implacable determination of the Assynt Crofters Trust, the liquidators at last accepted the bid. And history was made to turn.

Assynt had belonged to the notorious Marquis and Marchioness of Stafford. Just as in Strathnaver and the other glens in the east, they had ruthlessly evicted people who had lived there for generations. The interior had been largely emptied and those who clung on and survived the Clearances lived on the coast in twelve townships. These are strung along what is now the B869 that runs from Kylesku in the north to Lochinver in the south. The story of Assynt over the last three centuries may be seen as emblematic of events that disfigured the landscape of the Highlands and Islands for far too long. Led by Allan MacRae, the crofters called time on all that powerlessness and won the land at last. Six hundred people living in 187 tenanted crofts and more than fifty owner-occupied properties now at last had control of where they lived and worked.

The Assynt Crofters Trust has been run in a business-like manner. At Loch Poll, the Assynt Hydro Project was built with borrowed funds to supply energy, but also to sell it to the National Grid. The loan has been repaid and the scheme now generates income for the trust. Brown trout fishing in the hundreds of lochans of the interior has produced revenue from licences and deer-stalking is also earning cash. The landscape has been revived, become a place where a living can be made rather than withering into scenery.

The example of Assynt encouraged others. Communities in Skye, Lewis, Sutherland, on the island of Eigg, and in Knoydart soon followed suit. The former founder of the *West Highland Free Press*, Brian Wilson, had become a Labour MP and then a minister. He encouraged Highlands and Islands Enterprise, the successor body to the HIDB, to create a community land fund and successive Scottish governments have further facilitated community land buyouts. By 2022, more than 500,000 acres in the Highlands and Islands had passed into the ownership of the people who lived and worked on the land, and it seems that more will be purchased with every passing year. History turned in 1992 in Assynt and now it is moving as landlords slowly retreat. The third element of the *West Highland Free Press* masthead, *An Tìr, An Cànan, 'S na Daoine*, is gradually taking control of the first. The People are beginning to win the Land. But what of *An Cànan,* the Language?

*

More than forty years ago, I stood on the pier at Mallaig with two old friends waiting for the ferry. It was not the Calmac car ferry to Armadale on Skye or to the Small Isles but an altogether much smaller boat. Looking more like a fishing smack, nothing like the black and white leviathans with their signature red funnels, it would take no more than half an hour to sail into the mouth of Loch Nevis and tie up at the quay at Inverie. Little more than a row of white cottages on the shore, it was for us the gateway to a trackless wilderness, to adventure, to lungfuls of pure mountain air. Our plan, conceived in the convivial warmth of Leslie's Bar in Edinburgh's south side, was to walk up the glens and across the saddles between the mountains of Knoydart. Between Inverie and Glen Shiel, we would cross only one road, and without any designation on the map, neither an A, a B or a C, it was probably little more than a single track.

The walk would probably take three days if the weather was OK. On the first night we would sleep under the corrugated iron roof of a bothy but for the other two we would camp. Food – and drink – rather than accommodation was the logistical problem. In addition to carrying the tent, its gear and a stove, it would be prudent to take four days' worth of provisions in case the weather shut down, and that was too much for us to carry.

I had a plan. Some years earlier, an old schoolmaster who went hiking most summers in the Highlands told me he had sent food parcels ahead that could be collected at various points on his journey. In those days, the Post Office had a duty as well as an obligation to deliver to any address, no matter how remote. Dried food was much lighter and I had ordered a series of small packs, not much bigger than a cigarette packet, of dried beef stew, dried mashed potatoes and dried spinach (a mistake – I've never enjoyed spinach since) that would heat up well after being soaked for half an hour. About two-thirds of the way between Inverie and the A87 in Glen Shiel (and its buses) was Kinloch Hourn.

The unclassified road ended there and by means I've now forgotten, I had found the name of the farmer. Enclosing a stamped, addressed envelope, I wrote to Mr Macdonald to ask if he would mind accepting a large parcel from me that we would collect. He would not mind. And so off went a cardboard box full of dried food, many packets of biscuits (not heavy), most of them Jammy Dodgers, and a bottle of Glenlivet that had been carefully decanted into a Tupperware container with a good seal.

Like a snapshot on a clear day, I have a crystal memory of walking down a steep path on the flanks of Glen Barrisdale and making our way along the southern shore of Loch Hourn. The water was so clear that through the glint I could make out the stones on the bottom. But when we reached the farmhouse, there seemed to be no one about, and my friends began to shake their heads and raise an eyebrow. We had consumed almost all we had brought from Inverie, including the first lot of Glenlivet. But my knock on the door was quickly answered by an older lady. I guessed Mrs Macdonald had seen us coming. But when I asked her about the food parcel, she just smiled and shook her head a little. Wondering if she was deaf, I repeated my question more slowly and emphatically. The old lady stepped forward out of the doorway and looked up at the distant mountain side to the south of the loch. I could not see what she was looking at. 'Macdonald iss approaching', she said, pointing, before retreating indoors.

We all scanned the horizon but could make out no movement. A few minutes later, around a bend in the track, as if by magic,

Macdonald arrived with his dogs. Smiling, and nodding to me, he went into his farmhouse and moments later, emerged with the large cardboard box. Having thanked him profusely (out of the corner of my eye, I caught exhalations of relief from my sceptical companions), we shook hands and we walked on a little to unpack the box and divide its contents between our rucksacks. I realised that the old farmer hadn't said a word.

Looking back at that snapshot over forty years, I realise that it was a moment of fading, of the passing of an ancient culture. Mrs Macdonald was not deaf or her husband shy. It did not occur to me at the time but it became clear to me when I thought about it that neither of them wished to have a conversation in English. Macdonald certainly understood the language because he had written, admittedly briefly, to me a few weeks before. But in this spectacular, isolated place at the end of a long track, surrounded by mountains, streams and a loch named in their native tongue, why would Mr and Mrs Macdonald speak anything else except Gaelic to each other and their dogs?

As late as the census of 1891, there were almost 44,000 monoglot Gaelic speakers in a speech community of more than 200,000 and most of them lived west of the Great Glen. That's a statistic worth pausing to take in. Only a little more than a century ago, entire communities in Britain had no need of English. They lived, loved, worked, thought and dreamed in Gaelic. Before the advent of mass media in English, with the spread of newspapers, then radio, then television, why would the Macdonalds and others like them who worked the land want to speak anything but their native language? It had evolved to describe the land, the weather and the work they did much better than English, the nouns, adjectives and verbs much more precise – and beautiful. But the twentieth century changed that linguistic landscape forever.

When the question was first asked in the 1881 census, 231,594 people replied that they had Gaelic. Ten years later, a more complete and comprehensive set of statistics saw that number rise to 254,415 and for the first time, it was found there were 43,738 monoglots.

That latter figure was always likely to decline with the inevitable reach of English language media, and for other reasons linked to administrative centralisation. But between 1911 and 1921, it crashed. The disproportionate number of Highlanders killed in the slaughter of the First World War (and the loss of the *Iolaire*), and the departing shiploads of emigrants undoubtedly contributed significantly to the overall loss seen in the total number of speakers, falling from 192,398 to 158,779. But it is the difference between 18,400 monoglots in 1911 and only 9,829 ten years later that is most striking, a huge drop of 46 per cent. This was critical and a statistic that would resonate almost a century later.

Each successive census has seen decline. In 1971 there were only 477 monoglots, a number that might have included Mrs Macdonald of Kinloch Hourn. These were all almost certainly older people, for ten years later none are recorded. By 2011, the total number of Gaelic speakers had fallen to its lowest ever with only 57,602, or 1.1 per cent of the population of Scotland. That included me, ticking the box even though I scuff along on the edges of the language. But every little helps. Numbers matter very much because they encourage political support. Because of the Covid pandemic, and also the insistence by the Scottish government that they managed the census in Scotland for 2021 (which was delayed and deadlines extended), it may be that only 75 per cent of the population has sent a return. That makes all of census statistics unreliable and few will trust the count of Gaelic speakers or the percentage derived once they are finally announced.

Perhaps much more important was a study published in 2020 by the University of the Highlands and Islands. Led by Professor Conchúr Ó Giollagáin, an expert in Irish as well as Scots Gaelic, the findings of the research revealed a desperately fragile situation. Only around 11,000 who had Gaelic used the language habitually at home; they were people who lived their daily lives in its mouth-filling words and phrases. Professor Ó Giollagáin said: 'The situation is so critical; the vernacular community is falling apart and those charged with supporting Gaelic need to face up to these issues. More of the same [policies] will give you more of the same crisis.'

Above the story, newspaper headlines were unequivocal: 'Gaelic dead in a decade.'

With the Gaelic Language (Scotland) Act of 2005, the Scottish government put in place a series of supportive measures, including the creation of Bòrd na Gàidhlig to oversee development. But few of these initiatives seem to be working. The UHI study showed that a critical group in the native speech community, three- to seventeen-year-olds, is dwindling rapidly. Between 1981 and 2011, the number fell from just over 5,000 to 2,000. Gaelic speakers are dying faster than they are being born. With the powerful added influence of the internet and social media, especially on young people, all in English (or American English), this collapse can hardly be seen as surprising.

The political reality is that Gaelic will not be allowed to die. But at some point in the near future, no one will any longer live in the language, think in it or use it as their everyday speech. The future of Gaelic is with learners, but can they keep it truly alive if it is not their first language? What is clear is Gaelic's central place in the identity of the Highlands and Islands, and that distinctive identity is crucial to a successful, growing future for the region. Many of the pages of history that precede this one have shown that. Language is not a vehicle but a definition, the way a society understands its culture. Gaelic best describes the Highlands and many of the Islands, while English translates and approximates.

Envoi

In the grey half-light of early morning, my headlights swung around a sharp bend in the track leading from my farm and put up a covey of startled partridges. Their low, reluctant flight whirred over the thorn hedge as I turned towards the A7 and headed north towards the mountains. I had rented a cottage in Glenfinnan for four days, somewhere in the heart of the Highlands and Islands where I could find the peace to think about all that had happened in the midst of the drama and majesty of these singular landscapes I had come to love.

But they are not my landscapes, not my places. A Borderer born and bred, I had come back home more than twenty years ago from a working life spent in cities: Edinburgh, Glasgow, London and Los Angeles to live once more, to live out the rest of my life, in my home places – and with the people who had made me. I grew up in a council estate on the edge of a small town and summers were spent in the woods, around the farms, on the riverbanks and up the gentle valleys of the Cheviot Hills. On our ancient, ramshackle bikes, we cycled long distances, sometimes as far as the wide empty beaches of the Northumberland coast, sometimes west up the Tweed valley. I've written a good deal about the history of the Borders and know the intimate detail of its fertile countryside and busy little towns and villages well. Several times, people have asked me about favourites, the places especially beloved. There are many, a long list, but in truth it is the fields I love best, the patchwork produced by centuries of day-in and day-out labour somehow best seen in the evening, lit by a westering sun, flowing like a golden river down the Tweed towards the sea. Evening is best because the day's end brought rest for the numberless and nameless people who worked out their lives in these fields. And they are their common monument. Of all the other monuments, grand houses, romantic ruins and picturesque tableaux to be seen in the Borders, it is the fields that are most beautiful. They can be atmospheric, intimate. After the harvest, in early September, when round straw bales dot and accentuate their contours and the trees and hedges fringing them are beginning to turn russet, they look at their gentle best.

The Highlands and many of the Islands could not be more different. It is for the most part wild land, scarcely touched by the hands of men and women, except in the glens and the straths. And the tiny, carmine-red dots of settlements that speckled William Roy's Great Map were all but obliterated from the eighteenth century onwards and the sense of wilderness was allowed to return. The press and power of geography is everywhere to be seen, shaping routeways, forcing communities to the edges, turning the seaways into highways, slowing down time, moulding a language to describe its features and intricacies. Geography made history in the Highlands and Islands. And it also made the weather.

When at last I arrived at Glenfinnan and found my rented cottage near the shore of Loch Shiel, it was raining. Mountainsides rose sheer out of the water, like a Norwegian fjord, and when I looked down the long length of the loch, the cloud hid the tops, a sodden, slate-grey blanket. I had of course looked at the forecast and past experience had persuaded me not just to pack waterproofs, but two sets of waterproofs. Nothing keeps out West Highland rain for a whole day. I was glad to see a radiator next to the front door of the cottage with a drying rack above it.

Having walked up to the busy A830 to stretch my legs, I was surprised to see a large car park almost full. But the principal attraction at Glenfinnan was not the monument by the lochside that remembered the raising of the royal standard in 1745, it was the viaduct. And not because it was an elegant example of railway engineering, but because it featured in the enormously popular Harry Potter films. The trains that took Harry and his friends to the wizard school

at Hogwarts passed over the viaduct for no good reason except that
it is scenic. On a good day. What had filled the car park was not an
interest in a turning moment in the history of the Highlands, but the
travels of a boy wizard. Trains for Hogwarts departed from Platform
Nine and Three-quarters, and under that sign in the National Trust
Visitor Centre, a display of merchandise associated with the books
and films was the first thing to greet visitors. At the back, beyond
it and the shop selling high-class tartan rugs and mugs was a room
with information about the Jacobite Rising. One of the helpful ladies
behind the till told me that the vast majority of the visitors went to
look at the viaduct, their mobile phone cameras at the ready, and not
so many went down to the monument by Loch Shiel.

None of which is surprising, or regrettable. Harry Potter brings
people to the Highlands who buy things, who need to be fed and
accommodated, and that happy accident of a famous film location
brings jobs. But I couldn't help thinking much more could have been
made of the events that unfolded in the summer of 1745. They were
scenes in a different sort of drama from the stories of J. K. Rowling,
a real life and death drama that could be made accessible to Potter
readers and fans without the need for David Niven to say, 'Hello
Scotsmen'. As often, the realities of history are much more engaging
and memorable than the confections of romance, and Glenfinnan
would have been a good place to begin that story.

The following morning, in a steady drizzle, I walked down to the
pier at Slatach. I had booked a boat trip down Loch Shiel on the MV
Sileas to Acharacle at the south end. At fourteen miles, the loch is
long, leading sailors almost to the sea, but not much of it was visible
in the mirk. With two bird watchers, festooned with binoculars and
long-lensed cameras, I was one of only three passengers. The boat had
no heating and as the rain blurred down the clear plastic windows
of the awning stretched over the stern, I became very quickly chilled
and glad of the blankets piled on the benches. But when we finally
reached Acharacle, where tying up at the pier was made awkward
because days of rain had raised the level of the loch and submerged
much of it, the skies began to clear and a watery sun slowly emerged.

While the *Sileas* took on passengers for a bird-watching tour of the southern end of the loch, I walked up to the village in search of hot soup and warmth. At Café Tioram I found both and much more. The sign on the roadside had announced *Thigibh a-staigh*, 'Come on in'. The café was run by three welcoming young women whose Gaelic had been anchored by their time at the local primary school and its frequent use of the language. Eggs Stornoway was the strong recommendation, after excellent soup, and it was a version of Eggs Benedict that used Charlie Barley's black pudding instead of ham. It was equally warming to listen to Gaelic spoken in the kitchen and the young woman who brought me the superb food kindly told me that my *blas* was good. But much more than that, the language gave the little café real identity, made it memorable, singular, not part of any chain or standard offer.

Looking back through my notebook, I saw that I'd scribbled 'authentic'. In a grey world governed by algorithms and faceless transactions, a pungent, unique identity stands out, matters more than ever, helping establish coherence, a sense of place, of community. Throughout the process of writing this history of the Highlands and Islands, the story always sang when clichés were swept aside and authentic voices were heard rather than the fakery of tartanry or when bogus, mist-strewn romance and silly sentiment jigged and reeled across the screen. The builders of the temples at Ness of Brodgar were not mute witnesses to history, they created a new religion, a new worldview that spoke spectacularly not only on Orkney but down the length of Britain to Stonehenge. The prayers and chanted music of Columba, Brendan, Moluag and Maelrubha rose from the mouths of their monks up into huge Highland skies and beyond, to the vaults of Heaven. The clack and rattle of the weavers of Harris Tweed, whose colours reflected the island landscape, has echoed across the Minch and around the world. The soaring cadences of the Gaelic psalmody, the images made by Sorley MacLean, Alasdair macMhaighstir Alasdair, Sileas na Ceapaich, the war cries of the charging clans at Culloden echo down the centuries and make the story of the Highlands and Islands come alive.

Almost all of that rich seam of authenticity was originally spoken and sung in Gaelic: it was the music of the thing as it happened. And yet so few have it now, fewer than 60,000. Given the fact that all native speakers are bilingual in English, there is no practical motivation to learn what is a difficult, very different language. But it should be attempted, for it is key to understanding much of the culture of the north (sadly, the departure of Norn has meant that dialects of English are, almost, sufficient to grasp at least the gist of the distinctive stories of the Northern Isles) and the stories of 400 generations. *Linn gu linn, bho ainm gu ainm*, as Runrig sing in 'Sìol Ghoraidh'. From one generation to the next, from one name to the next.

My own Gaelic, arthritic and cobwebbed by lack of use here in the Borders, is now very poor but I still have just enough to hear the distant echoes of that ancient music, to understand the significance of the names of places, of people and the events that swirled around them. And when I falter, frequently, Edward Dwelly's great lexicon is at my elbow, a constant presence as well as an adornment.

Most of all, the writing of this book has been the telling of a love story. I feel no awkwardness in that sentence, none at all. For almost sixty years, most years, and often more than once, I have been going north from the Borders into the mountains and to the ocean shore because there are places there I have come to love, whose spirits work powerfully on me. In Arisaig, on the west side of Lewis, in Bayble on the east, in Applecross, in Sleat, by Loch Ness I have laughed with the people and wept at the beauty of it all. Looking across the Sound of Sleat in the evening from Isleornsay to the Rough Bounds of Moidart as the sun lights only the mountain tops, at the immovable, eternal majesty of the land, I have felt the tears prickle, not at sadness or regret, but for the passing of all that experience in one place, for the distant music of the thing as it happened.

Iain Noble was surely right when he said that the language, the reassertion of identity and the self-confidence those things brought would make these sparse places come alive once more. It is happening. People are coming back, not in a flood, not to every part of the Highlands and Islands. But they are coming back in part because of the reassertion and a rediscovery of the pride in a pungent identity, in a place like no other. Recovery is in the clear, clean air of the north.

*

For seven or eight years, between the early 1980s and the early '90s, we stayed for a week in the late autumn with a group of friends from London in an old hunting lodge on the southern shore of Loch Sunart. Built in the nineteenth century when sporting estates were further emptying the landscape of Morvern, the accommodation was basic, even Spartan, but there was a large sitting room with old sofas and armchairs to sink into and a vast fireplace that could burn and crackle logs two feet long. The other warm room was the kitchen and its dining room with an oil-fired Aga and a Rayburn to heat the water. One of the London couples were vegetarians, something much less common then, and they did all the dinners and lunches – which amazed us all, they were so delicious and inventive. Non-veggies were however catered for by my sausage, bacon, black pudding and fried egg breakfasts. Always an early riser, I was happy to be up and doing in the early dark to wash up the night before's clutter and get everything ready for the first bleary-eyed stumbler out of bed.

That routine was memorable. It gave me time to make some good coffee and pull on a warm coat and go outside in the half-light, a magical time. In front of the hunting lodge was a long grass paddock stretching down to the loch shore. Crunching over the gravel with my steaming mug, I liked to listen to the silence, breathe in the cold, clean air and wait for the dawn to wash over the Ardnamurchan mountains. When the morning sky was clear, I'd see the pale yellow light catch the tip of Beinn Resipol and wash down its flanks.

But the dawn I remember more than any other, like a tiny splash of sunshine in the dark mists of the past, was overcast, the gunmetal sky heavy with scudding clouds. Sipping my coffee, I leaned on the old cast-iron fence and looked down the sloping paddock. It was difficult to be sure at first but I thought I could make out movement by the loch side, shapes darker than the faint glimmer on the water. Then in a startling moment, I knew what I was peering at. A red deer stag suddenly roared. It was a deep, echoic, throaty bellow. Around him his hinds were grazing, and somewhere in the distance other stags heard his warning.

I must have watched and listened for some time, for when I looked over to the mountains, I saw the peak of Beinn Resipol lit by the butter-coloured rays of the morning sun as it pierced the fleeing clouds. Dawn seemed to light the land quickly, edging closer, the hundred colours of the Highlands beginning to glow. The stag raised up his head and roared again as a new day broke and the old land came alive once more. These were moments I've never forgotten.

Further Reading

Adomnán, *Life of St Columba* (trans. Sharpe, Richard; London, 1995)

Anderson, Peter, *The Stewart Earls of Orkney* (Edinburgh, 2012)

Armit, Ian, *Celtic Scotland* (Edinburgh, 2016)

Barthorp, Michael, *The Jacobite Rebellions, 1689–1745* (Oxford, 1982)

Birley, A.R., *Agricola and Germany* (Oxford, 2009)

Boardman, Stephen, *The Campbells, 1250–1513* (Edinburgh, 2019)

Bradley, Ian, *The Coffin Roads: Journeys to the West* (Edinburgh, 2022)

Burt, Edmund, *Burt's Letters from the North of Scotland* (Edinburgh, 1998)

Buxton, Ben, *Mingulay: An Island and Its People* (Edinburgh, 2016)

Buxton, Ben, *The Vatersay Raiders* (Edinburgh, 2012)

Caldwell, David, *Islay, Jura and Colonsay: A Historical Guide* (Edinburgh, 2019)

Caldwell, David, *Islay: The Land of the Lordship* (Edinburgh, 2017)

Caldwell, David, *Mull and Iona: A Historical Guide* (Edinburgh, 2018)

Cameron, Ewen, *Land for the People? The British Government and the Scottish Highlands, c. 1880–1930* (Edinburgh, 1996)

Clarkson, Tim, *Columba* (Edinburgh, 2024)

Clarkson, Tim, *The Picts: A History* (Edinburgh, 2016)

Cowan, E.J., *Montrose: For Covenant and King* (Edinburgh, 1995)

Cowan, E.J. (ed.), *The Wallace Book* (Edinburgh, 2010)

Cowan, E.J. and McDonald, R.A. (eds), *Alba: Celtic Scotland in the Medieval Era* (Edinburgh, 2012)

Craig, Maggie, *Bare-arsed Banditti: The Men of the '45* (London, 2022)

Craig, Maggie, *Damn' Rebel Bitches: The Women of the '45* (London, 2022)

Crawford, Barbara, *The Northern Earldoms: Orkney and Caithness from AD 870 to 1470* (Edinburgh, 2023)

Currie, Jo, *Mull: The Island and its People* (Edinburgh, 2001)

Davies, Norman, *The Isles: A History* (New York, 1999)

Devine, T.M., *The Great Highland Famine: Hunger, Emigration and the Scottish Highlands in the Nineteenth Century* (Edinburgh, 2021)

Devine, T.M., *The Scottish Clearances: A History of the Dispossessed, 1600–1900* (London, 2018)

Devine, T.M., *The Scottish Nation: A Modern History* (London, 2012)

Devine, T.M., *To the Ends of the Earth: Scotland's Global Diaspora, 1750–2010* (London, 2012)

Dodgshon, Robert A., *From Chiefs to Landlords: Social and Economic Change in the Western Highlands & Islands* (Edinburgh, 1998)

Dwelly, Edward, *Faclair Gàidhlig Gu Beurla le Dealbhan; Dwelly's Illustrated Gaelic to English Dictionary* (Glasgow, 1994)

Fleet, Christopher, Wilkes, Margaret and Withers, Charles, *Scotland: Mapping the Islands* (Edinburgh, 2012)

Fleet, Christopher, Wilkes, Margaret and Withers, Charles, *Scotland: Mapping the Nation* (Edinburgh, 2012)

Fraser, James E., *From Caledonia to Pictland: Scotland to 795* (Edinburgh, 2009)

Fraser, Sally M., *Picts, Gaels and Scots: Early Historic Scotland* (Edinburgh, 2014)

Fraser, Sarah, *The Last Highlander: Scotland's Most Notorious Clan Chief, Rebel and Double Agent* (London, 2013)

Goring, Rosemary, *Scotland. The Autobiography: 2,000 years of Scottish History by Those Who Saw It Happen* (London, 2008)

Goring, Rosemary, *Scotland. Her Story: The Nation's History by the Women Who Lived It* (Edinburgh, 2018)

Grant, Isabel, *Highland Folk Ways* (Edinburgh, 2018)

Gregory, Donald (ed.), *The History of the Western Highlands and Isles of Scotland, 1493–1625* (Edinburgh, 2008)

Haldane, A.R.B., *The Drove Roads of Scotland* (Edinburgh, 2019)

Hay, Robert, *How an Island Lost its People: Improvement, Clearance and Resettlement on Lismore, 1830–1914* (Edinburgh, 2023)

Hay, Robert, *Lismore: The Great Garden* (Edinburgh, 2015)

Horne, T., Pierce, E. and Barrowman, R. (eds), *The Viking Age in Scotland* (Edinburgh, 2023)

Hunter, James, *The Appin Murder: The Killing That Shook a Nation* (Edinburgh, 2021)

Hunter, James, *A Dance Called America: The Scottish Highlands, the United States and Canada* (Edinburgh, 2022)

Hunter, James, *Insurrection: Scotland's Famine Winter* (Edinburgh, 2021)

Hunter, James, *The Last of the Free: A History of the Highlands and Islands of Scotland* (Edinburgh, 1999)

Hunter, James, *The Making of the Crofting Community* (Edinburgh, 2018)

Hunter, James, *Set Adrift Upon the World: The Sutherland Clearances* (Edinburgh, 2023)

Hunter, John, *The Small Isles* (Edinburgh, 2016)

Hutchinson, Roger, *Martyrs: Glendale and the Revolution in Skye* (Edinburgh, 2015)

Hutchinson, Roger, *St Kilda: A People's History* (Edinburgh, 2014)

Hutchinson, Roger, *The Soap Man: Lewis, Harris and Lord Leverhulme* (Edinburgh, 2005)

Johnson, Samuel and Boswell, James (ed. R. Black), *To the Hebrides* (Edinburgh, 2011)

Lynch, Michael, *Scotland: A New History* (Edinburgh, 1991)

Keppie, Laurence, *The Legacy of Rome: Scotland's Roman Remains* (Edinburgh, 2004)

MacLean, Sorley, *Caoir Gheal Leumraich (White Leaping Flame): Collected Poems* (Edinburgh, 2023)

Macleod, John, *Highlanders: A History of the Gaels* (London, 1996)

Macleod, John, *When I Heard the Bell: The Loss of the* Iolaire (Edinburgh, 2010)

MacLeod Rivett, Mary, *The Outer Hebrides: A Historical Guide* (Edinburgh, 2021)

Macniven, Alan, *The Vikings in Islay: The Place of Names in Hebridean Settlement History* (Edinburgh, 2015)

Marsden, John, *Somerled and the Emergence of Gaelic Scotland* (Edinburgh, 2008)

Martin, J. and Wingfield, E. (eds), *Premodern Scotland: Literature and Governance 1424–1587* (Oxford, 2017)

Martin, Martin, *A Description of the Western Islands of Scotland Circa 1695: A Voyage to St Kilda* (Edinburgh, 2014)

McDonald, R. Andrew, *The Kingdom of the Isles: Scotland's Western Seaboard, c.1100–c.1336* (Edinburgh, 2008)

McDonald, R. Andrew, *The Sea Kings: The Late Norse Kingdoms of Man and the Isles c.1066–1275* (Edinburgh, 2019)

McKirdy, Alan, *Set in Stone: The Geology and Landscapes of Scotland* (Edinburgh, 2015)

McNamee, Colm, *Robert Bruce: Our Most Valiant Prince, King and Lord* (Edinburgh, 2018)

Meek, Donald E. (*ed.*), *Caran an t-Saoghail (The Wiles of the World): Anthology of 19th Century Scottish Gaelic Verse* (Edinburgh, 2019)

Mithen, Steven, *Land of the Ilich: Journeys into Islay's Past* (Edinburgh, 2021)

Moffat, Alistair, *Before Scotland: The Story of Scotland before History* (London, 2005)

Moffat, Alistair, *The Highland Clans* (London, 2010)

Moffat, Alistair, *The Scots, A Genetic Journey* (Edinburgh, 2012)

Moffat, Alistair, *The Sea Kingdoms: the Story of Celtic Britain and Ireland* (Edinburgh, 2012)

Moffat, Alistair, *War Paths: Walking in the Shadows of the Clans* (Edinburgh, 2023)

Murton, Paul, *The Hebrides* (Edinburgh, 2017)

Murton, Paul, *The Highlands* (Edinburgh, 2021)

Newton, Michael, *Warriors of the Word: The World of the Scottish Highlanders* (Edinburgh, 2009)

Nicolson, Alexander, *History of Skye* (Lewis, 2012)

Noble, Gordon and Evans, Nicholas, *The King in the North: The Pictish Realms of Fortriu and Ce* (Edinburgh, 2022)

Noble, Gordon and Evans, Nicholas, *Picts: Scourge of Rome, Rulers of the North* (Edinburgh, 2022)

Oram, Richard (ed.), *The Lordship of the Isles* (Leiden, 2014)

The Orkneyinga Saga (*trans.* Hjaltalin, J.A. and Goudie, G., Edinburgh, 1999)

Pennant, Thomas, *A Tour in Scotland, 1769* (Edinburgh, 2019)

Pennant, Thomas, *A Tour in Scotland, 1772 and Voyage to the Hebrides* (Edinburgh, 2019)

Perman, Ray, *The Man Who Gave Away His Island: A Life of John Lorne Campbell of Canna* (Edinburgh, 2022)

Pittock, Murray, *Scotland: A Global History, 1603 to the Present* (New Haven, 2022)

Prebble, John, *Culloden* (London, 2002)

Prebble, John, *Glencoe* (London, 2005)

Richards, Eric, *The Highland Clearances* (Edinburgh, 2008)

Rixson, Denis, *Arisaig and Morar* (Edinburgh, 2011)

Rixson, Denis, *Knoydart: A History* (Edinburgh, 2018)

Rixson, Denis, *The Small Isles: Canna, Rum, Eigg and Muck* (Edinburgh, 2018)

Sellar, David, *Pedigrees, Power and Clanship: Essays on Medieval Scotland* (Edinburgh, 2023)

Seward, Desmond, *The King Over the Water: A Complete History of the Jacobites* (Edinburgh, 2019)

Smout, T.C., *A History of the Scottish People 1560–1830* (London, 1998)

Smyth, Alfred, *Warlords and Holy Men: Scotland AD 80–1000* (Edinburgh, 1989)

Spiers, E., Crang, J. and Strickland, M., *A Military History of Scotland* (Edinburgh, 2012)

Stevenson, Katie, *Power and Propaganda: Scotland 1306–1488* (Edinburgh, 2014)

Strang, Dougie, *The Bone Cave: A Journey through Myth and Memory* (Edinburgh, 2023)

Thompson, William P.L., *The New History of Orkney* (Edinburgh, 2019)

Thomson, Derick S. (ed.), *Alasdair Mac Mhaighstir Alasdair: Selected Poems* (Edinburgh, 1996)

Thomson, Derick S., *Gaelic Poetry in the Eighteenth Century* (Aberdeen, 1993)

Watson, W. J., *The History of Celtic Place-names of Scotland* (Edinburgh, 2011)

Wickham-Jones, Caroline, *Orkney: A Historical Guide* (Edinburgh, 2015)

Withers, Charles W.J., *Gaelic in Scotland 1698–1981* (Edinburgh, 2021)

Woolf, Alex, *From Pictland to Alba, 789–1070* (Edinburgh, 2007)

Index